The Mahdi Paradigm

Ayatollah Sayyid Ahmad al-Ashkiwari

Translated by Ali N. Moughania, Ph.D.

THE MAINSTAY FOUNDATION

The Mahdī Paradigm

Author: Ayatollah Sayyid Aḥmad al-Ashkiwarī

Translator: Ali N. Moughania, Ph.D.

Printed in the United States.

ISBN: 978-1943393886

To our leader and savior.

To our Awaited Imām (a).

CONTENTS

ACKNOWLEDGEMENTS

First and foremost, we thank the truth for being there in a way that is accessible to some extent, regardless of all else. One's loving parents, supportive family, and reliable friends, especially – for those who are married – one's beloved spouse, are owed thanks that only God can truly fulfill. In the same spirit, we are forever grateful to our mentors and educators. Institutions and communities of learning across time and space command our lasting gratitude and reverence. We thank the author, the honorable Professor Sayyid Aḥmad al-Ashkiwarī of the *ḥawzah al-ʿilmīyah* in the holy city of Najaf. Special gratitude to those who sponsored this project. We ask God Almighty to pardon our shortcomings, bless the work and accept this modest deed with His all-encompassing generosity. To those we have not shown, but especially those we frankly *cannot* show, due thanks. "How can I truly thank you when being able to say, 'thank you,' calls for another, 'thank you'?"[1] Any good in our work is yours and the shortcomings are all our own.[2] - *Ali N. Moughania*

---

[1] T: My English rendering of words attributed to ʿAlī ibn al-Ḥusayn (d. 95 AH / 713 CE). ʿAlī ibn al-Ḥusayn Zayn al-ʿĀbidīn al-Sajjād, *al-Ṣaḥīfah al-Sajjādīyah al-Kāmilah*, ed. Muḥammad Bāqir al-Ṣadr (d. 1980 CE) (Beirut: Muʾassasat al-Aʿlamī lil-Maṭbūʿāt, n.d.), 162-165; 307-309.

[2] T: The text before you is an annotated English translation of the second edition (1434 AH) original Arabic work authored by Sayyid Aḥmad al-Ashkiwarī, titled, *al-ʿAqīdah al-Mahdawīyah.* The publisher of this English text, *The Mainstay Foundation*, in consultation with the author of the Arabic original, has omitted some of the front matter that appears in the Arabic version. It goes without saying that due acknowledgments noted in the original Arabic publication are, nonetheless, echoed here.

NOTE ON USAGE AND SPELLING

In the name of God, the Compassionate, the Merciful

It has been a distinct privilege and honor to participate in this humble attempt to convey into English such a valuable synthesis of Mahdī-related methodology, epistemology, primary sources, analysis of misconceptions and recommendations for Mahdī devotees. This is not merely a translation, as the reader will notice from the extensive footnotes (with the translator's comments preceded by "T:"), but it attempts to remain faithful to the author's wording while taking liberties related to syntax and idiomatic phrases, many of which are bracketed to signify the interventions made in the process. The hope is that this will allow students and scholars in the academic study of Islam, as well as Muslim community members, to more precisely access the Arabic original, including its excellent selection of excerpts from primary sources. Although this is not solely a translation, it is also not contributing an edition with a critical investigation into the text's citations (*taḥqīq*) --for that task was thankfully completed by the Arabic edition. However, the reader will notice that a number of footnotes attempt to engage closely with the author's references, which blessed this research and editorial team with opportunities to investigate and reflect, arguably beyond the duties of a translator. In many cases, the footnotes include the main translator's clarifying remarks, which draw on his training and lived experience in the ḥawzah of Najaf as well as his other readings. These remarks are meant to help ease the access to the text at hand and are not meant as a substitute for technical rigor found in reviewing the relevant literature in its original language. The remarks do not necessarily reflect the intricate disagreements that arise in the discussion of definition nuances within legal theory, for example. A disclaimer is thus in order and the detailed technicalities are to be explored in the appropriate place elsewhere. The translator has attempted to make the English reading accessible while remaining true to the technical precision of its author's scholarly language. Thus, the technical language in the English version is, arguably, an accurate reflection of the Arabic original. When original Arabic terms are transliterated in-text, it is meant to capture nuances that would seem to be lost in a solely English rendering. English technical terms are often used or coined when they appear to capture a sufficient sense of their definitions in the English phrase, but ultimately require reference to the relevant footnotes. For clarifications on Islamic jurisprudential / legal theory terminology, reference can be made to Shaykh Muḥammad Ṣanqūr ʿAlī's *al-Muʿjam al-Uṣūlī*, vols. 1-2.[1] The transcription of Arabic words in this document follows the American Library Association - Library of Congress (ALA-LC) Romanization Table. We dedicate this English rendering to the awaited one; may God make his public appearance sooner, rather than later, and make the best wishes of humanity come true.

Translation & Editorial Team

---

[1] Muḥammad Ṣanqūr ʿAlī, *al-Muʿjam al-Uṣūlī*, 3rd ed., vol. 1-2, 2 vols. (Manshūrāt al-Ṭayyār, 2007).

FOREWORD BY THE AUTHOR

قَالَ رَبِّي يَعْلَمُ الْقَوْلَ فِي السَّمَاءِ وَالْأَرْضِ ۖ وَهُوَ السَّمِيعُ الْعَلِيمُ

He said, 'My Lord knows every word [spoken] in the sky and the earth, and He is the All-hearing, the All-knowing.'[1]

All praise is due to God for bestowing grace, grants, and blessings. May God's blessings shower upon the valiant frontrunner of God's emissaries, the master of all creatures, our Prophet, the Messenger of Mercy, Abū al-Qāsim[2], Muḥammad[3]. Moreover, peace be upon his honorable progeny, the guiding lights in the darkness and the luminous beacons in the moonless nights.

---

[1] Qurʾān 21:4.

T: Qurʾānic translations here have generally considered the translation by Ali Quli Qaraʾi, as well as others to a lesser extent, at times with modifications after consulting Arabic Qurʾānic commentaries. As expected, the original Arabic should be referred to when assessing arguments that rely on Qurʾānic verses.

[2] T: The *kunyah* of Prophet Muḥammad; a *kunyah* is a kind of epithet starting with *Abū* (literally, "Father of"), for a man, or *Umm* (literally, "Mother of"), for a woman.

[3] T: Whenever Prophet Muḥammad is mentioned, it is a convention in Arabic Islamic writing to include a short prayer to God – may God shower peace and blessings upon him and his progeny. It is similarly a convention to make a prayer saluting other prophets and members of Ahl al-Bayt (Prophet Muḥammad's Household, including his daughter Lady Fāṭimah, and the Twelve Imams) – peace be upon them all. Although the translation here does not spell out such a prayer in every instance of their mention, since this is not a convention in English writing, the reader is nonetheless invited to vocalize the prayer or, at least, intend it at heart.

Excelling in the pursuit of knowledge, reaching the mountaintops, and extracting pearls and coral require the following foundations: freedom of thought and choice, on the one hand, and presentation characterized by integrity and excellent quality, on the other hand.

In the meantime, and all along, the enemies of truth and the forces of darkness strive to extinguish that light. They attempt to make way for spiders to spin their webs and for delusion to thrive in its lairs. They do not cease to take the path of temptation and misguidance. Our Lord says the following in the Holy Qurʾān,

> وَكَذَٰلِكَ جَعَلنا لِكُلِّ نَبِيٍّ عَدُوًّا شَياطِينَ الإِنسِ وَالجِنِّ يوحي بَعضُهُم إِلى بَعضٍ زُخرُفَ القَولِ غُرورًا [...]
>
> *That is how for every prophet We appointed as enemy the devils from among humans and jinn, who inspire each other with flashy words, deceptively. [...]*[1]

Consequently, there is a need for those who invite to what is right, scholars[2] of guidance, spokespersons of authenticity, torches of Oneness, and pulpits of knowledge, who function to renovate that which has been eroded of the religion's[3] guideposts and raise that which has been obscured of the faith's lighthouse.

The purpose of this book and other publications is to make it easy for all to get to know Imam Mahdī, to live with him in terms of their religious conduct[4], to carry him with them in terms of their report-based thought[5], to adopt him in terms of their reason-based creed, to have him deeply rooted in them in terms of their heartfelt emotion, and to endeavor in

---

1 Qurʾān 6:112.

2 T: *ʿUlamāʾ*; sing. *ʿālim*; Knowledgeable one, sage, etc.

3 T: *al-Dīn*; The holistic worldview and comprehensive way of life that it entails.

4 T: Sulūkan fiqhīyan

5 T: *Fikran riwāʾīyan*; Report-based thought. The reports referred to here are namely the reported sayings, actions, and/or silent approvals attributed to Prophet Muḥammad and the twelve appointed Imams.

paving the way for him and properly awaiting him. For awaiting him is not about standing idly by, being on the watch for and gazing out toward a future event and upcoming prediction. Rather, properly awaiting him is meant to be a prerequisite step paving the way for his public appearance[1]. The meaning of relief[2] is an expansive one. It includes in its folds even the present state of awaiting him, leading up to his public appearance. Thus, the faithful have come to compare Imam Mahdī to the savior of the world as conceived by others. The faithful have then proceeded to weave him into a single, integrated, harmonious religious system with the fragrance of monotheism, reading him in between the lines of the guideposts and finding him, "between the *rukn* and the *maqām*."[3]

There is still much that lies ahead. Intense determination is needed to continue the journey and reap the best fruit. God Almighty says,

[...] وَأَنزَلنا إِلَيكَ الذِّكرَ لِتُبَيِّنَ لِلنّاسِ ما نُزِّلَ إِلَيهِم وَلَعَلَّهُم يَتَفَكَّرونَ

> *[...] We have sent down the Remembrance to* you *so that* you *may clarify for the people that which has been sent down to them, and so that they may reflect.*[4]

Sayyid Aḥmad al-Ashkiwarī

---

[1] T: al-Ẓuhūr.

[2] T: *al-Faraj*; Associated with the public appearance of Imam Mahdī.

[3] T: The phrase, "between the *rukn* and the *maqām*," appears in reports attributed to the Imams, describing the location of an event in which the awaited Imam Mahdī is publicly present at the holy Kaʿbah in the pilgrimage city of Mecca.

[4] Qurʾān 16:44.

INTRODUCTION

The Mahdī system of thought is currently characterized by a state of ambiguity to some extent. There is a foggy and occult image of Mahdī culture and a similar lack of clarity when it comes to how the Mahdī system of thought is to be read. This is in light of the Mahdī system's program and controversies, on the one hand, and the lack of its reception by some due to differences in cultural and historical background, on the other hand. The Mahdī system experiences this ambiguity despite the precision, excellence and planning of its Maker, the splendor of its Designer, and the skill of its Codifier.

To the unreceptive group, from time to time the Mahdī system may even deviate from its outlined and planned Divine course. The crookedness and deviance manifest either in terms of thought, behavior, or both.

This is no surprise of course – the richer the idea, the more it is tested.[1] Religion itself, as a phenomenon, has not been immune to deviance. That is despite the intelligence, wisdom, precision, insight and metaphysical nature of its Legislator. Whether at its birth in the days of Prophet Muḥammad, during the period close to it, or subsequently, the religious phenomenon has fallen prey to deviance. Many schools of thought[2]

---

[1] T: *Iftitān*; Related to the word *fitnah*, which, depending on the context, can refer to a test or conditions such as calamity, sedition, and temptation.

[2] T: *Madhāhib* (sing. *madhhab*); Schools of thought and/or practice; sometimes referring to the community adopting the school.

developed in association with a single *sharīʿah*[1]. For the multiplicity of these schools was due to their mistaken understanding and the deviance of their leading patrons. This does not come as a shock, for being tested is an inevitable Divine precedent[2] applying to every religious phenomenon.

When its inner ingredients interact with the world of competing forces[3], it becomes susceptible to being tested, paving the roads of trial and examination. God Almighty says,

أَحَسِبَ النَّاسُ أَن يُتْرَكُوا أَن يَقولوا آمَنّا وَهُم لا يُفتَنونَ

> *Do the people suppose that they will be let off because they say, 'We have faith,' and they will not be tested?*[4]

It has also been reported that Imam Muḥammad al-Bāqir said:

لتمحصن يا معشر الشيعة شيعة آل محمد كمخيض الكحل في العين، لان صاحب الكحل يعلم متى يقع في العين ولا يعلم متى يذهب، فيصبح أحدكم وهو يرى أنه على شريعة من أمرنا فيمسي وقد خرج منها، ويمسي وهو على شريعة من أمرنا فيصبح وقد خرج منها

> *O community of the Shīʿah, the followers*[5] *of Muḥammad's progeny, you will indeed be sifted through similar to the remaining kohl*[6] *settling around the eye. For the one with kohl knows when the kohl is put on around the eye but does not know when it will wear off. Similarly, a person from among you will see himself to be on a path*[7]

---

[1] T: The Divine path/prescription to be followed, with all its rules, regulations, recommendations, etc.; particularly referring to the Sharīʿah of Islam here.

[2] T: *Sunnah*; Wont, manner, way.

[3] T: That is the world of crude matter, in which opposing forces are at play.

[4] Qurʾān 29:2.

[5] T: Shīʿah

[6] T: *Kuḥl*; A preparation used to darken the edges of the eyelids.

[7] T: Sharīʿah.

> *associated with our authority[1] in the morning but will have veered off course by the evening; and he will be on a path associated with our authority in the evening but will have veered off course by the morning.[2]*

Thus, human volition and freedom, on the one hand, and the philosophy behind creating, examining, and testing the human being, on the other hand, entail a margin of potential for error. In turn, that opens up room for the deviant to abuse their freedom and move toward the dark side out of their own volition. As God Almighty says,

---

[1] T: *Amr*; The Arabic root AMR, and more specifically the noun *Amr*, has its own web of interconnected connotations in the Qurʾān (e.g., command, authority, matter, affair, thing, etc.).

[2] Ṭūsī, *al-Ghaybah*: 339, 340 / Ḥadīth (Ḥ) 288; Also, on page 339 / Ḥ 287, it is reported that Jābir al-Juʿfī said:

> قلت لأبي جعفر عليه السلام متى يكون فرجكم؟ فقال : هيهات هيهات لا يكون فرجنا حتى تغربلوا ثم تغربلوا ثم تغربلوا، يقولها ثلاثا، حتى يذهب الكدر ويبقى الصفو

> *I asked Imam Muḥammad al-Bāqir, "When will come the time of your relief?" The Imam replied, "Far be it, the time of our relief will not come until you are sifted through, then sifted through, then sifted through – (he would say it thrice) – until the pollutants are removed and the finest remain."*

On page 472 / Ḥ 491, it has also been reported that Imam Jaʿfar al-Ṣādiq said:

> إن أصحاب موسى ابتلوا بنهر وهو قول الله عز وجل، "إِنَّ اللَّهَ مُبْتَلِيكُمْ بِنَهَرٍ،" وإن أصحاب القائم يبتلون بمثل ذلك.

> *Indeed, the companions of Moses were tested with a stream, as God Almighty says [in the Qurʾān], "God will test you with a stream [...]." [2:249] Indeed, the companions of the Qāʾim [Rising One; the Mahdī] will be tested with something similar.*

The relevance of this reference is based on the assumption that "the companions of the *Qāʾim*" include even those *awaiting* his public appearance (i.e. his followers during the period in which he is not publicly accessible – when he is hidden, in a state of occultation otherwise known as *ghaybah*).

وَنَفسٍ وَما سَوّاها

فَأَلهَمَها فُجورَها وَتَقواها

By the soul and Him who fashioned it,

and inspired it with [discernment between] its virtues and vices[1]

The Creator inspired human beings with discernment, giving them the freedom to unlock the door of following evil with the key of *mutashābih*[2] notions.

[...] فَأَمَّا الَّذينَ في قُلوبِهِم زَيغٌ فَيَتَّبِعونَ ما تَشابَهَ مِنهُ ابتِغاءَ الفِتنَةِ [...]

[...] As for those in whose hearts is deviance, they follow what tashābaha[3] *in it, in pursuit of mischief*[4] *[...]*[5]

---

[1] Qur᾿ān 91:7-8.

[2] T: *Mutashābih* notions; linguistically, the word *mutashābih* is related to the past tense verb *tashābaha* and the noun *tashābuh*, which expresses the *similarity/resemblance* between different matters. This can mean different things, depending on the context. In some contexts, *mutashābih* describes the *consistency* between the verses of the Qur᾿ān (i.e. verse 39:23). However, in other contexts, such as in the verse quoted here, *mutashābih* arguably refers to a form of *ambiguity* which arises when the intended meaning of a Qur᾿ānic verse is not straightforward *in a standalone fashion.* At first glance, in such verses, there would be multiple possibilities that would seem *similar* to what must be right, leading to uncertainty. In this sense, the *mutashābih* verses (as opposed to what are called the "*muḥkam*" verses) are supposed to be clarified by understanding them with reference to the *muḥkam* verses, which are already straightforward. The deviant choose to go after the *mutashābih* verses without referring them back to the *muḥkam* verses and thus end up with twisted interpretations. (See exegetical works such as al-Ṭabāṭabā᾿ī's *al-Mīzān* and Makārim's *al-Amthal* for a detailed discussion of *mutashābih* vs. *muḥkam* in this verse.)

[3] T: *tashābaha*; The past tense verb related to *mutashābih*; see previous footnote and refer to exegetical literature for discussion on *mutashābih* vs. *muḥkam* verses of the Qur᾿ān.

[4] T: *fitnah*; See earlier footnote on *iftitān*.

[5] Qur᾿ān 3:7.

The fact that the deviant of heart are guilty of wrongdoing and following *mutashābih* notions does not imply a deficiency in the Divinely prescribed system of thought. Neither does it dent that system's foundations, durability and righteousness, nor does it undermine the Omnipotence and Wisdom of its Theoretician. The Author of the Universe has written its chapters with a common goal and purpose. All of its different shapes and forms come together in a complete portrait. For if the journey of thought has faced thorns and obstacles on the way... If at some stages, such challenges have: taken away from its effectiveness and progress; diverted it from its intended natural course; left negative effects on the souls of its followers; and caused doubt and suspicion to enter their hearts, and the light of the sharīʿah to be put out in their souls because they did not discern the soundness of the idea; then the journey of thought has developed in a contaminated environment that distorts its appearance and deprives it of its well-being.

One of the most dangerous types of deviance is deviance in thought. That is especially the case when: it occurs under the impression that it is issuing forth from within the inner circle; it is established under the pretext of reforming the outlook of one's thought; it is broadcasted in the form of soundbites by those who dress up in an attempt to appear scholarly; the deviant idea is masked with a guise of holiness; and those opposing the deviance are described as being outside the folds of the religion. With this, the alarm of deviance begins to cry out. However, it is not necessarily the case that such deviance is comprehensive. Rather, it could be that the deviance is merely partial, occurring in only some matters. God Almighty says,

[...] أَفَتُؤْمِنُونَ بِبَعْضِ الْكِتَابِ وَتَكْفُرُونَ بِبَعْضٍ [...]

> *[...] What! Do you believe in part of the Book and defy another part? [...]*[1]

---

[1] Qurʾān 2:85.

Belief in Imam Mahdī, the very idea of a Mahdī figure, and the phenomenon of the *ghaybah*[1] are perhaps subject to this dilemma as well. For these notions have been caught between the two extremes of excess and deficiency. Our objective here is to pinpoint some of the causes for this dilemma and to identify the means of providing the relevant immunities. The latter serves a twofold purpose: [1] to safeguard the dilemma from exploitation; and [2] to present this belief in the fields of knowledge and thought in a digestible manner that does not invite belittlement and underestimation.

The preliminary outline is as follows:

- Part One: Establishing the *default principle*[2] and referring back to it in our day and age.
- Part Two: Examining terms/entries at the level of concepts[3] and beliefs[4].

---

[1] T: The period during which the Imam is not publicly accessible; when he is hidden, in a state of occultation; sometimes thought of as the period during which the Imam lives amongst the people incognito.

[2] T : al-Aṣl.

[3] T: *al-Taṣawwur*, Conceptualization alone, as opposed to *al-taṣdīq* (conceptualization accompanied by adoption/belief/assent).

[4] T: *al-Taṣdīq*, Conceptualization accompanied by adoption/belief/assent regarding the conceptualized proposition (i.e. that it is true, or that it is false).

PART ONE

ESTABLISHING THE DEFAULT PRINCIPLE

CHAPTER 1

THE TYPES OF PEOPLE ACROSS DIFFERENT SOCIETIES

It is a basic intuitive fact that the people of a given society and era can be categorized into several groups:

1) The Naïve: These are the simple-minded, for they are not intellectually equipped to enter the fields of [sophisticated] thought. It has been reported that Imam ʿAlī has said,

    الناس ثلاثة: عالم ربّاني، ومتعلّم على سبيل النجاة، وهمج رعاع، أتباع كلّ ناعق...

    People are of three types: [1] the godly sage[1]*; [2] the learner on the path of salvation; and [3] the insignificant*[2]*, the immature*[3]*, those who follow every herder's call*[4] *[...]*[5]

---

[1] T: *ʿĀlim*; Knowledgeable one, scholar, etc.

[2] T: *Hamaj* (sing. *hamajah*); This can refer to a small type of flies that fly around the faces of livestock; apparently used figuratively here to describe the misguidance and/or insignificance of this type.

[3] T: *Raʿāʿ* (sing. *raʿāʿah*); This can refer to the young of age; apparently used figuratively here to describe the immaturity and foolishness of this type.

[4] T: *Nāʿiq*; This can refer to a herder who calls out toward the herd; apparently used here to describe the similarities between this third type of individual and sheep in that they both behave absentmindedly; this third type follows the herder, regardless whether his call be good or bad.

[5] *Al-Khiṣāl*: 186 / Ḥ 257.

2) The Fools: These are the ones who [unreasonably] *suppose*[1] that their deeds are good. For their practical and intellectual choices are not based on reasonable[2] foundations and methods. Rather, their way is closer to a feeble-minded approach. For not only do they not make gains, they also bring harm to themselves or others. Imam Muḥammad al-Bāqir has said,

يا عبد الله بن عطاء قد أخذت تفرش أذنيك للنوكى

O ʿAbd Allāh ibn ʿAṭāʾ, you have been lending your ears to fools[3].[4]

3) Those Characterized by Compound Ignorance[5]: These are the ones who are frequently certain about matters that do not match up with reality. For they see themselves to be donning the garb of knowledge, but they are closer to ignorance and error than they are to reality. Moreover, they cannot bring themselves to accept that they have made a mistake. Rather, pride[6] carries them off to sin[7], as this group is inseparable from sin. Hence, their practical moves in the external

---

[1] T: The emphasis on *suppose* here is based on the understanding that their main flaw is the absence of due consideration in their choices. The author is likely alluding to verse 18:104 of the Qurʾān here.

[2] T: *ʿUqalāʾī*; Related to the plural noun *ʿuqalāʾ* (sing. *ʿāqil*); understood to be those of sound mind, reasonable individuals; careful in light of substantive considerations.

[3] T: al-Nawká (sing. al-anwak).

[4] *Al-Kāfī* 1:342 / Section on the *Ghaybah* / Ḥ 26.

[5] T: *al-Jahl al-murakkab*; the state of ignorance in which one is unaware of his/her ignorance.

[6] T: The word *al-ʿizzah* here is arguably translated as pride in this context, but not praiseworthy pride; it can also refer to worldly might/glory gained through sin (see exegetical literature on verses 2:205-206).

[7] T: This phrase can be translated differently depending on the exegetical interpretation considered for verse 2:206.

world are made according to the ignorance imprinted in their minds. God Almighty says:

وَإِذا تَوَلّىٰ سَعىٰ فِي الأَرضِ لِيُفسِدَ فيها وَيُهلِكَ الحَرثَ وَالنَّسلَ ۗ وَاللَّهُ لا يُحِبُّ الفَسادَ

وَإِذا قيلَ لَهُ اتَّقِ اللَّهَ أَخَذَتهُ العِزَّةُ بِالإِثمِ ۚ فَحَسبُهُ جَهَنَّمُ ۚ وَلَبِئسَ المِهادُ

And if he were to wield authority, he would try to cause corruption in the land, and to ruin the crop and the stock, and God does not like corruption.

And when he is told, 'Be wary of God,' pride carries him off to sin; so let hell suffice him, and it is surely an evil resting place![1]

4) The Weak[2]: These are the ones who surrender to the existing, corrupt social reality. They echo every herder's call and follow every path. For their way is to surrender to the other without due consideration of the truth behind that other. God Almighty says:

وَقالَ الَّذينَ كَفَروا لَن نُؤمِنَ بِهٰذَا القُرآنِ وَلا بِالَّذي بَينَ يَدَيهِ ۗ وَلَو تَرىٰ إِذِ الظّالِمونَ مَوقوفونَ عِندَ رَبِّهِم يَرجِعُ بَعضُهُم إِلىٰ بَعضٍ القَولَ يَقولُ الَّذينَ استُضعِفوا لِلَّذينَ استَكبَروا لَولا أَنتُم لَكُنّا مُؤمِنينَ

قالَ الَّذينَ استَكبَروا لِلَّذينَ استُضعِفوا أَنَحنُ صَدَدناكُم عَنِ الهُدىٰ بَعدَ إِذ جاءَكُم ۖ بَل كُنتُم مُجرِمينَ

وَقالَ الَّذينَ استُضعِفوا لِلَّذينَ استَكبَروا بَل مَكرُ اللَّيلِ وَالنَّهارِ إِذ تَأمُرونَنا أَن نَكفُرَ بِاللَّهِ وَنَجعَلَ لَهُ أَندادًا ۚ وَأَسَرُّوا النَّدامَةَ لَمّا رَأَوُا العَذابَ وَجَعَلنَا الأَغلالَ في أَعناقِ الَّذينَ كَفَروا ۚ هَل يُجزَونَ إِلّا ما كانوا يَعمَلونَ

The faithless say, 'We will never believe in this Qur᾽ān, nor in what was [revealed] before it.' But if you *were to see when the wrongdoers are made to stop before their Lord,*

---

[1] Qur᾽ān 2:205-206.

[2] T: *Mustaḍ῾afūn* (sing. *Mustaḍ῾af*); those abased, weak, oppressed; in a sense, disadvantaged.

casting the blame on one another. Those who were abased will say to those who were arrogant, 'Had it not been for you, we would surely have been faithful.'

Those who were arrogant will say to those who were abased, 'Did we keep you from guidance after it had come to you? No, you were guilty [yourselves].'

Those who were abased will say to those who were arrogant, 'Rather [it was your] night and day plotting, when you prompted us to forswear God and to set up equals to Him.' They will hide their remorse when they sight the punishment, and We will put iron collars around the necks of the faithless. Shall they be requited except for what they used to do?[1]

5) The Bigoted Conformists: These are the ones who submit to their own bigotry and blind allegiance to others. Hence, they blindly follow[2] those others, promote them, melt into their embrace, and devote themselves entirely to their elders. This blind following may be due to a range of bigotries: tribal, clan-based, nationalist, class-based, and the like. It has been reported that the Commander of the Faithful, Imam ʿAlī, has said,

أَلَا فَالْحَذَرَ الْحَذَرَ مِنْ طَاعَةِ سَادَاتِكُمْ وكُبَرَائِكُمْ الَّذِينَ تَكَبَّرُوا عَنْ حَسَبِهِمْ وتَرَفَّعُوا فَوْقَ نَسَبِهِمْ وأَلْقَوُا الْهَجِينَةَ عَلَى رَبِّهِمْ، وجَاحَدُوا اللهَ عَلَى مَا صَنَعَ بِهِمْ [...]

Indeed, beware, beware of obedience to your chiefs and elders who have aggrandized themselves beyond their legacy, raised themselves above their origins, attributed

---

[1] Qurʾān 34:31-33.

[2] T: Although the word "taqlid" is used here (i.e. a term that has come to represent the pious practice of most of the Twelver Shīʿah public when they defer to experts on matters requiring expertise), the context implies that it is being used here in the negative sense of, "blind following," not in the sense of, "reasonably referring to verified experts."

> *the trait [they] abhorred to their Lord, and rejected [due gratitude to] God for what He had made of them*[1] *[...]*[2]

6) Those of Unreasonable Stubbornness and Persistence[3]: Cautioning the individuals of this category is of no avail. Their only concern is to disagree with others. It has not been their aim to unveil what is right or true. Rather, their only interests lie in the desire for publicity through the notion that "controversy attracts attention."[4] God Almighty says,

> إِنَّ الَّذِينَ كَفَرُوا سَوَاءٌ عَلَيْهِمْ أَأَنذَرْتَهُمْ أَمْ لَمْ تُنذِرْهُمْ لَا يُؤْمِنُونَ
>
> *As for the faithless, it is the same to them whether you warn them or do not warn them; they will not have faith.*[5]

7) The Materialistic, the Concupiscent and Those Who Pursue the Worldly: The only aim of those in this group is worldly, animalistic utilitarianism[6]. In order to achieve this objective, they are willing to resort to any means. Guidelines and standards do not guide them or put them in check. Rather, utilitarianism[7] now has its own conceptual foundations and ideological underpinnings. Even more, those who promote it have not had any shame when presenting it. For in the field of ethics, what is presented is much worse. It has been reported that the Messenger of God, Prophet Muḥammad, said:

---

[1] T: I used the phrase, "made of them," to refer to the blessings that God has bestowed upon them, God's generous acts toward them.

[2] *Nahj al-Balāghah*: Sermon 192, called, "al-Qāṣiʿah."

[3] T: *Aṣḥāb al-Lajjah*; In this context, those of [unpraiseworthy] persistence.

[4] T: The Arabic saying goes, "*Khālif tuʿraf* (disagree with/violate [the status quo] and you will become known)."

[5] Qurʾān 2:6.

[6] T: The author uses the Arabic word "al-nafʿīyah," which can refer to the term Utilitarianism. However, in this context it appears to be a general sense of utilitarianism that is driven by materialistic, selfish, and hedonistic interests.

[7] T: In a very broad sense that includes the type of opportunistic, materialistic, selfish and concupiscent utilitarianism the author is referring to here.

ليغشين أمتي من بعدي فتن كقطع الليل المظلم، يصبح الرجل فيها مؤمنًا ويمسي كافرًا، ويمسي مؤمنًا ويصبح كافرًا، يبيع أقوامٌ دينهم بعرضٍ من الدنيا قليل

After me, trials[1] – like segments of the dark night – will befall my community. In those trials, a person will be faithful in the morning and become unfaithful by the evening, and will be faithful in the evening and become unfaithful by the morning. Groups of people will sell their religion for a petty worldly gain.[2]

God Almighty says:

وَما أَرسَلنا في قَريَةٍ مِن نَذيرٍ إِلّا قالَ مُترَفوها إِنّا بِما أُرسِلتُم بِهِ كافِرونَ

وَقالوا نَحنُ أَكثَرُ أَموالًا وَأَولادًا وَما نَحنُ بِمُعَذَّبينَ

We did not send a warner to any town without its affluent ones saying, 'We indeed disbelieve in what you have been sent with.'

And they say, 'We have greater wealth and more children, and we will not be punished!'[3]

8) Those of One-Sided and Domineering Thinking: These are the ones who marginalize and eliminate the thinking of others. For they do not allow others to speak, they close the doors of intellectual dialogue, and they think that they own everything, including the minds of others. Rather, they try to draw out the terms and way of thinking for others, forcing them not to transgress and go beyond these. God Almighty says:

قالَ رَبِّ إِنّي دَعَوتُ قَومي لَيلًا وَنَهارًا

فَلَم يَزِدهُم دُعائي إِلّا فِرارًا

[1] T: *Fitan* (sing. *Fitnah*).

[2] *Kanz al-ʿUmmāl* 11:127.

[3] Qurʾān 34:34-35.

وَإِنِّي كُلَّما دَعَوتُهُم لِتَغفِرَ لَهُم جَعَلوا أَصابِعَهُم في آذانِهِم وَاستَغشَوا ثِيابَهُم وَأَصَرّوا وَاستَكبَرُوا استِكبارًا

He said, 'My Lord! Indeed, I have summoned my people night and day but my summons only increases their evasion.

Indeed, whenever I have summoned them, so that You might forgive them, they would put their fingers into their ears and draw their cloaks over their heads, and they were persistent [in their unfaithfulness], and disdainful in [their] arrogance.[1]

9) The Hypocrites: These are the ones who have double standards. Their rhetoric does not match up with their reality. What they hide in their hearts conflicts with what rolls off their tongue. God Almighty says,

وَمِنَ النّاسِ مَن يَقولُ آمَنّا بِاللَّهِ وَبِاليَومِ الآخِرِ وَما هُم بِمُؤمِنينَ

And among the people are those who say, 'We have faith in God and the Last Day,' but they have no faith.[2]

In another verse, God Almighty says:

مَثَلُهُم كَمَثَلِ الَّذِي استَوقَدَ نارًا فَلَمّا أَضاءَت ما حَولَهُ ذَهَبَ اللَّهُ بِنورِهِم وَتَرَكَهُم في ظُلُماتٍ لا يُبصِرونَ

صُمٌّ بُكمٌ عُميٌ فَهُم لا يَرجِعونَ

Their parable is that of one who lighted a torch, and when it had lit up all around him, God took away their light, and left them sightless in a manifold darkness.

Deaf, dumb, and blind, they will not come back.[3]

---

[1] Qur'ān 71:5-7.

[2] Qur'ān 2:8.

[3] Qur'ān 2:17-18.

10) The Wavering: Neither with these nor with those, the members of this group waver in between. Every day they align themselves with a different camp. For they have not had a well-defined path, let alone a well-defined beginning and an identifiable end. In light of this, they have not had a gauge for determining the options to follow and go after. Hence, they have not become enlightened with knowledge nor have they taken a clear path[1]. As a result, the more they walk, the more lost they become. As God Almighty says,

مُذَبذَبِينَ بَيْنَ ذَٰلِكَ لا إِلَىٰ هٰؤُلاءِ وَلا إِلَىٰ هٰؤُلاءِ [...]

> *wavering in between: neither with these nor with those. [...]*[2]

11) Those of Frivolous, Exhaustive Thinking: These are the ones whose only fixation and concern is to think. They have not studied thought for the sake of reality. Rather, they have studied thought for the sake of thought.[3] Their concern is the terminology and the label, as opposed to the reality and substance which is being labelled. They postulate hypothetical scenarios that are closer to whimsical fantasy than to what is real and true. For their aim is not to explicate how to treat issues and solve problems. Rather, their aim is to increase skepticisms and hypothetical scenarios. Their aim is to further expound on empty ideas --ideas sprouting from the cool head of a soulless body. In his *Sharḥ al-Asmāʾ al-Ḥusná*, Mullā Hādī al-Sabzawārī writes:

فانحراف القوة الدراكة منه إلى جانبي الإفراط والتفريط يسمّى جربزة وبلاهة واعتدالها حكمة [...]

---

[1] T: *Manhaj*; Can also mean program, methodology/method, approach or system; the connotations implied are related to a systematic approach.

[2] Qurʾān 4:143.

[3] T: The author is apparently not criticizing the pursuit of theoretical knowledge, no matter how specialized and sophisticated, but is rather criticizing the pursuit of thought for the frivolous thinking alone (i.e. rid of any concern for reality -- whether that reality be theoretical knowledge or practical knowledge).

The deviance of the power of intellect in the human being can be in the direction of excess[1]*, in which case it is called unreasonable cunning*[2]*, or in the direction of deficiency*[3]*, in which case it is called thoughtlessness*[4]*. The golden mean*[5] *of the power of intellect in the human being is called wisdom*[6]*.*[7]

The author of *al-Asfār* writes:

ومن أتم حالات النفس الشيطانية أن تكون مكّاره محيّلة جربزة كذوبة مظهرة للأمور على غير ما هي عليه شأنها التدليس والتلبيس بإبراز المقدّمات الباطلة في صورة الحقّ وإظهار الأكاذيب الواهية بهيئة الصدق، فهي أبدًا عاشقه للمكر والحيلة والوسوسة والمواعيد الكاذبة والأماني الباطلة كما قال تعالى في صفة الشيطان: يعدهم ويمنيهم وما يعدهم الشيطان الا غرورا .

One of the most fully actualized states of the satanic soul[8] *is for it to be characterized by excessive plotting, deceit, unreasonable cunning, profuse lying, and making things out to be different than they actually are. Such a soul deals with fraud and causes delusion by making invalid premises out to be right and by making whimsical lies out to be true. Such a soul is ever infatuated with plotting, deceit, satanic*

---

[1] T: Ifrāṭ.

[2] T: *Jarbazah*; Although this word can be linguistically related either to a loss or to a form of deception, as a term in Islamic ethics it refers to an unreasonable use of cognitive abilities, such as being obsessively compulsive in one's thoughts, and being overly analytical or skeptical without sound judgment.

[3] T: Tafrīṭ.

[4] T: *Balāhah*; Linguistically and as a term, this word can be thought of to mean thoughtlessness. But as a term, it could be used in a slightly broader sense to refer to nuanced forms of imprudence that represent a deficient use of intellect.

[5] T: Iʿtidāl.

[6] T: *Ḥikmah*; Prudence.

[7] Sharḥ al-Asmāʾ al-Ḥusná 1:68.

[8] T: *Nafs.*

temptations, broken promises[1] *and false hopes. As God Almighty says, describing Satan,*

يَعِدُهُمْ وَيُمَنِّيهِمْ ۖ وَمَا يَعِدُهُمُ الشَّيْطَانُ إِلَّا غُرُورًا

He makes them promises and gives them [false] hopes, yet Satan does not promise them anything but delusion[2].[3]

12) The Sophists[4]: These are the ones who do not see that any reality exists or that any values are fixed. Otherwise, in their minds, *what is right* is that *what is right* is changeable. There is no such thing as truth or correctness or reality. In their minds, the realness of reality is that there is no reality to it. The person who does not see him or herself to be real, *a fortiori* would not see his or her thoughts to be real and true. For [their view implies that] they are nothing but a [mentally-concocted] convention[5], illusion, shadow, and imagination. ʿAllāmah Majlīsī has relayed the following words of Avicenna[6],

[...] لأنا لو جوّزنا أن يرى الإنسان صورًا ويشاهدها ويتكلّم معها ويسمع أصواتها ويرى أشكالها ثمّ إنّها لا تكون موجودة البتة في الخارج، جاز أيضًا في كلّ هذه الأشياء التي نراها ونسمعها من صور الناس والجبال والبحار وأصوات الرعود أن لا يكون لشيء منها وجود في الخارج، بل يكون محض الخيالات ومحض الصور المرتسمة في الحسّ المشترك، ومعلوم أنّ القول به محض السفسطة.

---

[1] T: *al-Mawāʿīd al-Kādhibah*; This literally refers to lies related to appointments (*mawāʿīd*).

[2] Qurʾān 4:120

[3] Al-Asfār 3:185.

[4] T: *al-Sūfisṭāʾīyūn*; Related to the word sophistry (*safsaṭah*); This word is used in Islamic philosophy to refer to unreasonable skeptics or outright deniers of reality. The degree of skepticism being referred to depends on the context. It can be skepticism/denial about the reality of existence beyond oneself, the reality of one's own existence, or the reality of knowledge, for instance.

[5] T: Iʿtibār.

[6] T: al-Shaykh al-Raʾīs; Ibn Sīnā.

> *[...] For if we were to allow for the possibility that a human being could see images, watch them, speak with them, hear their sounds, and see their shapes, and then also propose that they are not at all existent in the external reality, then in regards to all of these things that we see and hear, such as the images of people, mountains, and seas, and the sounds of thunder, it would also be possible that none of them exist in the external reality. In other words, they would be sheer figments of imagination, sheer images imprinted in the common sense*[1]*, and it is known that such a claim is sheer sophistry.*[2]

13) The Slaves: These are the ones who envision their ideal self as servants and assistants of others. They are the worst among their kind. The drive and initiative for their actions in the external world are their subservience to others. They have thus become a burning fire pit, being eaten up in order to fuel the worldly life of others. God Almighty says:

> وَإِذا قيلَ لَهُم تَعالَوا إِلىٰ ما أَنزَلَ اللَّهُ وَإِلَى الرَّسولِ قالوا حَسبُنا ما وَجَدنا عَلَيهِ آباءَنا ۚ أَوَلَو كانَ آباؤُهُم لا يَعلَمونَ شَيئًا وَلا يَهتَدونَ
>
> *And when they are told, 'Come to what God has sent down and [come] to the Messenger,' they say, 'Sufficient for us is what we have found our fathers following.' What, even if their fathers did not know anything and were not guided?!*[3]

14) The Faithful: This is the group of those who have organized their journey of thought and practice, determined their objectives, defined their path, risen above the material and sensory world, lived [with] broadened horizons and [figuratively basking] in the natural environment, breathed in the fragrant scent of the messages espoused

---

[1] T: *al-Ḥiss al-Mushtarak*; One of the four internal senses.

[2] *Biḥār al-Anwār* 58:202-203.

[3] Qur'ān 5:104.

by prophets, reformers and the free. Hence, they have revered knowledge and thought, honored the people of knowledge and thought, acted according to knowledge and thought, persevered in their journey, and risen above the outlined boundaries and the barriers obstructing them from achieving the excellence they are after. God Almighty says:

الَّذِينَ يُؤمِنونَ بِالغَيبِ وَيُقيمونَ الصَّلاةَ وَمِمّا رَزَقناهُم يُنفِقونَ

وَالَّذينَ يُؤمِنونَ بِما أُنزِلَ إِلَيكَ وَما أُنزِلَ مِن قَبلِكَ وَبِالآخِرَةِ هُم يوقِنونَ

أُولٰئِكَ عَلىٰ هُدًى مِن رَبِّهِم ۖ وَأُولٰئِكَ هُمُ المُفلِحونَ

[Those] who believe in the Unseen, and maintain the prayer, and spend out of what We have provided for them;

and who believe in what has been sent down to you and what was sent down before you, and are certain of the Hereafter.

Those follow their Lord's guidance, and it is they who are the felicitous.[1]

The existence of groups such as these is an innate, intuitive fact. No two individuals would disagree about this. That is unless our theorizing is to be based off of idealistic values, as not to hurt the feelings of our community and society. But we want to be realistic. We want to work on prevention and treatment in Mahdī-related education to the greatest extent possible. We want to treat the instances of deviance that can be treated by filling in the gaps and bringing about the means for sound understanding. Doing so requires the following:

Firstly: Admitting that society includes these different types of groups.

---

[1] Qur'ān 2:3-5

Secondly: Identifying and establishing the *default principle*[1] and the reference to refer to when a satisfactory solution, answer and treatment has not been reached.

For there is no doubt that in order for a physician to be successful at diagnosing and treating a particular illness, he or she must first admit that [the patient in] his or her society is carrying and living with the [cause of that illness]. It has been reported that our master, the 12th Imam, said,

> [...] قد آذانا جهلاءُ الشيعةِ وحمقاؤهم ، ومَن دينُه جناحُ البعوضة أرجحُ منه
>
> *[...] The ignorant among the Shīʿah, the foolish among them, and those whose faith*[2] *is outweighed by the wing of a gnat, have indeed hurt us.*[3]

---

[1] T: *al-Aṣl.*

[2] T: *Dīn*; Religion, including a relevant worldview and practices prescribed because of that worldview.

[3] *Al-Iḥtijāj* 2:289; *Biḥār al-Anwār* 25:267 / Bāb 10 / Ḥ 9.

CHAPTER 2

THE *DEFAULT PRINCIPLE* IS PRECAUTION

Acknowledging that society includes these categories of individuals is one premise --an intuitive one at that. Recognizing that, [in the greater scheme of things], we are living in the stage of being tried and tested is another premise. Noting and conceding that, historically, many have collapsed and failed in the face of the exam is yet another premise. In light of these premises, one must admit that the issue [at hand] is a difficult one which requires diligent efforts in understanding and also requires sound, good taste[1] in assessing. For the issue, this worldly life, [that is], is a vast sea which is not traversed by every aspiring swimmer, and a lofty target which is not hit by every archer.

It has been reported that Imam Mūsá the son of Jaʿfar al-Kāẓim said the following, in part of a lengthy address to Hishām:

> [...] إِنَّ لُقْمَانَ قَالَ لِابْنِه تَوَاضَعْ لِلْحَقِّ تَكُنْ أَعْقَلَ النَّاسِ وإِنَّ الْكُيِّسَ لَدَى الْحَقِّ يَسِيرٌ يَا بُنَيَّ إِنَّ الدُّنْيَا بَحْرٌ عَمِيقٌ قَدْ غَرِقَ فِيهَا عَالَمٌ كَثِيرٌ فَلْتَكُنْ سَفِينَتُكَ فِيهَا تَقْوَى اللَّه وحَشْوُهَا الإِيمَانَ وشِرَاعُهَا التَّوَكُّلَ وقَيِّمُهَا الْعَقْلَ ودَلِيلُهَا الْعِلْمَ وسُكَّانُهَا الصَّبْرَ [...]
>
> *[...] Indeed, Luqmān said the following to his son, "Be humble before what is right and you will be the one with the best [sense of] reason among the people. Indeed, the prudent when it comes to what is right are few. My son,*

---

[1] T: *al-Dhawq al-ḥasan al-salīm*; This can be understood as a sense of taste and sound judgment, used in different contexts, that enables one to identify suitable, befitting conclusions.

> *indeed this worldly life is a deep sea in which many people have drowned. Hence, let your ship be God-consciousness[1], its cargo be faith, its sail be reliance [on God], its captain be the intellect, its guide be knowledge, and its helm[2] be patience."*[3]

At this point, it has become clear that every individual must fall under the umbrella of one of the aforementioned categories, maybe even more than one, regardless of whether the individual means to do so or not, and regardless of whether the individual knows that is the case or not. For a human being is bound to be in some form of motion and must be on some sort of a journey. Every motion has an aim, even if that aim is nothing but observing traditions and customs, giving in to desires, or moving in the direction of matters which are agreeable to one's disposition. It has been reported that the Commander of the Faithful, Imam ʿAlī, wrote the following as part of a letter to his appointee[4] over Baṣrah, ʿUthmān ibn Ḥunayf al-Anṣārī, after he was told that the latter had been invited to the banquet of a group from the city and had attended it:

> [...] فَانْظُرْ إِلَى مَا تَقْضَمُه مِنْ هَذَا الْمَقْضَمِ - فَمَا اشْتَبَه عَلَيْكَ عِلْمُه فَالْفِظْه - ومَا أَيْقَنْتَ بِطِيبِ وُجُوهِه فَنَلْ مِنْه - أَلَا وإِنَّ لِكُلِّ مَأْمُومٍ إِمَاماً يَقْتَدِي بِه - ويَسْتَضِيءُ بِنُورِ عِلْمِه - أَلَا وإِنَّ إِمَامَكُمْ قَدِ اكْتَفَى مِنْ دُنْيَاه بِطِمْرَيْه - ومِنْ طُعْمِه بِقُرْصَيْه - أَلَا وإِنَّكُمْ لَا تَقْدِرُونَ عَلَى ذَلِكَ - ولَكِنْ أَعِينُونِي بِوَرَعٍ واجْتِهَادٍ وعِفَّةٍ وسَدَادٍ [...]

> *[...] Look to what you bite at from this food[5] – leave out whatever you are unsure about and take from that which you are sure is lawful in its various dimensions. Indeed,*

---

[1] T: *Taqwá Allāh*; Piety, vigilance regarding one's responsibility before God.

[2] T: *Sukkān*; In this context, the part of the ship responsible for its motion/stillness (hence, the connection to the root SKN); Associated with the steering mechanism.

[3] *Al-Kāfī* 1:15 / Kitāb al-ʿAql wa al-Jahl / Ḥ 12.

[4] T: ʿĀmil; In this case, the appointee was working for him as governor.

[5] T: Maqḍam; Object of biting; food.

> *every follower has a leader whom he follows and is enlightened by the light of his knowledge. Indeed, your Imam has contented himself with two worn-out pieces of clothing from his life in this world and two loaves [of bread] for his food. Certainly, you cannot handle doing so, but at least support me with piety[1], exerted efforts[2], chastity[3] and uprightness[4] [...][5]*

In order to achieve the aim, one must choose a school of thought and a particular ideology with a clear worldview that is to be studied and evaluated among other corresponding approaches. It is also a must to choose a spiritual and thought leader who outlines one's path in terms of values and course of action, guarantees the safety of the path, and safeguards one's arrival to the destination and successful, sound end. Moreover, the one treading the path should head toward and ascend to the clear, towering stage, and should keep the end in sight of his or her weary eyes.

For this reason, one must establish the *default principle* to be referred to [whenever in doubt] when it comes to determining one's line of thinking and choosing one's leader: Should one default to being on the safe side ([the *default principle of*] *precaution*) or is one, by default, permitted to take a risk ([the *default principle of*] *permissibility*)?

The correct *default principle* is the former – one must not give in easily, take matters lightly and obey rashly. The *default principle* that should be deferred to is the principle of precaution – verification, investigation, examination, and inspection; the principle of pausing to consider matters carefully and contemplate; the principle of reflecting, learning and reservation. The *default principle* is precaution ––not permissibility, not

---

[1] T: Wara'.

[2] T: Ijtihād.

[3] T: 'Iffah.

[4] T: Sadād.

[5] *Nahj al-Balāghah* 3:70 / Ḥ 45.

simple-mindedness, not taking things lightly, not inclining toward just any person who calls out, not hastiness, not melting away quickly, and not [having] a devalued price. One should not enter a deal in which the compensation and that which is being sold is trivial or abased. [When it comes to] the weakness of a thinker's [intellectual] merchandise, [it] is due either to the flimsiness of his or her evidence, to the weakness and meekness of his or her assumptions[1], or to the spurious nature of his or her thought.

It has been reported that Imam ʿAlī said,

كُنْ فِي الْفِتْنَةِ كَابْنِ اللَّبُونِ - لَا ظَهْرٌ فَيُرْكَبَ ولَا ضَرْعٌ فَيُحْلَبَ

> *In the midst of wrongdoing[2], be like an adolescent camel --[having] neither a back for riding nor an udder for milking.*[3]

Taking the position of spectator, avoiding any interference and staying out of and away from the fight is of no avail. Movement and thought that is rid of a worldview, that is removed from philosophy and philosophizing is of no avail. Being satisfied with a shallow theory, rid of intricacies, is of no avail. Why? Because the issue at hand is a double-edged sword, subject to a number of conflicting matters. The issue does not allow for sheer spectatorship and indifference, because every motion and step taken requires a drive and propelling fuel --a group of intellectual matters, worldviews and psychological states. This group of matters creates a close-knit fabric of aspirations and choices related to life and its modes, one's attire, nutrition, types of relationships, and social – and even individual – affiliations. Hence, [if one is to default on the side of precaution, then] there is no way out of choosing a spiritual and thought leader.[4] Such a leader must be chosen according to particular and established criteria. Even more,

---

[1] T: Muʿṭayāt; givens, premises.

[2] T: *Fitnah.*

[3] *Nahj al-Balāghah* 4:3 / Ḥ 1.

[4] T: Assuming one has not already developed into such a qualified leader, of course.

such a leader must be comprehensively tested in the founding stage and subsequently. This is what we meant by the *default principle* of verification[1].

In addition to this *default principle* being the verdict of intuitive, innate reasoning, it is also the case that reasonable individuals[2] would find it blameworthy for a person to walk through a valley of uncharted territory[3]. God Almighty says,

[...] وَلا تُلقوا بِأَيديكُم إِلَى التَّهلُكَةِ [...]

[…] and do not cast yourselves into destruction […][4]

God Almighty also says,

[...] فَإِن تَنازَعتُم فِي شَيءٍ فَرُدّوهُ إِلَى اللَّهِ وَالرَّسولِ [...]

[…] And if you dispute concerning anything, refer it to God and the Messenger […][5]

Prophet Muḥammad is reported to have said:

حلال بيّن، وحرام بيّن، وبينهما شبهات، لا يعلمها كثير من الناس، فمن اتّقى الشبهات فقد استبرى لدينه وعرضه. ومن وقع في الشبهات، وقع في الحرام، كالراعي حول الحمى، يوشك أن يقع فيه. ألا وإنّ لكلّ ملك حمى، وإنّ حمى الله محارمه

[There exist] Permissible matters which are clear, forbidden matters which are clear, and in between there

---

[1] T: *al-Tafaḥḥuṣ*; Verification, checking; the author used this idea to elaborate on the principle of precaution.

[2] T: *al-ʿUqalāʾ*.

[3] T: Without taking proper precautions, that is.

[4] Qurʾān 2:195.

[5] Qurʾān 4:59.

> *exist unclear matters[1] which are unknown to many people. So whoever guards against the unclear matters has sought to clear his or her conscience[2] for his or her religion and honor[3]. As for the one who tumbles into the unclear matters, he or she tumbles into that which is forbidden, similar to how the shepherd grazing [animals] around a protected area[4] is on the verge of tumbling into it. Indeed, every sovereign has a protected area, and indeed God's protected area is [the area of] that which He has forbidden.[5]*

For, indeed, what is meant by, "guards against the unclear matters," is that the person investigates the situation(s).

Imam Jaʿfar al-Ṣādiq is reported to have said:

> لا يسعكم فيما ينزل بكم مما لا تعلمون إلا الكف عنه والتثبت والرد إلى أئمة الهدى حتى يحملوكم فيه على القصد ويجلوا عنكم فيه العمى، ويعرفوكم فيه الحق، قال الله تعالى: "فَسْئَلُوا أَهْلَ الذِّكْرِ إِنْ كُنْتُمْ لا تَعْلَمُونَ"

> *When a matter befalls you that you do not know, it is not permissible for you [to do anything] but to hold back from it, to verify[6], and to refer it back to the Imams of guidance*

---

[1] T: *Shubuhāt* (sing. *Shubhah*); In this context, these unclear/ambiguous matters are arguably those which do not clearly fall under either the permissible designation or the forbidden designation.

[2] T: Although the Arabic from this source reads *istabrá*, which can be rendered, "sought to mend," given that many other sources read *istabraʾa*, it is likely that the former is a typographical error.

[3] T: ʿIrḍ

[4] T: *al-Ḥimá*; In this context, an area which is protected as not to allow for grazing.

[5] *ʿAwālī al-Laʾālī* 1:89 / Ḥ 24.

[6] T: *al-Tathabbut*; Verification; ascertainment; checking.

such that they may have you take the judicious position[1] *regarding it, remove your blindness regarding it, and show you what is right regarding it. God Almighty says,*

[...] فَسْـَٔلُوا أَهْلَ الذِّكْرِ إِنْ كُنْتُمْ لا تَعْلَمُونَ

[...] ask the People of Knowledge[2] *if you do not know*[3].[4]

Hence, one's choice of leader is not by default a sound selection. When a person chooses his or her purview of thought, it is not by default a sound selection. This is especially true if the issue of thought is comprehensive, permeating an individual's every movement and stillness at all times – even beyond this realm[5]. Hence, that which is at stake is vital, calling for diligent precautions.

But what about reports of teachings that urge people to give others the benefit of the doubt? For it has been reported that Imam Jaʿfar al-Ṣādiq has said:

---

[1] T: *al-Qaṣd*; This translation reflects the meaning of *al-qaṣd* to be "moderation." However, *al-qaṣd* can mean "intent" or "aim" as well.

[2] T: *Ahl al-Dhikr*; the People of the Remembrance (*al-Dhikr*). Commentators on the holy Qurʾān understand this phrase to refer/apply to the people of knowledge/acquaintance/awareness in various fields, but especially, if not exclusively, the people of the (Divinely Revealed) Remembrance (i.e. the Qurʾān in the Muslim context, whose People/Guardians are the Prophet Muḥammad and his Divinely appointed successors).

[3] Qurʾān 16:43.

[4] *Al-Kāfī* 1:50 / Ḥ 10.

[5] T: *al-Nashʾah*; The genesis/formation; "This" genesis/formation refers to the worldly realm we live in. The Qurʾān refers to other instances of genesis/formation beyond this one (e.g., 29:20 and 53:47).

قال أمير المؤمنين (عليه السلام) في كلام له: ضع أمر أخيك على أحسنه حتَّى يأتيك ما يغلبك منه ولا تظننَّ بكلمة خرجت من أخيك سوءًا وأنت تجد لها في الخير محملًا

In some of his remarks, the Commander of the Faithful, Imam ʿAlī, said the following, "Take what comes from your brother in the best way possible until something comes to you from him that overwhelms[1] you. Indeed, do not think ill of a word that came out of your brother['s mouth] so long as you can find a good way to take it.[2]

There are also other reports along these lines. What about such reports? Such reports are intended to map out life and order at the level of peaceful coexistence and brotherhood, not when it comes to identifying the leader and role model to be followed. [With such reports clarified, it stands,] then, that every individual must have his or her own exemplar, imam and gauge to identify his or her role model and course of action. For this reason, the Imam has said,

[...] من هجم على أمر بغير علم جدع أنف نفسه [...]

[...] One who engages in a matter without knowledge cuts off his or her own nose [...][3]

Hence, one must rely on a firm foundation.

The Commander of the Faithful, Imam ʿAlī, is reported to have said the following in a sermon of his:

---

[1] T: *Yaghlibuka*; Defeats you, not allowing for another interpretation or good way of taking it.

[2] *Al-Kāfī* 2:362 / Bāb al-Tuhmah wa Sūʾ al-Ẓann / Ḥ 3.

[3] *Al-Kāfī* 1:26 and 27 / Kitāb al-ʿAql wa al-Jahl / Ḥ 29.

وإنَّمَا سُمِّيَتِ الشُّبْهَةُ شُبْهَةً لأَنَّهَا تُشْبِه الْحَقَّ - فَأَمَّا أَوْلِيَاءُ الله فَضِيَاؤُهُمْ فِيهَا الْيَقِينُ ودَلِيلُهُمْ سَمْتُ الْهُدَى، وأَمَّا أَعْدَاءُ الله فَدُعَاؤُهُمْ فِيهَا الضَّلَالُ ودَلِيلُهُمُ الْعَمَى، فَمَا يَنْجُو مِنَ الْمَوْتِ مَنْ خَافَهُ، ولَا يُعْطَى الْبَقَاءَ مَنْ أَحَبَّهُ

A misconception[1] was only named a "misconception" because it exhibits resemblance to [but misses] that which is the right [conception]. As for the friends of God[2], in the midst of a misconception their light is sound knowledge[3] and their guide is the path[4] of guidance. As for the enemies of God, in the midst of a misconception their call is [the call of] misguidance and their guide is blindness. Those who fear death will not escape it and those who love immortality will not be granted it.[5]

It is also reported that Imam ʿAlī said:

أَلَا فَالْحَذَرَ الْحَذَرَ مِنْ طَاعَةِ سَادَاتِكُمْ وكُبَرَائِكُمُ الَّذِينَ تَكَبَّرُوا عَنْ حَسَبِهِمْ وتَرَفَّعُوا فَوْقَ نَسَبِهِمْ وأَلْقَوُا الْهَجِينَةَ عَلَى رَبِّهِمْ وجَاحَدُوا الله عَلَى مَا صَنَعَ بِهِمْ مُكَابَرَةً لِقَضَائِه ومُغَالَبَةً لِآلَائِه، فَإِنَّهُمْ قَوَاعِدُ أَسَاسِ الْعَصَبِيَّةِ، ودَعَائِمُ أَرْكَانِ الْفِتْنَةِ، وسُيُوفُ اعْتِزَاءِ الْجَاهِلِيَّةِ، فَاتَّقُوا الله ولَا تَكُونُوا لِنِعَمِه عَلَيْكُمْ أَضْدَاداً، ولَا لِفَضْلِه عِنْدَكُمْ حُسَّاداً، ولَا تُطِيعُوا الأَدْعِيَاءَ الَّذِينَ شَرِبْتُمْ بِصَفْوِكُمْ كَدَرَهُمْ، وخَلَطْتُمْ بِصِحَّتِكُمْ مَرَضَهُمْ، وأَدْخَلْتُمْ فِي حَقِّكُمْ بَاطِلَهُمْ، وهُمْ أَسَاسُ الْفُسُوقِ، وأَحْلَاسُ الْعُقُوقِ، اتَّخَذَهُمْ إِبْلِيسُ مَطَايَا ضَلَالٍ، وجُنْداً بِهِمْ يَصُولُ عَلَى النَّاسِ، وتَرَاجِمَةً يَنْطِقُ عَلَى أَلْسِنَتِهِمْ، اسْتِرَاقاً لِعُقُولِكُمْ، ودُخُولًا فِي عُيُونِكُمْ، ونَفْثاً فِي أَسْمَاعِكُمْ، فَجَعَلَكُمْ مَرْمَى نَبْلِه، ومَوْطِئَ قَدَمِه، ومَأْخَذَ يَدِه [...]

---

[1] T: *Shubhah*; Related to the root SH-B-H, which can have the meaning of being similar, exhibiting resemblance; (resemblance to *what is right* from some aspect, but mistaken).

[2] T: *Awliyāʾ*.

[3] T: *al-Yaqīn*; Certainty. Some commentators describe this to mean "sound knowledge" in this context.

[4] T: *Samt.*

[5] *Nahj al-Balāghah* 1:89 / Sermon 38.

Indeed, beware, beware of obedience to your chiefs and elders who have aggrandized themselves beyond their legacy, raised themselves above their origins, attributed the trait [they] abhorred to their Lord, and rejected [due gratitude to] God for what He had made of them[1], *stubbornly opposing His decree and contesting His blessings. For, indeed, they are the foundations for the basis of bigotry*[2], *the supports for the cornerstones of mischief*[3], *and the [ones who use their] swords for the pride of ignorance. Therefore, be mindful*[4] *of God, do not be antagonistic to His blessings, and do not be the envious [enemies]*[5] *of His grace. Do not obey the impostors*[6] *-- those whom you have drunk their polluted [drink] along with your pure one, [whom] you have mixed their disease with your sound health and [whom] you have injected their wrong into your right. That is while they are the basis of transgression and the ones who cling to ingratitude*[7]. *Iblīs*[8] *has used them as rides [carrying people] into misguidance, as soldiers with whom he attacks people, and as interpreters, speaking through their mouths, robbing you of your wits, infiltrating your vision, and blowing into*

---

[1] T: I used the phrase, "made of them," to refer to the blessings that God has bestowed upon them --God's generous acts toward them.

[2] T: al-ʿAṣabīyah.

[3] T: *fitnah*; see earlier footnote on *iftitān*.

[4] T: *Ittaqū*; be Godwary, God-conscious, God-fearing, pious in one's choices.

[5] T: Do not do that which causes the grace to be pushed away.

[6] T: *al-Adʿiyāʾ* (sing. *Daʿīy*); Those who are apparently Muslims but are actually hypocrites, or those who claim to descend from someone who is not really their father. This can be used to refer to unqualified individuals claiming a position requiring distinguished qualifications, impostors in a sense.

[7] T: al-ʿUqūq.

[8] T: Satan.

> *your ears. He has thus made you a target of his arrows, a stepping stone*[1] *for his feet, and an object taken by his hand [...]*[2]

It is also reported that he said,

> [...] أَلَا وإِنَّ أَخْوَفَ الْفِتَنِ عِنْدِي عَلَيْكُمْ فِتْنَةُ بَنِي أُمَيَّة [...]
>
> *[...] Indeed, the most frightening of trials*[3] *that I fear for you is the trial of the Umayyads [...]*[4]

"The trial of the Umayyads" apparently refers to the features of that trial, features which recur in every age. Hence, it includes the trial of the Abbasids as well.[5]

On the other hand, someone might make the following argument: Many people do not have an outlook and a vision. As such, they do not need to establish a *default principle*, go through the hassle and exhaust themselves, or spend their time with these types of matters.

But this is not the case. For even those individuals have an approach. Their approach is characterized by not caring about what lies beyond[6], by not deeply thinking about preparing provisions for their journey, by clinging to the sensory, by seeking after the short-term[7] and abandoning the long-term[8], and by satiating carnal, animalistic instincts. God Almighty says,

---

[1] T: *Mawṭiʾ qadamih*; A place for his foot to step.

[2] *Nahj al-Balāghah* 2:142-143 / Sermon 192 called al-Qāṣiʿah.

[3] T: *Fitan* (sing. *Fitnah*).

[4] *Nahj al-Balāghah* 1:183 / Sermon 93.

[5] T: In other words, the author understands the reference to the "Umayyads" in this report to be archetypal, not limited to the historical instance of the Umayyads but rather extending to those who resemble the historical Umayyads in the features pertinent to this report.

[6] T: Beyond this world as well as the metaphysical world.

[7] T: *al-ʿĀjilah*; The present worldly life.

[8] T: *al-Ākhirah*; The hereafter.

[...] إِنْ هُمْ إِلَّا كَالْأَنْعَامِ ۖ بَلْ هُمْ أَضَلُّ سَبِيلًا

[...] They are just like cattle; rather they are further astray from the way.[1]

In a few words, every individual – and I mean *every* individual – has a vision, a philosophy, and a set of intellectual principles, even if he or she does not make them explicit and even if he or she tries to fool him or herself to the contrary. God Almighty says,

بَلِ الْإِنسَانُ عَلَىٰ نَفْسِهِ بَصِيرَةٌ * وَلَوْ أَلْقَىٰ مَعَاذِيرَهُ

Rather, the human being is an [eye-witness] against him or herself,

even though he or she makes excuses.[2]

Thus, some philosophies, which are based on a *default principle* of utopianism[3] and taking a liking to conflicting ideas and warring leaders, can be traced back to the *default principle* of taking things lightly[4], of lazy thinking, of not going through the hassle of thinking matters through, of giving up the talk of the Hereafter, and of not becoming accustomed to accepting the Hour of Reckoning and Retribution. What gives away this *default principle* of theirs is that they do not apply these rules in their worldly matters. In other words, they are completely careful and precise when it comes to the mundane matters of this worldly life, while they do not delve into awareness about their Hereafter fate in the slightest. Thus, the double standard between the two realms suffices for them to delve into the path of deviance and transgression. For it has been reported that

---

[1] Qurʾān 25:44.

[2] Qurʾān 75:14-15.

[3] T: In a sense that is unrealistic, with an emphasis on being unrealistic, not on being ideal. For such notions may arguably not truly represent the "ideal" state of excellence.

[4] T: *al-Tasāmuḥ*; In this context, having too much tolerance for error, lacking the appropriate seriousness for what is at stake.

Masʿadah ibn Ziyād heard Imam Jaʿfar al-Ṣādiq address a question about the following verse in the holy Qurʾān:

[...] فَلِلَّهِ الْحُجَّةُ الْبَالِغَةُ [...]

[...] To God belongs the conclusive argument [...][1]

In this regard, Imam Jaʿfar al-Ṣādiq is reported to have said:

إنَّ الله تعالى يقول للعبد يوم القيامة: عبدي أكنتَ عالماً؟ فإن قال: نعم، قال له: أفلا عملتَ بما علمت؟ وإن قال: كنتُ جاهلاً، قال له: أفلا تعلَّمتَ حتَّى تعمل؟ فيخصمه، وذلك الحجة البالغة.

Indeed, God Almighty says the following to His servant[2] *on the Day of Judgment, "My servant, were you a knowledgeable person*[3]*?" If he or she says, "Yes," then God says to him or her, "[Why] did you not then act according to what you knew?" And if he or she says, "I was ignorant," then God says to him or her, "[Why] did you not then learn such that you may act [accordingly]?" Thus, God*

---

[1] Qurʾān 6:149.

[2] T: *ʿAbd*; Although the word "ʿabd" can refer to a "slave", the word "slave" as understood in English-speaking countries today is often associated with a history of human enslavement and inhumane practices. The so-called "slavery" of a human being before God, on the other hand, is an empowering experience, even a liberating one. For every creature, let alone human beings, depend on God Almighty for their very existence as well as their sustainment in every passing moment. A creature has no power, liberty, or existence without God Almighty, and thus it is only through "slavery" to God that one can *be*, let alone be *free*. I have used the word "servant" to avoid the oppressive connotations associated with the word "slave."

[3] T: *ʿĀlim*; In some contexts, the word ʿālim refers to a sagely, erudite scholar. However, in other cases, it more plainly refers to one who is learned. The range of knowledgeability implied by the word depends on the context in which it is used.

> *would win the argument. That is the conclusive argument*[1].[2]

The fact that God contends with and wins the argument against the unlearned servant indicates that seeking knowledge is mandatory and that the ignorant individual is not excused.

---

[1] T: *al-Ḥujjah al-bālighah*; from Qurʾān 6:149.

[2] *Amālī al-Mufīd*: 227-228.

PART TWO

MAHDĪ-RELATED TERMS/ENTRIES AT THE LEVEL OF CONCEPTS AND BELIEFS

One must admit from the get-go that there is an initial obscurity in dealing with the Mahdī proposition. Because of this, greedy hands have been able to take advantage of it and infiltrate it through the gaps in Mahdī culture that a collective of people experience. These hands have made their mark, robbed the Mahdī proposition of its splendor, portrayed it as being in a corner of some deviant monkhood, deprived it of its beauty, and disabled the role of reason in it. They have made way for those of poor knowledge to weigh in on it, for the weak of mind to wander in its alleyways, and for those of weak spirits to theorize about it. They have incited their followers to boycott the gatherings of knowledge and have inspired their friends with upside down ideas. Thus, values have been lost and the cards have been shuffled. The [one who long went figuratively] barefoot has put shoes on and has been pushed to the forefront.[1] Moreover, the one of lesser merit has taken the lead. They have entered the houses not from their doors[2]. They have brought the displaced outcast nearer. The person who was a nobody has been made out to be somebody. The one who would be careless regarding ritual purity[3] has been made out to be a leading scholar in the community. Goatherders [without intellectual credentials] have been made out to be the intellectual elite and the bare [of learning] have donned the garb of knowledge.[4]

Hence, one must open the way by being illuminated by the beacons of light, raising the curtain, clarifying concepts, explaining terms, removing ambiguity, presentation the image, filling the gap, and defining the

---

[1] T: The author seems to have in mind, for example, those who take the lead prematurely --without having a history of relevant credentials.

[2] T: Not from the designated entry points.

[3] T: *al-Bawwāl ʿalá ʿaqibayh*; The one who would urinate onto his heels. This expression can imply that the individual does not care about ritual purity, for urine is ritually impure.

[4] T: The implication here is not that a goatherder, for example, can never be part of the intellectual elite. Rather, the implication is that roles and qualifications have suffered such that a goatherder who does not have the qualifications for leading intellectual discourse has been put forward as part of the intellectual elite.

standard, the way to the water, and how the fertile land is watered with the water of life from the pure household of Muḥammad.

What follows are some terms that we wanted to clarify, removing the ambiguity associated with them. We will discuss each of them in a separate chapter.

CHAPTER 3

THE STANDING OF IMAM MAHDĪ

There is no doubt that, for the Shīʿah, the Mahdī idea and creed are an external reality, not a philosophically rational – yet merely hypothetical – issue and not merely a bunch of psychological delusions. For the Imam has an actual human existence, one connected to the Divine[1] in a way similar to how other Divinely appointed friends[2] of God are connected. He has characteristics of a broader scope than those applying to body, physique and matter. For he has moral and spiritual features and he extends a blessed family tree. God Almighty says,

قُلْ أَرَأَيْتُمْ إِنْ أَصْبَحَ مَاؤُكُمْ غَوْرًا فَمَن يَأْتِيكُم بِمَاءٍ مَّعِينٍ

> *Say, 'Tell me, should your water go deep [becoming hidden underground], who will bring you running water [that is apparent and accessible]?*[3]

At least when considered in light of the reports[4], it is perhaps apparent that what is meant by "water" in this holy verse is not merely "water" in the literal sense but also in a previously accustomed[5] sense. It is these attributes that paint a picture of the Imam's personality for us.

---

[1] T: *al-Samāʾ*; The heavens; the metaphysical realm.

[2] T: *al-Awliyāʾ*; The saintly, erudite sages. In this context, they are the prophets and Divinely appointed successors of those prophets.

[3] Qurʾān 67:30.

[4] For example: *Kifāyat al-Athar* 120; *Kamāl al-Dīn* 1:325; and al-Ṭūsī's *al-Ghaybah* 101.

[5] T: *Maʿhūd*; Meaning, there is an explanation for water that you have become accustomed to and that familiarity is being relied on here. The reports the author

It is important to emphasize the idea of becoming acquainted with the Mahdī, specifically, by tracing his general and specific traits as they appear in the reports [attributed to the Prophet and the Imams]. This is as opposed to relying on historical accounts [not attributed to the Prophet and the Imams] --a human approach that is based on the sensory, the accessible[1], and that which is observable. The latter is not the approach to be taken in this regard, because the Imam is hidden, in occultation, and not apparent except in very limited circumstances in terms of time and place. Hence, there is no point in referring to chroniclers for them to tell us about his features and merits. The report-based approach, on the other hand, is different, because it does not depend on or rely on the sensory and the accessible alone. Rather, it reveals that which is beyond [the sensory by drawing on the words attributed to the conduits of Divine revelation]. This means that the historical approach – and descriptive approaches more generally – are limited in the likes of these matters. Even more so, from a particular aspect, they may have a damaging effect.[2] Conversely, the report-based approach reflects the reality in question extensively and precisely.[3] Furthermore, it is through the report-based approach that all of the following are put in order within our outlook: the link for becoming known

---

is referring to explain the "water" in the verse to be the Imam and/or the Qāʾim (the Mahdī).

[1] T: *al-Ḥāḍir*; That which is present; presumably, as opposed to that which is metaphysical, Unseen, or otherwise beyond.

[2] T: The author seems to be referring to how a descriptive approach does not capture all angles of a historical reality because that is not what it is meant to do. Limiting evidence to external artifacts and documents, for instance, typically excludes admitting evidence based on elaborate philosophical arguments, let alone appealing to sensibilities of an ethical, aesthetic and/or mystical kind. Depending on the assumptions and other specifics of one's descriptive approach, such implications may even be reductively "damaging" to the objects of study being described and the individuals/societies with stakes in them.

[3] T: For those who accept the authority of the Prophet and the Imams to whom the reports are (verifiably) attributed.

to[1] the Imam, the means of connecting, our need for him[2], the prospects of interacting, the responsibilities, the disclosure of some fruits of his existence during the *ghaybah* era, acquaintance with the global campaign of bringing about reform and justice, reviving Divine[3] values, and arriving at the final chapter of the Divine's book of the Universe. In accordance with this study, we might have reservations about some reports and refine the report-heritage by filtering out planted fabrications and forgeries.[4]

The Twelver, Imāmīyah Shīʿah believe that the [Lord's] successor[5] on earth must not have any deficiencies when it comes to the different forms of excellence[6] that are possible[7] for him. There must not be any non-existential dimensions to his being. Moreover, there must not exist any evil or lacking aspects to him. Rather, his entire being is existentially good and beautiful. For, in his words, actions, character and knowledge, he is generosity and light. Hence, blessed souls yearn for him and are drawn toward him.

Divine selection of the friends[8] of God is by no means haphazard. For, indeed, they are the Godly lights – lights that existed before the creation of the universe. They are the complete creation of God, through whom the

---

[1] T: al-Taʿarrufu bihi.

[2] T: Or "it," meaning the connection to him.

[3] T: *al-Samāʾ*; The Heavens; the metaphysical realm.

[4] T: The methodology for doing so is partly elucidated in the book but remains an exercise of holistic reading (at the discretion of qualified specialists).

[5] T: *al-Khalīfah*; The viceroy or representative; This appears to allude to Qurʾān 2:30,

وَإِذ قالَ رَبُّكَ لِلمَلائِكَةِ إِنّي جاعِلٌ فِي الأَرضِ خَليفَةً [...]

When your Lord said to the angels, 'Indeed I am going to set a viceroy on the earth,'

[6] T: *Kamāl*; Existential excellence; lacking deficiency; perfection; form of completeness.

[7] T: That are possible for his level of existence, as a created, limited being, as the best of God's servants in a given age.

[8] T: *al-Awliyāʾ*; The Friends of God; the saintly, erudite sages. In this context, they are the prophets and Divinely appointed successors of those prophets.

Creator's attributes manifest. This statement does not mean that such perfect creatures and God's attributes are one and the same. For the Sacred Essence of God is infinite – by virtue of His very essence – let alone His attributes and qualities of excellence. There is a vast gorge between the infinite and the finite. Therefore, the fact that the [Twelver Shīʿah] Imams are the names of God[1] does not entail that they and God's Sacred Essence are one and the same. As such, the following has been reported in the signed document[2] attributed to the Twelfth Imam:

> بِسْمِ اللّه الرَّحْمَنِ الرَّحِيمِ، أُدع في كلّ يوم من أيّام رجب: اللَّهُمَّ إِنِّي أَسْأَلُكَ بِمَعَانِي جَمِيعِ مَا يَدْعُوكَ بِهِ وُلاةُ أَمْرِكَ الْمَأْمُونُونَ عَلَى سِرِّكَ الْمُسْتَبْشِرُونَ بِأَمْرِكَ الْوَاصِفُونَ لِقُدْرَتِكَ الْمُعْلِنُونَ لِعَظَمَتِكَ أَسْأَلُكَ بِمَا نَطَقَ فِيهِمْ مِنْ مَشِيَّتِكَ فَجَعَلْتَهُمْ مَعَادِنَ لِكَلِمَاتِكَ وأَرْكَانا لِتَوْحِيدِكَ وآيَاتِكَ ومَقَامَاتِكَ الَّتِي لا تَعْطِيلَ لَهَا فِي كُلِّ مَكَانٍ يَعْرِفُكَ بِهَا مَنْ عَرَفَكَ لا فَرْقَ بَيْنَكَ وبَيْنَهَا إِلا أَنَّهُمْ عِبَادُكَ وخَلْقُكَ فَتْقُهَا ورَتْقُهَا بِيَدِكَ بَدْؤُهَا مِنْكَ وعَوْدُهَا إِلَيْكَ أَعْضَادٌ وأَشْهَادٌ ومُنَاةٌ وأَذْوَادٌ وحَفَظَةٌ ورُوَّادٌ فَبِهِمْ مَلأْتَ سَمَاءَكَ وأَرْضَكَ حَتَّى ظَهَرَ أَنْ لا إِلَهَ إِلا أَنْتَ فَبِذَلِكَ أَسْأَلُكَ وبِمَوَاقِعِ الْعِزِّ مِنْ رَحْمَتِكَ وبِمَقَامَاتِكَ وعَلامَاتِكَ أَنْ تُصَلِّيَ عَلَى مُحَمَّدٍ وآلِهِ وأَنْ تَزِيدَنِي إِيمَانا وتَثْبِيتا يَا بَاطِنا فِي ظُهُورِهِ وظَاهِرا فِي بُطُونِهِ ومَكْنُونِهِ يَا مُفَرِّقا بَيْنَ النُّورِ والدَّيْجُورِ يَا مَوْصُوفا بِغَيْرِ كُنْهٍ ومَعْرُوفا بِغَيْرِ شِبْهٍ حَادَّ كُلِّ مَحْدُودٍ وشَاهِدَ كُلِّ مَشْهُودٍ ومُوجِدَ كُلِّ مَوْجُودٍ ومُحْصِيَ كُلِّ مَعْدُودٍ وفَاقِدَ كُلِّ مَفْقُودٍ لَيْسَ دُونَكَ مِنْ مَعْبُودٍ أَهْلَ الْكِبْرِيَاءِ والْجُودِ يَا مَنْ لا يُكَيَّفُ بِكَيْفٍ ولا يُؤَيَّنُ بِأَيْنٍ يَا مُحْتَجِبا عَنْ كُلِّ عَيْنٍ يَا دَيْمُومُ يَا قَيُّومُ وعَالِمَ كُلِّ مَعْلُومٍ [...]

> *In the name of God, the Compassionate, the Merciful. Every day in the days of Rajab, make the following prayer: "O God, I ask You by the meanings of all that which You are called upon by the guardians of Your authority[3] – those*

---

[1] T: *Asmāʾ Allāh*; Those reflecting, referring to, and directing attention toward God's perfect attributes.

[2] *Al-Tawqīʿ*.

[3] T: *Wulāt Amrik*; The Guardians of Your *Amr* (depending on the context, *amr* can refer to authority, matter, affair, command, etc.). This expression is closely

who are entrusted with Your secret, are delighted by Your command[1]*, describe Your might, and proclaim Your grandeur. I ask You by the aspect of Your wish which speaks within them and, thus, You made them treasure troves for Your words, and pillars for [professing] Your oneness*[2]*, Your signs and Your stations, which in every place are never left inactive*[3]*. It is through them that he or she who has come to know You comes to know You. There is no separating*[4] *between You and them except that they are Your servants and Your creation. Their disentangling and their entangling are in Your hands, their origin is from You and their return is to You. Aides, witnesses, testers, keepers, guardians and pioneers. With them You filled Your heaven and Your earth until it became manifest that there is no god but You. So, I ask You by that, and by the positions of might*[5] *from Your mercy and by Your stations*

---

related to, if not synonymous with *Ulū al-Amr* (see Qur'ān 4:59 for example) and is commonly understood to refer to the immaculate Imams. On the other hand, some reports refer to a limited number of individuals who secretly help the Imam, even when he is publicly inaccessible to the rest of his followers during the *ghaybah* (for example, see al-Ṭūsī's *al-Ghaybah*, 61). Such a servant is described as one who helps the Imam in his affairs (*yalī amraho*). The verb *yalī*, used in this sense to refer to a particular type of helper to the Imam, as opposed to the Imam himself, would arguably warrant further consideration.

[1] T: *Amr.*

[2] T: *Tawḥīdik*; unicity.

[3] T: Lā Taʿṭīla lahā.

[4] T: *Farq*; Difference, distinction or separation; these creatures are so perfect in their devotion to God, so spiritually close to God Almighty, that they draw attention to His Absolute Perfection by being spotless mirrors reflecting His Beauty and perfect role models for other creatures. The only distance between them and God is the distance that makes them so special – their absolute servitude to God and their nature as creatures testifying to the Absolute Perfection of their Creator.

[5] T: *al-ʿIzz*; Might, honor, or glory.

> *and marks, that You bless Muhammad and His progeny and increase me in faith and steadfastness. O [He who is] Hidden in His manifestation and Manifest in His hiddenness and inviolability*[1]*! O [He who] separates brightness*[2] *from darkness! O [He who is] described without being encompassed and is well-known while being beyond comparison*[3]*! [He who] limits every limited being! [He who is] Witness to all that is witnessed! [He who] brings into existence every being that has come to exist! [He who] keeps account of everything that can be counted! [He who] is devoid of every void*[4]*! There is no one to be worshipped but You, Possessor of Grandeur and Generosity! O He who is not described in terms of a condition or situated in a coordinate of space! O [He who] hides Himself from every eye! O Everlasting! O Self-Subsisting Being upon whom all rely, and Knower of all that is known! [...]*[5]

Even further, we can say the following: It is invalid to compare the infinite to the finite. As a figure of speech – just to bring the idea closer to home – one might say that they[6] are a droplet in the seas of Divine merit. God Almighty says,

> قُل لَّو كَانَ الْبَحْرُ مِدَادًا لِّكَلِمَاتِ رَبِّي لَنَفِدَ الْبَحْرُ قَبْلَ أَن تَنفَدَ كَلِمَاتُ رَبِّي وَلَوْ جِئْنَا بِمِثْلِهِ مَدَدًا
>
> *Say, 'If the sea were ink for the words of my Lord, the sea would be exhausted before the words of my Lord are*

---

[1] T: *Maknūnih*; His being beyond reach and sight; secure.

[2] T: *al-Nūr*; Light.

[3] T: *Shibh*; Someone comparable/similar to Him.

[4] T: *Fāqida kulli mafqūd*; Without any deficiency; free of every need.

[5] *Misbāḥ al-Mutahajjid:* 803-804 / Ḥ (9/866).

[6] T: The Imams described.

exhausted, even if We were to bring another like it for replenishment.'[1]

By, "the words of my Lord" what is meant are beings created by God, apparently --for it is clear that God[2] does not speak through a mouth opening. Rather, His speech is His action [in the world] and the existence that He emanates. The verse, then, speaks firstly about how the world of existence is not limited to the visible or known universe. Instead, it is so vast and great that even if the sea were to be ink, and God Almighty's attributes were to be written down, then the sea would dry up before the beings in the world of existence could be enumerated. This points to the grandeur of the Creator's attributes and the fact that words cannot encompass Him, even if the sea were to be ink and He were to bring us additional seas like it. Secondly, even if we cannot fully comprehend the words of God, they are still finite. They are a shadow of the One with a shadow, no matter how great those words are. In addition, the excellence

---

[1] Qur'ān 18:109

[2] T: The author is using the word "Allāh/God" as the one and only instance of the Necessary Being, who requires no explanation beyond His very essence for why He exists. That is, the Necessary Being is the one who exists by virtue of that being's very essence, not by being caused by another being (as all other beings are). In this vein, every other being besides the Necessary Being is contingent and, in that sense, is a creature dependent on the Necessary Being. The word "Allāh," translated as "God," here, is meant in this specific sense. Hence, the Trinitarian Christian understanding of the God-head does not entirely apply to the way the word "God" is used here. One might argue that the word "Allāh/God," in this Islamic view, can be thought of as devotionally reserving the word "Allāh/God" for the Essence/Being upon whom all other beings depend, but without allowing for the notion that any other being could truly share in the likeness of that nature/essence (i.e. "Father" only in the sense of having dependents, but not "Father" in the sense of having a "Son" or "sons" of the same nature; all besides the Necessary Being are contingent and, therefore, creatures of the Necessary Being. However, in line with Qur'ānic language, perhaps to avoid mistakenly conveying a Trinitarian Christian view of God's identity, Shī'a Muslims – as Muslims generally – typically do not use the word "Father" to refer to the Allāh/God or "sons/children" to refer to God's dependents).

of the lights who are His successors on earth is a borrowed excellence[1] that is powered up[2] by the Absolute, the One with No Need[3]. For the ultimate excellence of a created being lies in the intensity of that being's [experiential awareness of] need for the Absolute, the One with No Need. Having conviction in this regard pushes away the evil of [heretical/misguided] *exaggeration*[4] and ascribing partners to God. On the other hand, however, the successor is the mirror for God's attributes. For the successor is the spirit[5] of[6] God, the servant of God, the Face of God, and the Gateway of God. The successor has stations in the world of existence that cannot be left

---

[1] T: *Kamāl faqrī*; An excellence/perfection of deficiency, of impoverishment, of utter need for God; No matter how excellent this excellence is, it is being "borrowed" from God and is continuously indebted to Him and truly under God's absolute ownership.

[2] T: It is important to note that the author is primarily describing the ontological dimension of existence, as opposed to the moral responsibility dimension. In an analogy, taken with several grains of salt due to any analogy's limitations, God powering up existence is analogous to the electric current powering up a gaming system. As for the moral responsibility of decisions made by humans, that is analogous to the gaming system players using their controllers to make choices that show up in the game. The good chosen will always owe credit to God, for God has made good options within reach and provided freedom as the means for developing greater excellence, but responsible agents only have themselves to blame when crediting the moral responsibility for their bad decisions. The *undesirable* side effect, which is the *potential abuse* of freedom, is a natural consequence of enabling the *greater good* which is freedom. In a nutshell, God *empowers freedom directly*, within limits, with warnings through one's conscience and external messengers --all for a *greater wisdom* in the bigger picture, with a promised day to have justice served *for eternity*.

[3] T: *al-Ghanī*; The Self-Sufficient; the Independent; the One of Infinite Wealth.

[4] T: *al-Ghuluww*; Exceeding the bounds. This typically refers to believing that the Prophet and/or Imams are gods or independent creators, and similar beliefs and related practices that do not coincide with the teachings of the Prophet and the Imams about their true nature.

[5] T: *Rūḥ*; Soul.

[6] T: This can be understood similar to how servant of God is understood; the spirit made by God, owned by God.

inactive or delegated to others. Rather, the Imam assumes those stations himself, regardless whether he is behind the scenes or is publicly recognized. Hence, the Imam is not just like every other person. Otherwise, why would it be him who is the Imam and not somebody else? Is it conceivable that the way in which the Imam is selected and chosen is by means of drawing lots, chance or the like?

Prophet Muḥammad has said:

> [...] يا علي لولا نحن ما خلق الله آدم عليه السلام ولا حواء ولا الجنّة ولا النار ولا السماء ولا الأرض، فكيف لا نكون أفضل من الملائكة؟! وقد سبقناهم إلى معرفة ربّنا وتسبيحه وتهليله وتقديسه لأنّ أول ما خلق الله عز وجل أرواحنا فأنطقها بتوحيده وتمجيده [...]
>
> *[...] O ʿAlī, if it were not for us God would not have created Adam*[1]*, Eve*[2]*, Heaven, Hell, the sky or the earth. How, then, would we not be of greater merit than the angels?! For we have preceded them in becoming acquainted with*[3] *our Lord, praising Him*[4]*, declaring His Oneness*[5]*, and hallowing Him*[6]*. That is because the first thing that God Almighty created was our spirits – He had them pronounce His Oneness and Glory.*[7]

The concealment of the Imam – his *ghaybah* – does not mean that his works, mission and stations are inactive. It is similar to how God Almighty [is never inactive]. Because of God's transcendence and sublimity, those

---

[1] T: Ādam.

[2] T: Ḥawwāʾ.

[3] T: *Maʿrifah*; Knowing; becoming aware/conscious of.

[4] T: Tasbīḥihi.

[5] T: Tahlīlihi.

[6] T: Taqdīsihi.

[7] *ʿUyūn Akhbār al-Riḍā* 1:237 / Ḥ 22.

with understanding[1] cannot conceive of God Almighty being characterized by inactivity[2]. Sure, minds that are tied up with the sensory – which do not accept any horizons beyond the physical and the sensory – might conceive of God Almighty as being inactive. But after having established the proof for the Imam's existence, our ignorance of the particular benefit reaped from him does us no harm. For it suffices that the All-Wise and Omnipotent God Almighty is the One who prepared the Imam for his role, [whatever that role may be]. Moreover, the Universe's system has been founded based on a particular foundation and systematic methodology. It is similar to how a law governing matter is enshrined according to an established scientific equation – one that the world has been ignorant of for thousands of years. For example, the position of the Sun in the solar system is highly precise, such that if it were to change, then the system would collapse – even if we had been oblivious of it. Furthermore, the law of gravity[3] is the secret to the universe's organization – even though scientists had denied it[4] for long spans of time. In fact, science is still advancing and deciphering codes in the world of matter. All sciences, all fields of knowledge – with their various divisions, types, and subfields – have one message: The world, from the smallest particle to the greatest extent of the cosmos, is a harmonious world characterized and governed by the most precise systems. However, because the human mind only accesses a limited sphere of information, it is not capable of encompassing the benefits of things from all aspects. God Almighty says,

[...] وَما أُوتيتُم مِنَ العِلمِ إِلّا قَليلًا

---

[1] T: *Ulū al-Albāb*; Those of sound reasoning, those possessing intellect, those endowed with insight.

[2] T: *Taʿṭīl*; Disability, dormancy.

[3] T: Qānūn al-jādhibīyah; The author appears to be using this phrase to refer broadly to facts leading up to and related to the discovery of gravity.

[4] T: Meaning, denied facts leading up to and related to the discovery of gravity.

[...] and you[1] *have not been given of the [pieces of] knowledge except for a few.*[2]

Hence, what matters is that the proof for something's existence becomes clear and that one sticks to the evidence. When it comes to the Imam's existence, one must refer to reports[3] and other means in order to prove it. Given that such proof is established, discussion beyond it is superfluous. There will be more expounding on that later.

The *Ḥujjah*[4] is the path toward God, the remaining one who God has kept [preserved][5]; he is the rising sun, the luminous moon, and the scintillating star. For he is one of the Imams who guide by God's *Amr*[6]. God Almighty says,

وَجَعَلْنَاهُمْ أَئِمَّةً يَهْدُونَ بِأَمْرِنَا [...]

We made them imams*, guiding by Our amr [...]*[7]

---

[1] T: Plural pronoun.

[2] Qur'ān 17:85.

[3] T: *al-Naql*; In a broad sense, chronicles, ḥadīth literature or otherwise historical accounts. In some contexts, such as this one, *al-naql* can also refer more specifically to reported content that is ultimately associated with Divine revelation (as opposed to independent human reasoning), such as the Qur'ān, and the ḥadīth of Prophet Muḥammad and the Imams. Such a usage of *al-naql* would be contrasted with *al-ʿaql* (knowledge from reason).

[4] T: *al-Ḥujjah*; The proof/argument that establishes a case for or against something; in this context, the *Ḥujjah* is the Imam who serves as immaculate guardian of the Divine message, establishing the accountability to (*munajjizīyah*) [God to follow that proof] and excusableness for (*muʿadhdhirīyah*) [following that proof] as understood through reliable channels.

[5] T: Baqīyat Allāh.

[6] T: *Amr*; The Arabic root AMR, and more specifically the noun *amr*, has its own web of interconnected connotations in the Qur'ān (e.g., command, authority, matter, affair, thing, etc...).

[7] Qur'ān 21:73.

Guidance is not limited to words. As the exegesis *Tafsīr al-Mīzān* puts it, this guidance is truly by the *Amr* of God and not the guidance that is arrived at by thinking and reflecting. It is similar to how the Qur᾽ān used the word "word" to refer to an external reality as opposed to merely a statement. God Almighty says,

وَجَعَلَها كَلِمَةً باقِيَةً في عَقِبِهِ [...]

And He made it a lasting word among his posterity [...][1]

For in this verse, the word "made" refers to actually making – bringing about existence – in the world, not a matter of legal convention. The same applies to the notion of guidance in the earlier verse. Guidance in this sense means delivery to the intended goal. It is a type of existential acting upon souls to move them along the path of excellence, [not a matter of legal convention]. This form of guidance is an established role even for someone like the *hidden*[2] Imam. God Almighty says,

[...] وَاجعَلنا لِلمُتَّقِينَ إِماماً

[...] and make us imams *of those mindful of God*[3]*.*[4]

[1] Qur᾽ān 43:28.

[2] T: Emphasis is mine based on the understanding that what makes this guidance distinct in the case of the Imam Mahdī is that he retains this role despite being hidden.

[3] T: *al-Muttaqūn*; The Godwary, God-conscious, God-fearing, those pious in their choices.

[4] Qur᾽ān 25:74.

For he is *Āl Yāsīn*[1], God's summoner, godly[2] one among His signs, God's gateway, supporter of His right[3], guide[4] toward His will, reciter of His book and its[5] interpreter, and God's covenant and promise. He is the appointed[6] guidepost[7] and the outpoured knowledge. He is the salvation[8] and extensive mercy, guardian of the faithful, ruin of the faithless, one who lights up the darkness, one who brings light to what is right, the one who speaks with wisdom.

He is the one, "who will efface all traces of deviance [in belief] and hedonism [in action]," the one, "who will spring the traps of lies and fabrication [with the truth]." He is the one who, "shall unify all people upon the fear of God." He is, "the gateway to God that is the only way one can approach him." He is, "the focal point to which God's friends turn their attention." He is, "the lifeline linking the [denizens of] earth to [God] on high." He is, "the master of the Day of Conquest and the one who shall raise the banner of guidance." He is the one, "who will combine people's scattered interests into what is best for them and what pleases them." He is, "the awaited one who shall straighten [even the last vestiges of] crookedness, [no matter how] small or imperceptible." He is the one, "upon whom we rest our hopes so that he will end injustice and oppression." He is the one, "who has been preserved [by God] to renew the directives and recommendations found in the Qurʾān and the Prophet's example." He is the one, "upon whom we rest our hopes so that he will revive the Book [of God] and the injunctions set forth therein." He is the one, "who will revive Islamic symbols and [through them revive] Muslims." He is the one, "who

---

[1] T: *Āl Yāsīn*; The progeny of Yāsīn (understood to mean the progeny of Muḥammad, as a number of reports explain).

[2] T: Rabbānī.

[3] T: *Ḥaqq*; What is right (true and/or due).

[4] T: *Dalīl*; A guide toward or proof of [something].

[5] T: Or His interpreter.

[6] T: *al-Manṣūb*; Erect, designated, appointed.

[7] T: *ʿAlam*; Flag/banner, mountain, chief.

[8] T: *al-Ghawth*; The help.

will crush the military might of the transgressors." He is the one, "who will demolish the edifices of polytheism and hypocrisy." He is, "the destroyer of the corrupt, [and] the sinful." He is the one, "who will cut down errancy and division."[1] Furthermore, he is the partner and counterpart of the Qur'ān.

The scholar of ḥadīth, al-Nūrī, has described him as follows,

> عنقاء قاف العدم مرقاة الهمم الاسم الأعظم الأكبر الحاوي للعلم غير المتناهي قطب رحى الوجود، ومركز دائرة الشهود كمال النشأة ومنشأ الكمال، جمال الجمع ومجمع الجمال المتوشح بالأنوار الإلهية المربى تحت أستار الربوبية مطلع الأنوار المصطفوية ومنبع الأسرار المرتضوية، ناموس الله الأكبر وغاية نوع البشر إلى الوقت ومرج الزمان الذي هو للحق أمين وللخلق أمان ناظم المناظم الحجّة القائم.
>
> *Peak of the encircling of nonexistence, means for the ascension of determinations, the grandest and greatest name, the one encompassing infinite knowledge, pivot point for the quern of existence, center of the circle of spiritual witnessing, [utmost] excellence of the realm and basis of excellence, beauty of the collective and collecting point of beauty, the one donning the Divine lights, the one brought up under the veils of Lordship, sunrise of Muḥammad's spiritual lights, spring of ʿAlī's spiritual secrets, greatest one entrusted with secrets by God, epitome of human kind's excellence to date, meadow of the age, the one who is trustee over what is right, the one who is guarantor of the creation's security, organizer of the*

---

[1] T: The preceding quotes in this paragraph are translated from the supplication known as *Duʿāʾ al-Nudbah,* as the author acknowledges. I have benefited from the rendering of Islamic Texts Institute's publication *al-Nudbah: A Devotional Elegy for the Prophet Muḥammad and his Family,* published under the direction of Shaykh Rizwan Arastu. Please see the said publication and relevant footnotes, especially pages 80-85.

places of organization, the Ḥujjah, the Qā᾿im, [the rising one][1].[2]

In *Biḥār al-Anwār*, it has also been reported that Imām Mahdī said,

[...] فأنا بقيّة من آدم، و[ذ]خيرة من نوح، ومصطفى من إبراهيم، وصفوة من محمّد [...]

[...] For I am one remaining [preserved][3] *from [the descendants of] Adam*[4]*, kept in store from [the descendants of] Noah*[5]*, chosen [from the descendants of] Abraham*[6]*, elect [from the descendants of] Muḥammad [...]*[7]

In another account, Imam Mahdī is reported to have said:

[...] وليعلموا أنّ الحقّ معنا وفينا، لا يقول ذلك سوانا إلّا كذّاب مفتر، ولا يدّعيه غيرُنا إلّا ضالّ غوي، فليقتصروا منّا على هذه الجملة دون التفسير، ويقنعوا من ذلك بالتعريض دون التصريح إن شاء الله

[...] Let them know that what is right is with us and in us. No one besides us says that except for a liar, a fabricator. No one besides us claims it except for someone who is misguided and perverse. So let them limit themselves – on our account – to this sentence without explanation; from

---

[1] T: The *Qā᾿im*; the description typically associated with the 12th Imam, the Mahdī within Twelver Shī῾ah Islam.

[2] *Jannat al-Ma᾿wá* by Shaykh al-Nūrī, printed at the end of volume 53 of *Biḥār al-Anwār* (p. 200).

[3] T: *Baqīyah*; Preserved [in readiness/preparation].

[4] T: Ādam.

[5] T: Nūḥ.

[6] T: Ibrāhīm.

[7] *Al-Ikhtiṣāṣ*: 257; *Biḥār al-Anwār* 52:238 / Ḥ 105.

> *that, [let them] be satisfied with the hint as opposed to an explicit statement, God-willing.*[1]

Moreover, in a response issued by Imam Mahdī, the following was recorded:

> بسم الله الرحمن الرحيم عافانا الله وإياكم من الضلالة والفتن، ووهب لنا ولكم روح اليقين، وأجارنا وإيّاكم من سوء المنقلب. انّه أنهي إلي ارتياب جماعة منكم في الدين، وما دخلهم من الشكّ والحيرة في ولاة أمورهم، فغمّنا ذلك لكم لا لنا، وساءنا فيكم لا فينا، لأنّ الله معنا ولا فاقة بنا إلى غيره، والحقّ معنا فلن يوحشنا من قعد عنّا، ونحن صنائع ربّنا، والخلق بعد صنائعنا.
>
> *In the name of God, the Compassionate, the Merciful. May God: relieve us of misguidance and trials*[2]*, and [may God relieve] you [too]; grant us the spirit of certainty, and [may God grant it to] you too; and deliver us from a bad end, and [may God deliver] you [too]. [News] has reached me that a group of you has a misgiving related to the religion and [news has reached me] of the doubt and puzzlement*[3] *that has infiltrated them regarding the guardians of their affairs*[4]*. Thus, that has grieved us --for your sake, not for ours. It has saddened us --for your sake, not for ours. For God is with us and we do not have a need for anyone but Him; what is right is with us, so we will not feel desolate because of those who fail to support us; we are brought up*

---

[1] *Kamāl al-Dīn* 511 / Bāb 45 / Ḥ 42.

[2] T: *Fitan.*

[3] T: *Ḥayrah.*

[4] T: *Wulāt umūr* (sing. *Wālī umūr*).

by our Lord and the [remaining] creatures are, subsequently, brought up by[1] *us.*[2]

In another report, [he has been recorded to have said that]:

قلوبنا أوعية لمشيئة الله فإذا شاء شئنا

Our hearts are vessels for God's wish; such that if He wishes then we wish.[3]

Imam Mahdī has also said:

أنا المهدي أنا قائم الزمان أنا الذي أملؤها عدلًا كما ملئت ظلمًا وجورًا

I am the Mahdī [i.e. the guided one]. I am the Qāʾim [i.e. the rising one] of the age. I am the one who fills it with justice, just as it has been filled with inequity and tyranny.[4]

It has also been reported that Imam Mahdī exits from the vicinity of the Kaʿbah[5] with Gabriel[6] on his right and Michael[7] on his left; he has the awe-

---

[1] T: That is, they are the means by which God chooses to guide and channel mercy to others. Another related meaning is that they fulfill the primary purpose of creation through their exemplary servitude to God and for their sake, out of love for them, God created everything else. So by them, God brought about everything else.

[2] T: *al-Ghaybah* by al-Ṭūsī: 285 / Baʿḍ mā ẓahara min jihatihi min al-tawqīʿāt / Ḥ 245.

[3] *Al-Ghaybah* by al-Ṭūsī: 247 / Ḥ 216.

[4] *Kamāl al-Dīn*: 445 / Bāb 43 / Ḥ 18.

[5] T: *al-Kaʿbah*; The Kaʿbah, the cubed structure in Mecca, present-day Saudi Arabia, toward which Muslims direct themselves in prayer and circumambulate in pilgrimage.

[6] T: Jibrāʾīl.

[7] T: Mīkāʾīl.

inspiring presence[1] of Moses[2], the majesty[3] of Jesus[4], the judgment of David[5], and the patience of Job[6]; on him are collars of light blazing from the beam of holiness's radiance[7]. [The following are verses of poetry describing Imam Mahdī:]

ليس لفضله المبين كاتم * مبدأه ومنتهاه الخاتم

وقلبه مرآة ذات الباري * في سرّه لطائف الأسرار

مَنطِقُه منطقة السماء * في عالم الصفات والأسماء

منطقه البليغ في المعارف ميزان كلّ سالك وعارف

Nothing can silence his evident merit

His beginning and his end is the Seal[8]

His heart is a mirror for the Essence of God

Within him are the hidden secrets

His speech is the utterance of Heaven['s Divine Revelation]

In the world of [Divine] Attributes and Names

His eloquent speech in fields of knowledge --

---

[1] T: *Haybah.*

[2] T: *Mūsá.*

[3] T: *Bahā*ʾ.

[4] T: *ʿĪsá.*

[5] T: *Dāwūd.*

[6] T: *Ayyūb.*

[7] T: Another reading of this sentence would be rendered as follows in English, "Over him, [the faithful's] collars of light blaze from the beam of holiness's radiance." Yet another reading would be rendered, "Because of that, collars of light blaze from the beam of holiness's radiance."

[8] T: *al-Khātam*; Apparently, this is a reference to Prophet Muḥammad, the Seal of All Prophets. Imam Mahdī's existence, from beginning to end, revolves around the message of Prophet Muḥammad.

Is a standard for every [spiritual] wayfarer and sage[1].[2]

THE DESCRIPTION OF PROPHETS IN THE QUR᾿ĀN AND OTHER TEXTS

The holy Qur᾿ān described prophets[3] as having every beautiful attribute that they are supposed to have. Thus, their description in the Qur᾿ān includes every honorable achievement that goes hand-in-hand with the sanctity of their station and the integrity of Divine ambassadorship.

For they are the chosen ones. God Almighty says,

إِنَّ ٱللَّهَ ٱصْطَفَىٰٓ ءَادَمَ وَنُوحًا وَءَالَ إِبْرَٰهِيمَ وَءَالَ عِمْرَٰنَ عَلَى ٱلْعَٰلَمِينَ

> *Indeed God chose Adam and Noah, and the progeny of Abraham and the progeny of Imran[4] above all the nations;[5]*

Discussing the topic of knowing "the progeny of Abraham" and "the progeny of Imran" would go beyond the scope of this short publication. Moreover, what is meant by "the nations"[6] is the nations of their time.

They are "those with certainty."[7] God Almighty says,

---

[1] T: *ʿĀrif;* A sage in the sense of a spiritual master who follows the teachings of Prophet Muḥammad and his household; The awareness of the *ʿārif* in spiritual matters goes beyond mental concepts and is, rather, grounded in direct experiences and attainment of spiritual stations.

[2] *Al-Anwār al-Qudsīyah*: 119. Poetry by Shaykh Muḥammad Ḥusayn al-Iṣfahānī al-Kumbānī.

T: The English rendering is by this translator, as with the remaining excerpts, unless otherwise noted.

[3] T: Whenever the English word "prophet" is used in this text, it refers to a Divinely appointed, immaculate prophet, unless otherwise noted.

[4] T: ʿImrān.

[5] Qur᾿ān 3:33.

[6] T: al-ʿĀlamīn.

[7] T: al-Mūqinūn.

وَكَذَٰلِكَ نُرِىٓ إِبْرَٰهِيمَ مَلَكُوتَ ٱلسَّمَٰوَٰتِ وَٱلْأَرْضِ وَلِيَكُونَ مِنَ ٱلْمُوقِنِينَ

Thus did We show Abraham the dominions of the heavens and the earth, that he might be of those with certainty.[1]

They are the guided ones. God Almighty says:

وَوَهَبْنَا لَهُۥٓ إِسْحَٰقَ وَيَعْقُوبَ ۚ كُلًّا هَدَيْنَا ۚ وَنُوحًا هَدَيْنَا مِن قَبْلُ ۖ وَمِن ذُرِّيَّتِهِۦ
دَاوُۥدَ وَسُلَيْمَٰنَ وَأَيُّوبَ وَيُوسُفَ وَمُوسَىٰ وَهَٰرُونَ ۚ [...]

And We gave him Isaac and Jacob and guided each of them. And Noah We had guided before, and from his offspring, David and Solomon[2]*, Job, Joseph*[3]*, Moses and Aaron*[4] *[...]*[5]

In another verse, God Almighty says,

أُو۟لَٰٓئِكَ ٱلَّذِينَ هَدَى ٱللَّهُ ۖ فَبِهُدَىٰهُمُ ٱقْتَدِهْ ۗ [...]

They are the ones whom God has guided. So follow *their guidance. [...]*[6]

They are the ones who know through *knowledge by God's presence*[7]. God Almighty says,

وَلَقَدْ ءَاتَيْنَا دَاوُۥدَ وَسُلَيْمَٰنَ عِلْمًا ۖ وَقَالَا ٱلْحَمْدُ لِلَّهِ ٱلَّذِى فَضَّلَنَا عَلَىٰ كَثِيرٍ مِّنْ
عِبَادِهِ ٱلْمُؤْمِنِينَ

---

1 Qurʾān 6:75.

2 T: Sulaymān.

3 T: Yūsuf.

4 T: Hārūn.

5 Qurʾān 6:84.

6 Qurʾān 6:90.

7 T: *al-ʿIlm al-Ladunnī*, Knowledge *from* God in a way that is not commonly accessible.

Certainly We gave David and Solomon knowledge, and they said, 'All praise belongs to God, who favored us over many of His faithful servants.'[1]

They are the blessed ones. God Almighty says:

أُو۟لَـٰٓئِكَ ٱلَّذِينَ أَنْعَمَ ٱللَّهُ عَلَيْهِم مِّنَ ٱلنَّبِيِّـۧنَ مِن ذُرِّيَّةِ ءَادَمَ وَمِمَّنْ حَمَلْنَا مَعَ نُوحٍ
وَمِن ذُرِّيَّةِ إِبْرَٰهِيمَ وَإِسْرَٰٓءِيلَ وَمِمَّنْ هَدَيْنَا وَٱجْتَبَيْنَآ ۚ إِذَا تُتْلَىٰ عَلَيْهِمْ ءَايَـٰتُ ٱلرَّحْمَـٰنِ
خَرُّوا۟ سُجَّدًا وَبُكِيًّا ۩

They are the ones whom God has blessed from among the prophets of Adam's progeny, and from [the progeny of] those We carried with Noah, and from among the progeny of Abraham and Israel[2]*, and from among those We guided and chose. When the signs of the Compassionate were recited to them, they would fall down weeping in prostration.*[3]

They are the good doers. God Almighty says,

وَوَهَبْنَا لَهُۥٓ إِسْحَـٰقَ وَيَعْقُوبَ ۚ كُلًّا هَدَيْنَا ۚ وَنُوحًا هَدَيْنَا مِن قَبْلُ ۖ وَمِن ذُرِّيَّتِهِۦ
دَاوُۥدَ وَسُلَيْمَـٰنَ وَأَيُّوبَ وَيُوسُفَ وَمُوسَىٰ وَهَـٰرُونَ ۚ وَكَذَٰلِكَ نَجْزِى ٱلْمُحْسِنِينَ

And We gave him Isaac and Jacob and guided each of them. And Noah We had guided before, and from his offspring, David and Solomon, Job, Joseph, Moses and Aaron —thus do We reward the good-doers[4] *—*[5]

They are the righteous. God Almighty says,

وَزَكَرِيَّا وَيَحْيَىٰ وَعِيسَىٰ وَإِلْيَاسَ ۖ كُلٌّ مِّنَ ٱلصَّـٰلِحِينَ

---

1 Qurʾān 27:15.

2 T: Isrāʾīl; Commonly understood to refer to Jacob (Yaʿqūb).

3 Qurʾān 19:58.

4 T: *al-Muḥsinūn* (sing. *Muḥsin*); The virtuous.

5 Qurʾān 6:84

and Zechariah[1], John[2], Jesus and Elijah[3] – each of them among the righteous[4]

They are the favored ones. God Almighty says,

وَإِسْمَٰعِيلَ وَٱلْيَسَعَ وَيُونُسَ وَلُوطًا ۚ وَكُلًّا فَضَّلْنَا عَلَى ٱلْعَٰلَمِينَ

and Ishmael[5], Elisha[6], Jonah[7] and Lot[8] – each We favored over all the nations[9]

This is the gist of the Qurʾānic taste when speaking of the attributes of prophets. The position of the *guarded community*[10] follows suit.

As for accounts from the corrupted texts of earlier Divine revelations, they have described prophets and the *guardians* succeeding them[11] in terms that are unbefitting for their station and rank. Rather, such accounts are unbefitting even for an [ordinary,] upright person of faith, let alone someone who makes a [special] connection with God Almighty. For example, Chapter 12 of Genesis portrays Abraham as having claimed before Pharaoh that Sarah was his beautiful sister, not his wife. Pharaoh marries her and subsequently honors Abraham, giving him sheep, cows,

---

[1] T: Zakarīyah.

[2] T: Yaḥyá.

[3] T: Ilyās.

[4] Qurʾān 6:85

[5] T: Ismāʿīl.

[6] T: al-Yasaʿ.

[7] T: Yūnus.

[8] T: Lūṭ.

[9] Qurʾān 6:86.

[10] T: *al-Ṭāʾifah al-Ḥaqqah*; The right community, the community that is right; guarded by the immaculate Imam who maintains a threshold of immaculate guidance for the community.

[11] T: *Awṣiyāʾ* (sing. *waṣī*); trustees; deputies; successors; will-executors, etc.

donkeys and male and female slaves. After Pharaoh finds out that Sarah is Abraham's wife, Pharaoh reproaches him and returns Sarah to Abraham.[1]

Chapter 19 of Genesis tells the story of Lot and his two daughters on the mountain. As the story goes, the older sister tells the younger sister, "Our father is getting old, and there is not a man on earth to unite with us as was the custom everywhere. Come, let us ply our father with wine and then lie with him, that we may have offspring by our father."[2] The two had their father drink wine that night and the older sister lay with him. On the second night, they had their father drink wine and the younger sister lay with him. The two thus became pregnant by their father and each gave birth to a son.[3]

Chapter 27 of Genesis describes how Isaac wanted to give his special blessing [of prophet-hood] to his son Esau[4]. But then Jacob tricked Isaac, making him think that he was Esau. Jacob offered Isaac food and so he ate, drank and then gave Jacob the blessing of prophet-hood, withholding it from Esau.[5]

Chapter 1 of Matthew, while mentioning the genealogy of Jesus, the Messiah, in detail, presents the Messiah, Solomon, as well as his father David as descending from someone[6] who was born out of wedlock.[7] In Chapters 11 and 12 of 2 Samuel, David is said to have had relations with the wife of Uriah, the faithful warrior. She becomes pregnant. Fearing a scandal, David attempts to elude her husband. When David is unsuccessful,

---

[1] *Mawsūʿat al-Kitāb al-Muqaddas* / Book of Genesis / v. 1 / p. 65; also, see *Tafsīr al-Mīzān* 7:223.

[2] T: Translation from "The New American Bible - IntraText," accessed August 1, 2018, http://www.vatican.va/archive/ENG0839/__PL.HTM#-2X.

[3] See *al-Bayān fī Tafsīr al-Qurʾān* / Sayyid al-Khūʾī: 51.

[4] T: ʿĪsū.

[5] *Al-Bayān fī Tafsīr al-Qurʾān*: 51.

[6] T: Perez.

[7] *Al-Bayān fī Tafsīr al-Qurʾān*: 52.

he sends Uriah to the frontlines of battle where he is killed. David then takes Uriah's wife into his home and publicly marries her.[1]

It is baffling how educated nations, men of their times, and experts in their fields who examine the commonly circulated Torah and are aware of the tales[2] therein can believe that it is Divine revelation and an [entirely intact] Divine book. Sure, taking the position of one's forefathers for granted[3] is like a person's second nature. It is difficult to let go of that instinct and simply follow what is right and real. But when what is right is this clear, it cannot be overlooked.

That being said, the Qur᾿ān includes descriptions that might be misinterpreted to imply a deficiency in the station of a prophet. For example, some have imagined that the Qur᾿ān describes Prophet Muḥammad in unbefitting terms. This is due to misunderstanding God Almighty's words when He says,

عَبَسَ وَتَوَلَّىٰٓ

He frowned and turned away[4]

Indeed, parts of the Qur᾿ān explain its other parts. For in another verse, God Almighty says,

وَإِنَّكَ لَعَلَىٰ خُلُقٍ عَظِيمٍ

---

[1] Ibid.

[2] T: *al-Khurāfāt* (sing. *al-Khurāfah*); Myth; fiction; imagined story; using this word in Arabic implies that the author finds these stories to include fictional elements, even if part of the story is true. In the context, the author would consider the immoral behavior attributed to prophets to be fictional and likely evidence of corruptions in the text (as opposed to a preserved integrity of the original Torah revealed by God Almighty).

[3] T: *Taqlīd*; In this context, blind following. In other contexts, the term *taqlid* refers to a commonsensical practice of referring to the research of qualified experts.

[4] Qur᾿ān 80:1.

> *and indeed* you *are of an exalted character.*[1]

Furthermore, God Almighty says,

> إِنَّمَا يُرِيدُ ٱللَّهُ لِيُذْهِبَ عَنكُمُ ٱلرِّجْسَ أَهْلَ ٱلْبَيْتِ وَيُطَهِّرَكُمْ تَطْهِيرًا
>
> *Indeed God wills to keep all impurity*[2] *away from you [specifically], O People of the Household*[3]*, and purify you with a thorough purification.*[4]

Hence, misunderstanding the aforementioned verse to mean something unbefitting of Prophet Muḥammad's standing does not fit with, and is rather rejected by, the latter verses' affirmation of his sublime character.[5]

In any case, we believe that is it impossible to fully comprehend the spiritual stations of the prophets and friends[6] of God. We can only realize some of their standing and that is by means of the sound [report-based] channels

---

[1] Qur'ān 68:4.

[2] T: *al-Rijs*; Including all sins.

[3] T: Prophet Muḥammad and this specific, purified group. As Qur'ānic exegesis and ḥadīth literature in agreement with the commonly-held Shī'ah view on this verse confirm, wives of the Prophet are not part of this group even though they live in the home of the Prophet. According to one line of reasoning to that end, for instance, the exclusive description in the verse indicates that this special group is safeguarded from the impurity of sin, hence to be contrasted with those who are being addressed (with a different pronoun in Arabic) and admonished before and after this excerpt.

[4] Qur'ān 33:33.

[5] T: Meaning, the verses must be read holistically, and any unbefitting reading must be revised conceptually or applied differently. For example, the verse read to be exhibiting unbefitting character either has more context to explain it as exemplary conduct, or (as is the prevalent Shī'ī reading) applies to someone else entirely. Of course, this is all taking for granted that the references in question can be reasonably reconciled through holistic reading and reasonable assumptions (i.e. they are not obvious contradictions).

[6] T: *al-Awliyā'*; In this context, the reference is likely to Divinely appointed Imams.

accessible to us[1]. For this reason, it has been reported that one ought to recite the following when visiting[2] [the Imam(s)]:

[...] مَنْ أَرادَ اللهَ بَدَأَ بِكُمْ وَمَنْ وَحَّدَهُ قَبِلَ عَنْكُمْ وَمَنْ قَصَدَهُ تَوَجَّهَ بِكُمْ، مَوالِيَّ لا أُحْصِي ثَناءَكُمْ وَلا أَبْلُغُ مِنَ الْمَدْحِ كُنْهَكُمْ وَمِنَ الْوَصْفِ قَدْرَكُمْ، وَأَنْتُمْ نُورُ الأَخْيارِ وَهُداةُ الأَبْرارِ وَحُجَجُ الْجَبّارِ، بِكُمْ فَتَحَ اللهُ وَبِكُمْ يَخْتِمُ [الله] وَبِكُمْ يُنَزِّلُ الْغَيْثَ وَبِكُمْ يُمْسِكُ السَّماءَ أَنْ تَقَعَ عَلَى الأَرْضِ إِلاّ بِإِذْنِهِ [...]

[...] The one who wants God begins with you; the one who upholds the oneness of God accepts from you [what you say]; the one who seeks God turns [to Him] through you. My masters, neither do I enumerate your praise nor do I reach your essence in praising you or your value in describing you; and you are the light of the [upright], the guides of the righteous, and the Ḥujaj[3] of the Almighty. Through you, God began [everything] and through you God will conclude [everything]. Through you, He brings down the rain and through you He keeps the sky from falling upon the earth, except by His permission [...][4]

---

[1] T: Meaning, that have survived to this day. There may be other accounts that were lost.

[2] T: *Ziyārah*; Visit/visiting; saluting; This refers to a form of devotional literature recited while directing oneself to the holy figure being visited, either up close at a grave or from afar.

[3] T: *Ḥujaj* (sing. *ḥujjah*). *Al-Ḥujjah*: The proof/argument that establishes a case for or against something; In this context, the *Ḥujjah* is the Imam who serves as immaculate guardian of the Divine message, establishing the accountability to (*munajjizīyah*) [God to follow that proof] and excusableness for (*muʿadhdhirīyah*) [following that proof] as understood through reliable channels.

[3] T: Baqīyat Allāh.

[4] *Al-Mazār* by Ibn al-Mashhadī: 532, from al-Ziyārah al-Jāmiʿah al-Kabīrah.

But with this belief and commitment to it, we do not [and should not] fall into the trap of [heretical/misguided] *exaggeration*[1]. For we also believe in the following words reportedly quoting the Commander of the Faithful, Imam ʿAlī:

إيّاكم والغلو فينا قولوا إنّا عبيد مربوبون وقولوا في فضلنا ما شئتم

> *Beware of [heretical/misguided] exaggeration pertaining to us. Say that we are servants*[2] *[of God], those who have a Lord; and say what you wish regarding our merits*[3].[4]

In another report, he is quoted to have said,

هلك فيَّ رجلان محبّ غالٍ ومبغض قالٍ

> *Two [types of] men are ruined in [their disposition with] regards to me: a [heretical/misguided] exaggerating lover; and a loathing hater.*[5]

---

[1] T: *al-Ghuluww*; Exceeding the bounds. This typically refers to believing that the Prophet and/or Imams are gods or independent creators, and similar beliefs alongside related practices that do not coincide with the teachings of the Prophet and the Imams about their true natures. In that vein, it may also be considered *ghuluww* to describe the Prophets/Imams/saints as (actively) having certain stations/roles without knowledge (or authorization by them) to describe them as such ––that is even if such stations/roles are theoretically possible for them to have (i.e. even if they are still being described as fully dependent on God in those stations/roles).

[2] T: *ʿAbīd* (sing. *ʿabd*); Slaves in the sense that they belong to God and need God for everything; servants [of God]; devotees of God. Sometimes the word *ʿabd* is used specifically to honor a person who has chosen to be devoted to God. For example, Prophet Muḥammad is honored by the title, "*ʿabduhu wa rasūluh* (God's slave/servant and messenger)."

[3] T: *Faḍl*; Merit, virtue, favor.

[4] *Al-Khiṣāl*: 614.

[5] *Nahj al-Balāghah* 4:28 / Ḥ 117.

This is all in consideration of the references accessible to us dealing with defining their attributes.

DISTINCT FEATURES OF IMAM MAHDĪ

As for the distinct features of Imam Mahdī, as they appear in the accounts accessible to us, here are some examples:

1) It has been reported that Jābir said: I heard Sālim ibn ʿAbd Allāh ibn ʿUmar ibn al-Khaṭṭāb speaking to Abū Jaʿfar, [that is Imam] Muḥammad ibn ʿAlī [al-Bāqir] in Mecca. He[1] said: I heard my father, ʿAbd Allāh ibn ʿUmar, saying: I heard the Messenger of God, [Prophet Muḥammad,] saying:

[...] والحجّة القائم كأنّه كوكب درّي في وسطهم، فقلت: يا ربّ من هؤلاء؟ فقال: هؤلاء الأئمّة، وهذا القائم يحلّ حلالي ويحرّم حرامي وينتقم من أعدائي، يا محمّد أحببه فإنّي أُحبّه وأُحبّ من يحبّه.

[...] and the Ḥujjah[2], the Qāʾim (Rising One) – it is as though he is a glittering star[3] in their midst. Then I asked, "Lord, who are those [individuals]?" He replied, "Those are the Imams, and this is the Qāʾim; he makes lawful what I have deemed lawful, he forbids what I have deemed forbidden and he brings my enemies to justice[4]. O' Muḥammad, love him, for indeed I love him and I love those who love him."[5]

2) It has been reported that Abū Wāʾil said: The Commander of the Faithful, Imam ʿAlī, looked at Imam Ḥusayn and said:

---

[1] T: Sālim is saying this to Imam Muḥammad al-Bāqir.

[2] T: *al-Ḥujjah*; The proof/argument that establishes a case for or against something; In this context, the *Ḥujjah* is the Imam who serves as immaculate guardian of the Divine message, establishing the accountability to (*munajjizīyah*) [God to follow that proof] and excusableness for (*muʿadhdhirīyah*) [following that proof] as understood through reliable channels.

[3] T: Kawkabun durrīyy.

[4] T: Yantaqimu min aʿdāʾī.

[5] *Biḥār al-Anwār* 36:222-223 / Ḥ 21.

إن ابني هذا سيد كما سماه رسول الله (صلى الله عليه وآله) سيّداً ، وسيخرج الله من صلبه رجلا باسم نبيّكم يشبهه في الخَلق والخُلق، يخرج على حين غفلةٍ من الناس، وإماتةٍ للحقّ، وإظهارٍ للجور، واللهِ لو لم يخرج لضربت عنقه، يفرح بخروجه أهل السماوات وسكّانها، وهو رجل أجلى الجبين، أقنى الأنف، ضخم البطن، أزيل الفخذين، بفخذه اليمنى شامة، أفلج الثنايا، ويملأ الأرض عدلاً كما ملئت ظلماً وجوراً

This son of mine is a master (Sayyid) just as the Messenger of God [Prophet Muḥammad] called him a master; and God will bring out a man from his descendants[1] *whose name will be the name of your Prophet [Muḥammad], resembling him in features*[2] *and character*[3]*; he will mobilize*[4] *at a time when people are absentminded, what is right is being put to death, and tyranny is made manifest. [I swear] by God that were he not to mobilize [at that point in the future], he would have been beheaded*[5]*; the people of the heavens and its dwellers will be delighted by his advent*[6]*. He is a man of a broad forehead*[7]*, a [slightly] elongated nose with a curve midway and a fine tip*[8]*, a*

---

[1] T: *Min ṣulbih*; From his loins.

[2] T: *al-Khalq*; His physical features.

[3] T: *al-Khuluq*; Character/manners.

[4] T: *Yakhruj*; He comes out; likely referring to the beginning of an armed resistance (*khurūj bi al-sayf*), perhaps to be distinguished from the mere advent of his public appearance (*ẓuhūr*). See next footnote.

[5] T: Some would understand this to mean that the Imam must mobilize his armed resistance at that point because if he does not then his enemies will assassinate him. This may be hinting at how the Imam is publicly identified (*ẓāhir*), thus ending the period of *ghaybah*, before he mobilizes his movement (*yakhruj*). See al-Iṣfahānī's *Mikyāl al-Makārim*, vol. 1, p. 82.

[6] T: *Khurūjih*; His mobilization.

[7] T: Ajlá al-jabīn.

[8] T: Aqná al-anf.

[proportionately] sizeable abdomen[1]*, a separation between his [heavily built] thighs*[2]*; on his right thigh there is a beauty spot*[3]*; his front teeth are spaced*[4]*; and he fills the earth with justice just as it has been filled with injustice and tyranny.*[5]

3) It has been reported that the Sayyid, the son of Muḥammad al-Ḥimyarī, said the following as part of a longer discussion: I asked [Imam] al-Ṣādiq, [that is] Jaʿfar the son of Muḥammad, "O' [grand]son of God's messenger, reports attributed to your forefathers have been relayed to us concerning the *ghaybah* and its veracity. So [I ask you to] tell me, who does [the *ghaybah*] occur to?" Then he replied:

ستقع بالسادس من ولدي والثاني عشر من الأئمّة الهداة بعد رسول الله صلى الله عليه وآله أوّلهم أمير المؤمنين علي بن أبي طالب عليه السلام وآخرهم القائم بالحقّ بقيّة الله في أرضه صاحب الزمان وخليفة الرحمن، والله لو بقي في غيبته ما بقي نوح في قومه لم يخرج من الدنيا حتى يظهر فيملأ الأرض قسطاً وعدلاً كما ملئت جوراً وظلماً

It will occur to the sixth of my descendants, the twelfth of the guiding Imams after God's Messenger [Muḥammad]. The first of them is the Commander of the Faithful, ʿAlī, the son of Abū Ṭālib and the last of them is the Qāʾim [who rises with and to establish] what is right; the remaining one who God has kept [preserved][6] *on His earth; the master of*

---

1 T: *Ḍakhm al-baṭn*; This could be referring to the muscular anatomy of his abdomen area that is proportional to the remainder of his strong build.

2 T: Azyal al-fakhidhayn.

3 T: *Shāmah.*

4 T: *Aflaj al-thanāyā*; Having a slight gap between the front teeth, regarded as a sign of beauty.

5 *Al-Ghaybah* by al-Nuʿmānī: 222-223 / Bāb 13 / Ḥ 2.

6 T: Baqīyat Allāh.

the age[1] *and the successor*[2] *of the Merciful One. [I swear] by God, [even] if he remains in his ghaybah as long as Noah remained among his people, then he will not depart this world*[3] *until he appears [publicly] and fills the earth with fairness and justice just as it has been filled with tyranny and injustice.*[4]

4) It has been reported that Jābir ibn ʿAbd Allāh al-Anṣārī said: The Messenger of God said:

المهدي من ولدي، اسمه اسمي، وكنيته كنيتي، أشبه الناس بي خَلقاً وخُلُقاً، تكون به غيبة وحيرة تضل فيها الأمم، ثمّ يُقبل كالشهاب الثاقب يملأها عدلاً وقسطاً كما ملئت جوراً وظلماً.

The Mahdī [is] from among my progeny, his name is my name, and his kunyah[5] *is my kunyah. In terms of features*[6] *and character*[7]*, he is the closest in resemblance to me amongst [all] people. There will be a ghaybah and a puzzlement*[8] *associated with him, during which communities*[9] *will go astray. Then he will come like a*

---

[1] T: Ṣāḥib al-zamān.

[2] T: *al-Khalīfah*; The viceroy or representative.

[3] T: al-Dunyā.

[4] *Biḥār al-Anwār* 51:145 / Bāb 6 / Ḥ 12.

[5] T: A *kunyah* is a kind of epithet starting with *Abū* (literally, "Father of"), for a man, or *Umm* (literally, "Mother of"), for a woman. But if someone's *kunyah* is "Abū ʿAbd Allāh," for example, that does not necessarily mean his son's name is ʿAbd Allāh. He may not even have a son at all for that matter. Conversely, sometimes a person becomes known by a *kunyah* only after he or she has a child, in which case the *kunyah* would be associated with the name of his or her child.

[6] T: *al-Khalq*; His physical features.

[7] T: *al-Khuluq*; Character/manners.

[8] T: *Ḥayrah.*

[9] T: *al-Umam* (sing. *ummah*); Communities or nations.

penetrating star[1]*; he fills [the world] with justice and fairness just as it has been filled with tyranny and injustice."*[2]

It might be [argued that] what is apparently meant by "name" here is not the literal name [of the person]. Rather, what is meant is the one being named – meaning, the two have a single reality[3]. Moreover, what is meant by the *kunyah* here is that the two have the same attributes[4]. [The argument to this end would reason that] it is far-fetched for the report to be referring merely to a sameness[5] in terms of [literal] name and *kunyah*, as there is no merit in that [per se]. Indeed, such a thing might occur to anyone. That being said, it might be argued that this is a literal name that has been conferred by the Divine and that suffices as a merit because it is not shared by any other. Yes, a conferral by the Divine is a matter-of-fact[6] type [of conferral] that reveals an essential quality [of the person], not haphazard [mentally-concocted] convention[7]. Divine conferrals are not chaotic bestowals.

---

[1] T: Shihāb thāqib.

[2] *Kamāl al-Dīn*: 286 / Bāb 25 / Ḥ 1.

[3] T: *Ittiḥād al-ḥaqīqah*; having a shared meaning/nature/truth. This is not to negate the superiority of Prophet Muḥammad or to deny the dependence of the Mahdī on the earlier Imams, however. To use the analogy of light, for instance, the shared meaning here is more about the shared luminosity, not about the layers of dependency embedded between one instance of luminosity and the next.

[4] T: *Ittiḥād al-ṣifāt.*

[5] T: *Ittiḥād.*

[6] T: *Nafs amrīyah*; Related to *nafs al-amr*, which is arguably the intelligible plane on which existing beings and true statements are described to be as such, even if their referents do not have an actual existence in the mind or externally. For further details and other opinions, see Ṭabāṭabāʾī's *Nihāyat al-Ḥikmah* (al-Marḥalah al-ūlá, al-faṣl al-thānī).

[7] T: Iʿtibār.

5) It has been reported that Abū Baṣīr said: I heard Abū ʿAbd Allāh, that is [Imam] Jaʿfar, the son of Muḥammad [al-Ṣādiq], saying:

إنَّ في الليلة التي يولد فيها الإمام لا يولد مولود إلَّا كان مؤمناً، وإن ولد في أرض الشرك نقله الله إلى الايمان ببركة الامام.

On the night in which the Imam is born, every newborn born [that night] will be a believer. If [the newborn is] born in the land of [ascribing partners to the Absolute][1]*, then God will transport [the newborn] to faith*[2] *by the blessing of the Imam.*[3]

---

[1] T: *al-Shirk*; Taking false gods.

[2] T: *al-Īmān*; The faith.

[3] *Amālī al-Ṭūsī*: 412 / Ḥ (925/73).

Al-Majlisī says: I say: Shaykh [al-Ṭūsī] in his two books [with the word] *Miṣbāḥ* [in their titles], Sayyid Ibn Ṭāwūs in his *Iqbāl al-Aʿmāl*, and the remaining authors of prayer books have specified his birthday as being in the middle of Shaʿbān. The author of *al-Fuṣūl al-Muhimmah*, [Ibn al-Ṣabbāgh al-Mālikī, a non-Shīʿah] has written: "He was born in Sarra-Man-Raʾá (Samarra) on the eve of the middle of Shaʿbān, the year 255 [AH]."

[Al-Majlisī continues:] It has been relayed from [a text in the] handwriting of [the scholar known by the title] *al-Shahīd* that [Imam Jaʿfar] al-Ṣādiq has said:

إنَّ الليلة التي يولد فيها القائم عليه السلام لا يولد فيها مولود إلَّا كان مؤمناً، وإن ولد في أرض الشرك نقله الله إلى الإيمان ببركة الإمام

On the night in which the *Qāʾim* is born, every newborn born [that night] will be a believer. If [the newborn is] born in the land of ascribing partners [to the Absolute], then God will transport [the newborn] to faith by the blessing of the Imam.

Biḥār al-Anwār 51:28.

Regarding this feature, either: [1] we say that it is characteristic of all of the Imams, as the usage of the word "Imam" indicates in al-Ṭūsī's report. In this case, the mention of Imam Mahdī [the *Qāʾim*] in *al-Shahīd's* report would be an application [of the general principle], even if that be by *al-Shahīd* himself, or [2] we say that this feature is exclusively a feature of Imam Mahdī, in which case the first report

This is an exclusive merit specific to Imam Mahdī – that the day in which the Imam was born was an honorable day, honored and distinguished by the birth of the Imam. For it is the Imam who imparted such an honor and merit to that day. This is no surprise of course – places and times are honored because of the individuals associated with them, just like Karbalāʾ is distinguished due to the distinction of Ḥusayn.

6) It has been reported that al-Mufaḍḍal said: I heard Abū ʿAbd Allāh [Imam Jaʿfar al-Ṣādiq] saying:

إن لصاحب هذا الأمر بيتا يقال له: بيت الحمد، فيه سراج يزهر منذ يوم ولد إلى يوم يقوم بالسيف، لا يطفأ

Indeed, the one to whom this amr[1] *belongs has a house called the house of praise*[2]*. Inside, there is lamp that has been glowing since the day he was born and [will continue to glow] until the day in which he rises [up in arms]*[3] *– it is never turned off.*[4]

Apparently, neither is this referring to a physical house nor is the lamp referring to a physical lamp. Rather, perhaps what is meant by them both is the station of spirituality and excellence he has.

---

would either be ambiguous (*mujmalah*) or unqualified (*muṭlaqah*) [itself] but qualified by the second report.

[1] T: *Amr*; The Arabic root AMR, and more specifically the noun *amr*, has its own web of interconnected connotations in the Qurʾān (e.g., command, authority, matter, affair, thing, etc.).

[2] T: Bayt al-ḥamd.

[3] T: *Bil-sayf*; Literally, with the sword.

[4] *Al-Ghaybah* by al-Nuʿmānī: 245 / Ḥ 31.

Moreover, [here][1], the limit[2] is included in that which has the limit[3]. For, indeed, this station, this excellence, subsists so long as he exists and is not negated after he rises [up in arms] [4].

7) It has been reported the Jābir ibn ʿAbd Allāh al-Anṣārī quoted the Commander of the Faithful [Imam ʿAlī] to have said,

[...] المهدي من ذرّيتي، يظهر بين الركن والمقام، وعليه قميص إبراهيم، وحلة إسماعيل، وفي رجله نعل شيث

[…] The Mahdī [is] from among my progeny; he appears between the rukn and the maqām[5] *wearing Abraham's*

---

[1] T: Presumably, the author is not making a general statement on this notion discussed in legal theory but is merely commenting on this particular instance of using the *ghāyah* relative to the *mughayyah*. See the following footnotes.

[2] T: *al-Ghāyah*; The end, the utmost limit. The analogous reference here would be to, "the day in which he rises […]."

[3] T: *al-Mughayyá*; That which has the limit (*ghāyah*). The analogous reference here would be to the lamp continuing to glow.

[4] T: *Bil-sayf*; Literally, with the sword.

[5] T: The phrase, "between the *rukn* and the *maqām*," appears in reports attributed to the Imams, describing the location of an event in which the awaited Imam Mahdī is publicly present at the holy Kaʿbah in the pilgrimage city of Mecca.

shirt[1], *Ishmael's [two-piece set of clothing]*[2] *and Seth's*[3] *footwear*[4].[5]

Indeed, in all of such descriptions there are instances of *kināyāt*[6] and hints pointing to his spiritual stations and [Divinely-bestowed] honors[7].

8) It has been reported that Abū al-Ṣalt al-Harawī said: I asked [Imam ʿAlī, son of Mūsá] al-Riḍā, "What are the signs of the *Qāʾim* from amongst you [the Imams of Prophet Muḥammad's household] when he mobilizes[8]?" He replied,

---

[1] T: *Qamīṣ*.

[2] T: *Ḥullah*; two pieces of clothing. This word can also mean weapon.

[3] T: *Shīth*.

[4] T: *Fī rijlihi naʿlu Shīth*; On his leg/foot is the footwear of Shīth. The Arabic singular terms *rijl* (leg/foot) and *naʿl* (footwear/shoe) either refer to the *type* of thing, in which case could represent both feet and pair of shoes, or refer to the *singular* thing (as opposed to the plural), in which case would be specifying one particular foot and its footwear. I have allowed for both possibilities in the English rendering above. That being said, the author's commentary explains that these descriptions symbolize spiritual stations.

[5] *Muʿjam Aḥādīth al-Imām al-Mahdī* 3:121; referencing *Ithbāth al-Hudāt* 3:587 / Bāb 32 / Ḥ 804.

[6] T: Sing. *kināyah*; Linguistically, this refers to meaning something without saying it explicitly. As a term, it arguably refers to using a phrase in its literal meaning while intending to make an entailed meaning understood, but with the possibility of also meaning for the former to be understood as well. See Daqīq's *Durūs fī al-Balāghah*, page 157.

[7] T: *Karāmāt* (sing. *karāmah*); This can also refer to saintly "miracles" (extraordinary acts that reflect a person's closeness to God; albeit not as challenging and beyond reproducibility as miracles done by Divinely-appointed prophets.)

[8] T: *Kharaja*; when he sets out or comes out. The use of this word seems to refer to his mobilization after already having made himself known publicly. But it is possible that *kharaja* merely refers to coming out more generally, in which case it could mean he comes out of his secrecy and makes himself publicly known

علامته أن يكون شيخ السنّ، شاب المنظر حتّى أنّ الناظر إليه ليحسبه ابن أربعين سنة أو دونها، وإنّ من علاماته أن لا يهرم بمرور الأيّام والليالي حتّى يأتيه أجله.

His sign is that he will be an elder[1] in terms of his age and a youth in terms of his looks – to such an extent that if someone were to look at him, he or she would think he is forty years old or younger. Indeed, one of his signs is that he does not grow old with the passing days and nights, all the way up until his time[2] comes.[3]

9) The Mahdī is a "word"[4] among the "words" of God[5] and the "light" of God on earth[6]. For, indeed, the holy Qurʾān describes Jesus as God's word. God Almighty says,

---

(*ẓuhūr*). However, the word *kharaja* is often associated with setting out in the sense of mobilizing.

[1] T: Shaykh.

[2] T: Of death.

[3] *Kamāl al-Dīn*: 652 / Bāb 57 / Ḥ 12.

[4] T: Kalimah.

[5] It has been reported that Muḥammad ibn Muslim said: I heard Abū Jaʿfar [Imam Muḥammad al-Bāqir] saying [the following when commenting on Qurʾānic verse 42:24],

[...] "وَيَمْحُ ٱللَّهُ ٱلْبَٰطِلَ" يعني يبطله "وَيُحِقُّ ٱلْحَقَّ بِكَلِمَٰتِهِ" يعنى بالنبيّ وبالأئمّة والقائم من آل محمّد

[...] "and God effaces the falsehood," meaning he puts an end to it, "and confirms the truth with His words," meaning, through the Prophet, through the Imams and the *Qāʾim* from the progeny of Muḥammad.
(*Tafsīr al-Qummī* 2:275)

[6] It has been reported that Prophet Muḥammad said,

[...] معاشر الناس إنّي نبيّ وعلي وصيّ، ألا إنّ خاتم الأئمّة منّا القائم المهدي [...]
ألا إنّه الباقي حجّة ولا حجّة بعده ولاحقّ إلّا معه ولا نور إلّا عنده [...]

[...] O people, indeed I am a prophet and ʿAlī is a *guardian* (*waṣī*). Indeed, the seal of the Imams from among us is the *Qāʾim*, the Mahdī [...]
Indeed, he the one remaining as a *ḥujjah*; there is no *ḥujjah* after him; what is right is with none other than him; there is no light except with him.

إِذْ قَالَتِ الْمَلَائِكَةُ يَا مَرْيَمُ إِنَّ اللَّهَ يُبَشِّرُكِ بِكَلِمَةٍ مِّنْهُ اسْمُهُ الْمَسِيحُ عِيسَى ابْنُ مَرْيَمَ وَجِيهًا فِي الدُّنْيَا وَالْآخِرَةِ وَمِنَ الْمُقَرَّبِينَ

When the angels said, 'O Mary, God gives you the good news of a Word from Him whose name is the Messiah, Jesus, son of Mary, distinguished in the world and the Hereafter, and one of those brought near [to God].[1]

Similarly, the Imam has been described as one of God's words. There is also such a connection to "light"[2]. As God Almighty says,

اللَّهُ نُورُ السَّمَاوَاتِ وَالْأَرْضِ ۚ مَثَلُ نُورِهِ كَمِشْكَاةٍ فِيهَا مِصْبَاحٌ ۖ الْمِصْبَاحُ فِي زُجَاجَةٍ ۖ الزُّجَاجَةُ كَأَنَّهَا كَوْكَبٌ دُرِّيٌّ يُوقَدُ مِن شَجَرَةٍ مُّبَارَكَةٍ زَيْتُونَةٍ لَّا شَرْقِيَّةٍ وَلَا غَرْبِيَّةٍ يَكَادُ زَيْتُهَا يُضِيءُ وَلَوْ لَمْ تَمْسَسْهُ نَارٌ ۚ نُّورٌ عَلَىٰ نُورٍ ۗ يَهْدِي اللَّهُ لِنُورِهِ مَن يَشَاءُ ۚ وَيَضْرِبُ اللَّهُ الْأَمْثَالَ لِلنَّاسِ ۗ وَاللَّهُ بِكُلِّ شَيْءٍ عَلِيمٌ

God is the Light of the heavens and the earth. The parable of His Light is a niche wherein is a lamp – the lamp is in a glass, the glass as though it were a glittering star – lit from a blessed olive tree, neither eastern nor western, whose oil almost lights up, though fire should not touch it. Light upon light. God guides to His Light whomever He wishes. God draws parables for mankind, and God has knowledge of all things.[3]

[But why would these two attributes be considered some of Imam Mahdī's *distinct* attributes despite the fact that the other Imams are also God's words and lights?] It is in consideration of the fact that the report has made explicit and literal mention of Imam Mahdī. This is [enough of a consideration to deem these distinct attributes for Imam Mahdī] even if [the explicit mention may be] explained [not necessarily as indicating exclusivity but] as an application [of

(*al-Iḥtijāj* 1:80)

[1] Qur'ān 3:45.

[2] T: That is, just as the Imam is one of God's words, he is also one of God's lights.

[3] Qur'ān 24:35.

the concept to a particular instance, that of Imam Mahdī, while there are other applications as well], or the explicit mention may be explained as indicating an additional degree of distinction [for Imam Mahdī as an instance of application,] based on [assuming] the gradated-nature[1] of the existential meaning [being referred to].

10) He will carry the stone of Moses, the son of Amram[2], which is a camel's [heavy] load[3]. At every place he will stop[4], a spring will gush forth from it[5]. *Perhaps*[6] this is hinting at the heavy weight of the load and that no one can carry such a load except one distinguished by God to do so. As God says,

إِنَّا سَنُلْقِي عَلَيْكَ قَوْلًا ثَقِيلًا

Indeed, soon We shall cast on you a weighty word.[7]

God also says,

يَٰيَحْيَىٰ خُذِ ٱلْكِتَٰبَ بِقُوَّةٍۢ ۖ وَءَاتَيْنَٰهُ ٱلْحُكْمَ صَبِيًّا

'O John![8]*' [We said,] 'Hold on with power to the Book!' And We gave him judgement while still a child,*[9]

---

[1] T: *Tashkīkīyah*; From the word *tashkīk*, the term referring to a gradation, a spectrum with varying degrees of intensity. In this case, it would be referring to the various degrees of "word-ness" and "light-ness."

[2] T: Mūsá ibn ʿImrān.

[3] T: Wiqr baʿīr.

[4] T: Manzil; Station, abode.

[5] T: The stone.

[6] T: *Qad yuqāl*; It might be said that […]

[7] Qurʾān 73:5.

[8] T: Yaḥyá.

[9] Qurʾān 19:12.

There is a difference between "holding on with power"[1] and "carrying"[2]. Furthermore, the "spring" in the report[3] is a *kināyah* referring to wisdom and goodness. Similarly, the "place he will stop" is not a physical place but the heart of a believer. *However*, the apparent meaning indicates that the physical matters are intended here. This is further emphasized in light of a clue from another report[4] in the book *al-Kharāʾij* – it has been reported that Abū Saʿīd al-Khurāsānī said: [Imam Jaʿfar] al-Ṣādiq relayed that his father said:

إنَّ القائم إذا قام بمكّة وأراد أن يتوجّه إلى الكوفة نادى مناديه: ألا لا يحمل أحد منكم طعاماً ولا شراباً، ويحمل حجر موسى بن عمران وهو وقر بعير، فلا ينزل منزلاً إلّا انبعث عين منه، فمن كان جائعاً شبع ومن كان ظامئاً روي، فهو زادهم حتّى ينزلوا النجف من ظهر الكوفة، فإذا نزلوا ظاهرها انبعث منه الماء واللبن دائماً [...]

Indeed, when the Qāʾim rises in Mecca and he wishes to head toward Kūfah, his announcer will call out, "Indeed, none of you should carry food or water[!]" He[5] will carry the stone of Moses, the son of Amram, which is a camel's [heavy] load[6]. At every place he will stop[7], a spring will gush forth from it[8]. So, whoever is hungry is satisfied and

---

[1] T: al-Akhdh bi quwwah.

[2] T: al-Ḥaml.

[3] T: The report from which this idea came from. For example, see *al-Kāfī*, vol. 1, p. 231.

[4] T: The author seems to have quoted *al-Kāfī's* version up until the phrase *min Ẓahr al-Kūfah*, then the continuation comes from *al-Kharāʾij*. Perhaps this implies that the author is more confident regarding the wording in the manuscript for *al-Kāfī*, but because *al-Kāfī* did not include the continuation, he quotes it from *al-Kharāʾij*.

[5] T: Imam Mahdī.

[6] T: Wiqr baʿīr.

[7] T: Manzil; Station, abode.

[8] T: The stone.

whoever is thirsty [his thirst] is quenched. That is their provision until they stop at "al-Najaf"[1] *from the "back of Kūfah."*[2] *Once they stop at its outskirts*[3]*, water and milk*[4] *will gush forth from it constantly [...]*[5]

These are the things that Imam Mahdī inherits from the prophets, as the other reports describe, such as the shirt of Adam and Joseph, the ring of Solomon and other items.

11) The Ark of Tranquility[6] will appear at the hands of the Mahdī. It has been reported that Sulaymān ibn ʿĪsá said:

بلغني أنّه على يدي المهدي يظهر تابوت السكينة من بحيرة طبرية حتّى يحمل فيوضع بين يديه ببيت المقدس، فإذا نظرت إليه اليهود أسلمت إلّا قليل منهم، ثمّ يموت المهدي.

[News has] reached me that the Ark of Tranquility will appear at the hands of the Mahdī from Lake Tiberias[7]*; it will be carried and put before him in Jerusalem*[8]*. Once the Jews look at it, they will become Muslim – [all] but a few of them. Then the Mahdī will die.*[9]

---

[1] T: The name "al-Najaf" (or Najaf for short) has been used to refer to the burial site of Imam ʿAlī, because it lies on an elevation (which is related to the linguistic meaning of "najaf"). See al-Majlisī's commentary in *Mirʾāt al-ʿUqūl*, vol. 3, p. 39.

[2] T: Ẓahr al-Kūfah.

[3] T: Ẓāhirahā.

[4] T: *Laban*.

[5] *Al-Kharāʾij wa al-Jarāʾiḥ* 2:690 / Ḥ 1.

[6] T: *Tābūt al-Sakīnah*; This likely refers to what is known as "the Ark of the Covenant." However, the origin story and significance associated with it may differ across present-day Judeo-Christian-Islamic accounts.

[7] T: Buḥayrat Ṭabarayyah.

[8] T: Bayt al-Maqdis.

[9] *Al-Malāḥim wa al-Fitan*: 150.

Similarly, he will have the staff of Moses. As Abū Jaʿfar [Imam Muḥammad al-Bāqir] reportedly said:

كانت عصا موسى لآدم عليه السلام فصارت إلى شعيب، ثم صارت إلى موسى بن عمران، وإنّها لعندنا وإنّ عهدي بها آنفا وهي خضراء كهيئتها حين انتزعت من شجرتها، وإنّها لتنطق إذا استنطقت، أُعدّت لقائمنا عليه السلام يصنع بها ما كان يصنع موسى وإنّها لتروع وتلقف ما يأفكون وتصنع ما تؤمر به، إنّها حيث أقبلت تلقف ما يأفكون يفتح لها شعبتان: إحداهما في الأرض والأخرى في السقف، وبينهما أربعون ذراعاً تلقف ما يأفكون بلسانها.

The staff of Moses used to be for Adam. Then it went to Jethro[1] *and subsequently to Moses, the son of Amram. Indeed, [now] it is with us. I have just seen it. It is green, in its form the way it was when it was taken from its tree. Indeed, it speaks if it is asked to speak. It has been prepared for our Qāʾim – he will do with it that which Moses used to do with it. Indeed, it will frighten, "swallow up their deceptions,"*[2] *and do what it is commanded to do. Indeed, whichever way it turns, "it swallows up their deceptions." It will have its two jaws open up, one on the ground and the other toward the sky, between the two being [a height of] forty cubits*[3] *– it swallows up their deception with its tongue.*[4]

Indeed, it is known among the children of Israel that bringing forth the Ark of Tranquility[5] reveals the veracity of the claim being made by the one who brings forth the Ark. The report was meant to indicate that the Imam will argue with each people on the terms

---

[1] T: Shuʿayb.

[2] T: A reference to Qurʾān 7:117; 20:69; and 26:45 ––"deceptions" of the Pharoah's sorcerers.

[3] T: *Dhirāʿ*.

[4] *Al-Kāfī* 1:231 / Bāb Mā ʿInda al-Aʾimmah Min Āyāt al-Anbiyāʾ / Ḥ 1.

[5] T: Otherwise known as the Ark of the Covenant.

that they take for granted[1]. In addition, the [quality of] excellence does not reside in the staff per se; rather, the [quality of] excellence is in its association with Moses or the Imam.

12) The Mahdī is, "in a pool[2] of light." For it has been reported that Salām said: I heard Abū Salmá, the shepherd [of camels] for the Prophet, saying: I heard the Messenger of God saying [something] in a long report, until he said:

[...] قلت : نعم يا ربّ فقال : التفت عن يمين العرش، فالتفت فإذا أنا بعلي وفاطمة والحسن والحسين وعلي ومحمّد وجعفر وموسى وعلي ومحمّد وعلي والحسن والمهدي عليهم السلام في ضحضاح من نور، قيام يصلون [...]

[...] I said, "Yes, O' Lord." Then [God said], "Look to the right of the Throne[3]." So I looked. Thereupon, I [recognized] 'Alī, Fāṭimah, Ḥasan, Ḥusayn, 'Alī, Muḥammad, Ja'far, Mūsá, 'Alī, Muḥammad, 'Alī, Ḥasan, and the Mahdī, in a pool of light, rising in prayer [...][4]

This is considered one of the distinct features of the Mahdī based on the understanding that the preposition in ["in a shallow pool of light"] refers specifically to him. However, the apparent meaning indicates that the preposition refers to the entire group. Hence, it is actually a general feature [that describes the others in addition to the Mahdī].

13) Jesus will pray behind him. For it has been reported that Abū Sa'īd al-Khudrī said: Prophet Muḥammad said,

---

[1] T: The terms that they believe in; The arguments that they believe would establish something to be true or false.

[2] T: *Ḍaḥḍāḥ*; A shallow pool.

[3] T: al-'Arsh.

[4] *Al-Ghaybah* by al-Ṭūsī: 148 / Number 109.

[...] مهدي هذه الأمّة الذي يصلّي عيسى خلفه [...]

[...] The Mahdī of this community, the one whom Jesus prays behind [...][1]

14) The angels of Badr[2] support the Mahdī. It has been reported that Abū Ḥamzah al-Thumālī said: Abū Jaʿfar [Imam Muḥammad al-Bāqir] said the following to me:

يا ثابت ، كأنّي بقائم أهل بيتي قد أشرف على نجفكم هذا - وأومأ بيده إلى ناحية الكوفة -، فإذا هو أشرف على نجفكم نشر راية رسول الله (صلى الله عليه وآله)، فإذا هو نشرها انحطّت عليه ملائكة بدر [...].

O' Thābit, it is as if I [can see] the Qāʾim from my household as he approaches this Najaf[3] *of yours – [and he pointed to the direction of Kūfah]. When he approaches your Najaf, he will unfurl the banner of God's Messenger. Once he unfurls it, the angels of Badr will descend upon him [...].*[4]

---

[1] See: *al-Ṣirāṭ al-Mustaqīm* 2:238.

[2] T: This refers to the famous battle of Badr in the early days of Islam, during which the Muslims were vastly outnumbered and still emerged victorious. See Qurʾānic verses 3:123-126.

[3] T: The name "al-Najaf" (or Najaf for short) has been used to refer to the burial site of Imam ʿAlī because it lies on an elevation (which is related to the linguistic meaning of "najaf"). See al-Majlisī's commentary in *Mirʾāt al-ʿUqūl*, vol. 3, p. 39.

[4] *Al-Ghaybah* by al-Nuʿmānī: 321 / Bāb 20 / Ḥ 3.

15) His turn [in power][1] is God's turn [in power[2]]. It is reported that Zurārah relayed the words of Abū ʿAbd Allāh [Imam Jaʿfar al-Ṣādiq] regarding the following verse from the Qurʾān,

[...] وَتِلْكَ ٱلْأَيَّامُ نُدَاوِلُهَا بَيْنَ ٱلنَّاسِ [...]

[...] and We make such vicissitudes rotate among mankind [...][3]

[As the report goes, Imam Jaʿfar al-Ṣādiq] said:

ما زال مذ خلق الله آدم دولة لله ودولة لإبليس، فأين دولة الله أمَا هو الّا قائم واحد

Ever since God created Adam, there has been a turn [serving on behalf] of God [in power] and a turn [serving on behalf] of Iblīs[4] *[in power]. So where is the turn [serving on behalf] of God [in power]? Indeed, [there is] but one Qāʾim*[5].[6]

---

[1] T: *Dawlah* or *dūlah* (see al-Rāghib al-Iṣfahānī's *Mufradāt Alfāẓ al-Qurʾān*, p. 322); The root d-w-l relates to rotating, alternating, taking turns, or occurring periodically; thus, the "turn" of coming to power and/or wielding authority over resources.

[2] T: Of course, this is referring to *temporal* power that follows God's prescription. As for ontological power, God is the Omnipotent – all power flows from Him alone.

[3] Qurʾān 3:140.

[4] T: Satan.

[5] T: Other possible renderings include, "he is but one *Qāʾim* [rising one; the Mahdī]," or, "it will not be but Qāʾim [standing], one [without discrepancies; actualized by the *Qāʾim*, the Mahdī]". The English rendering here requires an interpretive assessment that the author has not elaborated on in the Arabic text. There are also variations in the report's wording to consider.

[6] *Tafsīr al-ʿAyyāshī* 1:199 / Ḥ 145.

16) The Mahdī is a [source of] safety[1] for the inhabitants of the heavens[2] and earth. For it has been reported that Isḥāq ibn Yaʿqūb said: I asked Muḥammad ibn ʿUthmān al-ʿAmrī[3] to deliver a letter for me – one in which I had included questions about issues that I could not figure out[4]. Then the reply came back signed in the handwriting of our guardian[5], the master of the age[6],

[...] وإنّي لأمان لأهل الأرض كما أنّ النجوم أمان لأهل السماء [...]

[...] and, indeed, I am a [source of] safety for the inhabitants of earth just as the stars are a [source of] safety for the inhabitants of the heavens [...][7]

It is possible that the report attempts to address a potential misconception – [the idea that] one who is absent[8] [physically and/or from the public's eye] has no impact. The end of the report provides a clue in this regard. If that is the case, then this report comes in the context of the general features [as opposed to distinct features of the Mahdī][9].

---

[1] T: Amān; Safety/security.

[2] T: al-Samāʾ.

[3] T: The second of the four directly appointed deputies of Imam Mahdī during the period of the *minor ghaybah* (*al-ghaybah al-ṣughrá*; as opposed to the subsequent *major ghaybah* period – *al-ghaybah al-kubrá* – during which Imam Mahdī has no directly appointed deputies and his followers refer generally to qualified, upright Twelver Shīʿah scholars.)

[4] T: *Ashkalat ʿalayy*; They were problematic to me; difficult to resolve.

[5] T: Mawlānā.

[6] T: *Ṣāḥib al-zamān*; Referring to the Twelfth Imam, Imam Mahdī.

[7] *Kamāl al-Dīn*: 483-485 / Bāb 45 / Ḥ 4.

[8] T: *Ghāʾib*; In the state of *ghaybah*.

[9] T: Because the notion of absence, the state of *ghaybah*, is not something that only the Mahdī has gone through.

CONCLUSIONS

In light of the aforementioned, we can deduce the following:

1) His attributes are the attributes of the [previous] prophets, of Prophet Muḥammad and of the immaculate Imams. Moreover, his [spiritual] station is [based on] Divine selection. For, indeed, seeing the dominions[1] of the heavens and the earth is a Divine matter. [As the Qur᾿ān states,]

وَكَذَٰلِكَ نُرِيٓ إِبْرَٰهِيمَ مَلَكُوتَ ٱلسَّمَٰوَٰتِ وَٱلْأَرْضِ وَلِيَكُونَ مِنَ ٱلْمُوقِنِينَ

Thus did We show Abraham the dominions of the heavens and the earth, that he might be of those who possess certitude.[2]

The Seal [of All Prophets, that is, Muḥammad,] and the guardian [he appointed, that is, the Imam,] have the excellent attributes of the [previous] prophets and more. It is in light of this that Prophet Muḥammad became the Seal [of All Prophets] and his *Sharī῾ah* became the seal [of all *sharī῾ah* updates]. It has been reported that our guardian, the awaited [Mahdī], has said:

يَا أَيُّهَا النَّاسُ، إِنَّا نَسْتَنْصِرُ اللهَ فَمَنْ أَجَابَنَا مِنَ النَّاسِ، فَإِنَّا أَهْلُ بَيْتِ نَبِيِّكُمْ مُحَمَّدٍ وَنَحْنُ أَوْلَى النَّاسِ بِاللهِ وَبِمُحَمَّدٍ صلى الله عليه وآله وسلم، فَمَنْ حَاجَّنِي فِي آدَمَ فَأَنَا أَوْلَى النَّاسِ بِآدَمَ، وَمَنْ حَاجَّنِي فِي نُوحٍ فَأَنَا أَوْلَى النَّاسِ بِنُوحٍ، وَمَنْ حَاجَّنِي فِي إِبْرَاهِيمَ فَأَنَا أَوْلَى النَّاسِ بِإِبْرَاهِيمَ، وَمَنْ حَاجَّنِي فِي مُحَمَّدٍ صلى الله

[1] T: *Malakūt*; This word arguably refers to the inner, spiritual and/or metaphysical dimension of the apparent world. Thus, the *malakūt* is contrasted with the *mulk*. The physical actions of bowing and prostrating belong to the world of *mulk*, while the reality of prayer with its spiritual effects of forbidding indecency and wrongdoing belong to the world of *malakūt*. The *malakūt* of the heavens and the earth would, then, refer to something beyond the physical dimensions of the heavens and the earth.

[2] Qur᾿ān 6:75.

عليه وآله وسلم فَأَنَا أَوْلَى النَّاس بِمُحَمَّدٍ صلى الله عليه وآله وسلم ، وَمَنْ حَاجَّنِي فِي النَّبِيِّينَ فَأَنَا أَوْلَى النَّاس بِالنَّبِيِّينَ، أَلَيْسَ اللهُ يَقُولُ فِي مُحْكَمِ كِتَابِهِ [...]

O people, we are seeking God's support[1]*; whoever among the people answers [our call, know that], indeed, we are the household of your Prophet Muḥammad and we of all people have the best claim*[2] *to God and Muḥammad, peace and blessings shower upon him and his progeny. Whoever argues with me regarding Adam, I of all people am the one with the best claim to Adam. Whoever argues with me regarding Noah, I of all people am the one with the best claim to Noah. Whoever argues with me regarding Abraham, I of all people am the one with the best claim to Abraham. Whoever argues with me regarding Muḥammad, peace and blessings shower upon him and his progeny, I of all people am the one with the best claim to Muḥammad, peace and blessings shower upon him and his progeny. Whoever argues with me regarding the [other] prophets, I of all people am the one with the best claim to the prophets. Does God not say in His precise*[3] *Book,*

إِنَّ ٱللَّهَ ٱصْطَفَىٰٓ ءَادَمَ وَنُوحًا وَءَالَ إِبْرَٰهِيمَ وَءَالَ عِمْرَٰنَ عَلَى ٱلْعَٰلَمِينَ
ذُرِّيَّةًۢ بَعْضُهَا مِنۢ بَعْضٍ ۗ وَٱللَّهُ سَمِيعٌ عَلِيمٌ

Indeed, God chose Adam and Noah, and the progeny of Abraham and the progeny of Imran above all the nations[4]*;*

---

[1] T: Nastanṣiru Allāh.

[2] T: Awlá al-nās bi [...].

[3] T: *Muḥkam*; Depending on the context, this can mean exact, coherent, or carefully done. It is also possible that the usage of *muḥkam* here is juxtaposed with *mutashābih*, in which case *muḥkam* would arguably be a description that applies to verses which are straightforward *in a stand-alone fashion.*

[4] T: al-ʿĀlamīn.

some of them are descendants of the others, and God is all-hearing, all-knowing.[1] *[?]*[2]

Those who undertake the likes of these Divine posts must be immaculate[3]. There are Qurʾānic and report-based examples showing that this selection is a Divine selection and a choice based on the Creator's wisdom. For instance, there are [reports referred to as the] reports of "the light,"[4] "the clay [piece],"[5] and [reports describing] them as, "the first [creatures] created."[6] As it has been reported, Abū ʿAbd Allāh [that is Imam Jaʿfar al-Ṣādiq] has said:

إنَّ الله خلقنا من نور عظمته ، ثمّ صوَّر خلقنا من طينة مخزونة مكنونة من تحت العرش، فأسكن ذلك النور فيه، فكنّا نحن خلقاً وبشراً نورانيين لم يجعل لأحد في مثل الذي خلقنا منه نصيباً، وخلق أرواح شيعتنا من طينتنا وأبدانهم من طينة مخزونة مكنونة أسفل من ذلك الطينة ولم يجعل الله لأحد في مثل الذي خلقهم منه نصيباً إلَّا للأنبياء، ولذلك صرنا نحن وهم الناس، وصار سائر الناس همج، للنار وإلى النار

---

1 Qurʾān 3:33-34.

2 *Al-Ghaybah* by al-Nuʿmānī: 290 / Bāb 14 / Ḥ 67.

3 T: *al-ʿIṣmah* is required; the person must be *maʿṣūm*, that is, immaculate; impeccable.

4 T: *al-Nūr.*

5 T: *al-Ṭīnah*; The piece of clay; used figuratively to refer to the original [substance] fashioning [of] a creature's being.

6 T: Awwal mā khuliq.

Indeed, God created[1] *us*[2] *from the light of His Greatness. Then he formed our bodies*[3] *from a stored*[4]*, guarded*[5] *clay [piece]*[6] *– from beneath the throne – and had that light settle in it. Hence, we were – as [souls]*[7] *and [bodies]*[8] *– beings of light. He did not give anyone [else] a share in the likes of that from which He created us. He created the souls of our Shīʿah from our clay [piece] and their bodies from a stored, guarded clay [piece] beneath that clay [piece]. God did not give anyone [else] a share in the likes of that from which He created them except the prophets*[9]*. Because of this, we and they became the [true] human*

---

[1] T: This arguably refers to their souls.

[2] T: Prophet Muḥammad and the *guardians* succeeding him.

[3] T: *Khalqanā*; Our creation/formation/makeup. This arguably refers to their [physical] bodies (see p. 395, vol. 6 of al-Māzandarānī's *Sharḥ Uṣūl al-Kāfī*). However, al-Majlisī proposes the supposition that this "forming" refers to the creation of their ideal-form bodies (*ajsād mithālīyah*), which are ideal forms resembling their original [physical] bodies. According to al-Majlisī, this indicates that they have such ideal-form bodies before, after and even during the association of their holy souls with their [physical] bodies. As for other humans, he appears to say that our souls become associated with ideal-form bodies after we [physically] die (see p. 272, vol. 4 of al-Majlisī's *Mirʾāt al-ʿUqūl fī Sharḥ Akhbār Āl al-Rasūl*). But, elsewhere, he leaves open the possibility that our ideal-form bodies are the same in this sense and that what we see during sleep is through those ideal-form bodies (see p. 45, vol. 58, of al-Majlisī's *Biḥār al-Anwār*).

[4] T: Makhzūn.

[5] T: *Maknūn.*

[6] T: *Ṭīnah*; Piece of clay; used figuratively to refer to the original [substance] fashioning [of] a creature's being.

[7] T: Khalqan.

[8] T: Basharan.

[9] T: The prophets other than Prophet Muḥammad, of course.

> *beings and all other people hamaj*[1]*, [for the hellfire, and to the hellfire]*[2].[3]
>
> [Be careful to note, however:] This should not be mistaken to mean that the movement of [Divinely appointed] messengers is coerced or deprived of free will.[4]

---

[1] T: *Hamaj* (sing. *hamajah*); This can refer to a small type of fly that flies around the faces of livestock, apparently used figuratively here to describe the misguidance and/or insignificance of this type. It is also possible that this word was used to draw attention to their similarity with flies in how they gather around to follow any herder's call and then might abandon him for the slightest reason.

[2] T: *Lil-nār wa ilá al-nār*; Some commentators mention that these two phrases are either describing the category of *hamaj* or represent two additional predicates, making three predicates in total for the subject "all other people." Is it reasonable to argue that these are three categories of people each described slightly differently because their destiny in the afterlife will differ? For example, the *hamaj* might be treated with God's mercy despite their shortcomings because of their intellectual or other handicaps; the potential category of those "for the hellfire" may be those whose actions deserve the hellfire but may not end up going there due to some Divine mercy catching up with them. Lastly, the potential category of those "to the hellfire" may be those who will surely end up in hellfire. Regardless of whether or not this tripartite division is intended by the final phrase, there must be some way to account for the categories of people who will be pardoned by God – whether it be because they tried their best and still failed or because there is still a receptor of God's mercy intact within them and God finds it wise to forgive them. Either the notion of "Shīʿah" in the report is more flexible than the apparent meaning understood or the treatment of the group which is neither the Imams nor the Shīʿah is more nuanced than it seems at first glance here.

[3] *Al-Kāfī* 1:389 / Bāb Khalq Abdān al-Aʾimmah wa Arwāḥihim wa Qulūbihim / Ḥ 2.

[4] T: One of the attempts to reconcile the "clay [piece] reports" with Divine justice and human free will is to explain them as a *reflection* of God's absolute knowledge of humanity's *freely chosen choices*. Based upon God's transcendent knowledge of their *freely chosen choices*, He fashioned different people from substances more befitting of their final destiny (the destiny that they would have reached of their own volition regardless and *do* end up reaching of their own volition). On p. 393-394, vol. 6 of *Sharḥ Uṣūl al-Kāfī*, al-Māzandarānī writes:

In any case, the Imam's platform[1] is not about establishing a [completely] novel culture. Rather, it is an extension of [the aforementioned culture involving] prophetic selection. Thus, he does not have a new religion, a new sharīʿah, or a special school of thought[2] particular to him. This assessment is based on the notion that the extended movement of prophets reveals a shared essence of Religion. As for the designation, "the Religion of Islam," as opposed to, "the religion of Judaism and Christianity," that is a distinction in light of the deviation which occurred in previous religions. Otherwise, it is but one Religion. As God Almighty says,

مَا كَانَ إِبْرَٰهِيمُ يَهُودِيًّا وَلَا نَصْرَانِيًّا [...]

[...] فلما علم أن بعضهم يعود بالحالات العلية إلى مكان القرب، خلقهم منه وهو لطف يعينهم على اكتساب تلك الحالات وعلم أن بعضهم يعود بالحالات الدنية إلى محل البعد خلقهم منه ليكون عود كل أحد إلى أصله ومحله المأنوس كما قيل « كل شيء يرجع إلى أصله » ، وبالجملة تلك الحالات علّة للإيجاد على نحو مخصوص ومحل معلوم دون العكس فليتأمّل فإنّه دقيق جدّاً ، وبذلك يندفع كثير من الشبهات والله الموفق للخيرات .

[...] So when He knew that some of them would return – through elevated states [attained by choice] – to the place of closeness [to God], He created them from it. This is a [form of] Divine Grace (*luṭf*) helping them to attain those [elevated] states. And [when] He knew that some of them would return – through lowly states [attained by choice] – to the place of distance [from God], He created them from it such that each person's return would be to his or her origin and place of fondness/familiarity (*al-maʾnūs*). As the saying goes, "Every thing goes back to its origin." In general, those states [attained by choice] are causes [God employs for] bringing about the [person's] existence in a particular way, a place [already] known [by God to be the choice of the individual]. The opposite is not true. [T: Meaning, the particular way of existence and known place which end up occurring are not the cause by which God defined the aforementioned states of choice]. This must be reflected upon, for indeed it is very nuanced. With this, many misconceptions/objections become addressed, and God is the One who gives success to achieve [the rest (*al-khayrāt*)].

[1] T: *Mashrūʿ*; Project, campaign, mission.

[2] T: *Madhhab*; School of thought and/or practice, sometimes referring to the community adopting the school.

Abraham was neither a Jew nor a Christian […][1]

إِنَّ ٱلدِّينَ عِندَ ٱللَّهِ ٱلْإِسْلَٰمُ [...]

Truly the Religion in the sight of God is Submission[2] *[…]*[3]

The same goes for the notion of *madhhab*, or school of thought. For what is meant by the Shī'ah "school of thought" is in juxtaposition with the Sunnī school of thought, which veered off course. Otherwise, in light of 'Alī's movement being a continuation extending back to the Messenger of God [Prophet Muḥammad], the Shī'ah school of thought should not be described as a "school of thought" [proper][4]. Rather, it is [plainly]: the Religion of Islam. In any case, Imam Mahdī's platform is to revive the neglected ways[5] [prescribed by God]. For it has been reported that [Imam Muḥammad] al-Bāqir said:

ثم يظهر المهدي بمكة عند العشاء ، ومعه راية رسول الله صلى الله عليه وسلم ، وقميصه وسيفه وعلامات ونور وبيان [...]

Then the Mahdī appears in Mecca in the evening. He will have with him the Messenger of God's banner, shirt and sword, along with signs, light and elucidation[6] *[…]*[7]

In another report, [the Mahdī] is described in the following terms,

[...] يقاتل على التأويل [...]

---

[1] Qur'ān 3:67.

[2] T: *al-Islām*; The submission [to the Absolute, Unlimited, God Almighty].

[3] Qur'ān 3:19.

[4] T: In the strict sense of being a subdivision of a religion. In other words, it is not to be thought of as a sect.

[5] T: *Sunan* (sing. *Sunnah*).

[6] T: *Bayān*.

[7] *Al-Malāḥim wa al-Fitan*: 137 / Bāb 130 / Ḥ 157.

[…] He will fight over the interpretation [of scripture][1]
[…][2]

---

[1] T: *al-Ta'wīl.* In this context, the word is being used in opposition to *tanzīl* (revelation [of the Qur'ān]). Hence, *al-ta'wīl* refers to a form of properly understanding/applying the revelation.

[2] It has been reported that Jābir ibn 'Abd Allāh al-Anṣārī said: I was at the Prophet's [place] in the house of Umm Salamah. Then God revealed this verse,

إِنَّمَا يُرِيدُ ٱللَّهُ لِيُذْهِبَ عَنكُمُ ٱلرِّجْسَ أَهْلَ ٱلْبَيْتِ وَيُطَهِّرَكُمْ تَطْهِيرًا

Indeed, God desires to repel all impurity away from you, O People of the Household, and purify you with a thorough purification.
[Qur'ān 33:33]
So then the Prophet called for Ḥasan, Ḥusayn and Fāṭimah, and had them sit before him. Then he called for 'Alī and had him sit behind his back; and he said,

اللّهمّ هؤلاء أهل بيتي فأذهب عنهم الرجس وطهّرهم تطهيراً.

O God, these are the People of my Household, so repel all impurity away from them and purify them with a thorough purification.
Then Umm Salamah asked, "And am I with them, O Messenger of God?" Then he said to her,

إنّك إلى خير

You are [headed] toward that which is good. [Implication: But you are not in this group specifically.]
Then I said, "O Messenger of God, indeed God has honored this pure group of close kin (*'itrah*) and blessed progeny (*dhurīyah*) by repelling all impurity away from them." Then he said:

يا جابر لأنّهم عترتي من لحمي ودمي، فأخي سيّد الأوصياء، وابني خير الأسباط، وابنتي سيّدة النسوان، ومنّا المهدي

O Jābir, [that is] because they are my close kin (*'itrah*), of my own flesh and blood. For my brother ['Alī] is the master of the *guardians* (*awṣiyā'*); my two [grand]sons are the best of grandchildren/descendants (*al-asbāṭ*); my daughter is the leader (*Sayyidah*) of all women; and the Mahdī is from among us.
Then I said, "And who is the Mahdī, O Messenger of God?" Then he said,

تسعة من صلب الحسين أئمّة أبرار، والتاسع قائمهم يملأ الأرض قسطاً وعدلاً كما ملئت جوراً، يقاتل على التأويل كما قاتلت على التنزيل

Nine from the progeny (*ṣulb*) of Ḥusayn are righteous Imams; the ninth is the Qā'im among them, who fills the earth with fairness and justice just as it has been

2) His platform is essentially based on innately intuitive[1] concepts such as justice and fairness. It is clear that the principle of justice encompasses wide spans of hearts[2] and minds, especially after the world's nations become bankrupt in that regard. Hence, his movement is an innately intuitive one and his charisma is an essential dimension of his character. The pure-hearted gravitate toward him, especially those who have been deprived of justice on various levels (such as social justice, economic justice and educational justice). His just platform includes legislative as well as executive dimensions. For, in practice, it is the realistic platform that is not limited to [looking good enough for coverage on] the media, [which would be] to motivate the cultivation of justice in one's individual capacity. Rather, justice is the [very] quern of his encyclopedia and the colorful spectrum of its related concepts. That is why he is known as the one who will fill the earth with fairness and justice.

3) Implementing the platform is subject to the norms and laws of the universe. For this reason, the same logic that applies when it comes to how prophets accomplish their missions and reach their goals also applies to him. Hence, the trials that befell all prophets will also befall him. The same applies to his companions and his community. This means he does not reach his aims through means that are purely beyond this world[3]. For it has been reported that Bashīr al-Nabbāl said: When I came to Medina, I said to Abū Jaʿfar [that is Imam Muḥammad al-Bāqir], "They say that when the

---

filled with tyranny; he fights over the interpretation [of scripture] (*al-taʾwīl*) just as I have fought over the revelation [of scripture] (*al-tanzīl*).

Kifāyat al-Athar: 66.

[1] T: *Fiṭrīyah*; Innately intuitive or related to human nature.

[2] T: *Nufūs* (sing. *nafs*); Spirits/souls. The expression "hearts and minds" seems more familiar in English.

[3] T: *al-Ghayb*; The Unseen, the metaphysical realm, the supernatural.

Mahdī rises, things will naturally fall into place for him and he will not shed even a bit of blood[1]." Then he said,

كلّا والذي نفسي بيده لو استقامت لأحد عفواً لاستقامت لرسول الله (صلى الله عليه وآله) حين أدميت رباعيته، وشج في وجهه، كلّا والذي نفسي بيده حتّى نمسح نحن وأنتم العرق والعلق.

No. [Rather, I swear] by the One in whose hands is my soul[2] that if things were to naturally fall into place for anyone, then they would have fallen into place [naturally] for the Messenger of God when blood was shed from his incisor [tooth] and his face was wounded. No. [Rather, I swear] by the One in whose hands is my soul that things will not fall into place until we, along with you, wipe off sweat and blood[3].

[Bashīr al-Nabbāl continued to say:] Then he wiped his forehead.[4]

Indeed, the norms [God has set in place] do not bring about involuntary action; they do not eliminate the role of choice and volition. Moreover, there is no contradiction between Divine prophecy about the future and the notion that one must make the necessary preparations to that end, because the movement is a voluntary one.[5]

---

[1] T: wa lā yuhrīqu miḥjamata dam.

[2] T: *Wa al-lathī nafsī bi yadih*; God Almighty, all things are under His control.

[3] T: *al-ʿAraq wa al-ʿAlaq*; This is in reference to the hardships that will entail sweating and bleeding wounds.

[4] *Al-Ghaybah* by al-Nuʿmānī: 294-295 / Bāb 15 / Ḥ 2.

[5] T: In other words, the prophecy may be speaking about the results of a voluntary movement. Hence, those who do their duty and carry out their responsibilities, by exercising their free will properly, naturally bring about the fulfillment of that

For example, Joseph spoke of his vision – a matter of the future – but engaged in life according to the law of norms in the universe; he did not organize his life based on the vision about the future. Rather, he organized his life based on the principle that he had choices to make in this life of examination. Also, while the holy books included prophecies [substantively] about Islam as the final message and about Prophet Muḥammad as the Seal of All Prophets, this did not eliminate the need for Prophet Muḥammad's hard work.[1] Consequently, the prophecy would be fulfilled without falling into the trap of fatalism[2]. Hence, there is no contradiction between the notion of the Imam's wars and necessary efforts, on the one hand, and the notion that the Divine Promise will be fulfilled, on the other hand.

In light of this, it becomes clear that when the reports describe the Mahdī in terms of his "fear"[3] and the like, these are references to the same type of fear that prophets had[4].[5] As such, what we hear

---

prophecy. As for how the prophecy can exist at all, it can be explained by Divine Omniscience – God, who is beyond time and space, is aware of all that was, is and will be, including whether it was, is or will be *voluntarily or involuntarily so.*

[1] T: In other words, the prophecy expressed the result, but the means to that result would involve the voluntary action of Prophet Muḥammad. Hence, there is no fatalism.

[2] T: *al-Jabr*; The notion that there is no free will and that all actions performed are essentially *forced* upon the individual.

[3] T: *Khawf.*

[4] T: That is, it is fear related to the choices being made in this life of examination, in this voluntary movement, in preparing the grounds for the fulfillment of prophecy. Even though a prophet and/or Imam is immaculate, with a tranquil heart filled with God's remembrance, fear of God has many degrees and is not limited to fear of "sins" (in the legal classification sense). "Fear" here can also be a reference to observance of precautions related to the object of fear. Moreover, the fear is not necessarily for the person of the prophet or Imam himself, but *fear for others* and/or the community at large.

[5] Such as when God Almighty says,

every now and then from pseudo-intellectuals and those claiming to have knowledge and awareness – about the unintelligibility of some of the descriptions pertaining to the Imam – is rather telling of their lack in familiarity with Qurʾānic concepts and their lack in conceiving them correctly.

4) His revolution is characterized by knowledge, intellect, development, freedom, and honoring scholars. His system is founded on [the following]: a recognition of scientific specializations, emphasizing the phenomenon of specialization and opening up room for specialists to share their input without being at odds with the Sharīʿah; recognizing and employing the law of causes and effects[1]; and employing *conflict of laws* [at the level

---

فَأَصْبَحَ فِى ٱلْمَدِينَةِ خَآئِفًا يَتَرَقَّبُ فَإِذَا ٱلَّذِى ٱسْتَنصَرَهُۥ بِٱلْأَمْسِ يَسْتَصْرِخُهُۥ ۚ قَالَ لَهُۥ مُوسَىٰٓ إِنَّكَ لَغَوِىٌّ مُّبِينٌ

He rose at dawn in the city, fearful and vigilant, when behold, the one who had sought his help the day before, shouted for his help [once again]. Moses said to him, 'You are indeed manifestly perverse!'
Qurʾān 28:18.

In another verse, God Almighty says,

فَخَرَجَ مِنْهَا خَآئِفًا يَتَرَقَّبُ ۖ قَالَ رَبِّ نَجِّنِى مِنَ ٱلْقَوْمِ ٱلظَّٰلِمِينَ

So he left the city, fearful and vigilant. He said, 'My Lord! Deliver me from the wrongdoing lot.'
Qurʾān 28:21.

God Almighty also says,

[...] لَّا تَخَٰفُ دَرَكًا وَلَا تَخْشَىٰ

[...] not fearing to be overtaken, nor being afraid.
Qurʾān 20:77.

[1] T: That is, planning and resolving matters based on their natural causes and effects.

of implementation][1] jurisprudence[2], neither based on the notion of, "be and it is,"[3] nor based on the notion of invoking the absolutely otherworldly.[4] For the general Qurʾānic proposition is intact,

وَأَن لَّيْسَ لِلْإِنسَـٰنِ إِلَّا مَا سَعَىٰ * وَأَنَّ سَعْيَهُۥ سَوْفَ يُرَىٰ

[...] that man shall have nothing but that for which he endeavored,

And that his endeavoring shall be seen[5]

But of course, Divine support is actualized once [conditions for] social and cosmic laws are fulfilled. As God Almighty says,

يَـٰٓأَيُّهَا ٱلَّذِينَ ءَامَنُوٓا۟ إِن تَنصُرُوا۟ ٱللَّهَ يَنصُرْكُمْ وَيُثَبِّتْ أَقْدَامَكُمْ

O you who have faith! If you help God, He will help you and make your feet steady.[6]

God Almighty also says,

وَلَيَنصُرَنَّ ٱللَّهُ مَن يَنصُرُهُۥٓ

---

[1] T: *al-Tazāḥum*; the state when conflicting legal prescriptions appear to apply to the same subject matter and, thus, an individual cannot comply with both at the level of implementation for a given situation. This term is not being used specifically to refer to conflicts related to different jurisdictions. Rather, it is used more broadly to refer to conflicts arising from any opposing legal prescriptions appearing to apply to the same subject matter, even within the same jurisdiction. That being said, the emphasis is on conflicts at the level of implementation, as opposed to conflicts at the level of legislation.

[2] T: That is, employing jurisprudence related to *conflicts of law* (at the level of implementation) in order to apply more important laws to given situations.

[3] T: *Kun fa yakūn*; a reference to God's words in Qurʾān 2:117, for example.

[4] T: Hence, the Mahdī will not simply be invoking supernatural knowledge/abilities at every juncture.

[5] Qurʾān 53:39-40.

[6] Qurʾān 47:7.

God will surely help those who help Him.[1]

Moreover, the reports have discussed how the sciences will come to fruition, such as medicine, engineering and communications – –[when it comes to ease of communication,] the world will become like a miniscule village. The same can be said of law and the judiciary. But what about the accounts recorded in some books about how he will fight the scholars of his day? Such accounts are baseless. As the saying goes, "A claim may be famous, but nonetheless baseless."[2] However, there is a basis for reports that condemn and speak of removing the scholars serving tyrannical and fraudulent authorities.

Moreover, his language is not the language of violence.[3] Rather, he speaks the language of reason and wisdom, utilizing various legitimate means in order to: *promote virtue and prevent vice*[4]; educate the uneducated; lift the veils of obscurity and ambiguity; address misconceptions and resolve quandaries; and establish proofs[5] such as the advent[6] of Jesus Christ[7], retrieving the Ark of Tranquility[8] and some inheritances from the prophets [of old], and having the voice – with all its charm, composure,

---

[1] Qurʾān 22:40.

[2] T: Rubba shuhratin lā aṣla lahā.

[3] T: His logic/language/discourse (*mantiq*) is not that of the sword and violence.

[4] T: *al-Amr bil-maʿrūf wa al-nahy ʿan al-munkar*; prescribing what is right and proscribing what is wrong; encouraging good and forbidding evil; commanding right and forbidding wrong.

[5] *Ḥujaj* (sing. *ḥujjah*). *Al-Ḥujjah*: The proof/argument that establishes a case for or against something.

[6] T: *Baʿth*.

[7] T: *al-Masīḥ*; The Messiah; a description of Jesus Christ in the Qurʾān (e.g., 3:45; 4:157; 4:171…).

[8] T: *Tābūt al-Sakīnah*; This likely refers to what is known as "the Ark of the Covenant." However, the origins narrative and significance associated with it may differ across present-day Judeo-Christian-Islamic accounts.

comprehensiveness, truthfulness, and transparency – reach all creatures in the far reaches of the universe. He will, thus, establish the case for all ears to hear. The voice of what is right[1] will reach everyone from a pure, crystal-clear source and on the right wavelength. Hence, all [other] ways will come to an end and no longer will anyone have a case to make [in his or her own defense],

قُلْ فَلِلَّهِ ٱلْحُجَّةُ ٱلْبَـٰلِغَةُ [...]

Say, *'To God belongs the conclusive argument. [...]'*[2]

Therefore, there is no doubt that everyone will answer the call of truth, except for souls plagued by illness, unreasonable stubbornness, bigotry, and selfish interests[3]. As God Almighty says,

فِى قُلُوبِهِم مَّرَضٌ فَزَادَهُمُ ٱللَّهُ مَرَضًا [...]

There is a sickness in their hearts; then God increased their sickness [due to their choices] [...][4]

5) In the age of the Mahdī, the community will split into two camps: the camp of sheer truth and the camp of sheer falsehood. Truth will not be mixed up with falsehood. Rather, the forces of darkness will forge an alliance and wage a war against him in order to extinguish his light and radiance.

Moreover, the war that the Imam engages in is a defensive war, militarily-speaking. For it has been reported that the ones to initiate the wars will be the enemies of the Imam, such as the Sufyānī.[5] The Sufyānī will only be

---

[1] T: *al-Ḥaqq*; The truth and/or what is right. Also, one of the Divine names.

[2] Qur'ān 6:149.

[3] T: *Ṣāḥib al-naf'*; The one of [selfish/materialistic/hedonistic] utilitarianism.

[4] Qur'ān 2:10.

[5] T: See next footnote for an example of a report describing the Sufyānī as an adversary to the Mahdī.

bent on [going after] the progeny of Muḥammad and their followers.[1] On an intellectual level, however, the war is an offensive one, because it occurs after having exhausted all means of argumentation and scientific dialogue. It is a war of Divine aims and in pursuit of happiness[2] in this world and the next. It has no selfish, factional or sectarian aims.

Hence, there will be no room for whimsical desires, satisfying spite[3], negative vengeance, and expansionist and dictatorial spirit. Instead, all theories, intellectual outlooks, and *positivist*[4] studies will dissolve with the rise of thought springing forth from the eternal fountain[5]. Such thought will reveal how other theories are corrupt, false and weak.

---

[1] It has been reported that Jābir al-Juʿfī relayed the following words from Abū Jaʿfar [Imam Muḥammad al-Bāqir]:

[...] الزم الأرض لا تحرّكنَّ يدك ولا رجلك ابداً حتى ترى علامات أذكرها لك في سنة [...]

[...] ويظهر السفياني ومن معه حتَّى لا يكون له همّة الَّا آل محمّد صلى الله عليه وآله وشيعتهم، فيبعث بعثاً إلى الكوفة، فيصاب بأناس من شيعة آل محمّد بالكوفة قتلاً وصلباً [...]

[...] Stand your ground [Stay put]; do not move your hand or your foot at all until you see the signs that I mention to you [...]

[...] and the Sufyānī appears along with those with him; such that he will only be bent on [going after] the progeny of Muḥammad and their followers. Hence, he dispatches an army to Kūfah. As a result, people from among the followers of Muḥammad's progeny in Kūfah will be killed and crucified [...]

Tafsīr al-ʿAyyāshī 1:64 / Ḥ 117.

[2] T: *Saʿādah*; Felicity; well-being; success; prosperity; excellence.

[3] T: *al-Tashaffī*; Feeling a sense of satisfaction/glee by spiting one's enemies.

[4] T: *Waḍʿī/waḍʿīyah*; The word "waḍʿī" can translate to "positive" (as in positive law, law established by human authority), or "positivist" (as in an empiricist approach to knowledge). The author appears to be using the word in a broad sense to describe fallible, particularly secular, human theories/studies.

[5] T: al-ʿAyn al-azalīyah.

Thus, the more that valid sciences[1] advance, the closer we come to the age of the Mahdī's public appearance[2], such that those sciences aid in serving the global campaign. For the accumulation of knowledge and intellect paves the way for Imam Mahdī's movement. The encyclopedic vitalization of this world is a stepping stone to Mahdī-minded thought and the rise of grand ideas. For his platform is not founded on a philosophy that disregards, gives up and neglects this world's civilizational development. There are some delusional individuals who have expressed the idea that the discourse[3] of religion is solely related to the hereafter and is founded on a neglect of this world's affairs. They went even further to claim (in light of their flawed view) that it is this [supposed nature of religious discourse] which is behind the backwardness of Islamic societies. This [view of Islamic religious discourse] is far from the truth. A review of the general ḥadīth reports that deal with evaluating this world in the eyes of a believer tell of a clearly different reality. These reports indicate that the faithful individual must express appreciation of this world. For example, this includes putting [the land of a former] grave and road to use[4], and the recommendation of planting trees even if it were the Day of Judgment[5]. Moreover, there is no conflict between reports that condemn loving the worldly life and having false hopes of longevity[6] and the reports that prescribe the vitalization of this world and the advancement of its civilization[7].[8] But will the Mahdī's

---

[1] T: *al-ʿUlūm*; Fields of knowledge.

[2] T: ʿAṣr al-ẓuhūr.

[3] T: *Khiṭāb*; language, logic, rhetoric…

[4] T: Iḥyāʾ al-qabr wa al-ṭarīq.

[5] T: al-Qiyāmah.

[6] T: *Ṭūl al-amal*; Extended false hopes that one will continue to live in this world without having to face death and the otherworldly consequences of moral shortcomings.

[7] T: Iʿlāʾ madanīyatihā wa ḥaḍāratihā.

[8] T: There is no conflict because each set of reports is emphasizing a different dimension to the experience of this world. On the one hand, the life of this world should not make an individual lose sight of its transitory nature and that there is another world to prepare for through one's pursuits in this world. On the other

sacred mission not have some unavoidable consequences, such as enemy[1] casualties, the destruction of buildings, instilling fear in the hearts of skeptics, and other matters that may give the illusion of being characterized as evil? If that is the case, then it would involve matters that are definitively unavoidable in order to bring about just governance[2]. It is analogous to how [justified] general legislation can coincide with restrictions to the individual interests of some people. This means it is prescriptible even if some selfish individuals do not happen to approve.

Indeed, while the concepts of justice, democracy, liberty, and modernization[3] are crystal clear, their applications can be elusive. It has been reported that Jābir ibn ʿAbd Allāh al-Anṣārī said: The Messenger of God said:

> المهدي من ولدي، اسمه اسمي، وكنيته كنيتي، أشبه الناس بي خَلقاً وخُلُقاً، تكون به غيبة وحَيْرة تضل فيها الأمم، ثمّ يُقبل كالشهاب الثاقب يملأها عدلاً وقسطاً كما ملئت جوراً وظلماً.

> *The Mahdī [is] from among my progeny, his name is my name, and his kunyah[4] is my kunyah. In terms of features[5]*

---

hand, developing this world with the right intention and long-term vision can enhance one's prosperity in this world as well as the next.

[1] T: *Qatl al-kāfirīn*; The death of combatants among the ranks of those rejecting the truth despite it having been presented reasonably.

[2] T: *al-Ḥukūmah al-ʿādilah*; The just governance/government.

[3] T: *al-Ḥadāthah*; The author may be referring to "modernity" but because that term can have connotations that are likely unintended, a better translation is arguably modernization/advancement.

[4] T: A *kunyah* is a kind of epithet starting with *Abū* (literally, "Father of"), for a man, or *Umm* (literally, "Mother of"), for a woman. But if someone's *kunyah* is "Abū ʿAbd Allāh," for example, that does not necessarily mean his son's name is ʿAbd Allāh. He may not even have a son at all for that matter. Conversely, sometimes a person becomes known by a *kunyah* only after he or she has a child, in which case the *kunyah* would be associated with the name of his or her child.

[5] T: *al-Khalq*; His physical features.

> *and character*[1]*, he is the closest in resemblance to me amongst [all] people. There will be a ghaybah and a puzzlement*[2] *associated with him, during which communities*[3] *will go astray. Then he will come like a penetrating star*[4]*; he fills [the world] with justice and fairness just as it has been filled with tyranny and injustice."*[5]

[Some might object with the following question:] If the Imam has all of those attributes and excellences, then why does he resort to violence, war and bloodshed – things that sound reason would judge to be reprehensible[6]? But this objection should not be made. For, indeed, one would not imagine this objection after realizing that his approach is [the one mentioned in the following verse],

وَلَكُمْ فِي الْقِصَاصِ حَيَاةٌ يَا أُولِي الْأَلْبَابِ لَعَلَّكُمْ تَتَّقُونَ

> *There is life for you in retribution, O you who possess intellects, that perhaps you will be mindful of God*[7]*!*[8]

In other words, his approach is based on removing the tumor in order to save the body. Consequently, the community will come to enjoy social and economic justice and will reach the promised land. The ship of humanity will arrive at its final destination:

---

[1] T: *al-Khuluq*; Character/manners.

[2] T: *Ḥayrah*.

[3] T: *al-Umam* (sing. *ummah*); Communities or nations.

[4] T: Shihāb thāqib.

[5] *Kamāl al-Dīn*: 286 / Bāb 25 / Ḥ 1.

[6] T: *Qabīḥ*; Literally, ugly; but as a term in this context refers to blameworthy acts, as opposed to praiseworthy acts (*ḥasan*). In some contexts, the word may be referring more generally to evil or the absence of excellence.

[7] T: *Tattaqūn*; be Godwary, God-conscious, God-fearing, pious in one's choices.

[8] Qur'ān 2:179.

وَما خَلَقتُ الجِنَّ وَالإِنسَ إِلّا لِيَعبُدونِ

I did not create the jinn and the humans except that they may worship Me.[1]

---

[1] Qur᾿ān 51:56.

CHAPTER 4

IDENTIFYING THE MAHDĪ SYSTEM OF THOUGHT

Every individual with a claim in the world of knowledge possesses what he or she takes to be evidence and clear testament to that claim. [He or she takes something to be proof of his or her claim, but they cannot all be right in actual fact.] For it is imperative to believe that there is a single reality -- that *what is right*[1] is one. We, thus, reject the notion that reality is relative and that there are multiple versions of what is right[2]. It makes no sense to maintain that two contradicting propositions are both true. The intellect is capable of distinguishing right from wrong, true from false, and a fact from a lie. On the other hand, the Shīʿah believe in the *takhṭiʾah*[3] of *ijtihād*[4] as opposed to the *taṣwīb*[5] of *ijtihād* – in all of *taṣwīb*'s proposed versions. As such, when it comes to the realm of *ijtihād*, for example, we do not assume that the legal rulings derived are correct when they conflict with God's

---

[1] T: al-Ḥaqq; What is true as well as the right thing to do.

[2] T: For any given instance/issue at stake.

[3] T: Fallibility; that the conclusions arrived at through the process of *ijtihād* (skilled derivation of legal rulings from the primary sources) are potentially fallible, that they may prove to be wrong. The reality does not change in order to adapt to the conclusions of a skilled *mujtahid* (person deriving those rulings through the process of *ijtihād*). Rather, the *mujtahid* may err. This is regardless of whether or not God will reward the mujtahid for his effort/devotion.

[4] T: Skilled derivation of legal rulings from the primary sources.

[5] T: Infallibility, in the sense that the mujtahid is always "right." This is more nuanced than the theological notion of *ʿiṣmah* (immaculacy) in which there is an inherent potential for error but the person with ʿiṣmah is protected from actually falling into error. With *taṣwīb*, the conclusions of a mujtahid do not go wrong. But there are different versions of this general theory, as the author points out.

knowledge of what the rulings are in actual fact. Sure, one can assume oneself relieved[1] of the legal responsibility according to specific criteria and guidelines, as discussed in the appropriate place, but that is not the same as claiming the ruling is correct and matches up with reality. For it is one thing to maintain that two groups are both relieved of their legal responsibility despite acting on the basis of two different rulings – due to the disagreement of two skilled legal scholars – and it is another thing to claim that both of those groups have arrived at the objective reality [of the law in God's knowledge].

Moreover, evidence that is meant to reveal something about the external world – not just the part accessible to the senses – is not created equal. Rather, evidence differs depending on the type of claim it substantiates. Evidence might be sensory and experimental; it might be historical and traditional; it might be rational, based on an inherent and reason-based good; it might be report-based[2]; it might also be something else, such as reasonability[3], inspiration[4], or mystical experience[5]. Furthermore, when the intellect is capable, if only in certain cases, of comprehending something through its rational arguments, methods, tools and domains, even then there is no problem with maintaining that the report-based evidence is meant to *mentor*[6] one's intellect, [guiding it] to the rational

---

[1] T: *Barā'ah*; The principle that allows one to assume him or herself relieved of legal responsibility.

[2] T: *Naqlī*; Usually, this refers to reports ultimately attributing something to the appointed Imams, the Prophet and/or God Almighty. Hence, it would include the Qur'ān and verifiable ḥadīth.

[3] T: al-ʿAqlānīyah; This term would include not only strictly rational demonstration (philosophical rigor), but also more generally reasonable forms of thinking that are prevalent among reasonable individuals.

[4] T: al-Ilhām; inspiration or, arguably, a form of intuition that arrives at a sense of sureness unexplainable merely by tracing the thought process.

[5] T: *al-Kashf*; Revealing/unveiling; this is associated with mystical experiences of God and may also refer to extrasensory perception.

[6] T: *Irshād*; That is, the report-based evidence would not be evidence from the aspect that it is reported speech of the Prophet or the Divine but from the aspect

evidence. If, however, the reported content contradicts rationally-established content, then it is necessary to interpret the reported content in a way that agrees with and confirms the meaning of the rationally-established content and what it entails. Otherwise, [if such an interpretation is not possible,] then the reported content is disregarded and considered flowery [but empty][1] discourse. As for that which does not enter the intellect's domain of comprehension and is beyond the reach of its tools, arguments and perception, simply because the intellect does not understand it does not justify rejecting it and denying it.

To speak of [general] religious awareness is one thing and to speak of [in-depth] knowledge[2] is another thing. The former rests on faith, conviction, submission, attaching one's heart [to something], and [a sense of] assurance[3]. This state can occur even to one who is not a scholar. It arises from the [faculty of] *practical reason*[4]. This [faculty of the] intellect is energized through supplication[5], invocations [remembering God][6], [regimens of] devotional acts[7], moral lessons, admonitions, mastering

---

that it draws attention to some rational principle discoverable through the power of reason. Thus, the report serves to guide a person to realize the rational argument underlying the report and that rationally accessible notion suffices on its own to urge one's action. This notion can be used in a sense which includes advisory directives that are not legally binding, so long as those rationally accessible advisable notions would have sufficed on their own to urge one's action (without the directives).

[1] T: *Zukhruf*; Specious, falsehood that is made out to be appealing. See Qurʾān 6:112.

[2] T: Maʿrifah.

[3] T: *al-Ṭumaʾnīnah*; Contentment and tranquility that is associated with being reasonably sure.

[4] T: *al-ʿAql al-ʿamalī*; According to some definitions, it is the intellect's capacity not only to understand propositions related to what actions should be taken but also the capacity to urge action according to those propositions.

[5] T: *Duʿāʾ*.

[6] T: al-Adhkār (sing. dhikr).

[7] T: *al-Awrād* (sing. *wird*).

oneself[1], avoiding sins and unrecommended[2] acts, and performing recommended acts [of devotion]. As for the latter, it is the product of *theoretical reason*[3]. For it is the outcome of setting up and organizing theoretical premises. It depends on the content and form of syllogisms. It is acquired by attending gatherings of learning and through study. It is in light of this that we can find some orientalists to have abundant information about the Islamic faith but not to have a share in the sphere of *practical reason*. The fleshy and inflated knowledge that such an orientalist possesses, without having a spiritual and moral feel to it, is due to engaging *theoretical reason* without similarly engaging *practical reason*.

The undying faith of Islam is a *sharīʿah* and way of life for the discovery of nature and society. It is a system that believes in both bodily and spiritual dimensions, in individual and social spheres. It has interconnected horizons as well as visible and metaphysical[4] dimensions. It is comprehensive in terms of its steadfast principles, variables, *devotionally reserved* [Divinely endowed prescriptions][5], as well as its novelty at addressing developments put forth in this age of ours, taking the specificities of time and place into account. As such, it was imperative for Islam to develop a science that would safeguard against the mischievous individuals who would toy with and distort Islam's ideas, veering it off course. It was imperative for Islam to develop a science that would precisely

---

[1] T: *Tahdhīb al-nafs*; Disciplining oneself, taming one's desires.

[2] T: Makrūhāt (sing. makrūh).

[3] T: *al-ʿAql al-naẓarī*; Speculative Reason; it is the intellect's capacity to understand propositions about the world. According to some definitions, this would include the *understanding* even of propositions about what acts should/should not be done.

[4] T: *Ghaybīyah*; hidden; beyond the physical senses or otherwise present but unrecognized.

[5] T: *al-Tawqīfīyāt* (sing. *tawqīfī*); Matters that are prescribed/coined/defined by Divine legislation.

determine the process of arriving at demonstrative[1], certain knowledge, and have conviction regarding it in order to discover the universe and life from values[2].

To say that the metaphysical[3] cannot be known is an outrageous assertion and a senseless claim. Also fallacious is the notion that the system of religious thought, similar to the nature of conviction regarding that system, is Divinely elaborated[4] in the sense of being purely based on faith in the Divine, as opposed to having a demonstrative[5] quality in its elaboration. For Islamic knowledge springs forth from reason as well as Qur'ānic revelation. Moreover, the Sunnah[6] as well as innate intuition[7] and [human] nature are all sources of religious knowledge that deserve their share of discussion. Furthermore, it is also worthwhile to reflect on the mechanisms that energize the dimension of devotional practice and religious awareness. It is imperative [now] to discuss each one of these epistemic sources.

---

[1] T: *Burhānī*; Related to rational proof that meets philosophical standards of certainty.

[2] T: The author appears to be pointing out the difference between having demonstrative knowledge, on the one hand, and submitting to that mental understanding at heart with conviction, on the other hand. To have such conviction is to (as objectively as possible) draw on one's repository of morality, one's values.

[3] T: al-Ghayb.

[4] T: *Lāhūtīyah*; Related to *lāhūt*, the Divine. It appears that the author is using this term to refer to the realm of the Divine as opposed to something accessible to human reason.

[5] T: *Burhānī*; Related to rational proof that meets philosophical standards of certainty.

[6] T: Wont, manner, way of the immaculate individual (i.e. Prophet Muḥammad).

[7] T: *al-Fiṭrah*; Innate intuition associated with human nature.

THE FIRST EPISTEMIC SOURCE: REASON

This is the verdict and conviction of reason. For reason is a faculty that takes on the job of discerning, remembering, revealing, and comprehending universals[1] as opposed to particulars[2], objects of sense perception[3], and other things. Hence, information that is so commanded, and reason's intelligible objects, must be decisively certain (regardless of whether they are intuitive[4] or theoretical[5], [requiring further calculation]). As for conjectural[6] comprehension, we do not call that rational comprehension[7], for the comprehension of a particular is not rational comprehension.

As for reason's epistemic domain, it includes:

1. Good[8] and evil[9] (regardless of whether defined on the basis of existential excellence[10] and deficiency[11], respectively, or due to

---

[1] T: *al-Kullīyāt* (sing. *al-Kullī*); Universals; concepts that apply to several instances.
[2] T: *al-Juz'īyāt* (sing. *al-Juz'ī*); Particulars; concepts that do not apply to more than one instance. Sometimes, this term is used to refer to the actual existence of individual instances.
[3] T: al-Maḥsūsāt (sing. maḥsūs).
[4] T: *Badīhī*; Self-evident, intuitive; these objects of understanding do not require an elaborate thought process to comprehend and, when in the form of propositions, such propositions do not require proof to command one's decisive conviction.
[5] T: *Naẓarī*; Theoretical in the sense that these objects require an elaborate thought process to comprehend and, when in the form of propositions, such propositions require proof to command one's decisive conviction. In other words, these require further calculation.
[6] T: *al-Ẓannī*; Related to *al-ẓann*, supposition/conjecture/speculation.
[7] T: *Idrāk 'aqlī*; The power of reason's comprehension.
[8] T: *al-Ḥusn*; Beauty/goodness; in the sense of what ought to be done.
[9] T: *al-Qubḥ*; Ugliness/evil; in the sense of what ought not to be done.
[10] T: al-Kamāl.
[11] T: al-Naqṣ.

harmony[1] and disharmony[2] with innate [human] nature[3] --that is, what they call interest[4] and harm[5], respectively). *Theoretical reason* comprehends these propositions because they are actual realities, meaning they have an external reality regardless of comprehension.[6]

2. *Rational corollaries*[7] and organizing the relationship between rulings (e.g., to order a particular action entails making its prerequisite step mandatory; to order a particular action entails forbidding its opposite...). Reason's verdict regarding the corollary is acceptable if its conclusion is decisively certain. As for the legal ruling[8] itself, reason is not privy to it, because the legal ruling is *devotionally reserved* [to a distinctly Divine prescription][9]. This view is contrary to the position held by the Shāfiʿī and Ḥanafī

---

[1] T: al-Muwāfiq.

[2] T: al-Mukhālif.

[3] T: al-Ṭabʿ. This rendering is based on understanding the usage of ṭabʿ here to be referring not to the animalistic nature of a human, shared by other animals, but the distinctly human nature that makes a human human. That is, it may be described as an upper level, spiritual dimension of the human being that is harmonious with having justice served, safeguarding trusts, fulfilling commitments, and being grateful for blessings. It is likewise disharmonious with that which is contrary to such actions. It is likely that the author is entertaining the usage of harmony/disharmony with ṭabʿ in this sense, and then having that as the basis for (collective, not selfish) interest/harm, and for defining good/evil.

[4] T: al-Maṣlaḥah.

[5] T: al-Mafsadah.

[6] T: These are objects of reason, decisively certain, because they are not merely comprehended but they are comprehended to be in such a way that regardless of one's individual/social comprehension they would still be true, actual realities.

[7] T: *al-Mulāzamāt al-ʿaqlīyah*; propositions that are rationally entailed by other propositions.

[8] T: *al-Ḥukm.*

[9] T: *Tawqīfī.*

> schools, which adopt the notion of *Istiḥsān*[1] in their legal reasoning. For the very same[2] reason, the power of reason does not have access to the underlying formula of variables[3] that bring about the legislation of Divine rulings.

This is all dealing with *theoretical reason*.

As for *practical reason*, meaning the propositions dealing with *beneficial disciplining*[4], it is the verdict of reasonable individuals, [in light of their collective][5], that such and such an act is good or evil. Good and evil here mean that the agent performing the action deserves praise or blame, respectively, in the eyes of reasonable individuals. These two attributes [good and evil] describe voluntary actions[6]. This sense of good and evil is the point of contention between the *ʿadlīyah*[7], who include the Shīʿah and the Muʿtazilah, on the one hand, and the Ashāʿirah, on the other hand. The Ashāʿirah argued the following: Obligations are only known to be

---

[1] T: It is a form of deriving the law based on deeming something fitting but without having decisive evidence. Thus, Shīʿah scholars reject this form of legal reasoning which is conjectural, similar to how they reject *qiyās* (in the sense of analogical *conjecture*).

[2] T: Because the religious legislation is a distinctly Divine prescription.

[3] T: *Milāk*. The root cause, the underlying interest or harm at stake, which is the reason why the Divine legislation deals with the issues it deals with.

[4] T: *al-Taʾdībāt al-ṣalāḥīyah.*

[5] T: *al-ʿUqalāʾ* (sing. *al-ʿāqil*); Reasonable individuals.

[6] T: al-Afʿāl al-ikhtiyārīyah (sing. al-fiʿl al-ikhtiyārī).

[7] T: Advocates of *ʿadl* or justice; this is understood to be a reference to rationally intelligible justice that is understood to be true not only in the abstract sense (i.e. justice is good) but also in relation to Divine action (i.e. God acts in a just way that is rationally intelligible to some extent; justice is not defined by convention but is a truth actualized by Divine action).

obligations by virtue of Divine revelation[1]; as for reason, it does not make anything mandatory and it does not entail judgments deeming such and such to be good or evil[2]. Therefore, according to their view, reason would not reveal anything about reality in such a manner as to motivate action [like an obligation would]. Coming to know God can occur through the power of reason but would become an obligation only through Divine revelation. This means that even though reason has the power to come to know God, if not for evidence from the Divine revelation the power of reason's verdict would not reach the point of knowing that achieving such knowledge is an obligation. Hence, without Divine revelation, without the *sharīʿah*, [so the Ashāʿirah view would have it], such a verdict by the power of reason does not motivate action [in the way that an obligation would].

On another note, there is a related discussion on *practical reason*: Is *practical reason* [a faculty of comprehension,] *the comprehension*[3] *of what should be done* or is it a faculty of conviction[4] and faith[5] [urging the adoption of the said comprehension]?

In the former case, *practical reason* is a branch of comprehension similar to *theoretical reason*, the difference being that their objects of comprehension differ – one comprehends that which should be done while the other comprehends that which should be known. In the latter case, meaning *practical reason* as a faculty of conviction and faith, *practical reason* is not a branch of comprehension [but a faculty of action, adopting the said comprehension]. Regardless, when it comes to good and evil – in the sense that the acting agent deserves praise or blame, respectively – the

---

[1] T: *al-Samʿ*; That which is "heard" from Divine revelation through a holy book or otherwise spoken by a Divine representative. This typically refers to the Qurʾān and the ḥadīth.

[2] T: In the sense discussed earlier.

[3] T: *Idrāk*.

[4] T: al-Idhʿān.

[5] T: al-Īmān.

relevant verdict of reasonable individuals must have some backdrop and foundation.

If *practical reason* passes a judgment deeming something to be good or evil (regardless of whether defined on the basis of existential excellence and deficiency, respectively, or due to harmony and disharmony with innate [human] nature) then the result is the verdict of *practical reason*, so long as the object of comprehension is a universal, not a particular. This definition for the verdict of *practical reason* excludes *natural-disposition propositions*[1], *emotional-response propositions*[2], and *customary propositions*[3]. Moreover, *practical reason* is capable of determining a religiously accountable individual's[4] practical duty if no religious evidence is established [from Qur'ān and ḥadīth]. For example, among the laws

[1] T: *al-Khuluqīyāt*; These praiseworthy views are adopted by reasonable individuals because human dispositional qualities dictate them, such as the praiseworthiness of defending one's homeland, the praiseworthiness of courage and generosity, and the blameworthiness of cowardice and stinginess. The dispositional quality is a *malakah*, or habitus, that results from relevant habitual activity. These types of propositions are *natural-disposition propositions* (*khuluqīyāt*) when regarded from this angle, the angle of being natural dispositions. Meaning, there could be another angle from which such a proposition, or at least the principle behind it, is a verdict of *practical reason*.

[2] T: *al-Infiʿālīyāt*; These views are accepted by the public due to the evocation of a general emotional response, such as feelings of tenderness, compassion, shyness, etc. These types of propositions are *emotional-response propositions* (*infiʿālīyāt*) when regarded from this angle, the angle of being emotional responses. Meaning, there could be another angle from which such a proposition, or at least the principle behind it, is a verdict of *practical reason*.

[3] T: *al-ʿĀdīyāt*; These views are accepted by the public due to customary practice, such as the custom of respecting someone who is arriving by standing up for the person, the custom of offering hospitality to a guest, the custom of kissing the hand of a religious figure or king, etc. These types of propositions are *customary propositions* (*ʿādīyāt*) when regarded from this angle, the angle of being customary practices. Meaning, there could be another angle from which such a proposition, or at least the principle behind it, is a verdict of *practical reason*.

[4] T: *al-Mukallaf*.

discovered by *practical reason* are the rule about *the evil of punishment without prior warning*[1]; the rule about *Divine right to obedience*[2]; the rule about *avoiding potential harm*[3]; the rule about *the obligation to thank the source of blessings*[4]; and the rule about *Divine Favor*[5].

---

[1] T: *Qubḥ al-ʿiqāb bi lā bayan*; The idea that it is evil to punish someone for something without having first explained sufficiently that the (in)action was mandatory/prohibited. Hence, God would not punish human beings without providing sufficient access to a prior explanation/warning.

[2] T: *Ḥaqq al-Ṭāʿah*; The idea that – regardless what God chooses to do out of His benevolence – He still has the absolute right to be obeyed by His creatures; Specifically, even if He hypothetically does not provide prior warning and explanation, so long as human beings think it is reasonably possible that there is a duty owed to God pertaining to a given matter then they must err on the side of caution. In other words, by default, humans are not relieved of their duty toward God simply because no prior explanation/warning is accessible. The rational recognition of the Divine right to obedience suffices to oblige taking seriously even the slightest reasonable possibility of God's obligations and prohibitions. Granted, beyond this rationally conceived default position, it can become established through Divine revelation (Qurʾān and ḥadīth) that God excuses human beings from taking precaution in such a manner.

[3] T: *Dafʿ al-ḍarar al-muḥtamal*; The rational imperative to avoid potential harm. Even in the extreme case that the harm's likelihood is slim, so long as it is reasonably possible and *what is at stake* is dangerously serious, there is a rational imperative to avoid the potential harm. This rule is appealed to in order to explain why it is necessary to explore and find answers to questions of worldview and code of conduct.

[4] T: *Wujūb shukr al-munʿim*; The rational imperative for the receiver of a blessing to express gratitude to the giver.

[5] T: *Qāʿidat al-Luṭf*; The rule of *Divine favor*/grace/benevolence/kindness, which understands Divine wisdom, justice and/or generosity as not sparing any reasonable means of bringing creatures closer to reaching their spiritual potential, so long as the test of free will is maintained. God, thus, benevolently bestows various manifest and disguised blessings upon His creatures. Among these blessings are: communicating the required prescriptions of practice to them through prophets; and appointing the Imam after the final Prophet, in order to guard, interpret and implement the message as intended. God, on His end,

It is now clear, then, that neither does the power of reason always have the answers nor does it always have nothing to say. Instead, the power of reason is reliable when it yields certainty. For, indeed, the authority[1] of decisive knowledge[2] and certainty[3] is inherent[4]. Rather, all legal authority ultimately rests on the authority of decisive knowledge and certainty. That being said, reason's independent discovery of some rules is not tantamount to doing away with the need for a Divinely-appointed Messenger and a Divinely-appointed channel [of communication/mercy]. Contrary to the views of [those who deny prophethood][5] as well as [those who reject the employment of reason in religion][6], there is no conflict between reason's independence, on the one hand, and the need for a Divinely-appointed channel, on the other hand. For reason [in its independent capacity] does not arrive at the particular, Divinely endowed prescriptions which are based on [actual] interests and harms, because, as described earlier, reason [in its independent capacity] does not have the ability to encompass the underlying formulae of variables that bring about the legislation of Divine rulings, let alone the ability to encompass the Divine ruling itself. Moreover, Divine revelation has not been limited to confirming

---

provides these blessings, but humans may – through their evil choices – create barriers preventing them from accessing the blessings.

[1] T: *Ḥujjīyah*; The extent to which something is established to count as evidence for legal purposes; if something has *ḥujjīyah,* then it makes one liable as well as excused to count it as evidence.

[2] T: *Qaṭʿ*.

[3] T: *Yaqīn*.

[4] T: *Dhātīyah*; Essential, of its essence, not requiring an appeal to anything beyond it.

[5] T: *al-Barāhimah*; In this context, the term is being used as a shorthand for those who deny the appointment of prophets as intermediaries between God and humanity.

[6] T: *al-Ḥashwīyah*; In this context, the term is being used as a shorthand for those who reject the employment of reason and stick to superficial and simplistic readings of scripture, perhaps under the pretext that the employment of reason is correlated with being at odds with Divinely-appointed prophecy.

acknowledged verdicts of reason. In other words, it is not always the case that the sharīʿah prescriptions are mere confirmations guiding humanity to the verdict of reason. Rather, the Divine revelation speaks on two levels: [1] *mentorship*[1] and [2] *initiation*[2].

That is, the Divine revelation's sphere transcends the sphere of reason. For example, Divine revelation includes discussion of [the otherwise unknown] past, present, future, and other matters that transcend time such as knowledge related to the existence of the Divine Essence [of God Almighty].

In light of this, with regard to the topic at hand, we can say the following: The notion of the *ghaybah*, that is [at least in the sense of] the concealment of the [Imam's] identity – and even in the sense of visual concealment [invisibility], for that matter – is not rationally impossible. Those who reject the prospects of this notion or find it outlandish have not offered any [sufficient] justification for that relegation of the idea. They do not claim, for example, that reason rejects the prospects of invisible[3] truths. Sure, the *ghaybah* is an ontological phenomenon that is unfamiliar to a typical mind, a mind that confines itself purely to objects of sense perception. But [the principle of] it is familiar to a scientific mind, a mind that navigates an orbit transcending the typical, obvious objects of sense perception to include the unfamiliar objects of sense perception as well as matters beyond sense

---

[1] T: *al-Irshād*; Guidance directing attention to something that the power of reason can discover. This type of guidance is a confirmation of reason's conclusions and those rationally accessible notions suffice on their own to urge one's action. This notion can be used in a sense which includes advisory directives that are not legally binding, so long as those rationally accessible advisable notions would have sufficed on their own to urge one's action (without the directives). Furthermore, it is likely that the author is using the word *al-irshād* here in the sense of *endorsement* [of already existing practices] (*al-Imḍāʾ* or *al-taqrīr;* related to the word *mumḍāh*), in which case the term *endorsement* is more appropriate than *mentorship*.

[2] T: *al-Taʾsīs*; Initiating and establishing a matter that is not discoverable by reason alone.

[3] T: *Khafī*; Hidden; subtle; invisible.

perception. The [principle of the] notion at hand is indeed an established phenomenon. [As the saying goes:] The fact that something has occurred is the best evidence that such a thing is possible.[1] For scientific minds in the natural sciences have detected many occurrences that are imperceptible to the senses.

As for the Mahdī's prolonged lifespan, although some describe it as nothing but legend and myth, modern science entertains a different assessment. Studies in genetics dispel the strangeness of a prolonged lifespan [in principle] and make the prospects of the "legend" a familiar actuality. Furthermore, the *ghaybah* is a religious, ontological phenomenon subject to the omnipotence and will of the Creator. [In this regard, the *ghaybah* is] similar to transporting [the Queen of Sheba's][2] throne and creating angels, jinn, the worlds, and miracles, as evidence from Divine revelation describes. Believers in God all have faith in these matters [in principle]. For no religious school of thought denies the existence of matters beyond sense perception. [As the logical principle dictates:] When things are the same[3], the same laws apply to them.[4]

THE SECOND EPISTEMIC SOURCE: THE HOLY QUR᾽ĀN

The Qur᾽ān is the Divine book, the miracle. It is everlasting in its deep meaning, which is harmonious with the voice of one's conscience[5], innate

---

[1] T: al-Wuqū῾ khayr dalīl ῾alá al-imkān.

[2] T: *Bilqīs.* See Qur᾽ān 27:38-40.

[3] T: *al-Amthāl* (sing. *al-mithl*); Things that are [sufficiently] similar; that is, they are the same in terms of what counts for the laws in question to apply or not apply to them. Provided that incomplete induction allows for the isolation of the effective "similarity," this logical principle extends the laws of a given set to "similar" cases with logical certainty. Isolating the effective similarity is either a matter of intuitive self-evidence or a matter of cumulative probability yielding sureness gradually.

[4] T: Ḥukm al-amthāl fī mā yajūz wa mā lā yajūz waḥid.

[5] T: al-Wijdān.

intuition[1], and reason. It baffles the most skillful sages, philosophers, legislators, and masters of the arts with its audacious challenge,

قُل لَّئِنِ اجتَمَعَتِ الإِنسُ وَالجِنُّ عَلَىٰ أَن يَأتوا بِمِثلِ هٰذَا القُرآنِ لا يَأتونَ بِمِثلِهِ وَلَو كانَ بَعضُهُم لِبَعضٍ ظَهيرًا

Say, 'Surely if all of humanity and the jinn banded together to bring the like of this Quran, they would not bring the like of it, even if they assisted one another.'[2]

The Qurʾān challenged the power of kings and the knowledge of the Jewish sages[3] and Christian priests[4]; it challenged the eloquent and well-spoken among the Arabs; it challenged the idol worshippers; it challenged all, saying,

[...] فَأتوا بِسورَةٍ مِن مِثلِهِ [...]

[...] then bring a chapter[5] like it [...] [6]

In the arrangement[7] of utterance, in choosing words that capture the meaning's essence, in attending to the context of speech with fitting significance, and in articulating with ease of deliverance, the Arabs had achieved excellence and eloquence. The Qurʾān then challenged the Arabs with that which would arouse their sense of zeal[8] and kindle the fire of pride[9] and group spirit[10] within them. It challenged their vanity[11] when it

---

[1] T: al-Fiṭrah.

[2] Qurʾān 17:88.

[3] T: *Aḥbār* (sing. *ḥabr*).

[4] T: *Qasāwisah* (sing. *qissīs*).

[5] T: *Sūrah.*

[6] Qurʾān 2:23.

[7] T: *Naẓm*; This can also refer more specifically to versified speech or metrical patterns of speech.

[8] T: al-Ḥamīyah.

[9] T: al-Anafah.

[10] T: al-ʿAṣabīyah.

[11] T: al-Ghurūr.

came to their [prized] merchandise[1]. It challenged their sense of superiority in their art, [as they would arrogantly dismiss anyone else as imprecise]. What's more is that the duration of the challenge has endured long beyond [what would suffice]. The rallying invitation to meet the challenge has been extended [till this very day, to be precise]. But they have not answered the call; they only turn away. The extended duration has only increased their inability[2]. Their only response has been to try to hide and retreat out of defeat. Moreover, it challenged them with regard to its internal harmony[3], for had it not come from God then there would have been discrepancies in the excellence and eminence of its arrangement, in the articulateness and eloquence of its words, and in the soundness, precision and robustness of its meaning. As God Almighty says,

[...] وَلَو كانَ مِن عِندِ غَيرِ اللَّهِ لَوَجَدوا فيهِ اختِلافًا كَثيرًا

Had it been from [someone] other than God, they would have surely found much discrepancy in it.[4]

Furthermore, it challenged them with the news relayed by its accounts, with the gracefulness of its parables, with the dignity of its legislation and with the sublimity of its values. Some retreated out of defeat, some assented with conviction and others remained silent, yielding the conclusion that no one has stood a chance at meeting the Qur'ān's challenge.

Distinct Features of the Qur'ān

If one wishes to understand the Qur'ān, if that is one's aim, then let us discuss some of the distinct features of the Qur'ān. For in order to

---

[1] T: *Biḍā'ah*; Merchandise/money; In this context, it is referring to their prized skills and talent in Arabic expression.

[2] T: *'Ajz*; In the sense that the miracle of the Qur'ān is so inimitable, so irreproducible, that humans stand utterly incapable before its challenge to bring forth the like of it.

[3] T: *La ikhtilāf fīh*; There is no discrepancy in it.

[4] Qur'ān 4:82.

understand the Qur'ān, one must have recourse to some prerequisites and established principles regarding it:

1. It is protected from distortion[1] of all types[2], for it is delivered by God from being tampered with, changed, or switched around; indeed, the book that we have in our midst is the very Qur'ān that was sent down upon the heart of the noble Messenger, Prophet Muhammad, without any alteration of its noble qualities, its effects and its blessings. As God Almighty says:

[...] وَإِنَّهُ لَكِتَابٌ عَزِيزٌ * لَا يَأْتِيهِ الْبَاطِلُ مِن بَيْنِ يَدَيْهِ وَلَا مِنْ خَلْفِهِ تَنزِيلٌ مِّنْ حَكِيمٍ حَمِيدٍ

[...] And truly it is a mighty Book.

Falsehood comes not upon it from before it or from behind it; a revelation from [One who is] Wise, [One who is] Praised[3]

Consequently, it has definitively been issued [by God through Prophet Muḥammad], so there is no place for a chain of transmission[4] discussion regarding it. To adopt the position that it has been distorted is to adopt a myth and an illusion: No one would utter such a thing except for one with a weak mind, one without even the slightest share in the fields of knowledge, or one who strays from the path of what is right due to partiality[5] – for love can make a person deaf and blind [as the saying goes].

---

[1] T: al-Taḥrīf.

[2] T: Of all types dealing with the text in the capacity that would alter its noble qualities, effects and blessings. As for distortion when it comes to explaining the text, that is the *tafsīr*, it is one of the main reasons for the Shī'ah argument about the necessity of Divinely appointed Imams.

[3] Qur'ān 41:41-42.

[4] T: *al-Sanad.*

[5] T: 'Aṣabīyah.

2. Considered separately, different parts of the Qur'ān have different degrees of explicitness in indicating their meaning: [1] Some parts of the Qur'ān are *explicit*[1]; [2] Other parts of the Qur'ān are *apparent*[2] [but not *explicit*], which means that it is possible for another meaning to be intended, but such a possibility would require a clue [from the context or otherwise, in order to be adopted]. In the absence of such a clue, the meaning is assumed to be the apparent one. This is justified based on it being the practice of reasonable individuals[3], which has been *endorsed*[4] by the Divine Legislator[5]. Moreover, common sense[6] judgments[7] refer back to the apparent meaning [of expressions]; [3] Yet other parts of the Qur'ān are *mutashābih*[8], allowing for more than one meaning.

   Both the explicit and the apparent types of verses belong to the *muḥkam*[9] category. There is no reservation or disagreement regarding the reliability of *explicit* indications of meaning. As for *apparent* indications of meaning, they are also reliable for the purpose of understanding the Qur'ān. For Prophet Muḥammad did not invent a new method of communication in order to convey and deliver his aims. Rather, he spoke with his people based on their customary methods and styles of understanding and

---

[1] T: *Naṣṣ ṣarīḥ*; The explicit, outright word.

[2] T: *Ẓāhir.*

[3] T: *al-Sīrah al-'Uqalā'īyah.*

[4] T: al-Mumḍāh.

[5] T: al-Shāri'.

[6] T: *al-'Urfī*; Customary; related to the common way of using language.

[7] T: al-Taḥākumāt.

[8] T: See earlier footnote.

[9] T: Depending on the context, this can mean exact, coherent, or carefully done. It is likely that the usage of *muḥkam* here is juxtaposed with *mutashābih*, in which case *muḥkam* would arguably be a description that applies to verses which are straightforward *in a stand-alone fashion*, while *mutashābih* verses would require reading in light of the *muḥkam* verses to be properly understood.

communicating. Had he adopted a different approach, then it would have become clear to us. For, indeed, he spoke in a clear Arabic language; he urged them to contemplate the Qur᾽ān; and he required them to put its teachings into action and to evaluate [alleged] reports [of his words, actions or silent approvals] by measuring them up against the Qur᾽ān. Furthermore, the Divinely appointed Imams would make arguments by using [verses from the] Qur᾽ān.[1] As is well known, it is noteworthy that relying on the *apparent* indications of meaning is not a *personal-opinion* form of exegesis[2]. Rather, it is an exegesis based on the common sense understanding of an expression after having searched for relevant *clues* indicating the meaning otherwise – whether those *clues* be from the *immediately connected context*[3] or *beyond the immediately connected context*[4], and whether they be from the Qur᾽ān, the Sunnah, or reason.

3. Abrogation[5]; There is no disagreement regarding the fact that abrogation has occurred. All agree on this. For, indeed, many legal rulings in sharīʿah systems prior to Islam have been abrogated by the legal rulings of the Islamic sharīʿah. Furthermore, a number of legal rulings within the Islamic sharīʿah have been abrogated by other legal rulings of the same sharīʿah. For example, take the legal ruling related to facing the *qiblah*[6] direction [during prayer]. What

---

[1] T: The implication here is that the Imams would argue in a fashion that was not relying on their *authority* as Imams but was rather relying on an understanding of the Qur᾽ān that was accessible to the listeners. Had the apparent indications of meaning not been reliable, then the argumentation of the Imams would not have stood its own ground without an appeal to their authority as Imams.

[2] T: *al-Tafsīr bil-Ra᾽y*; A subjective, conjectural form of explaining the Qur᾽ān.

[3] T: *al-Qarā᾽in al-Muttaṣilah* (sing. *al-Qarīnah al-Muttaṣilah*).

[4] T: *al-Qarā᾽in al-Munfaṣilah* (sing. *al-Qarīnah al-Munfaṣilah*).

[5] T: *al-Naskh.*

[6] T: Today, the *qiblah* direction is toward the Kaʿbah location in Mecca, present-day Saudi Arabia. In the early days of Islam, it was toward Jerusalem.

matters is [the answer to the following question:] Are there legal rulings in the Qurʾān that have been abrogated by other verses from the Qurʾān, by the definitively established Sunnah, by *ijmāʿ*[1], or by the definitively established verdict of sound reason?

Based on [this author's] investigation into the matter, the legal rulings established by the Qurʾān can be abrogated by *mutawātir*[2] Sunnah and ijmāʿ. There is no problem with that – neither a report-based[3] problem nor a reason-based problem. Similarly, the legal rulings established by the Qurʾān can be abrogated by another verse from the Qurʾān *if* the abrogating verse's legal ruling pertains to, clarifies, and supersedes the abrogated legal ruling. An example of this is the *Najwá* verse[4]. However, a legal ruling that is established by the Qurʾān cannot be abrogated by another verse

---

[1] T: A form of consensus among scholars that, in Twelver Shīʿah thought, counts as religious evidence if it reveals the position of the immaculate individual (e.g., The Prophet Muḥammad or one of the twelve Divinely appointed Imams). Otherwise, consensus among scholars is often taken into account when determining positions of precaution, even if it does not establish a legal ruling on its own merit.

[2] T: Reports that are characterized by *tawātur*, that is wide-scale transmission beyond the [practical] possibility of collusion to lie by its transmitters. It is important to note that this wide-scale transmission does not always translate into *popularity* among the general population. It may be only wide-scale transmission among a particular group within a broader populace. The reliability of such reports hinges on being beyond the practical possibility of collaborating to tell a lie. This can be satisfied in cases where the transmitters are relatively few in numbers, but, for example, come from diverse backgrounds and have different motivations, yet still agree as far as the reported contented is concerned. In light of this clarification, it is conceivable that reports naming the twelve appointed Imams may not have been popular among the general public at some points in time, but were nonetheless circulated widely enough among a sufficient number of transmitters such that their collaboration to tell such a lie would be a practical impossibility.

[3] T: That is based on reports ascribed to God and His representatives (e.g., the Qurʾān, the ḥadīth.)

[4] Qurʾān 58:12, abrogated by Qurʾān 58:13.

from the Qur᾿ān that does not pertain to the abrogated legal ruling. There is no case of this kind. Similarly, the Qur᾿ānic legal ruling cannot be abrogated by *āḥād* reports[1]. That being said, some have erroneously conceived of abrogation by such reports, thinking that abrogation occurs in the cases of *seeming conflict*[2] between reports (e.g., *General*[3] and *specific*[4] reports; *unqualified*[5] and *qualified*[6] reports; *al-ḥākim* and *al-maḥkūm* reports[7]; *al-wārid* and *al-*

---

[1] T: *Akhbār al-āḥād* (sing. *khabar al-wāḥid*); Reports related by one or very few individuals, not characterized by *tawātur.* Typically, this category of reports does not yield a sense of sureness regarding it being actually issued by the authority it is ascribed to. However, in some cases, when there is indisputable external evidence corroborating the report's ascription, one can be sure that the statement in question was indeed issued by the authority it is ascribed to. In this latter case, it is not entirely clear what the author's position would be regarding the potential for such a report to abrogate a Qur᾿ānic legislation.

[2] T: *al-Ta῾āruḍ al-badwī*; When considered separately, some reports would seem to be indicating conflicting meanings. However, when considered in light of one another, a common sense reading would resolve the seeming conflict between the reports.

[3] T: *al-῾Ām.*

[4] T: *al-Khāṣṣ.*

[5] T: *al-Muṭlaq.*

[6] T: *al-Muqayyad.*

[7] T: Related to the notion of *al-ḥukūmah.* According to some interpretations, this is the situation that arises when the *ḥākim* speech/text includes a specific, personal clue (not a common-sensical generic clue) that the speaker is explaining the final intended meaning of the *maḥkūm* speech/text.

mawrūd reports[1]; *equivocal*[2] and *expounded*[3] reports; *literal*[4] and *metaphorical*[5] reports...). But cases of *seeming conflict* are not cases of abrogation at all. This has been explained and established in the appropriate place [elsewhere].[6]

4. The rules of *common sense reconciliation*[7]; Making use of these rules helps one to understand the Qur'ān. For example, *āḥād* reports can make exceptions from general and unqualified Qur'ānic statements. This is possible because the specific evidence [making the exception] is a clue that serves to clarify the intended meaning of those other statements.

5. The Qur'ān, in terms of signified meaning[8], includes both that which is *muḥkam* and that which is *mutashābih*. Hence, [in order to be properly understood,] the *mutashābih* must be referred back to the *muḥkam*.

---

[1] T: Related to the notion of *al-wurūd*. This is the situation that arises when the *wārid* speech/text actually (not just figuratively) negates the subject matter of the *mawrūd* speech/text, making its ruling not applicable, but does so through the mediation of devotional convention (*al-ta'abbud*). Had the mediation of devotional convention been unnecessary for the subject matter negation, the situation would be called *al-takhaṣṣuṣ*. The latter is one in which the omissions are neither exceptions from the general statement (*al-takhṣīṣ*) nor were they included within the scope of the general statement to begin with. As such, *al-wurūd* has the outcome of *al-takhaṣṣuṣ*, but requires the mediation of devotional convention to negate the *mawrūd* subject matter.

[2] T: *al-Mujmal*.

[3] T: *al-Mubayyan*.

[4] T: *al-Ḥaqīqah*.

[5] T: *al-Majāz*; A form of figurative language.

[6] T: In the study of *Fiqh* and *Uṣūl al-Fiqh* at the *ḥawza*.

[7] T: *Qawā'id al-jam' al-'urfī*; The rules governing how common sense / customary usage would reconcile seemingly conflicting statements.

[8] T: al-Madlūl.

6. *Taʾwīl*[1], as it pertains to the Qurʾān, is a true reality. Qurʾānic teachings, from rulings to admonitions[2] to [pearls of] wisdom, rely on that true reality. *Taʾwīl* is an established [truth] pertaining to all Qurʾānic verses (*muḥkam* as well as *mutashābih* verses). The *taʾwīl* [understanding] is not a concept signified by the phrases [of language]. Rather, it is one of the hidden[3] matters that transcends the phrases [of language]. Indeed, God Almighty has tied those hidden matters down with the shackles of phrases merely to bring them closer to home. For the phrases are akin to parables[4] that are put forth to bring [moral] lessons closer to home and they are clarified in the way that is appropriate relative to the comprehension of the listener.

There are two forms of taʾwīl [in the general sense of the word]:

- Invalid taʾwīl; This form of taʾwīl is practiced by people of deviance and misguidance, who take the *mutashābih* verses without understanding them with reference to the *muḥkam* verses. They make taʾwīl interpretations based on their subjective opinions and convictions without referring back to and relying upon the principles which have already been established in their appropriate place; *the people of communication engagement*[5] have come to agree to those principles in their communications [for the purpose of mutual understanding. By abandoning those principles, invalid taʾwīl results.] Perhaps invalid taʾwīl includes the *personal-*

---

[1] T: A form of interpretation that is not readily apparent from the language used itself. The author will clarify its usage here in the next few lines. However, sometimes the word taʾwīl is used to refer to intepretation more broadly construed. At other times, a general sense of the word taʾwīl is used to include a specific form of *taʾwīl*, yet still opposed to *exegesis* (*tafsīr*). These usages will become identifiable in the course of this section.

[2] T: Mawʿiẓah.

[3] T: *Ghaybīyah*; Unseen; beyond the typical experience of the physical world.

[4] T: *al-Amthāl* (sing. *mathal*); Analogies, more generally.

[5] T: *Ahl al-ḥiwār* (or *ahl al-muḥāwarah*); The people of dialogue, of discourse.

opinion form of exegesis[1], which has been forbidden in so many reports [attributed to the Prophet and/or Divinely appointed Imams].

- Valid[2] and correct[3] ta'wīl; This form of ta'wīl is practiced by the people of *what is right*[4], who take the *muḥkam* as the root principle and the *mutashābih* as the branch, taking the two together. This form of ta'wīl can, in turn, be divided into another two types.

  One type falls back on the rules governing the use of language, logic, general common sense, and the results of contemplation. This reads the verses that include *mutashābih* sentences, for example, the verses describing God while using phrases that give the impression of corporeal form[5], confined dimensions[6], contingency[7], [temporal] origination[8], and attributes of contingent beings; or the verses that are *prima facie*[9] conflicting, such as those describing God as the one who brings about death, in some instances, while describing the angels as those who bring about death, in other instances; or the verses giving the impression

---

[1] T: *al-Tafsīr bil-Ra'y*; A subjective, conjectural form of explaining the Qur'ān.

[2] T: al-Ṣaḥīḥ.

[3] T: al-Ṣā'ib.

[4] T: al-Ḥaqq.

[5] T: al-Tajsīm.

[6] T: al-Taḥayyuz.

[7] T: al-Imkān.

[8] T: al-Ḥudūth; apparently temporal in this context, but there are other forms of origination discussed in metaphysics.

[9] T: *Ẓāhir*; Apparently, but only at first glance here.

of fatalism[1], in some cases, and [entirely] *independent freedom*[2], in other cases.

Assuming that this is indeed a type of ta᾿wīl, then it is the role of the specialist. The specialist does this and practices it [only] after having exhausted his or her efforts[3] in investigating and after having acquired the skills[4] of the sciences that are involved in the process of seeking to understand the apparent meaning of statements [taken holistically].

The second type of valid ta᾿wīl belongs to the category of the transcendental[5]. This type of ta᾿wīl is specific to those firmly

---

[1] T: *al-Jabr*; The notion that there is no free will and that all actions performed are essentially *forced* upon the individual.

[2] T: *al-Tafwīḍ*; The notion that is opposed to *al-jabr* but conceives of the agent's freedom as being entirely independent of God in its subsistence – independent in the sense that God "*fawwaḍa* (delegated/empowered)" the agent to act, turning things over to the agent entirely, without a need for God's continuous emanation of existence.

T: Twelver Shī῾ah reject both *al-jabr* and *al-tafwīḍ*. Instead, they adopt an understanding of human agency that is dependent on God's omnipotence, on the one hand, while being within the human agent's freedom to choose, on the other hand. One way to interpret this is to say that human agents make free choices with the power of God. Thus, the power is ultimately God's alone. However, the exercise of the choice with God's power is the human's responsibility. God opens up this limited space for human agents to exercise freedom because there is a greater potential for humans to achieve when they have to make a choice for themselves. Although many humans may abuse this power, many others will make good use of it, achieving their potential, and God accounts for all the good and evil with the appropriate retribution. Thus, human agents are neither forced fatalistically nor are they independently free in their capability, but rather they fall somewhere in between.

[3] T: Istifrāgh al-wis῾.

[4] T: *Malakāt* (sing. *malakah*); Ingrained attributes; dispositions; habitus (in Latin); hexis (in Greek).

[5] T: *Ghayb*; The Unseen; That which is beyond the typical experience of the physical world or is otherwise hidden.

rooted in knowledge[1] – that is the Messenger [Prophet Muḥammad] and the [Divinely appointed] pure Imams alone.

Question: Why is it that comprehension of the Qurʾān varies and, yet, that does not stop it from being an epistemic channel, one that reveals and overrules?

Answer: There is a danger associated with [one's choice of] the epistemic approach[2] for understanding the Qurʾān. Indeed, there are a number of philosophical, theological[3] and mystical[4] trends of thought, in addition to trends of natural scientific thought deeply involved in or infatuated with a sociological bent, all of which have attempted to impose their opinions on the exegesis[5] of the Qurʾān.

In this regard, there are two approaches:

The first approach: This approach attempts to discover the signified meaning of the verse in question by setting aside the educational and intellectual backgrounds of the individual involved, entering the field of exegesis without any preconceived baggage [beyond the common-sensical], while relying on the epistemic mechanisms and rules of exegesis, whose criterion revolves around common sense usage, without any motive except to understand the signified meaning of the verse. In this case, the role played by other theoretical sciences is an auxiliary role, [merely] supporting the Qurʾānic conclusion. It should be known

---

[1] T: *al-Rāsikhūn fī al-ʿilm*; Referring to Qurʾān 3:7.

[2] T: al-Manhaj al-maʿrifī.

[3] T: *al-Kalāmīyah*; Related to *kalām*, systematic argumentation in defense of theological claims.

[4] T: *al-ʿIrfānīyah*; The schools of theory and/or practice related to *ʿirfān*, experiential awareness of God's presence from the aspect of His names, attributes and manifestations/signs.

[5] T: *al-Tafsīr*; Commentary; explanation.

that *apparent meanings*[1] are objects of intuition[2], not rational demonstration[3]; they are relational[4], not stand-alone[5]; and they are based on common sense usage[6], not [usage that is wholly] subjective[7]. Sure, the *intentions in all seriousness*[8] are underlying issues that require other bases besides those of the *apparent meanings*.

The second approach: This approach is the opposite of the first. For, here, the exegete attempts to fit the verse into his or her preconceived baggage[9]. As such, the role of the Qurʾān takes the back seat relative to the theory. This mistaken methodology explains the rise of gaps like these, such that understanding the [supposedly] *apparent meaning* of the Qurʾān becomes reserved to a particular group and specific type [of individuals, those with the sophisticated theoretical background]. The Qurʾān, then, loses its

---

[1] T: *al-Ẓawāhir* (sing. *al-ẓāhir*); The readily apparent meanings, albeit not explicit.

[2] T: *Wijdānīyah*; Related to *wijdān*, one's innermost; Such matters are readily intuited and found to be present to/within oneself.

[3] T: *Burhānīyah*; Related to *burhān*.

[4] T: *Nisbīyah*.

[5] T: *Nafsīyah*.

[6] T: *ʿUrfīyah*; Related to *ʿurf*, common sense or custom.

[7] T: *Dhātīyah*. In other contexts, this can mean essential or of the essence. But, here, it is apparently referring to subjectiveness in reading (as opposed to a more customarily shared, less subjective sense).

[8] T: *al-Irādāt al-jiddīyah* (sing. *al-irādah al-jiddīyah*); Beyond ascertaining the intention in use [of the language] (*al-irādah al-istiʿmālīyah*), the intention in all seriousness (*al-irādah al-jiddīyah*) is about the actual intention of the speaker behind that usage. For it is possible that a speaker has an intention in use, wanting to use a phrase that has the capacity to indicate its signified meaning, but that speaker may or may not have the intention to be serious (to the letter) in describing its meaning as a matter of fact (e.g., he may be joking without the intention to be serious; or he may be using a general statement, but only being serious about its application in a qualified sense that becomes known to the listener after becoming aware of another qualifying statement).

[9] T: Baggage that is theoretical in nature, not commonsensical.

common-sensical potential and, instead, fits in with molds specific to certain types [of individuals]. Sure, it may be the case that those with the [customary] common sense[1] do not [readily] pick up on certain points that would lead to a mistaken understanding, but if those internal or external points are brought to their attention [to avoid the mistaken understanding] then they would have arrived at the same [customary] common sense understanding.[2]

No epistemic approach is left unafflicted by this disagreement. Consequently, the danger is not in the very principle of engaging in exegesis, but rather [the danger is to fall short in] what matters – that one sets forth guidelines and criteria for defining the epistemic approaches. For the Qur᾿ān was not revealed in order to be a book on the natural sciences, astronomy, medicine, or history. Rather, it is a book of guidance.

In summary, the purpose of exegesis is to reveal the meaning of the phrase and to manifest it in the sphere of *expressed meaning*[3] or *implied meaning*[4]. There are also other forms of signified

---

[1] T: *al-ʿUrf*; Here, this is referring to the individuals with customary, common sense, as opposed to those with particularly nuanced, theoretical backgrounds.

[2] T: That is, such a scenario is *not* an instance of the second approach but, rather, fits within the first approach.

[3] T: *al-Manṭūq*; The "enunciated" meaning, in the sense of the signification or signified meaning expressed by the words, not implied. According to some definitions, this term is technically used when speaking of complete sentences, not merely parts of sentences. This is what the sentence literally says (literally as opposed to what it means by *implication*; not literally vs. figuratively). Sometimes this literal meaning is *explicit* (*naṣṣ*) and sometimes it is *apparent* (*ẓāhir*) but not *explicit*. It is critical to be attentive to the nuanced usage of these English words in order to understand the differences between these technical terms.

[4] T: *al-Mafhūm*; The "understood" meaning, in the sense that it is understood by implication, it is implied, not expressed. According to some definitions, this is limited to *corollary meanings that are specifically obvious* (*lāzim bayyin bil-maʿná al-akhaṣṣ*), not requiring a consideration of anything beyond the phrase itself to

meanings that do not fall under either the *implied meaning* or *expressed meaning*, in the technical senses of those terms. Such signification is called the *sequence of speech signification*[1] and it can be divided into the following subdivisions:

Dalālat al-Iqtiḍāʾ: This signification refers to meaning that, according to common sense [that is, custom[2]], is intended by the speaker; the truth or validity of what is being said depends on it – whether it be by the dictates of reason, Islamic law, language [rules] or customary practice[3].

Dalālat al-Tanbīh: Also called *dalālat al-īmāʾ*. This signification refers to meaning that, according to common sense [that is, custom[4]], is intended by the speaker due to the sequence of speech by means of which one becomes decisively sure that the speaker means to convey the entailed meaning [beyond the phrase], or one finds it far-fetched that the speaker does not mean it.

Both of these forms of signification [can be counted as evidence for legal purposes][5], either from the aspect of them being a form of [acceptable] exegesis[6] or from the aspect of them being a form of

---

arrive at the corollary implication, not even a consideration of the relation between the two.

[1] T: al-Dalālah al-siyāqīyah.

[2] T: al-ʿUrf.

[3] T: *ʿĀdatan*; A matter of custom, habit.

[4] T: al-ʿUrf.

[5] T: *Ḥujjah*; Proof/argument that establishes a case for or against something; establishing the accountability to (*munajjizīyah*) [God to follow that proof] and excusableness for (*muʿadhdhirīyah*) [following that proof] as understood through reliable channels.

[6] T: *Tafsīr*.

forgivable taʾwīl that common sense arrives at after having employed scientific diligence[1].

Sure, there is a subdivision of taʾwīl that is exclusively reserved for Ahl al-Bayt[2], and that is a matter related to Divine Knowledge. It has nothing to do with the process of learning and *acquired knowledge*[3]. For, in some cases, the [Prophet Muḥammad's] pure, close kin[4] share in common with other people the understanding of the Qurʾān based on the *apparent meaning, dalālat al-iqtiḍāʾ*, *sequence of speech signification, dalālat al-īmāʾ*, and the like, and, in other cases, they have exclusive access to taʾwīl. For taʾwīl falls under a subcategory of *hidden knowledge.*[5]

Furthermore, when it comes to the *mutashābih* category, if something is *mutashābih,* that does not mean it has no meaning. Rather, it has a meaning that is identified from the phrase. Had it not had a meaning, then what would be intended when God says, "they follow (*yattabiʿūna*)," in the following verse? God Almighty says,

[...] الَّذِينَ فِي قُلوبِهِم زَيغٌ فَيَتَّبِعونَ ما تَشابَهَ مِنهُ ابتِغاءَ الفِتنَةِ وَابتِغاءَ تَأويلِهِ [...]

---

[1] T: *ʿInāyah*; Care, consideration.

[2] T: Prophet Muḥammad's Household, including his daughter Lady Fāṭimah, and the Twelve Imams, peace and blessings be upon them all.

[3] T: *al-ʿIlm al-Kasbī*; Knowledge that is attained through a process, gradually; as opposed to a form of awareness/knowledge that is instantaneous and/or experiential/mystical.

[4] T: ʿItrah.

[5] T: *al-ʿIlm al-ghaybī*; Knowledge of the Unseen, the metaphysical realm, the supernatural.

> *[...] those in whose hearts is deviance, they follow what tashābaha in it, in pursuit of mischief and in pursuit of its taʾwīl [...]*[1]

[What do they "follow" if no meaning is understood from a *mutashābih* phrase?] Indeed, what is meant by "similarity/resemblance (*tashābuh*)"[2] [in the etymologically related *mutashābih*] is the *tashābuh* when it comes to the instances[3] [of the concept in external reality, not the abstract concept]. This means that the precise application[4] [intended by citing the concept] is unknown, while the signified meaning used and intended by the blessed verse is, nevertheless, clear. This means they go after [what are meant to be] metaphysical[5] applications [of an idea], such as the Seat[6] [of God; and instead of understanding this correctly in light of *muḥkam* verses, which deny likening God to a physical being, for example, they take it to mean that God has a physical instance of "Seat" for Himself to literally sit on. Alternatively, they might take the idea of "Seat" to apply to some mistaken esoteric notion without reasonable evidence.][7] Moreover, sometimes the word "mutashābih" is used

---

[1] Qurʾān 3:7.

[2] T: Linguistically, the word *mutashābih* is related to the past tense verb *tashābaha* and the noun *tashābuh*, which expresses the *similarity/resemblance* between different matters. See earlier footnote on *mutashābih* notions. This *similarity/resemblance* can give rise to ambiguity when not read according to the proper approach, that is in light of *muḥkam* notions.

[3] T: *al-Miṣdāq* (pl. *al-maṣādīq*); The applications; the examples; the cases manifesting the concept externally.

[4] T: *al-Miṣdāq.*

[5] T: al-Ghaybī.

[6] T: al-Kursī.

[7] T: The segment preceding this extended bracket explanation was not entirely clear in the author's original. Therefore, I took the liberty to provide two feasible explanations of the blameworthy type of following the author is referring to with the "Seat" example.

to mean "mujmal,"[1] in the sense that [the statement in question] has no *apparent meaning* in terms of its [*signification in*] *use of the language*[2], even if it has a clear, *apparent meaning* in terms of its [*signification*] *in all seriousness*[3] [when considered holistically in light of *muḥkam* verses].

Furthermore, the *Bāṭinīyah*[4], the Sūfīs[5] , and [the like who have] invalid beliefs make conclusions about *hidden meanings*[6] of the Qurʾān without relying on linguistic and scientific methods. Rather, their approach is sheerly one of guesswork[7] and counting on conjecture, *istiḥsān*, and imposing preconceived theoretical positions.

In light of the aforementioned, it is possible to reconcile between two [*seemingly conflicting*] groups of reports [attributed to the Prophet and the Imams]: one group of reports that regards Ahl al-

---

[1] T: Depending on the context, it can mean different things, such as equivocal, ambiguous, abridged, whole…

[2] T: *Istiʿmālan*; [*al-dalālah al-istiʿmālīyah*]; Related to *al-irādah al-istiʿmālīyah*, but the latter is about the very intention of the speaker as opposed to the signification of the statement.

[3] T: *Jiddan*; [*al-dalālah al-jiddīyah*]; Related to *al-irādah al-jiddīyah*, but the latter is about the very intention of the speaker as opposed to the signification of the statement.

[4] T: Those who claim there is an esoteric, hidden, innermost meaning beyond every *apparent meaning*; Often used in association with trends of Ismāʿīlism. Others would find this emphasis on a supposed innermost dimension – deemphasizing *apparent meanings* – problematic because it is a claim without proof and can lead astray.

[5] T: At least some of those who associate with the label "Ṣūfī"; many different trends of thought/practice associate with the word; most likely, this is referring to a form of mystical/spiritual practice that does not establish its claims based on a careful, common sense understanding of the Qurʾān and Sunnah.

[6] T: *Bawāṭin* (sing. *Bāṭin*); Internal; innermost; inward; esoteric; as opposed to outward or *apparent* (*ẓāhir*).

[7] T: al-Takharruṣ; Making a fallacious claim, telling a lie.

Bayt as having exclusive authority when it comes to exegesis [of the Qur'ān], and another group of reports that conceives of the Qur'ān as a [more generally accessible source of] clarification and guidance. For, indeed, the first group of reports is referring to the fact that the *ta'wīl* of the Qur'ān, the *hidden knowledge*, and acquaintance with all the distinct features of the Qur'ān, can only be attained through acquaintance with the *revelation*[1] and references with its same relevant implication. As for the second group of reports, it is referring to the fact that the words[2] of the Qur'ān are neither equivocal[3] nor [void of a signified meaning][4]. Rather, they have a meaning, [an accessible one at that]. Thus, Ahl al-Bayt share in common with other people their knowledge of the Qur'ān's *apparent meaning*.

7. The Qur'ān's phenomenon of a notion's *applicability [in other instances]*[5]; This differs from *ta'wīl*[6], on the one hand, and exegesis[7], on the other hand, in the following manner.

The Qur'ān is the everlasting, transcendent miracle and its prescriptions apply to all people of all times. The verses revealed about one group also apply to others when the prerequisite conditions are provided. There is an inclusion of other cases so long as the occasion of the revelation is not an exclusive case of the

---

[1] T: *al-Waḥy*; The Divinely revealed knowledge, that is the Qur'ān and the actual Sunnah of the Prophet Muḥammad.

[2] T: *Alfāẓ* (sing. *lafẓ*); Utterances.

[3] T: Mujmal(ah).

[4] T: Muhmal(ah).

[5] T: *al-Jary wa al-inṭibāq*; An idea with one application can apply in other instances that may be very different in terms of their time and place; The same principles that "*go for*" one case may very well "*go for*" many other cases. There is, thus, an *applicability* to many cases.

[6] T: In the specific sense that is exclusively known to God, the Prophet and the Divinely appointed Imams.

[7] T: *al-Tafsīr*.

verse in question. This is what is meant by *applicability [in other instances]*: the applicability of a verse to the most prominent[1] of instances, established by referring to a report [attributed to the Prophet and/or Divinely appointed Imams]; however, the verse maintains its *generality*[2]. That is, specifying a (past or future) instance to which the verse applies does not harm the *generality* of the verse --indeed, *the occasion of application does not restrict the revelation.*[3]

As for the approach of *ta'wīl*, its *intended meaning in all seriousness*[4] is not the *generality* [of the verse's language]; rather, the *intended meaning in all seriousness* is an external application identified by the means of reports [attributed to Prophet Muḥammad and/or the Divinely appointed Imams]; thus, the verse no longer sustains a *generality* [in the sense of applying to other cases].

As for *exegesis*, it reveals the *intended meaning in all seriousness* and identifies [the scope of the statement] from the sequence of speech[5] surrounding the verse. To clarify this idea, we say the following. There are a number of reports [attributed to the Prophet and/or the Divinely appointed Imams] that exegetically explain some verses [of the Qur'ān]. Examples of these verses are:

1. God Almighty says:

---

[1] T: *Akmal*; "Most excellent," but this "excellence" is context-dependent – "most excellent" in manifesting the quality under consideration, whether it be praiseworthy or not. Hence, the choice, "most prominent."

[2] T: *'Umūm*.

[3] T: *al-Mawrid lā yukhaṣṣiṣ al-wārid;* A familiar saying in *ḥawzah* circles of learning; referring to how the general nature of a statement from the Qur'ān or the Sunnah is not restricted in its scope to the particular application it applies to or occasion for which it was revealed.

[4] T: *al-Murād al-jiddī.*

[5] T: *Siyāq.*

يُرِيدُونَ أَن يُطفِئوا نورَ اللّهِ بِأَفواهِهِم وَيَأبَى اللّهُ إِلّا أَن يُتِمَّ نورَهُ وَلَو كَرِهَ الكافِرونَ * هُوَ الَّذي أَرسَلَ رَسولَهُ بِالهُدىٰ وَدينِ الحَقِّ لِيُظهِرَهُ عَلَى الدّينِ كُلِّهِ وَلَو كَرِهَ المُشرِكونَ

They desire to extinguish the light of God with their mouths, and God refuses but to complete His light, though [those who unreasonably reject what is right][1] be averse.

It is He who has sent His Messenger with the guidance and the religion of what is right to make it prevail over all religion, though [those who ascribe partners to the Absolute][2] be averse.[3]

[Providing an exegetical explanation of the verse, it has been mentioned that God is describing [those who unreasonably reject what is right][4] among the Jews and the Christians in saying that, "they desire to extinguish the light of God," the light of God being the Qurʾān and Islam, "and God refuses but to complete His light." In other words, God will not have it any other way than to bring about the Qurʾān's affair, Islam's affair, and to make His case[5] completely, "though [those who unreasonably reject what is right]

[1] T: al-Kāfirūn.

[2] T: al-Mushrikūn.

[3] Qurʾān 9:32-33.

[4] T: *al-Kāfirūn* (sing. *al-Kāfir*); Although this word is often translated "disbelievers" or "faithless," its usage is arguably more nuanced, depending on the context. For instance, in some cases, it is a legal category that requires a specialist reading of Islamic legal sources to define its boundaries. In other cases, it can be used to refer to those who are ungrateful for God's blessings, a notion with multiple ethical manifestations and degrees. Hence, the translation of this word, as many others, should be taken with a grain of salt and a disclaimer, until it becomes the main focus of careful study.

[5] T: His *ḥujjah*; His proof/argument that establishes a case for or against something; establishing the accountability to (*munajjizīyah*) [God to follow that proof] and excusableness for (*muʿadhdhirīyah*) [following that proof] as understood through reliable channels.

be averse," that is, despite the aversion of [those who unreasonably reject what is right]. "It is He who has sent His Messenger," Muḥammad, and had him carry the messages to deliver them to his community; "with the guidance," that is, with the *ḥujaj*[1], clear proofs[2], indications[3], and rational proofs[4]; "and the religion of *what is right*," that is, Submission[5] [to the Unlimited, God] and the sharāʾiʿ[6] included within it – upholding which makes one eligible[7] for reward, and every other religion is invalid, [and] for which one

---

[1] T: *Ḥujaj* (sing. *ḥujjah*). *Al-Ḥujjah*: The proof/argument that establishes a case for or against something; establishing the accountability to (*munajjizīyah*) [God to follow that proof] and excusableness for (*muʿadhdhirīyah*) [following that proof] as understood through reliable channels.

[2] T: al-Bayyināt (sing. al-bayyinah).

[3] T: *al-Dalāʾil* (sing. *al-dalīl*); It can mean different things, depending on how it is used, such as guide, argument, indicator, etc.

[4] T: *al-Barāhīn* (sing. *al-burhān*); Rational proofs that meet philosophical standards of certainty; or proofs, in a broader sense.

[5] T: It is likely that the author is referring to the innately recognized, primordial religion of submission (*al-islām*) [to the Absolute, the Unlimited], not simply the final prescription brought to humanity at the hands of Prophet Muḥammad (Islam). Hence, the author writes that any other religion would be invalid, a reference to Qurʾān 3:85.

[6] T: sing. sharīʿah; The Divine paths/prescriptions to be followed, with all their rules, regulations, recommendations, etc.

[7] T: *Yastaḥiqq*; Deserves; is entitled to; in the context of God's action, however, it is out of His own benevolence, generosity and mercy that He chooses to make good-doers deserving of reward. God has made that promise binding upon Himself – there is no higher authority beyond Him. Sure, His justice dictates that He would never punish someone who did not know any better – let alone someone who did the right thing. But as for deserving a reward for doing the right thing, that is up to Him and humans only "deserve" it in the sense that God has promised to reward them and God does not break His promises. I have chosen to translate *yastaḥiqq* as "makes one eligible" in order for the English to allow for this reading more readily, for God is the final authority on what is "deserved."

deserves[1] punishment; "to make it prevail over all religion," that is, to raise that religion [of *what is right*] above all other religions by [elaborating] proof[2], [and by] exceeding and overcoming them, such that every remaining religion on the face of the earth is exceeded. No one will exceed the people of Submission [that is, *al-Islām*] when it comes to their [elaboration of] proof[3], and it is, rather, they who will exceed the people of all other religions with their [elaboration of] proof. As for prevailing by means of exceeding [others], it is [an expression of how] each group of the [Submitters, the] *Muslims* would have exceeded and overcome [the people who ascribe partners to the Absolute[4] in an area of theirs. Offering another explanation, the following] has also been said[5]: [By saying this, God] meant the descent of Jesus, son of Mary[6] – there will not remain a people of any religion except [those who] will have submitted [to God, becoming Muslim] or paid *al-*

---

[1] T: Although this sense of "deserving" can be taken more literally (i.e. humans who make the wrong choices *deserve* to face the consequences of those choses), it is possible that some individuals are excused because they do not know any better, having tried their best and yet still failed to reach the valid worldview and system of practice. Furthermore, "deserving" to be punished is different than *actually* being punished. God may choose to forgive those who "deserve" to be punished for a number of reasons, when it is possible.

[2] T: *al-Ḥujjah.*

[3] T: *al-Ḥujjah.*

[4] T: *Ahl al-shirk*; The people who ascribe partners to the Unlimited, Absolute God Almighty, believing those partners to have influence independent of God. This can have many manifestations, such as worshipping idols.

[Note: In some senses, the word *shirk* (ascribing a partner [to God]; idolatry) is used to refer to forms of insincerity in one's relationship with God, applying even among those who profess belief in the One God alone. For example, doing acts of worship for the sake of people's admiration/approval is a form of insincerity called *riyāʾ*, and in some reports this notion of *riyāʾ* is described as *shirk.*]

[5] T: *Qīla.*

[6] T: ʿĪsá ibn Maryam.

jizyah[1].[2] It has been reported by al-Ḍaḥḥāk that Abū Jaʿfar, [that is Imam Muḥammad al-Bāqir,] said,

إن ذلك يكون عند خروج المهدي من آل محمّد، فلا يبقى أحد إلّا أقر بمحمّد

Indeed, that[3] *will come to pass when the Mahdī [the guided one] from the progeny of Muḥammad mobilizes*[4]*; for [as a consequence,] there will remain no one except [those who] will have acknowledged*[5] *Muḥammad.*[6]

It has also been reported that al-Mufaḍḍal asked [Imam Jaʿfar] al-Ṣādiq about the taʾwīl[7] of the verse, after telling him that some of

---

[1] T: A form of taxation levied on non-Muslims who wish to live under the protection of Islamic rule; analogous to the various forms of religious dues that Muslims are required to pay as acts of devotion, such as *zakāt*. Non-Muslims pay this tax, agreeing to be subject to the authority of Islamic rule similar to their fellow Muslim citizens. The details regarding this tax and when it is levied are a matter of Islamic law and the discretion of the imam (leader of the Islamic community).

[2] T: This sentence's explanation as well as that of the next sentence would either be considered prominent instances to which the verse applies, not impacting the verse's *generality*, or examples of *taʾwīl* (if provided by the Prophet and/or Divinely appointed Imams).

[3] T: Referring to the verse cited above.

[4] T: *Khurūj*; His "coming out" in the sense of mobilizing; Likely referring to the beginning of an armed resistance (*khurūj bi al-sayf*), to be distinguished from the mere advent of his public appearance (*ẓuhūr*).

[5] T: Aqarra bi; Confessed or admitted [faith] in; Professed [truth] of; accepted [truth] of. This phrase may also be used more generally to refer to an acknowledgment of something or someone's standing. It is this last sense that would seem more in line with the notion that there will remain those who are not Muslims but pay the *jizyah* tax.

[6] Adapted from *Tafsīr Majmaʿ al-Bayān* 5:45.

[7] T: Apparently going beyond the general language of exegesis (*tafsīr*). For even though the word "taʾwīl" can be used in the sense of *tafsīr*, linguistically, the fact that the report is explaining the verse as a prophecy yet to be fulfilled gives the indication that this is not merely *tafsīr* via identifying a notable application but also *taʾwīl* requiring the Imam's guarded knowledge.

the Muslims claim Islam had [already] prevailed over all other religions. In response, he said:

يا مفضَّل لو كان ظهر على الدين كلّه ما كان مجوسية ولا نصرانية ولا يهودية ولا صابئة ولا فرقة ولا خلاف ولا شكّ ولا شرك ولا عبدة أصنام ولا أوثان ولا اللات ولا العزى ولا عبدة الشمس ولا القمر ولا النجوم ولا النار ولا الحجارة، وإنَّما قوله: (لِيُظْهِرَهُ عَلَى الدِّينِ كُلِّهِ) في هذا اليوم وهذا المهدي وهذه الرجعة، وهو قوله: (وَقاتِلُوهُمْ حَتَّى لا تَكُونَ فِتْنَةٌ وَيَكُونَ الدِّينُ كُلُّهُ لِلَّهِ)

O Mufaḍḍal, had it prevailed over all religion then there would be no [conflict with that fact arising from the religious collectives of the][1] Magi[2], Christians, Jews, or Sabaeans[3]; [there would be] no disunity[4], no disagreement, no doubt, no ascribing partners [to the Absolute][5], no worshipers of idols[6] or statues[7] or al-Lāt or al-ʿUzzá[8], and no worshipers of the Sun or the Moon or the stars or fire or stone. Rather, when God says, "to make

---

[1] T: According to a holistic reading alongside reports indicating the existence of those who may not be Muslim at the prophesied time but will pay the *jizyah* tax, the members of the named religions would not cause a rift in the worldwide rule of the Mahdī and Jesus even if they have sizeable populations --they would not be at conflict with the verse's description of God's message prevailing.

[2] T: Majūsīyah.

[3] T: Ṣābiʾah.

[4] T: If read *furqah*. If read *firqah*, it would refer to sect(s).

[5] T: *Shirk*. See earlier footnote on "*Ahl al-shirk*."

[6] T: *ʿAbadat aṣnām* (sing. *ʿabd aṣnām*); Those who worship *aṣnām* (sing. *ṣanam*).

[7] T: *Awthān* (sing. *wathan*). Some differentiate between *ṣanam* and *wathan*, claiming that the former is a form without a body, taken as an object of worship, while the latter includes a body. Others say there is no difference between the two. A conclusive assessment would go beyond the scope of the purposes of this work.

[8] T: *al-Lāt* and *al-ʿUzzá* are the names of some of the idols worshipped by pre-Islamic Arabs.

it prevail over all religion," it is about this day, this Mahdī, this return[1]*. It is about the verse in which God says,*

وَقَاتِلُوهُمْ حَتَّىٰ لَا تَكُونَ فِتْنَةٌ وَيَكُونَ الدِّينُ كُلُّهُ لِلَّهِ [...]

And fight them [off] so that there is no strife[2]*, and religion is wholly for God.*[3] *[...]*[4]

2. God Almighty also says,

وَلَقَدْ كَتَبْنَا فِي الزَّبُورِ مِن بَعْدِ الذِّكْرِ أَنَّ الْأَرْضَ يَرِثُهَا عِبَادِيَ الصَّالِحُونَ

And We have indeed written in the Psalms, after the Remembrance, that My righteous servants shall inherit the earth.[5]

This verse refers to the idea that inheriting the earth will be fulfilled; the righteous servants of God will inherit the earth. Indeed, the Qur᾽ān presents a comprehensive theory with an objective. There is no room for coincidence, aimlessness, or haphazardness in the Qur᾽ān. It speaks of the universe, the human being, nature, the beginning and the end, the journey of [Divinely appointed] emissaries and prophets, their distinct features, and [how His] selection of them is based on an [underlying] wisdom, not by drawing lots or coincidence. It thus presents the vision that the universe is founded by [the act of] the Wise, All-aware Maker, that in the beginning of the universe, there is the story of Adam[6] and that this caravan [of humanity] will journey toward the resurrection[7]. The Qur᾽ān also spoke[8] about the end of the

[1] T: al-Raj῾ah.

[2] T: *Fitnah.*

[3] T: Qur᾽ān 8:39.

[4] *Mu῾jam Aḥādīth al-Imām al-Mahdī,* 5:143 / Ḥ 1562.

[5] Qur᾽ān 21:105.

[6] T: Ādam.

[7] T: al-Ma῾ād.

[8] T: Transition to past tense is in author's original Arabic.

universe, about the Divine government [of end times], and about achieving that intended aim. For the virtuous [polity][1] is a Qur'ānic and [more broadly] Divinely revealed discussion and aim. There is no harm in that[2] --just as [there is no harm in the fact that] discussing an origin [of all creatures] is Qur'ānic and [more broadly] Divinely revealed, even if [an ultimate origin has been] discussed [not only] by Divinely revealed books, [but also by] philosophical books, and theological books. For the verse [cited above] explicitly states that this planning has had its historical reach; it was not originated in the Islamic[3] tradition. Rather, its seeds have been planted since ancient times in the Remembrance[4] and in the Psalms[5].[6]

---

[1] T: *al-Dawlah*; In modern usage, this word often refers to the modern nation state. In the context of early Islamic civilization, this word would refer to dynastic rule, a "turn" [to hold power]. However, since the author is referring to *al-dawlah* as a matter of Divine planning from the earliest times, it is unlikely that he means it in the sense of a modern nation state. Hence, the translation, "polity."

[2] T: The author appears to be anticipating a potential objection raised in the face of the notion of shared elements of faith across religious traditions. Instead of arguing that these elements are uniquely Islamic to avoid the accusation of plagiarism or charlatanism, he embraces that there is no harm in having shared elements of faith. For the Islamic claim is that Prophet Muḥammad came in a series of prophets carrying the same general message from the one and only Divine source.

[3] T: In the specific sense of "Islam," that of Prophet Muḥammad in history.

[4] T: *al-Dhikr*.

[5] T: *al-Zabūr*.

[6] ʿAlī ibn Ibrāhīm al-Qummī said: My father relayed to me that Ibn Abī ʿUmayr relayed that Manṣūr ibn Yūnus relayed that ʿAmr ibn Abī Shaybah said he heard Abū Jaʿfar, [that is Imām Muḥammad al-Bāqir] initiating the following statement: [...] "وَلَقَدْ كَتَبْنا فِي الزَّبُورِ مِنْ بَعْدِ الذِّكْرِ،" قال: الكتب كلّها ذكر، "أَنَّ الأَرْضَ يَرِثُها عِبادِيَ الصَّالِحُونَ،" قال: القائم عليه السلام وأصحابه، قال: والزبور فيه ملاحم وتحميد وتمجيد ودعاء، وقوله: "قالَ رَبِّ احْكُمْ بِالْحَقِّ،" قال: معناه لا تدعو للكفّار، والحقّ الانتقام من الظالمين، ومثله في سورة آل عمران: "لَيْسَ لَكَ مِنَ الأَمْرِ شَيْءٌ أَوْ يَتُوبَ عَلَيْهِمْ أَوْ يُعَذِّبَهُمْ فَإِنَّهُمْ ظالِمُونَ."

3. The Qur᾽ān speaks similarly in the verse when God says:

وَعَدَ اللَّهُ الَّذِينَ آمَنوا مِنكُم وَعَمِلُوا الصّالِحاتِ لَيَستَخلِفَنَّهُم فِي الأَرضِ كَمَا استَخلَفَ الَّذِينَ مِن قَبلِهِم وَلَيُمَكِّنَنَّ لَهُم دِينَهُمُ الَّذِي ارتَضىٰ لَهُم وَلَيُبَدِّلَنَّهُم مِن بَعدِ خَوفِهِم أَمنًا ۚ يَعبُدونَنِي لا يُشرِكونَ بِي شَيئًا ۚ وَمَن كَفَرَ بَعدَ ذٰلِكَ فَأُولٰئِكَ هُمُ الفاسِقونَ

God has promised those of you who have faith and do righteous deeds that He will surely make them successors in the land, just as He made those who were before them successors, and He will surely establish for them their religion which He has approved for them, and that He will surely change their state to security after their fear, while they worship Me, not ascribing any partners to Me. And whoever is ungrateful after that — it is they who are the transgressors.[1]

The verse points to the following:

- God will make a righteous community for the faithful.

[…] "And We have indeed written in the Psalms, after the Remembrance," [21:105], [commenting on this, he said:] all the books are remembrance, "that My righteous servants shall inherit the earth," [21:105 continued]. [Commenting on this, he said: This is referring to the] *Qā᾽im* (Rising One) and his companions. [Then he said:] As for the Psalms, it includes [mention of] battles (*malāḥim*), praise (*taḥmīd*), glorification (*tamjīd*), and supplication (*du῾ā᾽*). As for when God says, "He said, 'My Lord, judge with *what is right* (*al-ḥaqq*)!'" [21:112], [commenting on this, the said:] it means that you should not pray for the [oppressive, unexcused disbelievers to get away with their crimes]; *what is right* is that the oppressors should be brought to justice. A similar notion is in the chapter of *Āl ῾Imrān* when God says, "You have no hand in the matter, whether He accepts their repentance or punishes them, for they are indeed wrongdoers." [3:128].
See: *Tafsīr al-Qummī* 2:77-78.

[1] Qur᾽ān 24:55.

- God will make the faithful successors in the land and will make their religion prevail, lead, exceed and overcome others.
- The community will go through the stage of fear and then will be followed by the stage of security.

Moreover, the instance to which this verse applies has been identified as Imam Mahdī, according to the reports – either from the aspect of *applicability*[1] or from the aspect of *taʾwīl.*

Furthermore, many reports have made this identification with respect to other verses as well. For example, God Almighty says,

وَنُرِيدُ أَن نَّمُنَّ عَلَى الَّذِينَ اسْتُضْعِفُوا فِي الأَرْضِ وَنَجْعَلَهُمْ أَئِمَّةً وَنَجْعَلَهُمُ الوارِثِينَ وَنُمَكِّنَ لَهُمْ فِي الأَرْضِ [...]

And We wish to bestow favor upon those who were oppressed in the land, and to make them imams, and to make them the heirs, and to establish them in the land [...][2]

For al-Ṭūsī has reported that [Imam] ʿAlī commented on this, saying,

هم آل محمّد، يبعث الله مهديهم بعد جهدهم، فيعزّهم ويذل عدوّهم

They are the progeny of Muḥammad; God will bring forth their Mahdī after their hardship; he will strengthen them and humble their enemy.[3]

4. God Almighty also says,

[...] إِلّا مَنْ خَطِفَ الخَطفَةَ فَأَتبَعَهُ شِهابٌ ثاقِبٌ

---

[1] T: *al-Jary [wa al-inṭibāq].*

[2] Qurʾān 28:5-6.

[3] *Al-Ghaybah* by al-Ṭūsī: 184 / Ḥ 143.

[...] except one who snatches a fragment as a piercing flame pursues him.[1]

Al-Ṣadūq has reported that [Imam Jaʿfar] al-Ṣādiq said,

أمَا والله ليغيبنّ عنكم مهديكم حتّى يقول الجاهل منكم: ما لله في آل محمّد حاجة

Indeed, [I swear] by God, your Mahdī will be hidden from you until the ignorant among you will say, "God has no need[2] *for the progeny of Muḥammad."*[3]

It is also reported that he said,

ثمّ يقبل كالشهاب الثاقب فيملأها عدلاً وقسطاً كما ملئت جوراً وظلماً

Then he will come like a penetrating star[4]*; he fills [the world] with justice and fairness just as it has been filled with tyranny and injustice.*[5]

This is all in addition to the chapter of *al-Qadr*; the gist of verses indicating the inevitability of the [Mahdī's] advent; the verses regarding [proactively] waiting [for it]; the verses discussing the nature of the conflict between right and wrong; and the verses discussing that final stop on humanity's [journey]. These indicate that the idea of the Mahdī is a Qurʾānic one, regardless whether the approach [to reading the text] is: *exegetical*, known through contemplation and the *sequence of speech signification*; or taʾwīl-derived [in a broad sense], known through the reports of Ahl al-

---

[1] Qurʾān 37:10.

[2] T: Perhaps such a foolish/ignorant person would think that since the Mahdī is not publicly identifiable then there is no Mahdī, there is no guided one from the progeny of Muḥammad to wait for. Thus, there is no Divine plan to be fulfilled by Muḥammad's progeny.

[3] *Kamāl al-Dīn:* 342 / Bāb 33 / Ḥ 22.

[4] T: Shihāb thāqib.

[5] *Kamāl al-Dīn:* 342 / Bāb 33 / Ḥ 22.

> Bayt either in the sense of *applicability* or in a sense of *ta'wīl* [exclusively identifiable by them].[1]

It thus becomes clear what is meant by publications titled, "The Mahdī in the Qur'ān," or, "'Alī in the Qur'ān" [for example].

In any case, the approach taken by the Shī'ah in their exegesis of the Qur'ān differs from the approach taken by the Sunnīs[2]. For the Shī'ah consider the words of the Prophet [Muḥammad] to be authoritative[3] in exegesis, but do not consider the words of the [early] followers[4] to be authoritative unless it is established that those words are the Prophet's words relayed by them. Otherwise, they are like all other Muslims [in that their words are not authoritative on their own merit].

---

[1] T: The word "ta'wīl" can be used in different senses, some broader than others. When it is used in its more specific senses, it is used as opposed to the more generally accessible *exegesis* (*tafsīr*). For *exegesis* relies on common sense understanding of *apparent meanings*, contemplation and *sequence of speech signification* to understand the Qur'ān and its instances of application. In the face of this reading, there is another form of reading that is learned from the reports of Ahl al-Bayt. This ta'wīl (i.e. the ta'wīl as opposed to *exegesis*) includes two types of information: [1] identifying *applicability*, in which instances of application are identified by Ahl al-Bayt's reports, without limiting the *generality* of an exegetical reading of the verses; and [2] the specific sense of *ta'wīl*, in which the ultimate meaning of the verses is identified through Ahl al-Bayt's exclusive knowledge (i.e. the *generality* of the exegetical reading of the verses is not maintained).

[2] T: *Abnā' al-'Āmmah*; or simply, *al-'Āmmah*; The "common" [people] as opposed to the *khāṣṣah* (inner circle or initiated); This is understood to refer to the general Muslim population who do not believe in the Twelve Imams as Divinely appointed Imams; as opposed to the inner circle of Muslims who do believe in the Divinely appointed authority of the Twelve Imams and have been initiated as their Shī'ah.

[3] T: Ḥujjīyah.

[4] T: *al-Tābi'ūn*; Sometimes, this word is used to specifically refer to the subsequent generation of followers of Prophet Muḥammad's companions. But in the general sense, it refers to followers more broadly.

Furthermore, on the authority of [Prophet Muḥammad's words in] *ḥadīth al-thaqalayn* and the like, which have been established by *tawātur*[1], the Shī'ah also believe that the words of Prophet Muḥammad's close kin[2] [that is, Ahl al-Bayt,] are authoritative.

Generations of Exegetes

What follows are descriptions of the generations of exegetes[3] within the Shī'ah [school]:

First Generation: Those who relayed the exegetical reports on behalf of the Prophet [Muḥammad] and his close kin. This includes transmitters such as Zurārah, Muḥammad ibn Muslim and the like, may God be pleased with them

Second Generation: The first to author texts of exegesis, such as Furāt al-Kūfī, Abū Ḥamzah al-Thumālī, al-'Ayyāshī, 'Alī ibn Ibrāhīm al-Qummī, and al-Nu'mānī, may God be pleased with them. Their approach was to transmit the reports, mentioning the *chains of transmission*[4], but without mentioning their own views on the subject.

Third Generation: Masters of various sciences, such as al-Sharīf al-Raḍī in his literary exegesis, al-Ṭūsī in his theological exegesis, al-Shīrāzī in his philosophical exegesis, al-Gunābādī in his Ṣūfī exegesis, and the Shī'ī al-Ṭabarī in his exegesis which encompasses numerous arts, such as language, grammar, theology and ḥadīth.

---

[1] T: That is wide-scale transmission beyond the [practical] possibility of collusion to lie by its transmitters.

[2] T: al-'Itrah.

[3] T: *al-Mufassirūn* (sing. *mufassir*); Expounders of exegesis; Qur'ānic commentators.

[4] T: *al-Asānīd* (sing. *al-sanad*); The series of reporters who relayed the content, all the way back to the original speaker.

THE THIRD EPISTEMIC SOURCE: THE NOBLE SUNNAH

The Sunnah is also a source of Islamic knowledge, similar to how the Qur'ān is. The noble Sunnah has dealt with all Islamic affairs and has supplied [Islamic] thought with originality and rich [intellectual] productions. Alongside the Qur'ān, the Sunnah will remain a source which is rich with the aromatic treasure that crowns Islam with immortality and endurance until God inherits the earth and its inhabitants. There is no difference between the Holy Book [the Qur'ān] and the Sunnah from the aspect that they both issue from the source of revelation. They are two lights emanating from a single source.

DISPARITIES BETWEEN THE QUR'ĀN AND THE SUNNAH

However, the two differ, having a number of disparities[1], such as:

1. One of the purposes of the Qur'ān is to be inimitably miraculous[2] and to have the spirit of challenging [humanity to bring forth the like of it]. As for the Sunnah, while it is miraculous, its miraculous nature is [not in its use of language as with the Qur'ān] but in its legislation and its metaphysical dimensions[3].

2. The wording of the Holy Book [the Qur'ān,] as well as its meanings, both originate from the Divine presence of God Almighty, while the Sunnah's wording does not.[4]

---

[1] T: *Fawāriq* (sing. *fāriq*).

[2] T: *al-I'jāz*; To be a miracle so inimitable, so irreproducible, that humans stand utterly incapable before its challenge to bring forth the like of it.

[3] T: *Mughayyabāt*; Aspects hidden to typical experience; Dealing with variables typically unknown.

[4] T: This is not to say that the established Sunnah's wording is fallible, for Prophet Muḥammad is immaculate. But there is something distinct about the wording of the Qur'ān being Divine in origin beyond the mere fact of immaculacy – it is inimitable, beyond reproducibility by skilled experts.

3. The Qur'ān's *chain of transmission*[1] is decisively known[2], [hence, one is sure that it issued from the Prophet Muḥammad], while the Sunnah's *issuance*[3] [from the Prophet Muḥammad] is not decisively ascertained, except in the case of *mutawātir* reports.[4]

4. In most cases, the Qur'ān is concerned with the very principle of legislation, founding general rules pertaining to *intentions in use [of the language]* (*al-irādāt al-isti'mālīyah*), which become reference points in cases of doubt regarding certain features. Thus, it mentions universal rules that require elaboration and elucidation. The role of the Sunnah, then, is to elaborate and elucidate. Therefore, an unqualified Qur'ānic statement cannot be taken [at face value] to yield a conclusion until after investigating [in search] for a qualifier.

Furthermore, the Islamic community harbored two other lines of thinking [besides the one just described]:

---

[1] T: *Sanad.*

[2] T: *Qaṭ'ī.*

[3] T: al-Ṣudūr.

[4] T: The author likely also considers the *issuance* of non-*mutawātir* reports that are corroborated by sufficient external evidence to be decisively known (*khabar al-wāḥid al-maḥfūf bil-qarā'in al-qaṭ'īyah*).

The [early establishment][1] line of thinking: Its structure of thought is founded on the notion that, "The Book of God suffices for us."[2] Today, this has been translated into the statement, "Islam is the Qur'ān alone." Thus, the legislation is deduced from the Qur'ān alone, and the noble Sunnah is given up or relegated to merely supplementary [status, referred to] ceremonially, [merely] to invoke blessings and good fortune.

Another line of thinking: The line of *exaggeration*[3] pertaining to the ḥadīth, accepting it whatever way it comes, and having no measured [criteria for] ascertaining the Sunnah. Thus, [this line of thinking puts the supposed accounts of] the Sunnah first. Hence, it is a retreat from these epistemic tools [that we have been drawing attention to], such as investigating the chain of transmission, reconciling conflicting reports, searching for clues and other things we will refer to later. Such a line of thinking entails an abandonment of the *necessarily established truths*[4] of reason or the

---

[1] T: *Abnā' al-ʿāmmah*; Typically, this would have been translated as "Sunnī," but the author is clearly referring to a trend of thinking that was advanced by some early companions of the Prophet Muḥammad who formed the core ruling establishment (as opposed to following the Divinely appointed Imam) after the Prophet passed away. It is a principle which Sunnī schools historically and today would likely disagree with, at least when it comes to legal matters. Still, Sunnī defense of such statements by early companions would lend credence to reading this description as an evaluation of Sunnī foundations, even if Sunnī thought formally espouses the Sunnah as a source of knowledge.

[2] T: A statement attributed to an early companion who said this in response to the Prophet Muḥammad's request to write a will of sorts that would safeguard the community from misguidance. It has been recorded in the major Sunnī collections of ḥadīth such as *Ṣaḥīḥ Muslim* (e.g. vol. 5, p. 76) and *Ṣaḥīḥ al-Bukhārī* (e.g., vol. 5, p. 138). See: "Razīyat yawm al-khamīs."

[3] T: al-Ghuluww.

[4] T: *al-Ḍarūrī*, a category of necessarily established truths (within a certain sphere of knowledge). For example, there are *necessarily established* rational truths within the sphere of human knowledge, *necessarily established* Islamic truths within the sphere of Islam, and *necessarily established* Shīʿah truths within the sphere of Shīʿah Islam.

Qur᾽ān. Moreover, we will later mention our position regarding *fabricated*[1] ḥadīth, *unestablished*[2] ḥadīth, *bizarre and unusual*[3] ḥadīth, ḥadīth which violates *necessarily established truths*, and the like. We will also shed light on the means of preserving the Sunnah, the tools used to ascertain it, and relevant treatments [of issues that come up with respect to it].

Furthermore, discussing the Sunnah deals with the following points, briefly put:

1. [Addressing the question:] What is the evidence proving that the Sunnah is [meant to be] an epistemic channel for Islam's legislation, creed[4] and ethics?
2. The mutual support between the Qur᾽ān and the Sunnah.
3. Some misconceptions[5] that [attempt to] disprove its epistemic instrumentality[6].
4. How we discover the Prophetic Sunnah according to the guideposts of the two schools [of thought; that is the Shīʿah and the Sunnī schools], assuming that "the other" [that is, the Sunnī] is indeed a school [of thought].
5. The phenomenon of *ijtihād*[7] as it pertains to the efficacy and persistence of the Sunnah.

---

[1] T: *al-Mawḍūʿ*.

[2] T: *al-Ḍaʿīf*.

[3] T: al-Shādhdh wa al-nādir.

[4] T: ʿAqīdah.

[5] T: *Shubuhāt* (sing. *shubhah*); Related to the root SH-B-H, which can have the meaning of being similar, exhibiting resemblance; [resemblance to *what is right* from some aspect, but mistaken].

[6] T: al-Ālīyah al-maʿrifīyah.

[7] T: Skilled derivation of legal rulings from the primary sources.

6. The "Imam Mahdī" proposition as it appears in the reports [attributed to the Prophet Muḥammad and the Divinely appointed Imams].

1- Proof that the Sunnah is an Epistemic Channel

All Muslims agree that the noble, prophetic Sunnah is to be counted [as evidence for religious arguments]. Whether they be exegetes, theologians, legal scholars or others, all agree that the Sunnah is an epistemic source and a way of revealing religious truths. This is regardless of the existence of some early [establishment-aligned] individuals that sufficed themselves with the Qur'ān, as described earlier in the lines of thinking harbored by Islam. [It does not violate the requirement of *ijmā'*[1]]. Thus, the Sunnah is on par with the Qur'ān in terms of being a source as well. The evidence proving this claim – in addition to *ijmā'* – is found in many verses.

For example, God Almighty says,

يا أَيُّهَا الَّذِينَ آمَنُوا استَجِيبوا لِلَّهِ وَلِلرَّسولِ إذا دَعاكُم لِما يُحيِيكُم [...]

> *O you who have faith! Respond to God and the Messenger when he calls you to that which will give you life. [...]*[2]

This verse issues a command requiring one to answer the call of the Messenger. Regardless whether this command is taken in the sense of

---

[1] T: A form of consensus among scholars that, in Twelver Shī'ah thought, counts as religious evidence if it reveals the position of the immaculate individual (e.g., The Prophet Muḥammad or one of the twelve Divinely appointed Imams). Otherwise, consensus among scholars is often taken into account when determining positions of precaution, even if it does not establish a legal ruling on its own merit.

[2] Qur'ān 8:24.

mentorship[1] or *legislation*[2], it gets across that the word of the Messenger is authoritative[3]. In addition, [the requirement of answering the call of] the Messenger being on par with the requirement of answering the call of God proves this point.

God Almighty also says,

وَما يَنطِقُ عَنِ الهَوىٰ * إِن هُوَ إِلّا وَحيٌ يوحىٰ

Nor does he speak out of [his own] desire:

It is just a revelation that is revealed [to him],[4]

This holy verse implies a number of notable points, such as the following:

The Messenger is supported with an *immaculate* type of support, for it is far-fetched that such praise would be relayed merely to elucidate an honorific status of the noblest Prophet [that is, Muḥammad]. Rather, the *apparent meaning* of the statement points to the fact that everything the noblest Messenger utters is a Divine revelation and an epistemic source.

Moreover, God Almighty says,

[...] وَمَن يَعصِ اللَّهَ وَرَسولَهُ فَإِنَّ لَهُ نارَ جَهَنَّمَ [...]

---

[1] T: *al-Irshādīyah*; Guidance directing attention to something that the power of reason can discover. Guidance directing attention to something that the power of reason can discover. This type of guidance is a confirmation of reason's conclusions and those rationally accessible notions suffice on their own to urge one's action. This notion can be used in a sense which includes advisory directives that are not legally binding, so long as those rationally accessible advisable notions would have sufficed on their own to urge one's action (without the directives).

[2] T: *al-Mawlawīyah*; Related to a command issued by God in order to urge action, in the sense that the object of the command would not have sufficed on its own to evoke that urge. It is not a matter of merely directing attention to something that would have been discoverable by reason. Rather, it initiates and establishes a matter that is not discoverable by reason alone.

[3] T: Ḥujjah.

[4] Qurʾān 53:3-4

[...] and whoever disobeys God and His Messenger, indeed there will be for him the fire of hell, [...][1]

Argumentation on the authority of this verse is clear, for it deems disobeying the Prophet to be similar to disobeying God Almighty, and both entail intensified punishment in the hereafter; thus, we conclude that taking the Prophet's word is a must. Furthermore, since the statement is unqualified, the word of the Prophet must be reliable and authoritative in [all the] various arts [of thought and practice]. This is also a prime testament to the necessity of accepting [as authoritative not only] the word, [but the] action and silent approvals[2] of the Prophet as well.

God Almighty also says,

[...] أَطِيعُوا اللَّهَ وَأَطِيعُوا الرَّسولَ [...]

[...] Obey God and obey the Messenger [...][3]

The verse couples obedience to the Messenger with obedience to God in a single sequence of speech, repeating the verb ["obey"]. This is to emphasize the requirement of taking the Prophet's word on matters and obeying him, as well as the fact that his Sunnah is an epistemic source. For the verse refers to [obeying the Prophet in] an independent sense and is perhaps a testament to establishing the Prophet's *legislative authority*[4].

---

[1] Qurʾān 72:23.

[2] T: *Taqrīr*; Tacit endorsements.

[3] Qurʾān 4:59.

[4] T: *al-Wilāyah al-tashrīʿīyah*; The Prophet's authority to legislate Divine rulings in the sense that he does not simply relay (or even merely reveal) Divine legislations, but is tasked by God with the role of a legislator, legislating in light of his assessment, through Divinely inspired knowledge, of the underlying interests. Note: This does not imply the fallibility of such legislation; the Prophet is immaculate and thus the Prophetic legislation would also be immaculate. It also does not imply that Prophetic legislation is an exercise of the typical human attempt at deriving rulings from sources of legislation (*ijtihād*) --even if one were to entertain that such *ijtihād* is immaculate in its conclusions; for the Divine inspiration empowering the Prophet, and Divine knowledge accessible by the

In another verse, God Almighty says:

فَلا وَرَبِّكَ لا يُؤمِنونَ حَتّىٰ يُحَكِّموكَ فيما شَجَرَ بَينَهُم [...]

> *But no, by* your *Lord! They will not believe until they make* you *a judge in their disputes [...]*[1]

For them to make him a judge assumes that they will also accept his judgment. This can be extended to all other rulings and the like, either because [there is *no third position*][2] or by means of *disregarding particularity*[3].

God Almighty says in yet another verse,

وَما كانَ لِمُؤمِنٍ وَلا مُؤمِنَةٍ إذا قَضَى اللَّهُ وَرَسولُهُ أَمرًا أَن يَكونَ لَهُمُ الخِيَرَةُ مِن أَمرِهِم [...]

Prophet, would mean that Prophetic legislative authority transcends typical human attempts at *ijtihād.*

[1] Qur'ān 4:65.

[2] T: *'Adam al-qawl bil-faṣl*; literally, "the absence of [evidence for] a third position." The author apparently means that this is or can be shown to entail the same effect as one verifying "the position stating there is, indeed, no third position that is potentially correct on the matter" (*qawl bi 'adam al-faṣl*). It is either "this" or "that." Since we know it is not "this," then it must be "that" because there is no third position to be considered in this discussion. Both those who claim it is "this" and those who claim it is "that" agree that there is no credible third position.

[3] T *Ilghā' al-Khuṣūṣīyah*; When there is no *impactful* particularity about the instance to which the rule applied which would prevent the rule from applying to another case. Therefore, by *disregarding particularity* from this respect, one can apply the rule of one instance to another instance which is the same in other respects understood to be required by the rule. These become different instances/examples to which the rule applies because it is understood that the first instance was mentioned merely in the sense of an example, not that its particularity qualified the rule itself.

> *A faithful man or woman may not, when God and His Messenger have decided on a matter, have any option in their matter [...]*[1]

God Almighty also says,

> وَإِذَا قِيلَ لَهُمْ تَعَالَوْا إِلَىٰ مَا أَنزَلَ اللَّهُ وَإِلَى الرَّسُولِ رَأَيْتَ الْمُنَافِقِينَ يَصُدُّونَ عَنكَ صُدُودًا

> *And when they are told, "Come to what God has sent down and to the Messenger," you see the hypocrites turn away from you indeed.*[2]

There is no need to explain these verses – for the point is clear, especially based on the position maintaining the immaculacy[3] of the Prophet and the position that his knowledge is not [prone to error] like the *ijtihād* of a legal scholar[4]. Sure, different positions [on such matters] would require further clarification to maintain the argument.

Thus, the *authoritative*[5] status of the Sunnah to be followed is not in the sense of it *revealing*[6], *showing*[7], *being a means of reaching the reality*[8] [of], and [merely] *indicating* the religious legislation. Rather, its *authoritative* status is in the sense of it [itself] establishing the Sharīʿah and its religious

---

1 Qurʾān 33:36.

2 Qurʾān 4:61.

3 T: *ʿIṣmah*; protection from error (despite the freedom to choose error in principle); often translated "infallibility" but "infallibility" gives the impression that there is no inherent possibility for error. As such "infallibility" is better suited as a translation for (versions of) *taṣwīb*, as opposed to *ʿiṣmah*.

4 T: *Faqīh*; jurist. The expertise of a *faqīh* typically extends beyond matters of religious law to religious truths more broadly. But the non-technical sense of the word applies, generally, to one of deep understanding (even if not specialized in jurisprudence).

5 T: al-Ḥujjīyah.

6 T: al-Kashf.

7 T: al-Iẓhār.

8 T: al-Ṭarīqīyah.

legislations. This *authoritative* status is similar to how knowledge is *authoritative*, for knowledge is itself [the aim to be] revealed[1], [itself the sought out] clarity, [itself the manifest] appearance. This is also what is meant by the *authoritative* status of the Qur᾽ān. For the Sunnah includes the word, action and silent approval of the Prophet and [other] immaculate individual[s], and there is a difference between the Sunnah itself, on the one hand, and the evidence of the Sunnah, on the other hand[2]. The Messenger is a judge and God Almighty is the Judge; both are judges but God Almighty is the Principal[3] Judge while the Messenger is the agent[4] judge who becomes judge by the will of the Creator. [But the point is that both are *actually* judges]. As such, the judgment of the Messenger is a legal judgment that reveals legislation just as knowledge reveals the object of knowledge, not as [distant as how] an argument reveals its conclusion. [As previously cited,] God Almighty says,

[...] أَطِيعُوا اللَّهَ وَأَطِيعُوا الرَّسُولَ [...]

[...] Obey God and obey the Messenger [...][5]

This verse indicates that God's word *itself* constitutes the legal judgement, not that it leads one to it and is [merely] a *means of discovering*[6] it. Rather,

---

[1] T: Meaning, it is an end in itself when it comes to being authoritative; it is not authoritative merely because it is going to reveal something else, but rather it is authoritative because of its own clarity, and revealed quality.

[2] T: Do the words, actions and silent approvals of the immaculate individuals constitute the Sunnah, constitute the legal ruling itself, or are they merely *evidence* of the Sunnah, evidence to *reveal* the legal ruling and not the legal ruling itself? The author is making this distinction and explaining that the correct view of the Sunnah (when established) is the former.

[3] T: *Bil-aṣālah*; He is the *aṣīl* (Principal).

[4] T: *Bil-taba῾*; He is the *tābi῾* (follower) or *wakil* (agent) of the principal.

[5] Qur᾽ān 4:59.

[6] T: *Wāsiṭah fī al-ithbāt*; Means of discovery; of arriving at the knowledge of [something]; as opposed to *wāsiṭah fī al-thubūt*, which deals with the means at the level of causality in reality, not at the level of knowledge.

it is a *means of causing*[1] it. [The same applies to the word of the Messenger here, even though the Messenger is the agent and God is the Principal].[2] This distinction has very significant theological implications.

2- The Mutual Support and Influence between the Qur᾽ān and the Sunnah

Sometimes, this mutual support is in the area of *authoritativeness* and at other times it is in the area of defining and restricting.

As for the former (authoritativeness): There is no doubt that the Qur᾽ān is a source [of knowledge]. This is established and reiterated by the *explicit* word of the revelation. Moreover, the Qur᾽ān is the strongest proof for the *authoritativeness* of the Message and the Messenger, in terms of both word and action. For the *authoritativeness* of the Sunnah derives from the Holy Qur᾽ān.

---

[1] T: *Wāsiṭah fī al-thubūt*; Means of causation; of yielding the causal relationship at the level of reality, not merely linked to the notion of discovery; as opposed to *wāsiṭah fī al-ithbāt.*

[2] T: It appears this is the line of thinking the author intends by citing the verse once more. The author had pointed out earlier that this verse might be a suitable testament to establishing the *legislative authority* of the Prophet Muḥammad, as it commands obedience to Prophet Muḥammad with a repetition of the verb "obey." Is that what the author is getting at here? Arguably not. Regardless whether the Prophet has *legislative authority* or not, the author is making the case that the Sunnah defines the legal ruling and does not simply lead one to discover it the way an argument would lead to a conclusion. In other words, God Almighty's legislation is to make the Qur᾽ān and the Sunnah authoritative in defining the legal rulings. Hence, when the Sunnah is discerned, the legal ruling is known as the object of that knowledge. Hence, the question of whether or not the Prophet has *legislative authority* (beyond the authority of being the agent judge) or not remains a separate and distinct question. For it is possible that God has delegated the legislation step to the Prophet, at least in some cases, and not merely chosen to legislate that the Sunnah defines the legal rulings. Keeping in mind the difference between judgment (*ḥukm*) and legislation (*tashrī*ʿ) is key to capturing the nuance here.

As for the latter (defining): From one aspect, the ḥadīth has an influence [on understanding] the Qurʾān. For if [reported] ḥadīth is in line with the Qurʾān then it supports and reinforces [one's understanding of] the Qurʾān, but otherwise it serves to define and restrict [the scope of a Qurʾānic statement]. Consequently, [although] the Qurʾān is the reference point, the ḥadīth is an explanation and elucidation of the Qurʾān [to some extent].[1]

From another aspect, the Qurʾān has an influence on the ḥadīth. For the [reported] ḥadīth that [at first glance] is at odds with the Qurʾān is either *actually at odds*[2] [with it or merely *seemingly at odds*[3] with it]. Being *actually at odds* is to be at odds with the clear text of the Qurʾān or its agreed upon judgments/rulings. In this case, [the reported ḥadīth] is flowery [but empty][4] discourse.

As for [reported ḥadīth that is merely] *seemingly at odds*, this includes, for example, when a ḥadīth elucidates a detail of the legislation by adding a qualifier, stipulation or the like. That ḥadīth thus becomes a *clue* [from *beyond the immediately connected context* of the Qurʾānic verse] for the *apparent meaning* of the Qurʾānic [statement]. This includes, for instance, the ḥadīths[5] that elucidate the conditions and qualifiers for [buying and

---

[1] T: That is, when there is room in the *apparent meaning* of the Qurʾān for qualifiers and caveats, the ḥadīth may use more explicit language to spell them out and thus serve to reveal what was intended by the Qurʾānic statement.

[2] T: *Mukhālafah mustaqirrah*; a case of actual conflict, not merely first-glance/fleeting conflict.

[3] T: *Mukhālafah ghayr mustaqirrah*; a case of first-glance/fleeting conflict, reconcilable via the common sense rules used by people engaged in communication.

[4] T: *Zukhruf*; Specious, falsehood that is made out to be appealing. See Qurʾān 6:112.

[5] T: *Aḥādīth* (sing. *ḥadīth*).

selling][1], as these are clues used to understand the following verse, for example:

[...] وَأَحَلَّ اللَّهُ الْبَيْعَ [...]

[...] God has permitted buying and selling [...][2]

Ibn al-Qayyim has said:

> والسُنّة مع القرآن ثلاثة أوجه: أحدها: أن تكون موافقة له من كلّ وجه فيكون توارد القرآن والسُنّة على الحكم الواحد من باب توارد الأدلّة وتظافرها، والثاني: أن تكون بياناً لما أريد بالقرآن وتفسيراً له، والثالث: أن تكون موجبة لحكم سكت القرآن عن إيجابه أو محرّمة لما سكت عن تحريمه.
>
> *There are three possibilities when it comes to the relationship between the Sunnah and the Qurʾān: One [possibility] is that the Sunnah is in line with the Qurʾān in every dimension. In such a scenario, when the Qurʾān and the Sunnah are evidence addressing the same ruling, it falls under the category of accumulating and corroborating evidence; a second [possibility] is that the Sunnah elucidates and exegetically explains what is meant by the Qurʾān; a third [possibility] is that the Sunnah requires a ruling while the Qurʾān was silent about its required status, or [the Sunnah] prohibits something while the Qurʾān was silent about its prohibited status.*[3]

---

[1] T: al-Bayʿ.

[2] Qurʾān 2:275.

[3] See: *al-Uṣūl al-ʿĀmmah lil-Fiqh al-Muqāran* by Muḥammad Taqī al-Ḥakīm: 242.

3- Some Misconceptions[1] Attempting to Disprove the Sunnah's Epistemic Instrumentality

Those who deny [the epistemic instrumentality of the Sunnah] have mentioned a number of [causes for] doubt, such as: the legal prohibition on writing down ḥadīths; the fear of intermixing between the Qur᾿ān and the ḥadīth; the fear of abandoning the Qur᾿ān and being preoccupied with other matters; the ḥadīth transmitters' lack of acquaintance with writing; the lack of the need to compile ḥadīth in books; and other things. We will mention here some of those misconceptions and how to address them.

First Misconception: The Humanness of the Messenger

[This misconception states] that the Messenger of God is a human being who speaks in states of anger as well as satisfaction. So how can his words and actions be *authoritative*, to be followed [in all cases], when it may be the case that [the particular speech or action in question] issued from him while he was angry[? According to the person with the misconception,] this notion is supported by a report from [the ḥadīth compiler] Muslim in part of a ḥadīth, where he quotes [the Prophet Muḥammad as having said]:

> يا أمّ سليم أمَا تعلمين أنَّ شرطي على ربّي أنّي اشترطت على ربّي فقلت: إنَّما أنا بشر أرضى كما يرضى البشر وأغضب كما يغضب البشر فأيّما أحد دعوت عليه من أمّتي بدعوة ليس لها بأهل أن [يـ]جعلها له طهوراً وزكاةً وقربةً يقرّبه بها منه يوم القيامة
>
> *O Umm Sulaym, do you not know that I stipulated a condition [in an agreement] with my Lord[?] That is, I said, "I am merely a human being, I become satisfied like human beings become satisfied, and I become angry like human beings become angry. So whoever I supplicate against with a supplication [invoking God's wrath] upon*

[1] T: *Shubuhāt* (sing. *shubhah*); related to the root SH-B-H, which can have the meaning of being similar, exhibiting resemblance; [resemblance to *what is right* from some aspect, but mistaken].

> *them, from among my community, while that person does not deserve [such an invocation of wrath, my condition is] that God make it a [cause of] purity, blessing and closeness, bringing the person closer to Him on the Day of Judgment."*[1]

Answer: It has been established in the knowledge of the Book [of God] that Prophet Muḥammad is immaculate. For even though the noblest Messenger [Muḥammad] is a human being, the Divine has supported him and [made him a guide] in his external actions throughout his blessed life, both before the commencement [of the Prophetic mission] as well as after it. Some of the best testaments to his elevated station are as follows. [First,] the reports that have reached us through [the chains of transmission that include the Prophet's] pure, close kin. For they clearly indicate that [the Prophet Muḥammad is immaculate]. It is not surprising for the one with that misconception, [posing the objection], to utter such nonsense and disinformation. Rather, what such individuals conceal is even more outrageous. [Second,] in addition, God Almighty says,

وَإِنَّكَ لَعَلَىٰ خُلُقٍ عَظِيمٍ

> *and indeed* you *are of an exalted character.*[2]

How can one reconcile between this holy verse and what Muslim reported [above]? Someone who [invokes the wrath of God against someone and, as recounted in another report,] uses abusive language against someone without the person deserving it, simply acting out of anger, is not someone of character, let alone someone of [distinctly] exalted character. Every report that is at odds with the *explicit* text [of the Qur'ān] must be thrown out the window[3].

---

[1] *Ṣaḥīḥ Muslim* 8:27 / Bāb Man Laʿanahu al-Nabī.

[2] Qur'ān 68:4.

[3] T: *Lā budda min ḍarbihā ʿarḍ al-jidār*; Literally, "it must be struck against the width of the wall" --that is, it must be disregarded, left aside.

Second Misconception: Conflict between Reports Attributed to the Messenger

There is a quote [attributed to] the first caliph, saying:

إنّكم تحدّثون عن رسول الله صلى الله عليه وآله وسلم أحاديث تختلفون فيها والناس بعدكم أشدُّ اختلافاً فلا تحدّثوا عن رسول الله شيئاً

> *Indeed, you relay ḥadīths, attributing them to the Messenger of God while you disagree regarding them. People [who come] after you will [thus] be even more intensely in disagreement. Therefore, do not relay anything while attributing it to the Messenger of God.*[1]

Answer: Numerous reports [attributed to] Prophet Muḥammad explicitly require that one act according to the Sunnah. This is despite his knowledge that fabricators would make up plenty of reports and attribute them to him.[2] In addition, numerous treatments have been reported regarding how to overcome the phenomenon of fabricators [fabricating ḥadīth]. Sure, those who turn away from the counterpart of the Qurʾān, [that is, *Ahl al-Bayt*], get lost in such mazes.

Third Misconception: The Messenger Being Bewitched

Al-Bukhārī has reported that some Jews bewitched the Messenger of God to such an extent that it was made to seem to him that he would do

---

[1] *Tadhkirat al-Ḥuffāẓ* 1:2-3.

[2] In one of his sermons, Prophet Muḥammad said:

أيّها الناس قد كثرت عليّ الكذّابة فمن كذب عليّ متعمّداً فليتبوء مقعده من النار

> *O people, [the gang of liars] who ascribe lies to me has grown into many. So whoever ascribes a lie to me intentionally, let them take their seat in the fire of hell.*

Al-Kāfī 1:62 / Bāb Ikhtilāf al-Ḥadīth / Ḥ 1.

something even though he would not have [actually] done it.[1] Therefore, not everything ascribed to the Prophet must be followed, so long as there is

---

[1] It has been reported that ʿĀʾishah said: The Messenger of God was bewitched to such an extent that it was made to seem to him that he would do something even though he would not have [actually] done it. One day, when he was at my place, he supplicated to God, supplicated to Him [some more], and then he said,

أشعرت يا عائشة أنَّ الله قد أفتاني فيما استفتيته فيه؟

> *Did you sense, O ʿĀʾishah, that God had answered me regarding the question which I had asked Him?*

[ʿĀʾishah continues:] I said: What is that, O Messenger of God? He replied:

جاءني رجلان فجلس أحدهما عند رأسي والآخر عند رجلي ثمّ قال أحدهما لصاحبه: ما وجع الرجل؟ قال: مطبوب، قال: ومن طبه؟ قال: لبيد بن الأعصم اليهودي من بني زريق، قال: فيما ذا؟ قال: في مشط ومشاطة وجف طلعة ذكر، قال: فأين هو؟ قال: في بئر ذي أروان)، قال: فذهب النبيّ صلى الله عليه وآله وسلم في أناس من أصحابه إلى البئر فنظر إليها وعليها نخل ثمّ رجع إلى عائشة فقال: (والله لكأنَّ ماءها نقاعة الحناء ولكأنَّ نخلها رؤس الشياطين)

> *Two men came to me. One of them sat near my head and the other sat near my legs. Then one of them said to the other, "What is the pain this man [suffers from]?" He replied, "He has been bewitched (maṭbūb)." Then he asked, "and who bewitched him?" He replied, "Labīd ibn al-Aʿṣam, the Jew of Banū Zurayq." Then he asked, "What is it in?" He replied, "In a comb, fallen hair from combing and the spathe of a male date tree." Then he asked, "Then where is it?" He replied, "In the well of Dhī Arwān."*

[The transmitter of the report then said:] So the Prophet went with a group of his companions to the well. He looked toward at it, and date trees were over[hanging] it. Then he returned to ʿĀʾishah and said,

والله لكأنَّ ماءها نقاعة الحناء ولكأنَّ نخلها رؤس الشياطين

> *I swear by God that it is as if its water was [infused with Henna] and its date trees the heads of [satanic creatures].*

[ʿĀʾīshah then said:] I said, "O Messenger of God, did you then remove it?" He replied,

a likelihood[1] that what issued from him was perhaps due to the act of Jewish sorcerers.

Answer: God Almighty says,

وَما يَنطِقُ عَنِ الهَوىٰ * إن هُوَ إلّا وَحيٌ يوحىٰ * عَلَّمَهُ شَديدُ القُوىٰ

Nor does he speak out of [his own] desire:

It is just a revelation that is revealed [to him];

Taught by one of great powers[2]

In light of these verses, the first generation of the companions took the word of [Prophet Muḥammad] to be right on the target of inevitable[3]

لا، أمّا أنا فقد عافاني الله وشفاني وخشيت أن أثور على الناس منه شرّاً

No. As for me, God relieved me and healed me; and I feared that [by doing so] I would provoke evil from it at the [expense] of the people.

Then he ordered that it [be brought] and it was buried.
Ṣaḥīḥ al-Bukhārī 7:30.

[1] T: *Maẓannah*; Related to *ẓann*, which often means "supposition/conjecture" but can also refer to "knowledge" in some cases. In this context, in one sense "knowledge" works – for the claim of the misconception is that the Prophet was known to be bewitched in some cases – but otherwise "supposition/conjecture/likelihood" is what applies to suspect reports in this regard.

[2] Qur'ān 53:3-5.

[3] T: *Ḥatmī*; It is likely that the author is using this word as opposed to reality that is not inevitable. The latter includes cases in which free will allows for multiple trajectories from the human perspective. With regard to non-inevitable reality, the Prophet's words describing it may reflect the possibility of "*badā*'" or the change in outcomes, within some layers of destiny, based on a human's exercise of freedom in making choices. This would be done perhaps to emphasize the role of human agency, encouraging healthy lifestyle choices. For example, someone may be on a trajectory to have three years longer to live but then chooses to have a change of heart and connects with his/her relatives, triggering a change in the trajectory to be thirty years longer to live. The Prophet may at times describe non-

reality. Furthermore, there is no room for sorcerers to impact the soul[1] of God's Messenger. Even assuming that there is potency to the influence of sorcerers on *external reality*, their influence only extends to those of weak [hearts and minds][2], not to a Blessed person. The story of the sorcerers with the Prophet of God, Moses, in the Qur'ān is a testament to this. For, indeed, they bewitched all the people but were not able to influence the *actions* of Moses.[3]

Fourth Misconception: The Messenger Being a Mujtahid

[This misconception states] that the Messenger is merely a *mujtahid*[4]. Hence, it is the right of others to arrive at a different *ijtihād*-based conclusion as well. Thus, his word is not [the verbatim] Divine revelation [which would be] forbidden to disobey. This is the misconception known as, "the humanness of the Qur'ān." Most recently, this misconception has been draped with a secular garb.

Answer: It has been mentioned in the appropriate place that the knowledge of and information shared by the Prophet are Divinely revealed and that he

---

inevitable reality with appropriate terms to account for this. Of course, from God's perspective, transcending all variables and layers of reality, all final outcomes are inevitable, albeit some inevitable with a free-will trajectory to get there.

[1] T: *Nafs.*

[2] T: al-Nufūs.

[3] T: See, for example, Qur'ān 7:116. If the pronoun in Qur'ān 20:66 refers to Prophet Moses, then it appears that the author is referring to how bewitchment, in the sense that it causes something to seem like what it really is not, extends to all people, even in such a way that Prophet Moses recognized its effect. However, the difference is that while many people's external actions are also impacted by sorcery (e.g. dwelling on *unholy* fear, making rash decisions, accusing someone without evidence), the actions of Prophet Moses would not be impacted by the sorcery. That is for at least two reasons: [1] as with other Blessed persons, the influence of sorcery is too weak to influence his external actions; and [2] Moses would receive Divine revelation to see beyond any illusory effect of sorcery.

[4] T: A person deriving legal rulings through the process of *ijtihād*, that is the skilled derivation of legal rulings from the primary sources.

is immaculate. In the sermon of his farewell pilgrimage, Prophet Muḥammad said:

معاشر الناس، وكلّ حلال [وما يكون فيه سبب سعادتكم قد] [1] دللتكم عليه، أو حرام [وما يكون فيه سبب شقاوتكم قد] [2] نهيتكم عنه فإنّي لم أرجع عن ذلك ولم أبدّل

O people, [when it comes to] every lawful [matter and things that would include a cause for your happiness[3]][4], I have shown you [the way to] it; [and when it comes to the] prohibited [matters and things that would include a cause for your misery[5]][6], I have forbidden you from it. Indeed, I have not retreated from doing so and I have not changed.[7]

Earlier, it was mentioned that it is impossible for what issues from the Prophet to issue out of his [personal] *ijtihād* and interpretation[8]. This answer is not contingent on requiring an adoption of the view regarding Prophet Muḥammad's [Divinely authorized, independent] *legislative authority*[9]. Regardless of whether his *legislative authority* is established as

---

[1] T: I did not find this bracketed portion in the source cited. It seems to be an explanatory remark clarifying "kullu ḥalāl."

[2] T: I did not find this bracketed portion in the source cited. It seems to be an explanatory remark clarifying "ḥarām."

[3] T: Saʿādah; Felicity; well-being; success; prosperity; excellence.

[4] T: I did not find this bracketed portion in the source cited. It seems to be an explanatory remark clarifying "lawful."

[5] T: Shaqāwah; Failure; wretchedness; opposite of saʿādah.

[6] T: I did not find this bracketed portion in the source cited. It seems to be an explanatory remark clarifying "forbidden."

[7] See: *al-Iḥtijāj* 1:81.

[8] T: *Ḥads*; Depending on the context, this can mean a form of intuition; but it often means a form of interpretation as opposed to *ḥiss* (i.e. that which is readily an object of sense perception). Here, the latter appears to be the intended meaning, suitable with the meaning of *ijtihād*.

[9] T: See earlier footnote on "*al-Wilāyah al-tashrīʿīyah*."

fact or not, there is no doubt that Prophet Muḥammad is not [acting as] a *mujtahid*, except according to an [unusual][1] position among Sunnī views.[2]

Fifth Misconception: The Messenger's Command to Erase Things

It has been ascribed to the Messenger of God that he said,

لا تكتبوا عنّي، ومن كتب عنّي غير القرآن فليمحه

> *Do not write down anything on my behalf[3]; whoever has written anything on my behalf other than the Qurʾān, let him[4] erase it.[5]*

Answer: This ḥadīth is a fabrication[6]. One of the best testaments to this is that even those who prohibited the writing down of the Prophetic Sunnah did not cite this ḥadīth [to support their actions]. If [for argument's sake] we were to grant this report's reliability, then the compilers[7] of the *Ṣiḥāḥ*, the *Sunan*, and the *Masānīd* [categories of] compilations have violated the command of God's Messenger [in compiling written records of non-Qurʾānic statements by the Prophet]. In light of this, we see that the Sunnī scholars have objected to [the notion that] this ḥadīth issued from the

---

1 T: *al-Shādhdh*; bizarre; highly uncommon.

2 T: The issue with *ijtihād* is that it is associated with a fallible or, at least, *human attempt* in its process and conclusion. However, the arguments for Prophet Muḥammad's infallibility (in the sense of immaculacy/ʿ*iṣmah*), including the Qurʾānic descriptions of him, indicate that not only is his conclusion infallible, it is *Divinely revealed*. Hence, the *ijtihād* notion – which is by definition a *human attempt*, not *Divinely revealed* – is not a suitable explanation for Prophet Muḥammad.

3 T: ʿ*Annī*; In some contexts, it could mean, "about me," or [copy] "off of me."

4 T: In the sense of an imperative, "have him" or "he must."

5 *Ṣaḥīḥ Muslim* 8:229 / Bāb al-Tathabbut fī al-Ḥadīth.

6 T: *Mawḍūʿ*; "Placed" there, in the sense that it is not original; it is made-up; ascribed falsely.

7 T: *Muʾallif*; author.

Prophet; or they claimed that it did issue from the Prophet [but is qualified,] specific to particular areas.

4- How Do We Discover the Noble Prophetic Sunnah According to the Guideposts of the Two Schools?

According to both schools, [both the Sunnī and the Shīʿah schools, that is], the fact that memorization and writing down of the ḥadīth took place during the time of the Prophet Muḥammad is a given. It has been reported that Prophet Muḥammad encouraged doing so, saying,

أكتب فوَالذي نفسي بيده ما يخرج منه إلاّ حق

Write down [what I say], for, by the One in whose hand is my soul, nothing but what is right comes out of it.[1]

It was his mouth that he was referring to [by "it"].

However, after the passing of the Prophet, disagreement occurred. So some of [those in disagreement] would prohibit and prevent people from writing down [the ḥadīth], considering it an illegal matter. This included individuals such as Abū Bakr, ʿUmar, Ibn Masʿūd[2], Abū Saʿīd al-Khudrī, and others such as Zayd ibn Thābit, ʿUthmān and Muʿāwiyah[3]. On the other hand, there were those who encouraged writing down [the ḥadīth], such as the Commander of the Faithful, [Imam ʿAlī].

Writing down the ḥadīth flourished during the time of [Imam Ḥasan, the second Imam, and Imam Ḥusayn, the third Imam, and during the time of

---

[1] *Sunan Abī Dāwūd* 2:176 / Bāb fī Kitāb al-ʿIlm / Ḥ 3646.

[2] Review: the report of al-Khaṭīb al-Baghdādī, with his chain of transmission reporting from ʿAbd al-Raḥmān ibn al-Aswad, who relayed from his father, on the case of destroying the manuscript [which included ḥadīth regarding Ahl al-Bayt]. T: Aḥmad ibn ʿAlī al-Khaṭīb al-Baghdādī (d. 463 AH / 1071 CE), *Taqyīd al-ʿIlm*, ed. Yūsuf al-ʿIshsh, 2nd ed. (Daar Iḥyāʾ al-Sunnah al-Nabawīyah, 1974 CE), 54.

[3] Review: *Tadwīn al-Sunnah al-Sharīfah* by Sayyid Muḥammad Riḍā al-Jalālī.

Imam Muḥammad al-Bāqir, the fifth Imam, and Imam Jaʿfar al-Ṣādiq, the sixth Imam]. So many books were authored that it is not possible to enumerate them and to enumerate their authors. However, four hundred such books by four hundred or fewer authors were compiled. Since these codices were dispersed around and some of them were lost, some companions of [the eighth Imam,] Imam al-Riḍā took the initiative to compile the available content and secure it in a separate book he called "al-Jāmiʿ."[1] These collections are different than the books composed by the companions of the Imams up until the time of the *ghaybah*. Furthermore, since the time of Imam al-Riḍā, these collections have been a reference and [primary] source for the Shīʿāh in religious and legal matters up until the time of the *Four books*[2]. The latter are the ḥadīths extracted from the *Four hundred codices*[3] as well as all the [remaining] books from the early generation of the Imams' companions.

[Writing Down Ḥadīth within the Shīʿah School]

The vast majority of [Twelver Shīʿah] Imāmīyah scholars have the opinion that the ḥadīths in the *Four books* are susceptible to [scholarly] critique, both in terms of indicated content as well as chain of transmission. [They also agree] that some of the ḥadīths are *ṣaḥīḥ*[4], while the remainder are

---

[1] T: The all-inclusive; comprehensive; exhaustive; universal.

[2] T: *al-Kutub al-arbaʿah.* These are: *al-Kāfī* by al-Kulaynī; *Man Lā Yahḍuruhu al-Faqīh* by al-Ṣadūq; *Tahdhīb al-Aḥkām* by al-Ṭūsī; and *al-Istibṣār*, also by al-Ṭūsī.

[3] T: al-Uṣūl al-Arbaʿmiʾah.

[4] T: In the more recent technical sense in Imāmī/Twelver Shīʿī circles (i.e. as opposed to *ḥasan, muwaththaq*, and *ḍaʿīf*), a *ṣaḥīḥ* report is one that is transmitted by an (unbroken chain of) upright (*ʿadl/ʿādil*) Imāmī transmitter(s). In an earlier technical sense (i.e. as opposed to *ḍaʿīf* alone), the term *ṣaḥīḥ* would describe any report that is deemed reliable to the Twelver Shīʿī community, regardless whether that reliability stems from the trustworthiness of its transmitter(s), its *tawātur*, or because of relevant clues that cumulatively authenticate it.
Ṣanqūr ʿAlī, a*l-Muʿjam al-Uṣūlī*, vol. 2, 87.

either *muwaththaq*[1], *ḥasan*[2], or *ḍaʿīf*[3]. For simply including the ḥadīth in the collection is not proof of the ḥadīth's reliability. Moreover, the mere fact that a ḥadīth is acceptable to the authors who included it does not necessitate such a ḥadīth's *authoritativeness.*

As for the position of Ahl al-Bayt in relation to the Sunnah, the holiness of the Sunnah is established because it expresses the will of God through the words of the Prophet. Moreover, the decisively ascertained Sunnah (his words, actions and silent approvals) is present with Ahl al-Bayt because they are the true successors of the Messenger. For they are the counterpart

---

[1] T: A *muwaththaq* report is one that is transmitted by an (unbroken chain of) trustworthy (*thiqah*) transmitters, albeit not particularly characterized as upright (in the *ʿadālah* sense), and/or one transmitted by a combination of trustworthy transmitters, and upright transmitters. There is a discussion regarding how to classify a report transmitted by a combination of trustworthy and praiseworthy transmitters, depending on what how "praiseworthy" the transmitter in question is, as a report is typically classified (when classifying with respect to the chain of transmission, in the more recent system) based on the weakest link in its chain.
Ṣanqūr ʿAlī, a*l-Muʿjam al-Uṣūlī*, vol. 2, 90.

[2] T: A *ḥasan* report is one that is transmitted by an (unbroken chain of) praiseworthy *(mamdūḥ*), Imāmī transmitter(s), albeit not particularly characterized as upright (in the *ʿadālah* sense), and/or one transmitted by a combination of praiseworthy and upright transmitters. There is a discussion regarding how to classify a report transmitted by a combination of praiseworthy and trustworthy (*thiqah*) transmitters, depending on what how "praiseworthy" the transmitter in question is, as a report is typically classified (when classifying with respect to the chain of transmission, in the more recent system) based on the weakest link in its chain.
Ṣanqūr ʿAlī, a*l-Muʿjam al-Uṣūlī*, vol. 2, 84.

[3] T: In the more recent technical sense in Imāmī/Twelver Shīʿī circles, a *ḍaʿīf* report is one that does not satisfy the conditions of the other three types of reports (i.e. *ṣaḥīḥ*, *ḥasan*, and *muwaththaq*). In an earlier technical sense (i.e. as opposed to *ṣaḥīḥ* alone), the term *ḍaʿīf* would describe any report that is deemed unreliable, regardless whether that unreliability stems from the unreliability of (some/all of) its transmitters, not being transmitted from the earliest reliable extant sources, or other clues that undermine the report's credibility.
Ṣanqūr ʿAlī, a*l-Muʿjam al-Uṣūlī*, vol. 2, 87.

of the Qurʾān, as *ḥadīth al-thaqalayn* and others entail. The Prophetic Sunnah shines in the heritage of Ahl al-Bayt because they know it best, as the Prophet said,

علي المحيي لسُنّتي، ومعلّم أمّتي، والقائم بحجّتي

> *ʿAlī is the reviver of my Sunnah, the teacher of my community [Ummah], and the one who establishes my proof [ḥujjah]*[1]

As for ʿAlī, he has said,

ما نريد أحداً يعلّمنا السُنّة

> *We do not want anyone to teach us the Sunnah*[2]

ʿUmar would say the following to ʿAlī,

أنت خيرهم فتوى

> *You are the best of them in [issuing] rulings [addressing legal questions]*[3]

ʿĀʾishah would say the following about ʿAlī,

علي أعلم الناس بالسُنّة

> *ʿAlī is the most knowledgeable of all people when it comes to the Sunnah.*[4]

In light of this, the Sunnah is the word, action and silent approval of the immaculate individual, thus extending beyond the [strictly] Prophetic

---

1 *Al-Iḥtijāj* 1:155.

2 *Wasāʾil al-Shīʿah* 12:483 / Bāb 42 / Ḥ (16842/2).

3 *Kanz al-ʿUmmāl* 8:600 / Ḥ 24329.

4 *Al-Tārīkh al-Kabīr* by al-Bukhārī 2:255 / Bāb al-Wāḥid / Ḥ 2377.

Sunnah to include the *Sunnah of the guardian*[1] [appointed after Prophet Muḥammad] as well.

As for the ways in which the Sunnah is established within our [school as Shīʿah], it is through both *tawātur* as well as *āḥād* reports. Studying the types of *tawātur* and the conditions for the *authoritativeness* of *āḥād* reports, such as: the plausibility of the content rationally and religiously; the trustworthiness[2] of the transmitters; the bases for trustworthiness, such as the statement of a specialist on transmitters, whose *authoritativeness* is in turn examined as to whether such a specialist's statement is *authoritative* because he is *a person of expertise*[3] or because it is an instance of *the testimony of two just individuals*[4] or because of the *authoritativeness* of *āḥād* reports; the distinguishing between reliable[5] and [unreliable] *mursal*[6] reports; the study about *ijmāʿ*, *shuhrah*[7], the statement of a [language specialist][8], the statement of a specialist[9] [in other areas], *the practice of reasonable individuals*[10], *the practice of practicing individuals*[11], *common*

---

[1] T: *al-Sunnah al-mawlawīyah.*

[2] T: Wathāqah.

[3] T: *Min ahl al-khibrah*; From among the people of expertise.

[4] T: Shahādat al-ʿAdlayn.

[5] T: al-Muʿtamadah.

[6] T: Generally speaking, it is a report in which the transmitter relays from the immaculate individual without having met him on that occasion (i.e. there is a missing link in the chain of transmission).

[7] T: Popularity; either describing a report or a legal opinion, typically; used for cases that are popular/famous but do not reach the level of *ijmāʿ*.

[8] T: al-Lughawī.

[9] T: al-Mutakhaṣṣiṣ.

[10] T: al-Sīrah al-ʿUqalāʾīyah.

[11] T: *Sīrat al-Mutasharriʿah*; Generally speaking, the practice of the followers of the Prophet and the Imams.

sense[1], and *criterion determination*[2]; and other means of discovering the Sunnah, such as the studies on *equivalent [conflicting] evidence and outweighing factors*[3] [...] Although all of these studies are important, they require a separate treatise [to treat them]. To discuss them here would go beyond the scope of this work's purpose.

Writing Down Ḥadīth within the Sunnī[4] *School*

During the three-year caliphate of Abū Bakr, the Muslims who followed the way of Abū Bakr concerned themselves solely with reciting the Qur᾿ān and sufficed themselves with that without referring to exegesis and explanations. They abandoned writing down and transmitting ḥadīth. So was the case in the ten years of rule by the second [caliph, ʿUmar]. He did not stop at the prohibition of writing down and transmitting ḥadīth but, rather, used violent measures to enforce it. For he imprisoned three of the companions: Ibn Masʿūd, Abū al-Dardā᾿, and Ibn Masʿūd al-Anṣārī. The situation continued during the reign of ʿUthmān. As such, he exiled Abū Dhar al-Ghifārī to Shām then to al-Rabadhah because he transmitted ḥadīth and because of other positions [he took]. ʿUthmān also struck ʿAbd Allāh ibn Masʿūd in the middle of the Mosque until he broke his ribs. He also struck ʿAmmār ibn Yāsir. ʿUthmān even explicitly stated the following:

لا يحلُّ لأحد يروي حديثاً لم يسمع به في عهد أبي بكر ولا عهد عمر فإنّي لم يمنعني أن أُحدّث عن رسول الله صلى الله عليه وآله وسلم أن لا أكون من أوعى أصحابه عنه إلاّ أنّي سمعته صلى الله عليه وآله وسلم يقول: (من قال عليَّ ما لم أقل فقد تبوأ مقعده من النار)

---

[1] T: *al-ʿUrf*; The sense which is *common/customary* among people; custom. (Not "common sense" as in rationally intuitive first principles).

[2] T: *Tanqīḥ al-manāṭ*; Determining the underlying criterion for the application of a ruling so that the ruling can be generalized to other cases.

[3] T: *al-Taʿādul wa al-tarājīḥ*.

[4] T: *Abnā᾿ al-ʿāmmah*; This does not necessarily refer to the Sunnī school as it exists today in every respect.

> *It is not permissible for anyone to relay a ḥadīth that was not heard of during the reign of Abū Bakr or the reign of ʿUmar. For, indeed, that I am not among the most [knowledgeable of the Prophet's companions about his words] is not what prevented me from relaying ḥadīth from the Messenger of God. However, I have indeed heard him saying, "Whoever ascribes to me what I did not say has taken his seat in the fire of hell."*[1]

As for Muʿāwiyah, he recruited fabricators [of ḥadīth] during his reign. He honored those who would report a ḥadīth regarding the merits of ʿUthmān and he encouraged them to make up ḥadīths and transmit lies. The situation continued until the second half of the second century AH when the Sunnī transmitters of ḥadīth realized the mistakes and slipups of their predecessors in preventing ḥadīth from [being transmitted and] written down. Thus, the science of ḥadīth was set in motion. Many books came on the scene carrying the [descriptive] titles, "*al-Ṣiḥāḥ*,"[2] "*al-Masānīd*,"[3] and "*al-Mustakhrajāt*."[4] The goal was to collect ḥadīths without categorizing them into chapters, and without differentiating between reliable ḥadīths and others. This was the case until [such attempts were made in] the times of: al-Bukhārī (d. 256 AH); his student Muslim al-Naysābūrī (d. 261 AH); Muḥammad ibn Yazīd al-Qazwīnī, known as Ibn Mājah (d. 273 AH); Abū Dāwūd al-Sijistānī (d. 275 AH); al-Tirmidhī (d. 279 AH); and al-Nisāʾī (d. 303 AH).

Through the six works [of compilation] by these authors, the cornerstone collections of ḥadīth within the Sunnī school were formed. These

---

[1] *Al-Ṭabaqāt al-Kubrá* 2:336.

[2] T: Sing. *al-Ṣaḥīḥ*; The reliable; authentic.

[3] T: Sing. *al-Musnad;* The ḥadīth with a chain of transmission linked back to the Prophet.

[4] T: Sing. *al-Mustakhraj*; An attempt to identify alternative chains of transmission for reports collected in another work.

collections became known as, "*the six authentic collections*[1]," or, "*the two authentic collections and the traditions*[2]."[3] After that, the *musnad*[4], *mustadrak*[5], and *mustakhraj*[6] types of works were authored.

As for the Sunnī view – with the exception of a few among them, such as Shaykh al-Albānī – regarding the Prophetic Sunnah ḥadīth collections, they consider the authentic collections, especially [al-Bukhārī and Muslim's *ṣaḥīḥ* collections] to be the most reliable and well-written books after the Qur'ān. They made those two books [by al-Bukhārī and Muslim] the focal point for matters of creed and legal rulings. They deemed it decisively known that the two collections [as a whole] issued [from their authors] and they deemed it reliable[7] to consider the ḥadīths contained therein to have issued [from the Prophet]. That is why Faḍl ibn Rūzbihān has said,

> لو أنّ أحداً حلف يميناً بأنّ كلّ ما ورد في الصحاح الستّة من الأحاديث فهو صحيح وهو قول رسول الله، لكان يمينه صحيحاً ولا عليه الحنث
>
> *If someone were to [take an oath, swearing] that everything reported in the six authentic collections of ḥadīth is authentic (ṣaḥīḥ) and it is the word of the Messenger of God, then his oath is valid and [there is no burden of violation on him].*[8]

---

[1] T: *al-Ṣiḥāḥ al-sittah.*

[2] T: *al-Sunan* (sing. Sunnah); Practices of the Prophet Muḥammad.

[3] T: *al-Ṣaḥīḥān wa al-sunan.*

[4] T: Collection of ḥadīth organized according to who the main transmitter of the report is, as opposed to topical arrangement.

[5] T: Collection of ḥadīth that serves to complement another work by including the relevant ḥadīth that were not included in the earlier work.

[6] T: An attempt to identify alternative chains of transmission for reports collected in another work.

[7] T: *Ṣiḥḥah.*

[8] See: *Aḍwā' 'alá al-Ṣaḥīḥayn* by Muḥammad Ṣādiq al-Najmī, 73.

Thus, the difference between ḥadīth books in the Shīʿah school and the Sunnī school becomes clear. For the Shīʿah scholars have [a very different view of their own *four books*]. Even though the *four books* were transmitted by Shīʿah chains of transmission, the Shīʿah scholars take a position far from exaggeration and excess [when it comes to assessing the authenticity of the reports therein]. Although they benefit from the advantages of the *four books,* they do not ignore the flaws and deficiencies therein. For there is not a book without flaws and deficiencies, no matter how careful [people are] regarding it.[1] This is opposed to the Sunnī view regarding the [so-called] *six authentic collections*, as was mentioned earlier.

The difference between the two approaches in terms of scientific critique thus becomes clear when one considers reports that violate some *necessarily established truth* – whether it be an innately intuitive one, a rational one or a religious one. Such a violation would underscore a solid objection to the [so-called] *six authentic collections* or the [so-called] *two authentic collections* [of al-Bukhārī and Muslim] because they [i.e. those regarding everything in those collections to be authentic, effectively] claim infallibility for those collections. As for the Shīʿah, the existence of such unusual and violating reports does not harm the core of the book [and the Shīʿah do not claim that *every* report in a ḥadīth collection book is reliable to begin with[2]]. This is despite [the possibility] that some who have no

---

[1] T: Of course, the author is referring to humanity's flaws and deficiencies in the preservation process. The author would not doubt the perfection of the Qurʾān, or the Divinely appointed Imam as providing the perfect preservation of the Qurʾān, for example. Rather, he is referring to the general case with fallible individuals.

[2] T: At least not as understood at face value. For there are two dimensions to the accuracy of an account: [1] whether or not there is sufficient evidence that the report issued from the authority it is quoting; [2] whether or not the authority meant the content as the content has reached us. Even when the first dimension is claimed, the second dimension often allows room for interpretation. Although the Sunnīs might also, hypothetically-speaking, invoke this line of reasoning, in practice it would arguably require them to open up to more holistic readings of the reports in light of *muḥkam* Qurʾānic verses and decisively established ḥadīths.

expertise in ḥadīth may attempt to hang on to [such an unusual and violating report].

5- The Phenomenon of Ijtihād as It Pertains to the Efficacy and Persistence of the Sunnah

Human society, or a human being in general, has a need to quench [its/his/her] intellectual thirst, prepare the means for psychological stability, and create a social order – since the human being is by nature a social animal. The Creator did not leave the human being on his or her own without giving him or her [the power of] reason, an innate intuition, a conscience, and without sending prophets. [Explaining the latter, the power of] reason cannot independently manage a human being's life after it has been established that reason is too weak to resist temptations and desires, which may influence its characterizations and legislations. Moreover, because legislation has a changing dimension to it as a result of social advancement and change, there is a need for opening up the gate of *ijtihād* for inspecting and keeping up and advancing. What we mean by *ijtihād* in the Shīʿah school is *ijtihād* within the [parameters of the] religious texts, [which are the Qurʾān and the ḥadīth], not that the Imams [of the Shīʿah] performed *ijtihād* using their own opinions. For the Imams were an extension of the Prophethood [in this regard, without being prophets] – they know [the religion] without [a need for] *ijtihād* as this is what Imāmah entails.

Ijtihād, in our school, up until the time of the *ghaybah*, has gone through a number of stages:

1. From the passing of Prophet Muḥammad until the beginning of [Imam Muḥammad al-Bāqir and Imam Jaʿfar al-Ṣādiq's] time, that is, the end of the first century AH.
2. From the beginning of [Imam Muḥammad al-Bāqir and Imam Jaʿfar al-Ṣādiq's] time until the end of the *minor ghaybah* period.
3. From the beginning of the *major ghaybah* period until present day.

During the first stage, the sources of knowledge were the Qur'ān and the Sunnah. What is meant by the Sunnah includes the word, action and silent approval of the immaculate individual. The Imams rejected the principle of *al-qiyās*[1] and *al-istiḥsān*[2]. As for *ijmā'*, to us, it is not considered a source [sufficient] for legislation unless it reveals the view of the immaculate individual. This is contrary to the status of *ijmā'* according to the Sunnīs, for they consider it an independent source [for legislation]. As the Greatest Shaykh, [that is, Shaykh Murtaḍá al-Anṣārī] has said,

هم الأصل له وهو الأصل لهم

> *They are the principle [justification] for it, [that is, the supposed "consensus (ijmā')" counting as evidence] and it is the principle [justification] for them.*[3]

In other words, the legitimacy of the first caliphate was [justified] by *ijmā'*, whether that be the *ijmā'* of the Saqīfah conveners, or the people of Medina, or others. This is also regardless of the inconsistency that befell [the Sunnī predecessors] regarding the determination of [who would take on] the Imāmah – *ijmā'* in the case of the first [caliph], *appointment*[4] in the case of the second [caliph], and *consultation*[5] in the case of the third [caliph]. It is also known that the *authoritativeness* of *ijmā'*, according to the Sunnīs, has no basis except the very act of those [predecessors] who joined one another in consensus to install their [first] caliph.

---

[1] T: In the sense of analogical *conjecture*.

[2] T: It is a form of deriving the law based on deeming something fitting but without having decisive evidence. Thus, Shī'ah scholars reject this form of legal reasoning which is conjectural, similar to how they reject *qiyās* (in the sense of analogical *conjecture*).

[3] *Farā'id al-Uṣūl* 1:184.

[4] T: *Naṣṣ*; In the sense of appointing someone by utterance/text. When used with reference to the Shī'ah Imams, it is God appointing them through the words of the Prophet Muḥammad and/or each preceding Imam.

[5] T: Shūrá.

However, scholars have many [objections to and discussions about] this *ijmāʿ*, which are mentioned in their appropriate place [of study, elsewhere].

As such, to us, *ijtihād* is to take the *apparent meanings* of the Qurʾān and the Sunnah [read holistically]. During this [first stage], *ijtihād* had not [yet] expanded much [in its complexity] – rules and principles to refer back to for epistemic purposes were not yet spelled out. Rather, when it came to problems that would arise, the Shīʿah would refer to the Imams. By tracking the scientific[1] activity of the Imams, we find that they did not rely on either *ijmāʿ* or *qiyās*, neither in action nor in word.

As for the second stage: This stage starts from the early second century AH until around the end of the third century AH. During this stage, the process of *ijtihād* and inspecting the evidence was prevalent or preferable. Rather, the Imams encouraged the vitalization of the *ijtihād* process in the sense that Ahl al-Bayt [i.e. Prophet Muḥammad's household and appointed guardians of his message] had outlined. For Imam al-Bāqir had ordered Abān ibn Taghlib to sit in the mosque of God's Messenger and answer people's questions, [issuing legal rulings][2]. As the Imam said to him,

> اجلس في مسجد المدينة وافت الناس فإنّي أُحبُّ أن يُرى في شيعتي مثلك
>
> *Sit in the mosque of Medina and issue verdicts for people; for, indeed, I would love for the likes of you to be seen amongst my Shīʿah*[3]

The most important signpost of this stage was planting the seed of the general rules for dealing with the religious text. This distinguished the Shīʿah school from others, in terms of its methodologies and rules, preparing for it the means of continuity and keeping up [with the times/changes].

---

[1] T: *al-ʿIlmīyah*; Intellectual; related to science/field of knowledge.

[2] T: Yuftī al-nās.

[3] *Rijāl al-Najāshī*: 10/ # 7.

As for the third stage: This stage starts with the beginning of the *major ghaybah*. The most important distinct features of this stage are the absence [of public access] to the Imams and delegating problem-solving to the scholars, the jurists, by the command of the Imam. Thus, the scholars became the only reference point [authorized by the Imam] for solving the problems that people faced on all levels. Sure, some [who are unqualified] have intruded upon this sensitive position, but that is no surprise when [one realizes that] hypocrites had intruded upon [even greater positions,] the position of [God's] Messenger and [his] close kin as well.

This stage involved several phases of checking the reports, collecting them, categorizing them, spelling out the rules of [jurisprudence] principles[1], identifying that which falls under the *muḥkam* category, distinguishing that which falls under the *muḥkam* category from that which falls under the *mutashābih* category, establishing epistemic approaches and means, establishing some sciences such as *al-Dirāyah*[2], explaining the impact of some sciences on others (e.g., the impact of *uṣūl [al-fiqh]*[3] on report-based sciences[4]), and opening up the prospects of specialized branches of study.

As such, throughout its entire history, the Shīʿah school has never gone through a period of closing the gate of *ijtihād* and investigation. In this light, the spirit of scientific critique grew in our midst according to demarcated and measured criteria [taught by the Imams]. Scientific activity continues to advance in inspecting our heritage, spelling out its principles, and keeping it up to date. Hence, discussion has been invigorated in terms

---

[1] T: *Qawāʿid al-Uṣūl*; The rules related to the principles of jurisprudence (*uṣūl al-fiqh*).

[2] T: A science that studies ḥadīth reports from the aspect of the content as well as their chains of transmission as a whole, but not the individual transmitters; as opposed to the science of *rijāl* (transmitters), which studies the reliability of the individual transmitters.

[3] T: The principles of jurisprudence.

[4] T: *al-ʿUlūm al-naqlīyah*; Sciences dealing with "reported" knowledge, that is the Qurʾān and the ḥadīth.

of [assessing a scriptural account's] issuance [from God, the Prophet and/or Imams], indication, *aspect* [from which a statement was issued][1], [its] branching off of the [established] principles, and [in terms of] treating conflicting reports. Thus, *ijtihād* has been a flowing spring, gushing with goodness, and feeding new ideas and pioneering scientific theories into Islamic thought[2]. These ideas and theories have – without a doubt – contributed to the enrichment of Islam's civilization and thought[3].

This does not mean that *ijtihād* is infallible, [of course]. For we see that our scholars are not immune to error. In light of this, we have been described as, "*mukhaṭṭiʾah*[4]," as opposed to others who have been described as, "*muṣawwibah*[5]." The Shīʿah have deconstructed the hallow-of-sanctity-

---

[1] T: *al-Jihatīyah*; related to *jihah*. The technical term *jihah* refers to the "aspect" from which a given statement is meant to be meaningful (e.g. to reflect reality vs. to practice precautionary secrecy (*taqīyah*) vs. to make a joke, etc.). When in doubt, a common-sensical, customary reading would understand the (holistically read) *apparent meaning* (*ẓāhir/ẓuhūr*) of a statement to be issuing from the *aspect* that it actually describes reality (e.g. that the Prophet or Imam made the statement seriously and frankly, neither stating it from the *aspect* of practicing precautionary secrecy nor to be taken jokingly, for instance).
Ṣanqūr ʿAlī, a*l-Muʿjam al-Uṣūlī*, vol. 1, 625.

[2] T: al-Thaqāfah; education, culture. The word "al-thaqāfah" is often used to refer to general awareness/knowledge, as opposed to more specialized thought. However, here and in the following footnote, the usage appears to be a broader sense of "al-thaqāfah" that may also include more specialized thought.

[3] T: Thaqāfah.

[4] T: Related to *takhṭiʾah*. Those who adopt fallibility, in the sense that the conclusions arrived at through the process of *ijtihād* (skilled derivation of legal rulings from the primary sources) are potentially fallible, that they may prove to be wrong. The reality does not change in order to adapt to the conclusions of a skilled *mujtahid* (person deriving those rulings through the process of *ijtihād*). Rather, the *mujtahid* may err. This is regardless of whether or not God will reward the mujtahid for his effort/devotion.

[5] T: Related to *taṣwīb*. Those who adopt infallibility, in the sense that the mujtahid is always "right." This is more nuanced than the theological notion of *ʿiṣmah* (immaculacy) in which there is an inherent potential for error but the person with

complex associated with any personality besides the Messenger and the Imams. Hence, the Shīʿah community has continued to stay up to date, advance and pulsate with life. Moreover, the factors of time and place have [had] their effective impact on the advancement trajectory. This distinct feature is not clearly present in other schools of thought.

It has been reported in *Maʿānī al-Akhbār*, through its author's [Shaykh al-Ṣadūq's] chain of transmission, that Dāwūd ibn Farqad said: I heard Abū ʿAbd Allāh, [that is, Imam Jaʿfar al-Ṣādiq,] saying:

> أنتم أفقه الناس إذا عرفتم معاني كلامنا، إنَّ الكلمة لتنصرف على وجوه فلو شاء إنسان لصرف كلامه كيف يشاء ولا يكذب
>
> *You are the most knowledgeable of [all] people if you have become acquainted with the meanings of our words. Indeed, a word can have meaning in many respects, [it can be taken in different ways]. So if a person wishes, he can have his words go which way he wishes without him telling a lie.*[1]

The process of critiquing ḥadīth is not an easy one. It is not manageable for [just] anyone to [simply] review the books of ḥadīth and [books discussing report] transmitters and the like. Rather, it requires the skill[2] of *ijtihād* in this craft[3] and comprehensive engagement with the rigorous rules of critique.

ʿ*iṣmah* is protected from actually falling into error. With *taṣwīb*, the conclusions of a mujtahid do not go wrong. But there are different versions of this theory, as the author points out.

[1] *Maʿānī al-Akhbār*. 1 / Ḥ 1.

[2] T: *Malakah*; Ingrained attribute; disposition; related to habitus (in Latin) and hexis (in Greek).

[3] T: *al-Fann*; Art.

6- THE "IMAM MAHDĪ" PROPOSITION IN THE REPORTS

When regarded according to the Sunnī epistemic approach, a number of [causes for] doubt pertaining to the "Imam Mahdī" proposition have been noted.

First Misconception: The Criterion for Accepting Ḥadīth is Being Reported in [al-Bukhārī or Muslim's] Authentic Collections, None Else

Neither al-Bukhārī nor Muslim included even a single ḥadīth about the coming of the Mahdī. Had the matter of the Mahdī been taken from the Sunnah, then it would have been relayed to us in *the two authentic collections*, [al-Bukharī's and Muslim's, according to Sunnīs].[1]

Answer:

1. It has not been proven that al-Bukhārī and Muslim were immaculate such that they must have been comprehensive, including every matter [in their collections]. Rather, they themselves explicitly state that they were not entirely comprehensive.[2] For this reason, some have written postscripts for

---

[1] As is attributed to Ibn Khaldūn. Review: *al-Mahdī wa al-Mahdawīyah* by Aḥmad Amīn; and *al-Imām ał-Ṣādiq* by Abū [Zahrah].

[2] In his commentary on *Ṣaḥīḥ Muslim* (vol. 1 / p. 24), al-Nawawī states:

صنَّف الدارقطني وأبو ذر الهروي في هذا النوع الذي ألزموهما وهذا الإلزام ليس بلازم في الحقيقة فإنَّهما لم يلتزما استيعاب الصحيح بل صحَّ عنهما تصريحهما بأنَّهما لم يستوعباه وإنَّما قصدا جمع جمل من الصحيح كما يقصد المصنّف في الفقه جمع جملة من مسائله لا أنَّه يحصر جميع مسائله)

Al-Dāraquṭnī and Abū Dharr al-Harawī authored [books] of this type in which they [objected and] required [al-Bukhārī and Muslim to have included many ḥadīths that they did not include, despite those ḥadīths meeting the standards of reliability for the ḥadīths they did include]; But this [attempt at demanding such a] requirement [of al-Bukhārī and Muslim] is not entailed [by al-Bukhārī and Muslim's action] in truth. For, indeed, they did not commit to comprehensively including all the authentic ḥadīths. Rather, it has been reliably relayed that they explicitly stated they did not comprehensively include all the authentic ḥadīths. Instead, their intent was to compile a collection of authentic ḥadīths, similar to those two texts, [including many authentic reports not mentioned by their original collections], such as *al-Mustadrak ʿalá al-Ṣaḥīḥayn* [by al-Ḥākim al-Naysābūrī]. This is in addition to the fact that al-Bukhārī mentioned ḥadīths about the Mahdī in his work on history.

2. The minor premise is false. For we do not grant that al-Bukhārī and Muslim neglected to relay reports giving glad tidings about the Mahdī. Rather, al-Bukhārī has reported [that Prophet Muḥammad said],

   كيف أنتم إذا نزل ابن مريم فيكم وإمامكم منكم

   How will you be if [Jesus,] the son of Mary descends [to be] in your midst while your Imam is from among you[1]

   This is based the *apparent meaning* of the Imam from among them being a reference to Imam Mahdī, as is indicated by the remaining [ḥadīth collections]. Moreover, Muslim has reported [that Prophet Muḥammad said],

   يكون في آخر الزمان خليفة يحثو المال حثياً لا يعدّه عدّاً

---

how an author of jurisprudence compiles a collection of legal rulings, and does not comprehensively encompass all the legal rulings [there are].
Moreover, in *Muqaddimat Fatḥ al-Bārī* (p. 5), Ibn Ḥajar says:
[وقال أبو] علي الغساني رو[ي] عن [البخاري] أنّه قال: خرّجت الصحيح من ستّمائة ألف حديث. وروى عنه الإسماعيلي أنّه قال: لم أخرج في هذا الكتاب إلاّ صحيحاً وما تركت من الصحيح أكثر
Abū ʿAlī al-Ghassānī said that it has been reported that al-Bukhārī said, "I [tracked down citations for] the authentic ḥadīths out of six hundred thousand ḥadīths." Moreover, al-Ismāʿīlī reported that [al-Bukhārī] said, "I have not included in this book anything but authentic ḥadīth, and the authentic ḥadīths that I have left out are greater in number."
Hence, al-Bukhārī's assessment was not that every ḥadīth he chose not to report was unreliable. Rather, what he considered to be authentic reports are tens of times more numerous than the entirety of the ḥadīths he [selected and cited for his collection].

[1] *Ṣaḥīḥ al-Bukhārī* 4:143.

At the end of time, there will be a Caliph who [distributes wealth, pouring it out], not counting it [sparingly].[1]

3. We do not accept [the assumption] that al-Bukhārī and Muslim alone are the measure for evaluating [the status of a report]. Ḥadīths regarding the Mahdī have been relayed in the *Sunan* works by Abū Dāwūd, Ibn Mājah and al-Tirmidhī, as well as [by al-Ḥākim al-Naysābūrī in his] *Mustadrak [ʿalá] al-Ṣaḥīḥayn.* Furthermore, it is not known of any Sunnī scholar to deem everything not reported by [al-Bukhārī and Muslim] to be unreliable. Rather, their practice indicates the very opposite. By reviewing their definition of a *ṣaḥīḥ ḥadīth,* one does not find it to be contingent on being reported in [al-Bukhārī's and/or Muslim's authentic collections]. Similar is the case when it comes to their definition of a *mutawātir* report. Rather, according to Sunnīs, even if al-Bukhārī and Muslim both neglected to relay a *mutawātir* report, their agreement to do so would not harm the *tawātur* status of the report.

Second Misconception: The Infiltration/Fabrication of the Reports

[This misconception holds] that the ḥadīths regarding the Mahdī are [instances of] infiltration and fabrication. For the following has been relayed by Muḥammad Muḥyī al-Dīn ʿAbd al-Ḥamīd in a comment he made on [al-Suyūṭī's *al-Ḥāwī lil-Fatāwī,* in] the last volume, on [Suyūṭī's] *al-ʿArf al-Wardī fī Akhbār al-Mahdī,*

يرى بعض الباحثين أنّ كلّ ما ورد فيه عن المهدي وعن الدجّال من الإسرائيليات

[1] *Ṣaḥīḥ Muslim* 8:185.

> *It is the view of some researchers that all of the reports in it regarding the Mahdī and the Dajjāl*[1] *are Israelite*[2] *reports.*[3]

Answer: How can it be possible to claim that these reports are infiltrations/fabrications when they have been recorded in the authentic collections of ḥadīth – collections for which they deem everything therein to be authentic (as discussed earlier)? Indeed, the reports about the Mahdī have been deemed authentic by al-Tirmidhī, al-Dhahabī, Ibn Kathīr, al-Naysābūrī, al-Taftazānī, al-Suyūṭai, and al-Haythamī. Rather, some of them have even judged the Mahdī reports to be characterized by *tawātur*, such as al-Shawkānī.[4]

Third Misconception: The Unreliability of the Reports

[This misconception states] that the ḥadīths regarding the Mahdī are unreliable reports. This claim has been attributed to Ibn Khaldūn and those

---

[1] T: Also a figure associated with the end times; the word *Dajjāl* refers to one who practices deception.

[2] T: The implication of being "Israelite" reports is not that there is an issue with being associated with the children of Israel. For all Muslims believe in the Prophet Jacob, son of Isaac, and the subsequent prophets from his line. They believe that God has shown favor to the children of Israel by choosing prophets from among them, making it an even greater responsibility for the Israelites to live up to a higher standard of morality, including humility. However, by neglecting to follow Prophet Muḥammad and the "updated" revelation God sent with him, non-Muslim Israelites choose to keep themselves to what Muslims regard as an "outdated" and corrupted version of God's prescription for humanity. Being referred to as "Israelite reports" in this context implies that the report's content has been corrupted (for whatever reason) over time and is thus unreliable, perhaps even associated with an attempt to infiltrate/corrupt Islamic thought.

[3] Review: *al-Mahdī al-Muntaẓar fī Ḍaw' al-Aḥādīth wa al-Āthār al-Ṣaḥīḥah* by ʿAbd al-ʿAlīm al-Bastawī, 36.

[4] Review: *ʿAqīdat Ahl al-Sunnah wa al-Athar* / ʿAbd al-Muḥsin ʿIbādah / Majallat Risālat al-Thaqalayn / Issue 25.

who followed him [in his view], such as Aḥmad Amīn, Abū Zahrah, and Muḥammad Farīd Wajdī.

The answer to this is two-fold:

1. So long as the claim to *tawātur* holds its ground, even if only in some[1] of the reports about the Mahdī, then there is no harm in proposing unreliability [when it comes to individual reports]. In his *al-Idhā'ah*, al-Qinnawjī has said:

   لا شكَّ في أنَّ المهدي يخرج في آخر الزمان من غير تعيين لشهر وعام لما تواتر من الأخبار في الباب واتّفق عليه جمهور الأمّة سلفاً عن خلف إلاَّ من لا يعتدّ بخلافه

   [...]

   إنكار ذلك جرأة عظيمة في مقابلة النصوص المستفيضة المشهورة البالغة حدّ التواتر

   There is no doubt that the Mahdī will mobilize at the end of time – [but there is no evidence to claim that he will mobilize in a specific month and year. There is no doubt about this] for the reports in this regard are [mutawātir]; the mass of the community[2] is in agreement on it, [the agreement being passed down from one generation to the next][3]; [all agree on it] except for those[4] whose disagreement is inconsequential.

---

[1] T: *al-Tawātur* wa law *ijmālan.*

[2] T: *Jumhūr al-ummah.*

[3] T: *Salafan 'an khalaf;* [Apparently, more commonly expressed *khalafan 'an salaf,* that is, succeeding generation relaying from preceding generation].

[4] T: *Man lā yu'taddu bi khilāfih;* That is, such individuals who disagree are either not scholarly authorities, or they have not had sufficient exposure to the sources in question and/or their disagreement does not harm the overwhelming evidence they are up against, even if they are scholarly authorities.

[…]

To deny that would be [an expression of] grave insolence in the face of the abundant[1], famous[2] textual reports -- [reports] which reach the threshold of tawātur.[3]

2. The originator of the misconception – Ibn Khaldūn, that is – has said,

وهي كما رأيت لم يخلص منها من النقد إلاَّ القليل

As you have come to see, none of the reports [about the Mahdī] are spared critique save a few […][4]

This is an admission that there is no critique of some of [those reports about the Mahdī]. So, what excuse do they have not to take the reports that are free from critique after his own admission in this regard?

Even if [for argument's sake] we are to accept Ibn Khaldūn's [assessment of] unreliability and authenticity, then we say the following: Indeed, he deemed four reports to be authentic out of a total of twenty-three reports that he mentioned about the Mahdī.

Fourth Misconception: The Mahdī Idea is a Shī'ah Idea

[This misconception states] that the Mahdī idea only exists within the Shī'ah school of thought, not in any other schools of thought. For, [in a footnote on Muḥammad 'Abd al-Raḥmān al-Mubārakfūrī's commentary] *Tuḥfat al-Āḥwadhī* [*bi-Sharḥ Jāmi' al-Tirmidhī*], in the chapter on "What was reported regarding the Caliphs," [v. 6, p. 474, the editor 'Abd al-Wahhāb 'Abd al-Laṭīf, apparently comments:]

---

[1] T: *al-Mustafīḍah.*

[2] T: *al-Mashhūrah.*

[3] See: *al-Mahdī al-Muntaẓar fī Ḍaw' al-Aḥādīth wa al-Āthār al-Ṣaḥīḥah,* 45. Referencing: *al-Idhā'ah,* 145-146.

[4] *Tārīkh ibn Khaldūn* 1:322.

[يرى الكثيرون من العلماء أن كل ما ورد في أحاديث عن المهدي –– إنما هي موضع شك، وأنها لا تصح عن الرسول صلى الله عليه وسلم بل إنها من وضع الشيعة.]

Many scholars view that [--when it comes to] all of what has been reported in ḥadīths about the Mahdī --they are, indeed, suspect and there is no reliable way to link them back to the Messenger, peace and blessings be upon him. Rather, they are fabrications by the Shīʿah.

Answer: The ḥadīths regarding the Mahdī are not specific to the Shīʿah. Rather, the reports mentioned [in Sunnī sources] are no less than the ones mentioned in Shīʿah sources. Many of the leading Sunnī scholars have written about Imam Mahdī, such as: Kamāl al-Dīn Muḥammad ibn Ṭalḥah al-Shāfiʿī; Muḥammad ibn Yusuf al-Kanjī al-Shāfiʿī; Nūr al-Dīn ibn Ṣabbāgh al-Mālikī; Sibṭ ibn al-Jawzī; Muḥyī al-Dīn ibn al-ʿArabī; ʿAbd al-Raḥmān Jāmī; ʿAbd al-Wahhāb al-Shaʿrānī; Sayyid Jamāl al-Dīn al-Naysābūrī; al-Ḥāfiẓ Muḥammad ibn Muḥammad al-Bukhārī; al-ʿĀrif ʿAbd al-Raḥmān al-Ṣūfī; Shaykh Ḥasan al-ʿIrāqī; Aḥmad ibn Ibrāhīm al-Balādhurī; ʿAbd Allāh ibn Aḥmad al-Khashshāb; al-Faḍl ibn Rūzbihān; Shams al-Dīn Muḥammad ibn Ṭūlūn al-Ḥanafī; Aḥmad ibn Yusuf al-Qaramānī; Sulaymān ibn Ibrāhīm al-Qundūzī al-Ḥanafī; Aḥmad ibn Ḥajar al-Haytamī al-Makkī al-Shāfiʿī; Saʿd al-Dīn al-Ḥamawī; Abū al-Majd al-Dahlawī al-Bukhārī; Salāḥ al-Dīn al-Ṣafadī; ʿAlī Akbar ibn Asad Allāh [al-Mawdūdī]; Jalāl al-Dīn al-Suyūṭī; Ibn Saʿd, the author of *al-Ṭabaqāt al-Kubrá*; Ibn Abī Shaybah; Aḥmad ibn Ḥanbal; Ibn Mājah; Abū Dāwūd; al-Bayhaqī; Ibn ʿAsākir; Ibn Manẓūr; Ibn Ḥajar al-ʿAsqalānī; and [many] others [among their scholars have written much about the Mahdī].

Fifth Misconception: The Notion of the Mahdī is a Doubtful Matter of the Unseen[1]

There is no ambiguity or hesitation regarding the fact that there exists skepticism and a lack of knowledge when it comes to the notion of the Mahdī. Because it is a matter of the Unseen, it cannot be accepted [as fact].

The answer to this is two-fold:

1. A *complicating answer*[2]: The notion of the Resurrection[3] is also a matter of the Unseen and there are doubts about its details. But that does not harm the certainty [all Muslims have] regarding the very existence of the Resurrection, and so is the case with the notion of the Mahdī.

2. A *resolving answer*[4]: [For argument's sake,] if we were to grant the existence of skepticism regarding the notion of the Mahdī, then it is skepticism regarding the details, the particulars, and not the very principle of there being such a reality (i.e. the existence of an Imam named "the Mahdī" who will mobilize at the end of time). For that is a matter of agreement, *ijmāʿ*, and an Islamic *necessarily established truth.* Rather, the very principle of the existence of a savior is a *necessarily established* religious truth [across the spectrum of religion – Islam and others].

Sixth Misconception: The Mahdī is a Concocted Idea

[This misconception states] that, indeed, we suspend judgment when it comes to accepting the reports about the Mahdī because the idea of the Mahdī has been exploited by worldly people, caliphs, and tyrannical

---

[1] T: *Ghaybīyah*; Belonging to the category of the hidden; the unknown; the metaphysical; beyond typical experience.

[2] T: *Jawāb naqḍī.*

[3] T: *al-Maʿād*; sometimes, broadly used to refer to the Day of Judgment or the beginning of the Hereafter.

[4] T: *Jawāb ḥallī.*

sultans. So perhaps these reports have been concocted by such individuals in order to push for their [agenda and solidify their] rule.

I, [the author, that is,] say:

This misconception is similar in spirit to the saying that goes, "Indeed, religion is the opium of the people." What is offered as an answer in that regard also applies here. This is the general answer.

The detailed answers, both *complicating* and *resolving*, are [as follows].

As for the *complicating answer*: If this misconception were credible, then one would have to also suspend judgment when it comes to the matter of prophethood. For, indeed, prophethood has been exploited by the aforementioned groups of individuals as well.

As for the *resolving answer*: Simply granting the existence of exploitation and doing harm to the likes of the Imam Mahdī's notion does not call for suspending judgment with respect to the Mahdī notion [in principle]. There are so many cases similar to this! For there is not a [field of] knowledge that has not been exploited for wrong purposes[!] Does this mean that one should suspend judgment regarding [the truth of such knowledge]? One of the best testaments to this is the science of medicine, for example.[1]

Seventh Misconception: The Reports About the Mahdī Are at Odds with Reason

[This misconception states] that the group of reports relayed regarding the Mahdī are unreasonable.

Answer: If what is meant [in this misconception] is merely the conflict between the reports about the Mahdī and the *necessarily established truths* of the decisively certain [power of] reason, [then the answer is as follows].

---

[1] T: While the knowledge of medicine can be used to exploit people, that does not affect its status as a reality. It does not lead one to suspend judgment regarding its truth, particularly since it is effective at treating people.

Even though this would [hypothetically] entail the unreliability of those reports, how could that be the case? For we do not recall [even a single] example that indicates an explicit conflict [between the two]. Even if [for argument's sake] one were to grant such a thing, then it would [only] be in the rare details – the rejection of which would not harm the idea of the Mahdī in our school of thought.

If, however, what is meant [in this seventh misconception] is the conflict between the reports and reason's [capacity for] sense perception – for the sense perception capacity of reason does not find the notion of Imam Mahdī to be familiar, but rather finds it [beyond the physical senses] – [then the answer is as follows].

There are so many cases in which something is at odds with the [familiarity of] reason's sense perception, but that does not entail that one is to reject those matters. For how can reason's sense perception capture matters that are beyond its arena of performance and accessibility? Reason's sense perception deals with sheerly material matters and [serves] within the scope of the natural sciences. Moreover, based on [this author's] investigation into the matter, *reason's [capacity for] suppositional perception*[1] is not *authoritative* in and of itself. [Rhetorically,] then how can it possibly overcome the reports with authentic chains of transmission, whose *authoritativeness* has been established according to the criteria of the [science of Transmitters], as mentioned in the appropriate place elsewhere[?]

Eighth Misconception: The Reports About the Mahdī Conflict with a Sociological ["]Rule["]

[This misconception states] that the reports about the Mahdī conflict with the sociological ["]rule["] established by Ibn Khaldūn. As he has stated:

---

[1] T: *al-ʿAql al-ẓunnī;* reason's capacity for perception that is less than decisively certain, as opposed to *reason's decisive certainty* (*al-ʿaql al-qaṭʿī*).

والحقّ الذي ينبغي أن يتقرّر لديك أنّه لا تتمّ دعوة من الدين والملك إلاّ بوجود شوكة وعصبية تظهره وتدافع عنه من يدفعه حتّى يتمّ أمر الله فيه [...] وعصبية الفاطميين، بل وقريش أجمع قد تلاشت من جميع الآفاق ووجد أمم آخرون قد استعلت عصبيتهم على عصبية قريش، إلاّ ما بقي بالحجاز في مكّة وينبع بالمدينة من الطالبيين من بني حسن وبني حسين وبني جعفر وهم منتشرون في تلك البلاد وغالبون عليها وهم عصائب بدوية متفرّقون في مواطنهم وإماراتهم وآرائهم [...]

And the truth that you should take away [from this] is that no call toward a religion or [reign of power] can be successful unless power and [group spirit][1] are available to support it [to victory] and defend it against those who reject it until God's will with regard to them is fulfilled. […] The group spirit of the Fāṭimids and, indeed, that of all the Quraysh, has disappeared from all over. Other communities have appeared whose group spirit has gained the upper hand over that of the Quraysh. The only exception are the remaining Ṭālibids, Ḥasanids, Ḥusaynids, and Jaʿfarites in the Ḥijāz – in Mecca – and al-Yanbuʿ in Medina. They are spread over these regions and are preponderant there. They are Bedouin groups that are of diverging hometowns, dominions and opinions […][2]

To clarify: The one with this idea views sociological phenomena [i.e. specifically related to the rise to power as in the excerpt above] to be a product of [having group spirit][3]. That is, every [such] phenomenon must

---

1 T: al-ʿAṣabīyah.

2 *Tārīkh Ibn Khaldūn* 1:327.

3 T: *al-Taʿaṣṣub*; This word can be used to mean bias or bigotry, but in the context of explaining Ibn Khaldūn's idea related to al-ʿaṣabīyah, *al-taʿaṣṣub* arguably refers to putting "group feeling/spirit (*al-ʿaṣabīyah*)" into action. That is, it does not necessarily have a negative connotation here.

be explained in light of [a group] having group spirit. Since the phenomenon of Imam Mahdī is also [such] a sociological phenomenon which [would have] had [to] spread during that time [of the rise of the Mahdī], it [would have] inevitably [been] a product of having group spirit toward the Hāshimites.

Answer:

Firstly: The intrusion[1] of a scholar of history upon a specialization which is not his own – by deeming a [ḥadīth] report to be unreliable – is the utmost abomination[2].[3] It is even more abominable to accept [as authoritative] the statement of an intruder [upon an area which is not his or her specialization].

Secondly: This theory [of Ibn Khaldūn] itself requires evidence to be proven before it can be used to refute[4] something else.

Thirdly: It also requires evidence to prove its generalizability[5].

Fourthly: Is this theory adequate in explaining the movement of Prophets and Messengers?[6]

---

[1] T: Taṭafful […] ʿalá […].

[2] T: Ghāyat al-qubḥ.

[3] T: The author is assuming that Ibn Khaldūn is not a specialist in ḥadīth studies.

[4] T: In other words, Ibn Khaldūn can argue that he sees a pattern which his theory provides an explanation for, but this is not decisive proof that can refute other possibilities and matters his theory does not account for.

[5] T: ʿUmūmīyah.

[6] T: This is apparently the author's attempt to offer instances in which Ibn Khaldūn's theory likely does not apply. For as a believer in prophets sent by God, Ibn Khaldūn would have to admit that there are cases in which supernatural factors have influenced the course of history, despite the absence of significant group spirit, or find a way to explain the intervention of prophets naturally without forsaking their Divine connection. If Ibn Khaldūn grants either or both, then the author would extend the argument analogously to explain the rise of the Mahdī, as one of Prophet Muḥammad's prophecies, despite the potential absence of much group spirit.

Fifthly: It conflicts with the intuitive principle in Islam that views [unjust group spirit][1] as an abomination.

Ninth Misconception: The Disagreement among the Shīʿah is a Sign of Negation [Regarding the Truth of the Mahdī]

[This misconception refers to] the disagreement among the Shīʿah sects regarding the Mahdī due to the division among the Shīʿah after the eleventh Imam, [that is Imam Ḥasan al-ʿAskarī]. For they had reported ḥadīths about the necessity of there being a *Ḥujjah*[2] on earth [at all times], and since Imam al-ʿAskarī did not have offspring [who were known to the broader public], they were forced to adopt the notion of a hidden[3] Imam.

Answer: Disagreement alone does not necessitate invalidation. Otherwise, not a religion on the face of the earth would be spared [of being deemed invalid]. Moreover, Prophet Muḥammad foretold that, after his passing, his community would split up into seventy-three factions.[4] Furthermore, the Shīʿah community, in general, did not disagree [in such a way that departed] from the notion of the *ghaybah*. For the reports had paved the way for [accepting] the phenomenon of the *ghaybah*, [reports starting] from the time of Prophet Muḥammad and all the way until the time of [Imam Ḥasan] al-ʿAskarī.

---

[1] T: *al-Taʿaṣṣub*; Here used in the sense of group feeling/spirit that is regardless of *what is right*. If Ibn Khaldūn considers *al-ʿaṣabīyah* to be such an important factor for sociological phenomena, regardless of moral considerations that are supposed to discipline instincts, then this theory requires tweaking in order to apply to the development of civilization according to Islamic principles.

[2] T: The proof/argument that establishes a case for or against something; in this context, the *Ḥujjah* is the Imam who serves as immaculate guardian of the Divine message, establishing the accountability to (*munajjizīyah*) [God to follow that proof] and excusableness for (*muʿadhdhirīyah*) [following that proof] as understood through reliable channels.

[3] T: *al-Ghāʾib*; In this context, the one who is in the state of *ghaybah*, occultation; one who is publicly inaccessible, living incognito.

[4] *Kifāyat al-Athar*, 155.

Tenth Misconception: The Idea of the Mahdī Comes from Misguided Religions

[This misconception states] that the *ghaybah* is an idea shared by Jews, Christians and the Magi. For it is foreign to Islam and the Shīʿah have popularized it. As for the reports about the Mahdī, they are reports of Israelite origin that have been planted in the Shīʿah heritage [of ḥadīth].

Answer: Indeed, the existence of an idea and[/or] belief shared in common among Divinely revealed religions is something that cannot be denied. But simply sharing [ideas and/or beliefs] in common does not entail unreliability, infiltration and fabrication. Rather, [recognizing such commonalities] demands one to establish principles regarding the commonalities of religions in those matters.

Eleventh Misconception: The Misconception About His Birth

[This misconception states] that we grant the idea of the Mahdī [as an idea] but we are skeptical about his birth. Hence, he does not exist at the present time, even if [proving so requires us to argue] based on some *default principles* such as the *default of nonexistence*[1] and the *presumption of continuity*[2].

This can be addressed with the following answer:

Firstly: It is the one who is closer in relevance to the matter in question who is in the position to confirm or deny occurrence [of the relevant issue]. Such a person is more acquainted with the distinct features and details of that matter because it is his or her concern and pertains to him or her. As such, confirming and denying is not to be accepted from a confirmer or denier, [respectively,] who is distant in relevance from the matter in question. [Let the objector contemplate the following question:] Would the objector accept our affirmation that he or she has a belief which he or she actually

---

[1] T: *Aṣālat al-ʿadam.*

[2] T: *Istiṣḥāb.*

does not have or our negation [that he or she has a belief which he or she actually does have]?[1]

Secondly: Setting aside our first answer, there are indeed many [non-Shīʿah] who have recognized[2] his birth, such as: Muḥammad ibn Ṭalḥah al-Shāfiʿī in *Maṭālib al-Saʾūl*[3]; Ibn Khallikān[4]; and, [Ibn al-Ṣabbāgh al-Mālikī], the author of *al-Fuṣūl al-Muhimmah*[5]. Rather, there is not [even a

---

[1] T: The objector knows what beliefs he or she has or does not have better than us because he or she is closer in relevance to his or her own self than us. The one who is closer in relevance to the matter is more acquainted with it. As such, it is the Twelver Shīʿah community who has passed down their shared knowledge about the birth of Imam Mahdī [in the person of the twelfth Imam, the son of Imam Ḥasan al-ʿAskarī,] generation after generation, from parents to offspring, based on the many indications of his birth, including the witness testimonies of Imam Ḥasan al-ʿAskarī's inner circle.

[2] T: *Iʿtarafa*; admitted to; confessed regarding; confirmed.

[3] He said the following in his book *Maṭālib al-Saʾūl* (p. 480):

الباب الثاني عشر: في أبي القاسم عليه السلام [...]
فأمّا مولده فبسُرَّ من رأى في ثالث وعشرين رمضان سنة ثمان وخمسين ومائتين للهجرة

> *Chapter Twelve: Regarding Abū al-Qāsim [...]*
>
> *As for his birth, it was in Samarra, on the twenty third of Ramaḍān of the year two hundred fifty-eight AH.*

T: Quoting this non-Shīʿah reference does not imply that the author agrees on the specific year, let alone month or day, of birth given here. The author is merely highlighting the recognition of the birth in the general time frame expected for Imam Ḥasan al-ʿAskarī's son.

[4] He said the following in his book *Wafiyāt al-Aʿyān* (vol. 2 / p. 94 / # 169):

أبو محمّد العسكري... وهو والد المنتظر صاحب السرداب

> ***Abū Muḥammad al-ʿAskarī [...] And he is the father of the awaited one (al-muntaẓar), the one associated with the underground structure (al-sirdāb) [where he was known to have been seen].***

[5] He said the following in his book *al-Fuṣūl al-Muhimmah* (vol. 2 / p. 1095):

single] textual [source] in and around the time of his birth [that indicates] the birth was not established [as fact].

Thirdly: It is possible to say that the search for him by the oppressors is evidence that they admitted he was born, for – even though they did not find him – the search itself is perhaps evidence of the birth and [the birth] being an object of their [suspicion][1]. Otherwise, had it been clear to them that there was no birth, then their action [in searching for him] would be unreasonable. With this answer, we are [obviously][2] not trying to say that the search is a sign of the birth. Rather, we are arguing that it was not obvious that there was no birth.

Twelfth Misconception: There is No Benefit from an Absent Imam

What is the benefit from an absent Imam? It goes without saying that there must be some benefit reaped from appointing an Imam. For the Shīʿah have professed that it is impossible to cater to all the affairs of the Islamic community after the passing of Prophet Muḥammad except by the [function] of an Imam. But the *ghaybah* of the Imam negates this.

Answer: Proof has established that he exists, so there is no room for inquiring about his activities [in an effort to deny his existence]. For not realizing the benefit [he brings about] does not warrant deeming the reports [about the Mahdī] unreliable and, thus, denying his existence as

---

الفصل الثاني عشر: في ذكر أبي القاسم محمّد الحجّة الخلف الصالح ابن أبي محمّد الحسن الخالص عليه السلام وهو الإمام الثاني عشر وتاريخ ولادته ودلائل إمامته

Chapter Twelve: Regarding the mention of Abū al-Qāsim, Muḥammad, the Ḥujjah, the righteous successor, son of Abū Muḥammad, al-Ḥasan al-Khāliṣ [that is the eleventh Imam, Imam Ḥasan al-ʿAskarī]; [I am referring to him] who is the twelfth Imam; the date of his birth; and the proofs of his Imāmah.

[1] T: *Maẓannah*; this could also refer to knowledge, not merely likelihood.

[2] T: Or, "With this answer, we are not trying to say that the search is a sign of the birth; for that is obvious."

well as his existential influence and metaphysical effect beyond the physical senses. Indeed, the Shīʿah belief is that the [existence of the] Imam is an inevitability – even if [only] established by an appeal to the maintenance of a [metaphysical,] existential effect [of the Imam's existence], let alone that there are a number of established, physical effects [of the Imam's existence] based on the rule of *Divine Favor.*

Accordingly: The Mahdī creed is proven by *tawātur* and it must be conceded, either because it is a matter of the Unseen[1] [and the faithful believe in the established matters of the Unseen] or because the Prophet foretold about the Mahdī and it is necessary to have faith in the words of the Prophet [regardless whether they be about the Unseen or not].

Thirteenth Misconception: The Idea and Its Origin [Being] in Psychological Factors

[This misconception states that] the idea of the *ghaybah* arose in order for the Shīʿah to cope with the psychological suppression they have experienced as a result of being oppressed by tyrannical governments.

Answer: This kind of talk has been mentioned as a form of explaining away the belief [people have] in God Almighty. As they have said: The reason for believing in God is a psychological matter, according to Freud. Moreover, even a quick review[2] of the terms used in the Mahdī system of thought and its educational culture dispel this misconception. Furthermore, what evidence is there for the basis of their claim? For it is possible to rebut with the following: Indeed, the basis of their claim is that they are psychologically bent against the Shīʿah school of thought, the expansion of its movement and its increased reception.

---

[1] T: *al-Ghayb*; The hidden, metaphysical, supernatural, or otherwise beyond the typical physical experience.

[2] T: Adná murājaʿah.

Fourteenth Misconception: The Absence [Ghaybah] of Benevolence

The Imam is a [manifestation of] *benevolence*, meaning a drawing of one closer[1] to God Almighty. How can it be okay for *benevolence* to be in a state of absence, [that is, *ghaybah*]? For *benevolence* is meant to be manifest, [out in the open and publicly accessible]. Hence, *benevolence* and absence [*ghaybah*] cannot coincide.

Answer: Indeed, the Shīʿah do not say that the Imam is inactive. What contradicts *benevolence* is inactivity, not [being in the state of public inaccessibility, that is,] *ghaybah*. There is a difference between the two matters. The reports have indicated that the Imam is not inactive. Rather, he is in a state of *ghaybah*. That is, narrow minds do not realize [his existence]. It has been likened to how physical vision does not realize [the existence of] the Sun when [different forms of] clouds conceal it – does such [a phenomenon] mean that we forsake [recognition of] the Sun's benefit when it is being concealed? In addition, withholding benevolence, [keeping it from being entirely accessible during the *ghaybah*,] is unbefitting[2] [of God] and at odds with [the principle of *Divine Benevolence*] if it is God Almighty's fault [in terms of moral responsibility][3]. However, if [the withholding of benevolence] is the fault of creatures [in terms of moral responsibility], then the shortcoming is on their end and the blameworthiness is directed at them.

Fifteenth Misconception: The Mahdī Will Be Born Later

[This misconception includes an] acceptance of the Mahdī idea but [holds that] he will be born later. This is the view of the Sunnīs who refer to the reports that describe him as being born at the end of time.

---

[1] T: al-Muqarribīyah.

[2] T: *Qabīḥ*.

[3] T: That is if God chose to withhold manifesting a level of His *benevolence* for *no* overriding wisdom, no superseding excellence of allowing creatures the freedom to choose and face consequences.

Answer: Despite the vast quantity of reports in their sources, [the reports] do not use the phrase, "he will be born […]." Rather, the reports use the phrase, "he will appear," at the end of time. Clearly, "appearing[1]" describes a prior state of being hidden. In light of this, there is emphasis on the word "appearing" in the words of the immaculate ones. This serves to indicate that one of the attributes of the promised [one] is [his state of] *ghaybah*, as the phrase, "appearing" in their expressions indicates.

Sixteenth Misconception: The Notion of the Ghaybah Conflicts with Islamic Legal Rulings

The *ghaybah* violates [the commandment to] promote virtue and prevent vice[2], and [the commandment to] express concern for the affairs of Muslims[3].

Answer: [The commandment regarding] *promoting virtue and preventing vice* has conditions. Among those conditions are that the one undertaking the *promotion of virtue* must make use of natural, recognized means. As for the Imam, his act of *promoting virtue* would entail that it falls in the sequence of his [public] appearance. For, indeed, the Sharīʿah has an *outward*[4] [dimension] and an *inward*[5] [dimension]. As is mentioned in conflict of laws[6] [at the level of implementation] jurisprudence, that which is most important takes precedence [over that which is of less importance]; thus, the importance of his concealment takes precedence over [his public act of] *promoting virtue*. Indeed, this objection applies even to [surviving righteous personalities, such as] al-Khiḍr and the like. Furthermore, it is possible for the *ghaybah* to coincide with the *promotion of virtue* because

---

[1] T: al-Ẓuhūr.

[2] T: *al-Amr bil-maʿrūf wa al-nahy ʿan al-munkar*; Prescribing what is right and proscribing what is wrong; encouraging good and forbidding evil; commanding right and forbidding wrong.

[3] T: al-Ihtimām bi umūr al-muslimīn.

[4] T: *Ẓāhir*; Apparent.

[5] T: *Bāṭin*; Innermost, internal.

[6] T: *al-Tazāḥum*.

what is meant by the *ghaybah* is the concealment of identity, not the person.[1]

Seventeenth Misconception: The Existence of Multiple Mahdī-related Claims Warrants a Rejection of the Mahdī Idea

[This misconception states that multiple individuals have falsely claimed to be the Mahdī.] Perhaps this Mahdī too is a false one. For many have claimed or it was claimed for them that they are the Mahdī, such as the Sudanese Mahdī; Muḥammad ibn al-Ḥanafīyah; Muḥammad ibn ʿAbd Allāh ibn al-Ḥasan; the ʿAbbāsids; and others.

Answer: If there were such a [corollary relationship][2] then it would be valid to deny many other matters. For example, justice – it has been claimed by all tyrants on earth. [Is there no such thing as justice, then? If the aforementioned corollary relationship were true,] then we would deem scholars to be ignorant – for there are so many who [falsely] claim to be knowledgeable. We would similarly [deny] courage and generosity [for example] – as there is not a [single] noble attribute that has not been claimed by someone empty of it.

In addition, there are a number of objections and answers addressing them that have been mentioned by Shaykh al-Mufīd in his valuable book *al-Fuṣūl al-ʿAsharah fī al-Ghaybah.*

SUMMARY

Establishing [the fact of the] Mahdī notion [in principle], his mobilization and awaiting him are not [matters that] conflict with reason, Islamic legal principles, an agreed upon rule, or an established law[3]. This is with regard to the principle of the Mahdī notion, the fact that there is an actual instance

---

[1] T: That is, Imam Mahdī is living incognito, so he may perform the duty of *promoting virtue and preventing vice* publicly, albeit not while being recognized as Imam Mahdī when doing so.

[2] T: al-Mulāzamah.

[3] T: *Far*ʿ.

of the Mahdī [notion] in the person of a hidden Imam and that one must await him.

As for the details of this creed, if – hypothetically speaking – any of the details conflict with a rational or Islamic legal principle, or even an agreed upon law, then that detail is rejected. Otherwise, if the chain of transmission is not deemed *authentic*, such as in cases of *unreliable* reports, then it is impermissible to ascribe [the report] to the Divine Legislator, except when based on [accepting] the rule of *high tolerance [regarding the evidence for recommendations]*[1] or the reports about *whoever [news] reaches him or her [that there is a reward for a given act…]*[2] if they apply in this situation. On the other hand, if the chain of transmission is deemed *authentic*, such as in cases of *ṣaḥīḥ* reports, *ḥasan* reports, and *muwaththaq* reports, then it is an ordinary report and it is valid to ascribe it [to the Divine Legislator]. Moreover, in terms of religious accountability[3], it is not mandatory to believe in the details, so long as [the absence of such belief] does not entail some other danger. However, if some other danger *is* [in fact] entailed by not believing [in a detail], and there is no harm in believing in [the detail], then it is imperative to believe in [that detail]. Otherwise, if no other danger is entailed by not believing [in something], such as a very minor detail, or if believing in it entails harm [which must be avoided, legally speaking], then one should not believe in it. [This is] either because there is no evidence substantiating [the object of belief], or due to the legal ruling about [avoiding] harm and the like. This is clear, according to the criteria that have been mentioned in their appropriate place [of study, elsewhere].

As a matter of creed, belief in the Mahdī is proven by *tawātur* and it must be conceded, either because it is a matter of the Unseen[4] [and the faithful

---

[1] T: *al-Tasāmuḥ [fī adillat al-sunan].*

[2] T: *Riwāyāt man balagh[ahu thawabun ʿalá ʿamalin…].*

[3] T: Taklīfan.

[4] T: *al-Ghayb*; The hidden, metaphysical, supernatural, or otherwise beyond the typical physical experience.

believe in the established matters of the Unseen] or because the Prophet foretold about the Mahdī and it is necessary to have faith in the words of the Prophet that definitively issued from him [regardless whether they be about the Unseen or not]. As for the details, it is not mandatory to believe in them, even if we need most of them[1] – as is the case with other matters of creed.

In any case, being acquainted with the Imam is a *necessarily established* religious truth. For it has been reported that [Imam Muḥammad] al-Bāqir said:

> بني الإسلام على خمس: الصلاة والزكاة والصوم والحجّ والولاية ولم يناد بشيء كما نودي بالولاية، فأخذ الناس بأربع وتركوا هذه _ يعني الولاية _
>
> *Islam has been built on five [pillars]: prayer[2]; charity[3]; fasting[4]; pilgrimage[5]; and guardianship[6]. Indeed, there is not a thing that has been called for with as much [emphasis] as guardianship has been called for. But the*

---

[1]T: Details regarding matters of creed have different functions than merely being objects of belief. Details open up horizons of possibility to imagine more vividly and investigate more creatively, on the one hand, and to elicit awe, reverence and other emotional responses, on the other hand.

[2] T: *al-Ṣalāh.*

[3] T: *al-Zakāh.*

[4] T: *al-Ṣawm.*

[5] T: *al-Ḥajj.*

[6] T: *Wilāyah/Walāyah*; Some scholars say that *wilāyah* refers more to authority in the sense of right to rule [on various levels], while *walāyah* would refers more to love and support. However, the word *wilāyah* has been used and understood in Shīʿah circles to refer to all of these interrelated meanings, depending on the context. For the purpose of this text, *wilāyah/walāyah* are taken to refer to this interrelated collective of meanings, including authority, love, guardianship, allegiance, support, etc., all of which are commanded by Prophet Muḥammad and the twelve Divinely appointed Imams.

> *people adopted the [first] four and they neglected this [fifth one], that is, guardianship.*[1]

It has also been reported that he said,

> ذروة الأمر وسنامه ومفتاحه وباب الأشياء ورضا الرحمن تبارك وتعالى الطاعة للإمام بعد معرفته

> *The climax of the matter [of faith]; its [peak]*[2]*; its key; the gateway of [all] things; and the pleasure of the Merciful One, Blessed and High, is the obedience to the Imam, after becoming acquainted with him.*[3]

Answering a question from Zurārah, he said,

> الولاية أفضل لأنّها مفتاحهنّ والوالي هو الدليل عليهنّ

> *Guardianship is the best among them because it is their key; and the guardian is the one who guides to the others.*[4]

It has also been reported that he said,

> لا يعذر الله يوم القيامة أحداً يقول: يا ربّ لم أعلم أنَّ ولد فاطمة عليها السلام هم الولاة على الناس كافّة

---

1 *Al-Kāfī* 2:18 / Bāb Daʿāʾim al-Islām / Ḥ 3.

2 T: *Sināmuhu*; Its most honorable part [the peak of the "hump"].

3 *Al-Kāfī* 1:185-186 / Bāb Farḍ Ṭāʿat al-Aʾimmah / Ḥ 1.

4 *Al-Kāfī* 2:18 / Bāb Daʿāʾim al-Islām / Ḥ 5.

> *God will not excuse[1] anyone on the Day of Judgment who says, "O Lord, I did not know that the children of Fāṭimah are the guardians [with authority] over all people."[2]*

God Almighty says,

> إِنَّمَا وَلِيُّكُمُ اللَّهُ وَرَسُولُهُ وَالَّذِينَ آمَنُوا الَّذِينَ يُقِيمُونَ الصَّلَاةَ وَيُؤْتُونَ الزَّكَاةَ وَهُمْ رَاكِعُونَ
>
> *Your guardian is only God, His Messenger, and the faithful who maintain the prayer and give charity[3] while bowing down.[4]*

It has also been established, in the appropriate place [elsewhere], that when God Almighty says this, he means by *guardianship* [*wilāyah/walāyah*] not merely love, but the meaning of the Imāmah that the Shīʿah adopt.

It has also been reported that Abū Ḥamzah said: Abū Jaʿfar, [that is Imam Muḥammad al-Bāqir], said:

> إنَّما يعبد الله من يعرف الله، فأمَّا من لا يعرف الله فإنَّما يعبده هكذا ضلالاً
>
> *Indeed, only one who is acquainted with God [truly] worships God. As for one who is not acquainted with God, he or she worships Him as such misguidedly.*
>
> *[Abū Ḥamzah said:] May I be sacrificed for your sake, what is being acquainted with God?*

---

[1] T: Divine justice dictates that God would not punish someone who does not deserve to be punished. Then would God not excuse someone who claims to have an excuse? It could be that the person is not being sincere in claiming the excuse. It could also be that even if the person has an excuse for not having known something, s/he did not have an excuse for not trying to learn, for example.

[2] *Tafsīr al-Qummī* 2:250; *Biḥār al-Anwār* 23:80 / Bāb wujūb maʿrifat al-Imām […] / Ḥ 16.

[3] T: *al-Zakāh.*

[4] Qurʾān 4:55.

[Abū Ḥamzah said:] Then [the Imam] replied:

تصديق الله عز وجل وتصديق رسوله صلى الله عليه وآله وسلم وموالاة علي عليه السلام والائتمام به وبأئمّة الهدى عليهم السلام والبراءة إلى الله عز وجل من عدوّهم، هكذا يعرف الله عز وجل

Believing[1] *in God Almighty, believing in His Messenger, [allegiance to] the guardianship of ʿAlī, taking him and the Imams of guidance as Imams, and turning to God Almighty, disavowing*[2] *their enemies – that is how one becomes acquainted with God Almighty.*[3]

Thus, becoming acquainted with [matters of] the Imam is a component of the hereafter's [perpetual] happiness, a cause of assurance[4], one of the signs of a believer, and among many positive effects.

---

1 T: Taṣdīq; taking [something] to be true; taking [someone's] words to be true.

2 T: al-Barāʾah.

3 *Al-Kāfī* 1:180 / Bāb Maʿrifat al-Imām wa al-Rad ilayh / Ḥ 1.

4 T: *al-Iṭmiʾnān*; contentment; tranquility; peace of mind. Depending on the context, this can also refer to a degree of sureness in which the opposing possibility is negligible in the view of reasonable individuals (even though it is still *rationally* possible). In this context, the meaning is apparently more in line with the former, more general, sense.

CHAPTER 5

SEEING THE HIDDEN IMAM (*MUSHĀHADAH*)

THE *GHAYBAH* PHENOMENON AND THE DISTINCT FEATURES OF THIS STAGE

The *minor ghaybah* stage extended from 260 AH until 329 AH. This period of time has its distinct features. For it is a tangible reality that a selection of people engaged in --people who were the pioneers of this stage.

Among the distinct features of this stage are the following:

1. A number of those who lived during and were contemporaries of the *minor ghaybah* period had been among the companions Imam [Muḥammad] al-Jawād, [Imam ʿAlī] al-Hādī, and [Imam Ḥasan] al-ʿAskarī, such as: ʿAlī ibn Jaʿfar, Abū Hāshim; Dāwūd ibn al-Qāsim al-Jaʿfarī, who saw five of the Imams; Dāwūd ibn Abī Yazīd al-Naysābūrī; Muḥammad ibn ʿAlī ibn Bilāl; ʿAbd Allāh ibn Jaʿfar al-Ḥimyarī; Isḥāq ibn al-Rabīʿ al-Kūfī; Abū al-Qāsim Jābir ibn Yazīd al-Fārisī; and Ibrāhīm ibn ʿUbayd Allāh ibn Ibrāhīm al-Naysābūrī.

2. A number of those who were contemporaries of the *minor ghaybah* were *agents*[1] of Imam Mahdī [and/or notable companions of his father Imam Ḥasan al-ʿAskarī], such as: Muḥammad ibn Aḥmad ibn Jaʿfar; Jaʿfar ibn Suhayl; Muḥammad ibn al-Ḥasan al-Ṣaffār; ʿAbdūs al-ʿAṭṭār; Sindī

[1] T: *Wukalāʾ* (sing. *wakīl*).

ibn al-Naysābūrī; Abū Ṭālib al-Ḥasan ibn Jaʿfar al-Faʾfāʾ; and Abū al-Bukhtarī.[1]

3. The *deputies*[2] of the Imam during the *minor ghaybah* were the following four individuals: ʿUthmān ibn Saʿīd al-ʿAmrī; Muḥammad ibn ʿUthmān; al-Ḥusayn ibn Rawḥ; and ʿAlī ibn Muḥammad al-Samirī.
4. A group of those who were contemporaries of the *minor ghaybah* were among the legal scholars, such as al-Kulaynī, al-Ṣadūq and his father.
5. This stage was also distinct in that the answers [from the Imam] would appear in [the form of written correspondence][3].
6. This stage was also distinct in that there existed rank and file [public support] which: had a culture of connecting with the Divinely appointed Imam and believing in the previous Imams; carried a specific identity and particular sense of belonging; and, in its sphere of practice, relied on a specific jurisprudential approach.

---

[1] T: Some editions of Muḥammad Ibn Shahrʾāshūb's *Manāqib Āl Abī Ṭālib* read, "Sarī ibn Salāmah" (apparently instead of Sindī al-Naysābūrī) and "al-Fāfānī" (instead of al-Faʾfāʾ). For instance, see:
Muḥammad ibn ʿAlī Ibn Shahrʾāshūb (d. 588 AH / 1192 CE), *Manāqib Āl Abī Ṭālib*, ed. Yūsuf al-Biqāʿī, 2nd ed., vol. 4, 4 vols. (Beirut: Dār al-Aḍwāʾ lil-Ṭibāʿah wa al-Nashr wa al-Tawzīʿ, 1991 CE), 456.

[2] T: *Nuwwāb* (sing. *Nāʾib*); more than simply an agent, the *nāʾib* of this period delivered messages on behalf of the Imam to the agents and functioned as the main gateway to the Imam. In this context, the reference to *nāʾib* is to the *specifically designated deputy* (as opposed to *generally designated deputies* --the unspecified, qualified scholars who fit the description required in the Imam's reported words). This type of specific *nāʾib* appointment ended with the end of the *minor ghaybah* (i.e. there were only four, serving one after the other).

[3] T: Mukātabāt wa murāsalāt.

We will later pause to analyze and become acquainted with how these members of the public rank and file [among the Shīʿah] referred to Imam Mahdī after the martyrdom of [Imam Ḥasan] al-ʿAskarī, without being afflicted with confusion[1]. For had there been [such confusion among the core of the rank and file] then it would have become apparent.[2]

It is known that these members of the public rank and file had distinct features in thought and practice – features that reveal many benefits for [our analysis].

All [in the Twelver Shīʿah school] have agreed that the means of communicating with the awaited Imam was through the *deputies*. Moreover, there are no indications from the pioneers of this period, such as al-Kulaynī, that there was a practical effort to witness and see the Imam. Rather, it was a given that there was no such thing [as an active attempt in practice to do so] --even if only because there was a *barrier*[3] [of some sort] preventing [sight of the Imam to take place by one's intentional effort], and despite the existence of the entire *reason*[4] for seeing [the Imam]. Although one might entertain the notion that some individuals in that situation did seek out [the opportunity of seeing the Imam], as it has been reported regarding Abū al-ʿAbbās, Aḥmad ibn al-Khiḍr ibn Abī Ṣāliḥ al-Khujandī, it has also been reported that this pursuit was forbidden and prohibited. After being enticed into investigating and seeking out [the opportunity to see the Imam], leaving his hometown, looking for leads, a signed

---

[1] T: Irbāk.

[2] T: *Law kāna la bāna*; This is a famous saying which can be understood to mean that if something so drastic existed, then its ripple effects should have become manifest.

[3] T: al-Māniʿ.

[4] T: *al-Muqtaḍī*; The acting component of the complete cause (*al-ʿillah al-tāmmah*); when all conditions are fulfilled and all barriers are removed, thanks to this acting component, an effect is yielded. However, merely the existence of this acting component does not suffice in order to yield the effect, for all conditions must be fulfilled and all barriers must be absent first.

document[1] from the master of the age[2], [that is, the Twelfth Imam, was issued and] read,

من بحث فقد طلب، ومن طلب فقد دلّ، ومن دلّ فقد أشاط، ومن أشاط فقد أشرك

> *One who searches has sought out; one who seeks out has led to; one who leads to has spilt blood; and one who spills blood has ascribed a partner [to God]*

[The individual relaying the report then said:] So he stopped seeking out [the Imam] and returned.[3]

Some might claim that the barrier exists for the particular individual searching – that the statement is a *particular*[4], an *external proposition*[5]. But this argument is rejected because the *apparent meaning* of the cause [cited by the Imam] aptly fits with [understanding the statement in terms of] *generality.*

For had the matter of seeing the Imam – practically and actually striving to do so, especially in the situation of the *minor ghaybah, with the stipulation of the predicate*[6], [that is, seeing him while the situation is the situation of the *minor ghaybah*] – been an excellence and something beloved [by God], then why did not the *agents* [of the Imam], the companions [of the Imams], the scholars, and the people of faith aim for such an objective? This is despite their intense keenness on performing [unrequired,] recommended

---

[1] *Al-Tawqīʿ*

[2] T: Ṣāḥib al-zamān.

[3] *Kamāl al-Dīn*: 509 / Bāb Dhikr al-Tawqīʿāt / Ḥ 39.

[4] T: *Juzʾīyah.*

[5] T*: al-Qaḍīyah al-Khārijīyah.*

[6] T: *Bi sharṭ al-maḥmūl.*

prayers[1]. Rather, history records that they requested other things of the Imam by way of the [Imam's] *deputies.*[2]

EXAMPLES OF MAKING REQUESTS OF THE IMAM

For example, it has been reported that Abū Ja'far, Muḥammad ibn 'Alī al-Aswad, said: After the death of [the second *deputy*], Muḥammad ibn 'Uthmān al-'Amrī, 'Alī ibn al-Ḥusayn ibn Mūsá ibn Bābawayh asked me to ask Abū al-Qāsim al-Rawḥī, [that is, the third *deputy*, al-Ḥusayn ibn Rawḥ al-Nūbakhtī], to ask our master, the master of the age, to pray to God Almighty that He bless him with a baby boy. [The transmitter then] said: So I asked him and he delivered that [message to the Imam]; then three days later, he told me that he, [the Imam, that is], had prayed for 'Alī ibn al-Ḥusayn[3] and that he would have a blessed baby through whom God would benefit [others]; and after him [several] children.[4]

Another example is that of the questions which were sent to [the Imam]. For al-Ṭūsī has reported the following, [quoting Abū 'Abd Allah, al-Ḥusayn ibn 'Alī ibn al-Ḥusayn ibn Mūsá ibn Bābawayh], in his *al-Ghaybah*[5],

حدّثني جماعة من أهل بلدنا المقيمين كانوا ببغداد في السنة التي خرجت
القرامطة على الحاجّ وهي سنة تناثر الكواكب أنّ والدي رضي الله عنه كتب

---

[1] T: *al-Nawāfil* (sing. al-nāfilah).

[2] T: That is, they could have – hypothetically – asked to see the Imam, but what is recorded in history is that they asked for many other things and did not ask to see the Imam. There was, thus, a general understanding that the meeting – no matter how desirable on a personal level – was not something to seek out directly for one reason or another. The document referenced indicates the reason as protecting the Imam's safety, which is directly tied to sincerity toward God Almighty.

[3] T: The father of the renowned scholar, Shaykh al-Ṣadūq.

[4] *Kamāl al-Dīn*: 502 / Bāb 45 / Ḥ 31.

[5] *Al-Ghaybah* by al-Ṭūsī: 322 / # 270.

إلى الشيخ أبي القاسم الحسين بن روح رضي الله عنه يستأذن في الخروج إلى الحجّ [...]

A group from the people of our country, residing [therein], who were in Baghdad during the year in which the Qarmatians[1] *mobilized against the pilgrimage [Ḥajj, in Mecca], the year of the [meteor shower]*[2]*, relayed to me that my father, God be pleased with him, wrote to the Shaykh Abū al-Qāsim al-Ḥusayn ibn Rawḥ, God be pleased with him, asking permission to head out for the pilgrimage […]*

An additional example was relayed by [ʿAlī ibn Muḥammad] al-Kulaynī. As he said,

كتب محمّد بن زياد الصيمري يسأل صاحب الزمان عليه السلام كفناً يتيمّن بما يكون من عنده

Muḥammad ibn Ziyād al-Ṣaymarī wrote, asking the master of the age for a shroud [coming from him such that he may consider it blessed][3]

Yet another example is the al-Zurārī's request of al-Ḥusayn ibn Rawḥ that the Imam pray for him – pray to mend his affairs with his wife Umm [Abū al-]ʿAbbās. This is relayed in *al-Ghaybah.*[4]

An additional example has been reported by Shaykh al-Mufīd in his *al-Irshād*[5]. He reports that ʿAlī ibn Muḥammad said: Some of our

---

[1] T: al-Qarāmiṭah.

[2] T: *Tanāthur al-kawākib*; The dispersion of celestial objects. Apparently, this was an astronomical event in the year 329 AH.

[3] Al-Ṭūsī relayed it in a chain ending with [ʿAlī ibn Muḥammad] al-Kulaynī in al-Ṭūsī's *al-Ghaybah*: 297-298 / # 253.

[4] *Al-Ghaybah* by al-Ṭūsī: 303 / # 256.

[5] *Al-Irshād* 2:363-364.

companions have relayed the following to me, saying, "I had a baby, so I wrote, asking permission to circumcise him on the seventh day [...] And I prepared for the *pilgrimage*, bid people farewell and was about to head out when a message [from the Imam] reached me,

نحن لذلك كارهون، والأمر إليك

We dislike that [you do so], and it is up to you.

[The transmitter continued to say,] "So my chest tightened up, I became saddened and wrote, '[Your wish is my command], but I am sad over not heading out for the *pilgrimage*.' Then he replied,

لا يضيقنَّ صدرك، فإنَّك ستحجّ قابلاً إن شاء الله

Let not your chest tighten up, for indeed you will go on the pilgrimage next year, God-willing.

Here the transmitter requested the *pilgrimage* alone[1]. Similarly, at the end of the report, he says: I wrote, "I have taken Muḥammad ibn al-ʿAbbās as a *ʿadīl*[2] and I am assured regarding his religiosity. [What guidance can you share in this regard?]" Here too the transmitter merely requests information about the friend.

DISCUSSION AND ANALYSIS OF REPORTS AND SUPPLICATIONS RELATED TO SEEING [THE IMAM]

Sure, there are some reports that support the notion [of striving to see the Imam]. It may [indeed] be the *apparent meaning* of such reports to [encourage] the pursuit of seeing [the Imam] during the *ghaybah*. Assuming that these reports are sound in terms of their chain of transmission and their content, they are conducive to establishing a general culture [of striving to see the Imam], so long as there is no barrier and no

---

[1] T: That is, he did not request to meet the Imam.

[2] T: Literally, a counterpart/equal; a [form of] brother in-law.

prohibition by the Imam. We point to the most important of these [reports], along with our assessment in their regard, as follows:

It was reported in *al-Ghaybah*[1] that ʿAbd Allāh ibn Jaʿfar asked the first *deputy,* [that is, ʿUthmān ibn Saʿīd al-ʿAmrī, a question], saying,

> فأسألك بحقّ الله وبحقّ الإمامين اللذين وثّقاك هل رأيت ابن أبي محمّد الذي هو صاحب الزمان عليه السلام؟
>
> *So I ask you, by the right of God and by the right of the two Imams who deemed you trustworthy, have you seen the son of Abū Muḥammad, [the son of Imam Ḥasan al-ʿAskarī], that is, the master of the age?*

So [the first *deputy*] wept and then said,

> على أن لا تخبر بذلك أحداً وأنا حي[؟]
>
> *On [the condition] that you do not tell anyone of that while I am alive[?]*

[ʿAbd Allāh ibn Jaʿfar] then said, "Yes."

[The report then quotes the first *deputy* confirming that he did indeed see the twelfth Imam].

The argumentation using this report cites how [the first *deputy*] Abū ʿAmr prohibited [others from telling that he saw the Imam] during his lifetime ––so he did not prohibit that at all times. Therefore, the barrier is not perpetual.

However, the flaw of this argument lies in [neglecting] the *apparent meaning* understood from the report, which indicates that ʿAbd Allāh ibn Jaʿfar did not request of Abū ʿAmr to intercede [on his behalf] in order to see [the Imam] but, rather, at most [was simply] asking him if he actually had seen [the Imam himself]."

---

[1] *Al-Ghaybah* by al-Ṭūsī: 355 / # 316.

It has also been reported in *al-Ghaybah*[1] that Muḥammad ibn Aḥmad ibn Khalaf said:

[...] وصلّيت الظهر في أوّل وقتها، ودعوت بالطعام وسألت الشيخ أن يأكل معي فأجابني، فلمّا طعمنا سألت عن اسمه واسم أبيه وعن بلده وحرفته ومقصده، فذكر أنّ اسمه محمّد بن عبد الله، وأنّه من أهل قم، وذكر أنّه يسيح منذ ثلاثين سنة في طلب الحقّ ويتنقّل في البلدان والسواحل، وأنّه أوطن مكّة والمدينة نحو عشرين سنة يبحث عن الأخبار ويتبع الآثار.

[...] And I prayed the noon [prayer] at the beginning of its time; I called for food and asked the elderly man (al-shaykh) to eat with me; he accepted my invitation. When we had eaten, I asked him about his name, the name of his father, about his town, trade and where he was headed. In response, he mentioned that his name was Muḥammad ibn ʿAbd Allāh[2]*, that he was from the people of Qom. He mentioned that he had been roaming for thirty years in pursuit of what is right, going from town to town and coast to coast, that he took Mecca and Medina as homes for about twenty years, searching for news and following leads.*

The argument using this report is based on assuming that, "searching for news and following leads," refers to seeing Imam Mahdī. However, the following points rebut this:

Firstly, the *trustworthiness* of the elderly man (*al-shaykh*) has not been established. Rather, he was an unknown personality even to the transmitter [of this report] – that is why he asked him about his name [and other matters].

---

[1] *Al-Ghaybah* by al-Ṭūsī: 254-257 / # 224.

[2] T: The name ʿAbd Allāh means, "servant of God," and thus could be a generic description of the father as opposed to a name.

Secondly, it is not known that the man was a Shīʿah individual and that he was seeking to see the Imam. But if we were, [for the sake of argument,] to grant this, then [we are still confronted with] the barrier to [reaching the] Imam. For at the end of the report, there is a prohibition. As [the transmitter relays that Muḥammad ibn ʿAbd Allāh] says:

> فلمّا قربتُ منه إذ أنا بأسود مثل الفنيق قد اعترضني فصاح بي بصوت لم أسمع أهول منه: (ما تريد عافاك الله؟)، فأرعدت ووقفت، وزال الشخص عن بصري [...]
>
> *When I came close to him, I was confronted by a black individual who was [so grand and honorable][1]. He stood in my way and called out with a voice which I have never heard as grave, saying, "What do you want, may God grant you relief?" So I was shaken and stopped; and the person disappeared from my sight [...]*

Sure, at the very end of the report, which is very lengthy, it mentions that he succeeded in seeing [the Imam].

Al-Ghaybah[2] also reports the following:

> فقال: يا أحمد رأيت طلبتك؟ فقلت: ومن ذاك يا سيّدي؟ فقال: الذي رأيته في عشيتك هو صاحب زمانك.
>
> *[In a dream, the Prophet Muḥammad] said: O Aḥmad, have you seen the one you were after?*
>
> *I said: And who is that, my master?*
>
> *He said: The one you saw in the evening is the master of your age.*

[1] T: *Mithl al-Fanīq*, Like a bull (male camel) that is neither ridden nor violated.

[2] *Al-Ghaybah* by al-Ṭūsī: 262 / # 227.

But in this report, there are unknown individuals. Moreover, it is a dream. Sure, it is plausible that he is a faithful [Shīʿah] individual, for there is a line that reads,

> فذكر أنّه مكث سبع سنين يدعو ربّه ويسأله معاينة صاحب الزمان عليه السلام
>
> *Then he mentioned that he spent seven years praying to his Lord, asking him for [an opportunity] to see the master of the age.*

Another report in *al-Ghaybah*[1] reads:

> عن حبيب بن محمّد بن يونس بن شاذان الصنعاني، قال: دخلت إلى علي بن إبراهيم بن مهزيار الأهوازي فسألته عن آل أبي محمّد عليه السلام، فقال: يا أخي لقد سألت عن أمر عظيم، حججت عشرين حجّة كلاً أطلب به عيان الإمام فلم أجد إلى ذلك سبيلاً.
>
> *It has been reported that Ḥabīb ibn Muḥammad ibn Yūnus ibn Shādhān al-Ṣanʿānī said: I entered into the place of ʿAlī ibn Ibrāhīm ibn Mahziyār al-Ahwāzī and then I asked him about the progeny of Abū Muḥammad, [that is, Imam Ḥasan al-ʿAskarī]. He replied, "My brother, you have asked about a grave matter. I performed the pilgrimage for twenty years, in all of which I would request to see the Imam, but I found no means of doing so."*

In his *Muʿjam Rijāl al-Ḥadīth*[2], the scholarly investigator[3] Sayyid al-Khūʾī has said:

> [الرواية] ضعيفة السند جدّاً على [أنّها متعارضة] من جهة نسبة القصّة إلى علي بن إبراهيم بن مهزيار، أو إلى إبراهيم بن مهزيار، والله العالم

---

1 *Al-Ghaybah* by al-Ṭūsī: 262 / # 228.

2 See: *Muʿjam Rijāl al-Ḥadīth* 12:212.

3 T: al-Muḥaqqiq.

> *[The report's] chain of transmission is seriously unreliable. Moreover, there is a conflict regarding the attribution of the story, [with one account attributing it] to ʿAlī ibn Ibrāhīm ibn Mahziyār and [the other] to Ibrāhīm ibn Mahziyār. God knows [what the reality of the matter is].*

Another report appears in both *al-Ghaybah* and *al-Iḥtijāj*[1], which goes as follows:

> قال: طلبت هذا الأمر طلباً شاقّاً حتّى ذهب لي فيه مال صالح، فوقعتُ ــ أي ذهبتُ ــ إلى العَمْري وخدمته ولزمته وسألته بعد ذلك عن صاحب الزمان عليه السلام؛
>
> *He said: I sought out this matter with such an exhaustive seeking, until much of my wealth was spent in this way. So I went to al-ʿAmrī, served him, remained [in his company] and then later asked him about the master of the age.*

The argument using this report points out "this" [matter] as referring to seeing the master of the age.

But the argument is flawed. For as the account is relayed in *al-Wasāʾil*[2]:

> أنّه طلب من العمري أن يوصله إلى صاحب الزمان عليه السلام فأوصله، وذكر أنّه سأله فأجابه عن كلّ ما أراد، ثمّ قام ودخل الدار، قال: فذهبت لأسأل فلم يستمع [...]
>
> *He requested of al-ʿAmrī to bring him to the master of the age. So [al-ʿAmrī] brought him to [the master of the age]. He mentioned that he asked [the Imam] and he answered*

---

[1] *Al-Ghaybah* by al-Ṭūsī: 271 / # 236; *al-Iḥtijāj* 2:298; In the latter, "a panacea [sort of] seeking (ṭalaban shāfiyan)," [appears] instead of, "an exhaustive seeking (ṭalaban shāqqan)."

[2] *Wasāʾil al-Shīʿah* / Āl al-Bayt 4:201 / Ḥ (4919/7).

> *his questions about all that which he wished, then he rose and entered the home. [The transmitter of the report then] said: So I went to ask, but he would not listen [to further questions]*[1] *[…]*

This report's chain of transmission is missing some link(s)[2] and its accounts are conflicting. Furthermore, the [fact that the] Imam prohibited [the transmitter,] al-Zuhrī, is a better support for our claim.

In the book *Kamāl al-Dīn*[3], the following report is relayed:

> فسألته _ أي محمّد بن شاذان سأل الكابلي _ عن خبره فذكر أنّه لم يزل في الطلب وأنّه أقام بالمدينة فكان لا يذكره لأحدٍ إلاّ زجره، فلقي شيخاً من بني هاشم وهو يحيى بن محمّد العريضي، فقال له: إنّ الذي تطلبه بصرياء، قال: فقصدت صرياء فجئت إلى دهليز مرشوش، وطرحت نفسي على الدكّان فخرج إليّ غلام أسود فزجرني وانتهرني، وقال لي: قم من هذا المكان وانصرف [...]
>
> *I asked him [meaning, Muḥammad ibn Shādhān asked al-Kābulī] about his news. So he mentioned that he was still seeking him out, that he settled in Medina, and whenever he would mention him to someone, the person would rebuke him. [At one point,] he met an elderly man (shaykh) from the Hāshimite clan, Yaḥyá ibn Muḥammad al-ʿUrayḍī, and the latter told him, "Indeed, the one you seek is in Ṣaryāʾ*[4]*." [al-Kābulī] said: So I headed out toward*

---

[1] T: Fa lam yastamiʿ […]

[2] T: *Marfūʿ*; a report attributed to someone without a complete chain of transmission to the supposed source.

[3] *Kamāl al-Dīn*: 440 / Bāb 43 / Ḥ 6.

[4] T: According to Ibn Shahrʾāshūb, Ṣaryā[ʾ] is a village, founded by Imam Mūsá al-Kaẓīm, about three miles (in their unit system) outside Medina at the time. Ibn Shahrʾāshūb, *Manāqib Āl Abī Ṭālib*, vol. 4, 414.

> *Ṣaryā*ʾ, *came to an entryway that had been sprayed*[1] *and threw myself onto the bench*[2]. *A black young man came out to me, cautioned and reprimanded me, and said, "Rise out of this place and leave." […]*

The argument uses this report because of the phrase, "he was still seeking him out." However, this is a flawed argument because the Imam described the person as a liar in the very same report.

Another report is relayed in the book *al-Nujūm*, as accounted in *al-Biḥār*[3],

> قال: كنت قد سألت مولانا المهدي صلوات الله عليه أن يأذن لي في أن أكون ممَّن يشرَّف بصحبته وخدمته، في وقت غيبته، أسوة بمن يخدمه من عبيده وخاصَّته.
>
> *He said: I had asked our master, the Mahdī, to grant me permission to be among those who are honored by accompanying and serving him during the time of his ghaybah, similar to those servants and [members of his] inner circle who serve him.*

In addition to the unreliability of this report's chain of transmission, the following might be said to refute the claim. Indeed, the servants and [members of his] inner circle who serve him might not know the Imam's identity. [So they might see him without knowing they are seeing the

---

[1] T: Dihlīz marshūsh; a passage or corridor, which in this case is described as "sprayed (marshūsh)." Assuming "marshūsh" is not meant to be a proper noun for a specific entryway, but is rather an adjective describing that this particular entryway was washed recently, the description likely functions as an explanation for stopping at this spot (e.g. there is someone who has used water recently there who can be asked for further directions or the like). There are also other possibilities to consider.

[2] T: al-Dukkān.

[3] *Biḥār al-Anwār* 52:54 / Bāb Dhikr man raʾāhu ṣalawāt Allāh ʿalayh / Ḥ 38.

Mahdī]. Since the man requested that, [to be among the servants], it is not proof that [he will see the Imam while knowing the person as the Imam].

There may be other reports of this caliber of unreliability as well, and this remains an *incomplete survey*[1]. God knows [the reality of the matter].

[When it comes to reports attributed to the Prophet and the Divinely appointed Imams], there are reports,, including supplications, such as the following, as well as other noble supplications:

> اللّهمّ أرني الطلعة الرشيدة، والغرة الحميدة، وأكحل مرهي[2] بنظرة منّي إليه [...]
>
> *O God [please do] show me the magnificent countenance and the praiseworthy forehead, and [delight my eyes] by letting me have a look at him [...]*[3]

With regard to such supplications, their *apparent meaning* is unqualified. Hence, it encompasses the time of *ghaybah* as well as the time of public accessibility. However, it is possible that such expressions are *kināyāt*, referring to the request to be honored to be under his banner and part of his campaign, even if only as part of the *return from the dead*[4]. It could also mean, "Show me the person [of the Imam], even if I am not acquainted with his identity [when I see him]," for this is also among the highest forms of excellence. It could also mean a prayer for removing the *barrier* [which prevents seeing the Imam].

---

[1] T: *al-Istiqrā' al-nāqiṣ*; Incomplete/imperfect induction; inexhaustive survey.

[2] *Marihat al-'ayn marahan*: [*Marihat* is a verb describing an eye that has deteriorated due to abandoning kohl and attributing kohl to the noun *marah* is figurative. Alternatively, the noun *marah* is being used to describe an eye characterized by *marah*, figuratively.] In some versions, it reads, "wa akḥil nāẓirī," [i.e. "eye (nāzir)" instead of, "marah."]

[3] *Al-Miṣbāḥ* by al-Kaf'amī: 551; *Biḥār al-Anwār* 83:285 / Ḥ 47.

[4] T: *Raj'ah*; The return to life on earth after death; different from the final resurrection for the Day of Judgment.

The aforementioned has made it clear that the practical striving for and travel to different countries, traversing mountains and valleys, in order to meet with the beloved and be honored to see him is not a [Divinely] desirable matter. Rather, it may even be said that it is forbidden, as we discussed in the beginning of the chapter. We can also say the following: In our course of investigating the process of the community's connection to its leadership for the resolution of its problems during the time of the immaculate Imams, especially the time of [Imam Muḥammad] al-Jawād, [Imam ʿAlī] al-Hādī, and [Imam Ḥasan] al-ʿAskarī, it did not become apparent to us that they [i.e. the Imams] used to prefer in-person meetings. This was either because there existed a *barrier* [of some sort] or because they wanted [to give room for] the community's preparation for the *ghaybah* phenomenon. In light of this, we find that, in their own time, they established the ideas of *deputyship* and *agency*, or at least activated them. *The two Imams* ([i.e. Imam ʿAlī] al-Hādī and [Imam Ḥasan] al-ʿAskarī), especially while they were in Samarra, worked to deeply entrench the system of *agency*. The political, social and economic systems' pyramid was founded and based on the *agency* system. Rather, the system of *agency* and *deputyship* was in use during the time of the earlier Imams as well (due to political terrorism, imprisonment and the spread of the Shīʿah over different regions that were mostly distant from the Imams). Sure, this system became elaborate and took on a new dimension after preparing for the *ghaybah*, and the limited access to the later Imams. For al-Ṭūsī has relayed a report by Muḥammad ibn ʿĪsá, in which he said,

> كتب أبو الحسن العسكري عليه السلام إلى الموالي ببغداد والمدائن والسواد وما يليها: (قد أقمتُ أبا علي بن راشد مقام علي بن الحسين بن عبد ربّه، ومن قبله من وكلائي...
>
> *Abū al-Ḥasan al-ʿAskarī [i.e. the tenth Imam, ʿAlī al-Hādī] wrote to the supporters (mawālī) in Baghdad, al-Madāʾin, and [the rural areas]*[1] *and their surroundings, "I have*

[1] T: al-Sawād.

appointed Abū ʿAlī ibn Rāshid in the station of ʿAlī ibn al-Ḥusayn ibn ʿAbd Rabbih and his predecessors among my agents [...][1]

In another report, [the transmitter of the report mentions that Abū ʿAlī, Aḥmad ibn Isḥāq, asked Imam ʿAlī al-Hādī],

مَن أعامل أو عمَّن آخذ، وقول مَن أقبل؟

Who do I deal with or who should I take [knowledge/news] from, and whose word should I take?

[Imam ʿAlī al-Hādī] replied,

العمري ثقتي فما أدّى إليك عنّي فعنّي يؤدّي وما قال لك عنّي فعنّي يقول، فاسمع له وأطع، فإنّه الثقة المأمون

Al-ʿAmrī is my trusted [point of contact]; so what he delivers to you, on my behalf, he is [indeed], on my behalf, delivering [it]; and what he says to you, on my behalf, he is [indeed], on my behalf, saying [it]; so listen to him and obey, for indeed he is the trustworthy, fail-safe[2].

[The transmitter then] mentions Abū ʿAlī asking Abū Muḥammad, [that is, Imam Ḥasan al-ʿAskarī], a similar question. In response, [Imam Ḥasan al-ʿAskarī] said to him,

العمري وابنه ثقتان، فما أدّيا إليك عنّي فعنّي يؤدّيان وما قالا لك فعنّي يقولان، فاسمع لهما وأطعهما فإنّهما الثقتان المأمونان

Al-ʿAmrī and his son are two trustworthy individuals; so what they deliver to you, on my behalf, they are [indeed], on my behalf, delivering [it]; and what they say to you, on my behalf, they are [indeed], on my behalf, saying [it]; so

---

1 *Al-Ghaybah* by al-Ṭūsī: 350 / # 309.

2 T: al-Maʾmūn.

listen to them and obey them, for indeed they are the trustworthy, fail-safe.[1]

In the report of Muḥammad ibn ʿĪsá and Ḥasan ibn ʿAlī ibn Yaqṭīn, both relay an exchange with [Imam ʿAlī] al-Riḍā:

قال: قلت: جُعلت فداك إنّي لا أكاد أصل إليك أسألك عن كلّ ما أحتاج إليه من معالم ديني، أفيونس بن عبد الرحمن ثقة آخذ عنه ما أحتاج إليه من معالم ديني؟

فقال: (نعم)

[The transmitter] said, "May I be sacrificed for your sake; indeed, I am not able to reach you at all times in order to ask you about all that which I need [to know] regarding the guideposts of my religion. So is Yūnus ibn ʿAbd al-Raḥmān a trustworthy [reference] for taking what I need regarding the guideposts of my religion?" Then [Imam ʿAlī al-Riḍā] said, "Yes."[2]

It has also been reported that ʿAbd al-ʿAzīz ibn al-Muhtadī said the following to [Imam ʿAlī] al-Riḍā:

إنَّ شُقتي بعيدة فلست أصِلُ إليك في كلّ وقت، فآخذ معالم ديني عن يونس مولى آل يقطين؟

Indeed, my [travel coming here] is long-distance, so I am not able to reach you at all times. Should I take the guideposts of my religion from Yūnus [ibn ʿAbd al-Raḥmān], the mawlá[3] *of the Yaqṭīn family?*

---

[1] *Al-Kāfī* 1:330 / Bāb fī Tasmiyati Man Raʾāh / Ḥ 1.

[2] *Ikhtiyār Maʿrifat al-Rijāl* 2:784 / Ḥ 935.

[3] T: This word can mean different things depending on the context. In this context, it likely refers to a freedman.

[Imam al-Riḍā] replied, "Yes."[1]

Moreover, it has been reported that ʿAlī ibn al-Musayyab al-Hamadānī said:

قلت للرضا عليه السلام: شقتي بعيدة فلست أصل إليك في كلّ وقت فممّن آخذ معالم ديني؟ قال: (من زكريا بن آدم القمي المأمون على الدين والدنيا)

I asked [Imam ʿAlī] al-Riḍā, saying, "My [travel coming here] is long-distance, so I am not able to reach you at all times. Who should I take the guideposts of my religion from?" [Imam ʿAlī al-Riḍā] replied, "From Zakarīyah ibn Ādam al-Qummī, the fail-safe[2] *[when it comes to matters of] religion as well as the worldly life."*[3]

Moreover, it has been reported that Isḥāq ibn Yaʿqūb has relayed the following:

سألت محمّد بن عثمان العمري رضي الله عنه أن يوصل لي كتاباً قد سألت فيه عن مسائل أشكلت عليّ، فورد التوقيع بخطّ مولانا صاحب الزمان عليه السلام: (أمّا ما سألت عنه أرشدك الله وثبّتك...) إلى أن قال: (وأمّا الحوادث الواقعة فارجعوا فيها إلى رواة حديثنا..

I asked [the second deputy], Muḥammad ibn ʿUthmān al-ʿAmrī, may God be pleased with him, to deliver a letter [to the Imam – a letter] in which I had asked about [several] matters that had stumped me. Then the signed document[4] *[response] came, written in the handwriting of our master, the master of the age, stating, "As for what you asked about, may God guide you and keep you steadfast [...] As*

---

1 *Wasāʾil al-Shīʿah* /al-Islāmīyah 18:107 / Bāb 11 / Ḥ 35.

2 T: al-Maʾmūn.

3 *Al-Ikhtiṣāṣ*: 87.

4 T: al-Tawqīʿ.

> *for the events*[1] *that occur, refer*[2] *– concerning them – to the transmitters of our ḥadīth [...]*[3]

Hence, the phenomenon of referring to the legal scholars did not begin [only] following the *minor ghaybah.* Rather, scientific investigation reveals that this phenomenon existed in the earlier ages and [during the times of] the earlier Imams. Moreover, this matter was deeply ingrained within the minds [of Muslims who recited the Qur᾽ān, at least], due to the Qur᾽ānic teachings in this regard. For example, God Almighty says:

وَما كانَ الْمُؤمِنونَ لِيَنفِروا كافَّةً ۚ فَلَولا نَفَرَ مِن كُلِّ فِرقَةٍ مِنهُم طائِفَةٌ لِيَتَفَقَّهوا فِي الدّينِ وَلِيُنذِروا قَومَهُم إِذا رَجَعوا إِلَيهِم لَعَلَّهُم يَحذَرونَ

> *Yet it is not for the faithful to go forth en masse. But why should not there go forth a group from each of their sections to become learned in religion, and to warn their people when they return to them, so that they may beware?*[4]

The question was, rather, about the identity of the trustworthy individual to refer back to. The fact that the Shīʿah asked this question confirms that the Shīʿah were not satisfied with a *default principle* of taking things [too] lightly[5] when it came to their referring back to and following individuals. Indeed, investigation is what ensures that a person can become relieved of

---

[1] T: *Ḥawādith*; Events; occurrences; things that come up, etc.

[2] T: *Irjiʿū;* Refer (in the imperative form); this is etymologically related to the contemporary term *marjiʿ* which is used to designate a leading Grand Ayatollah, for he is the individual who people refer to.

[3] *Kamāl al-Dīn*: 483-484 / Bāb 45 / Ḥ 4.

[4] Quran 9:122

[5] T: *al-Tasāmuḥ*; In this context, having too much tolerance for error, lacking the appropriate seriousness for what is at stake.

the religious legal responsibility, arriving at the shores of safety and clearing their conscience.

In any case, seeing the Imam, witnessing his appearance, in principle, in and of itself, is a [form of] excellence, even if it does not mean that the one who sees [him] is better than others or that he or she is his trustworthy [point of contact] and that his or her word is authoritative. This is the meaning of there being an entire *reason*[1] for excellence [in seeing the Imam]. The generalities [understood from various pieces of evidence] in this regard suffice us [to make this point]. Examples include seeing an erudite sage[2], the Kaʿbah, the Qur'ān or a faithful individual.[3] [At the same time, the notion of] seeking out [the opportunity] to see [the Imam] – in the sense of the practical pursuit discussed earlier – had not issued from the scholarly, the virtuous, and those of piety and reason. Furthermore, *the practice of practicing individuals*[4] is to join [the Imam], coming under his banner, without the necessity of seeking out [an opportunity] to see him. Rather, what matters is to gain his approval, to be acquainted with his goal, to accomplish his mission, and to fully apply oneself in preparing the prerequisite steps leading up to his public appearance, such as mastering oneself[5], spreading the religion and mending the world. Sure, if seeing [the Imam] is considered the inevitable corollary of these prerequisites, then there is no issue with it.

As for reported supplications and acts of worship that [are described as] entailing the [opportunity] to see the Imam, what is meant by them – based on the *apparent meaning* – is the honor of meeting him. Some of the friends

---

[1] T: *Tamām al-muqtaḍī*; The completeness of the acting component of the complete cause.

[2] T: *ʿĀlim*.

[3] T: Meaning, there are reports that consider seeing these individuals/things to be meritorious/forms of worship.

[4] T: *Sīrat al-Mutasharriʿah*.

[5] T: Tahdhīb al-nafs.

of God[1], not only the most excellent [among them], have indeed seen [the Imam]. But it is not necessarily the case that whoever saw [the Imam] is the best. It is also necessary to pay attention to the difference between *seeking out* [an opportunity] to see [the Imam] and the *occurrence* of seeing [the Imam]. If we were to accept that seeing [the Imam] – without qualification – in all circumstances and for all individuals, is a [praiseworthy] distinction and [form of] excellence, then it would have been a [form of] excellence attributed to everyone who was with the Prophet Muḥammad or the other Imams. This is similar to the theory about *the probity of the companions*[2], adopted by others [of different schools of thought, not the Shīʿah. The Shīʿah reject this because] companionship as well seeing [the Imam] are [praiseworthy] distinctions when certain conditions and stipulations [are met] – and in light of those conditions, [not just the fact of companionship or seeing]. Their case is like the case of the verses in which God Almighty says:

يا نِساءَ النَّبِيِّ مَن يَأتِ مِنكُنَّ بِفاحِشَةٍ [...]

يا نِساءَ النَّبِيِّ لَستُنَّ كَأَحَدٍ مِنَ النِّساءِ ۚ إِنِ اتَّقَيتُنَّ [...]

> *O wives of the Prophet! Whosoever among you commits a flagrant indecency, [...]*
>
> *O wives of the Prophet! You are not like any other women if you are wary [of God] [...]*[3]

Moreover, when dealing with a claimant, the *default principle* [when in doubt] is not to believe him or her, not to accept his or her claim, especially if it would profit the claimant – that is, if it would create substantial results for the claimant's way, method, or personal project. This includes most of those who claim to have

---

[1] T: *al-Awliyāʾ*.

[2] T: *ʿAdālat al-ṣaḥābah*; Assuming the trustworthiness of all [the Prophet Muḥammad's] companions by default.

[3] Qurʾān 33:30-32.

seen [the Imam] – the default principle in that regard should be not to believe him or her. For it cannot possibly be valid to prove the rightfulness of one's school of thought by means of seeing [the inaccessible Imam] and meeting with him, as some Ṣūfīs claim in order to prove the rightfulness of their issues.

SUMMARY

Thus, the following matters are revealed:

1. Seeking out [the opportunity] to see [the Imam], in the sense of actively pursuing it, during the *ghaybah* age is not preferable, because there exists a *barrier.* Moreover, there is a difference between *seeking out* [an opportunity] to see [the Imam] and the external *occurrence* of seeing [the Imam]. Furthermore, we do not grant that there exists a corollary relationship between the external *occurrence* of seeing [the Imam] and the person seeing [the Imam] becoming more virtuous in terms of knowledge and piety.

2. The *default principle* is not to accept the claim of someone claiming to have seen [the Imam], unless it is established with decisive sureness[1] and assurance[2].

3. It is possible to accept the claim of having seen and witnessed [the Imam] after establishing testaments [indicating the truth of it, presented] to someone who does not take such a claim for granted, and provided [that the person making the claim] is void of personal motivations, [someone who is] concerned only with confirming the existence of the Imam.

4. The [impact on the] scope of one claiming to have seen [the Imam] must not go beyond personal, external matters; [the scope must] not include fateful decisions. Rather, the practice of the early

---

[1] T: al-Qaṭʿ.

[2] T: al-Iṭmiʾnān.

predecessors among our fellow [Shīʿah] was [to limit the scope] as such.

Had Ahl al-Bayt approved the approach [of having no limits to the scope of impact], then they would have endorsed it, especially since the issue is such a central and substantial one. Rather, the opposite is the case, for [they] activated the phenomenon of general *agency*. Furthermore, it has been reported that the one who claims to have seen [the Imam] is to be deemed a liar, [if such a claim is] in the following manner: Seeing [the Imam] is framed as a legitimate proof of an idea, legal position, political endorsement or the like. For it has been reported [that Imam Mahdī said],

وسيأتي شيعتي من يدّعي المشاهدة، ألا فمن ادّعى المشاهدة قبل خروج السفياني والصيحة فهو كاذب مفتر

> *There will come to my Shīʿah those who claim to have witnessed my appearance [in such a manner that conflicts with the major ghaybah period]. So, indeed, whoever claims to have witnessed my appearance [in such a sense] before the mobilization of the Sufyānī and the outcry*[1] *is a liar, a fabricator.*[2]

---

[1] T: *al-Ṣayḥah*; believed to be a distinct call made by the Angel Gabriel, testifying to the truth regarding the Mahdī's identity.

[2] *Kamāl al-Dīn*: 516 / Bāb 45 / Ḥ 44.

T: The prevalent reading of this report in the Twelver Shīʿah community is that it arguably does not conflict with the possibility of seeing the Imam. For the notion of "claiming to witness" in this report has been understood as making the claim of being a *specifically appointed deputy* of the hidden Imam, which would conflict with the *major ghaybah* period before the official end of the *major ghaybah* (which would be known by the *signs* that precede it, some of which are noted in this report). As for seeing the Imam, without making such a claim to *specifically appointed deputyship*, or any other issue, that would not be impossible/forbidden by this report.

5. There is no doubt that there is a cause for the subsistence of the Shīʿah school of thought. For this school of thought has endured throughout this long duration of the *ghaybah* age until this very day. But history does not record this cause of subsistence as being those who claim to have seen [the Imam]. Rather, history records that the Shīʿah school of thought has subsisted thanks to the efforts of legal scholars such as al-Kulaynī, al-Ṭūsī, al-Murtaḍá, al-ʿAllāmah [al-Ḥillī] and al-Shahīd [Muḥammad ibn Makkī], who followed the path of the Imams – that is, the appointment [of the legal scholars] and reference back to them as *general deputies*[1] [not *specifically appointed deputies*].

6. There exists a unanimous[2] position, in word and in action, when it comes to disregarding the claim of the one who claims to have seen [the Imam, in the sense that conflicts with the *major ghaybah*]. This *ijmāʿ* reveals that the precise, practical position [to be taken] is so, and that the practice of the scholars has been to [not take seriously][3] those who claim to have seen [the Imam] and [who by doing so] wish to prove fateful matters. The answer [of the scholars to such claimants] has been, "Peace!"[4]

7. Had the approach of seeing and witnessing the appearance [of the Imam] been taken for characterizing important matters, it would entail [disorder and chaos][5]. For there are many claimants and they contradict one another. It is noteworthy that most of those [claimants] have unknown histories and, furthermore, some of them have dark histories. Examining the behavior of such individuals is worthy of [further] contemplation. Indeed, the goal

---

[1] T: *al-Niyābah al-ʿāmmah*; General deputyship.

[2] T: *Iṭbāq*.

[3] T: al-Istihānah.

[4] T: Likely a reference to how one is commanded to address the ignorant in Qurʾān 25:63.

[5] T: al-Harj wa al-marj.

adopted by the proponents of these deviant paths has been to separate the community from the legal scholars – [the legal scholars] who, we have reaffirmed, are the way [to go, as reference points] endorsed by Ahl al-Bayt before and after the *ghaybah*.

With this matter clear, [one must recognize that] to follow the deviants who claim to have seen [the Imam, without proof,] is not acceptable. For God Almighty says,

وَقِفُوهُمْ ۖ إِنَّهُم مَّسْئُولُونَ

And stop them. Surely, they are to be questioned.[1]

8. Spreading a culture of misinformation in some uneducated societies and/or societies that are disconnected from authentic Islamic education for a time due to political and despotic reasons and circumstances plaguing them – such a culture [of misinformation] becomes a cause for hallucination in the minds of some naïve individuals. Thus, they make claims and become followed. Moreover, it becomes a cause for some behavior that is not authorized by legitimate legal evidence, and that entails harming the Shīʿah school of thought and insulting its glory. For a culture of darkness, one without foundations, provides its carrier with a share in incomplete knowledge and this education may lead its carrier to some social positions and expand his or her sphere of influence on the public masses. This is because the community, in its makeup, is subject to different considerations in terms of [its members'] awareness, [their] comprehension, and [their] education level. The community is influenced by many notions without delving into the background, objectives, and dimensions of those notions. Rather, the community innocently[2] gets carried away behind things that are prepackaged, without discussing and analyzing [them].

---

[1] Qurʾān 37:24.

[2] T: *Bi shakl ʿafwī*, Automatically; naturally; spontaneously; intuitively.

Thus, the criterion for accepting a cultural understanding is to subject it to rational considerations, logical rules, principles of scientific research, and measures for distinguishing right from wrong. Otherwise, the corollary will be the absence of truth – something which runs up against innate intuition, logic, law, and conscience, and is unacceptable by one who has even the least share of knowledge. Therefore, having a "filter," a safety valve, is necessary. For the measure of any [system of] thought is its resilience in the face of scientific critique and its possession of scientific[1] components. Abundance in numbers is of no avail; neither are social and political realities. If one lives [in a state of] ignorance and distance from true Islamic education, then the measure [of what is right] is determined by referring to the one with the specialized and experienced [knowledge of the relevant] scientific qualification, the one who has well-established standing in research, analysis, and transcending subjective whims[2]. For [the one with the] qualification is the scientific and practical benchmark for distinguishing [right from wrong in such matters of specialization] – not the one who takes [the topic] up at a distance, far from observation[3] and critique.

---

[1] T: Scientific in the sense that includes all fields of knowledge approached systematically.

[2] T: al-Tajarrud ʿan al-ahwāʾ.

[3] T: *al-Murāqabah*; Oversight; being closely monitored. In this context, it is likely referring to the *ḥawzah* scholarly community's close watch over its members' intellectual and ethical lives, being held accountable by fellow members of the scholarly community.

CHAPTER 6

PUZZLEMENT (*ḤAYRAH*) AND ABSENCE (*GHAYBAH*)

It has been reported that the Commander of the Faithful, [that is Imam ʿAlī], said,

تكون له ـ أي للمهدي ـ غيبة وحيرة، يضلُّ فيها أقوام

> *In relation to him, [the Mahdī, that is], there will be an absence (ghaybah) and a puzzlement (ḥayrah), in which [some] groups of people will go astray [...]*[1]

So what is meant by the said puzzlement (*ḥayrah*)?

Is the puzzlement with regard to religious beliefs due to an intellectual vacuum in the community? Or is the puzzlement regarding Imam Mahdī, meaning that the long duration of his *ghaybah* leads people to fall into doubt and disagreement pertaining to him? Or is the puzzlement with regard to the destiny of the world? Or is the puzzlement regarding the dominance of oppressors and people of falsehood, and losing hope of Divine support?

Why does the *ghaybah* entail puzzlement and going astray?

The *ghaybah* phenomenon is a new condition, one not familiar to the general Muslim population – even though the Qurʾān has trained [the mind of its careful readers] in this regard. Belief in the existence of an Imam, coupled with the belief that he is in a state of *ghaybah*, gives the false impression of [the Imam being characterized by] inactivity. Hence, awareness and sufficient knowledge is required in order for the puzzlement

---

[1] *Al-Kāfī* 1:338 / Bāb fī al-Ghaybah / Ḥ 7.

to dissipate. The longer the duration [of the *ghaybah*], the more the ambiguity increases. This is especially the case if the issue is surrounded by contributing factors such as the [relative] secrecy of [the Imam's] birth, the unfamiliar extended duration of the *ghaybah*, the complete disconnection [of accessibility to him during the *major ghaybah*], the early age of commencing his Imāmah role, the [relative] secrecy and uncertainty[1] regarding his mother's name, [the fact that] the Divine blessings bestowed upon him surpass the Divine blessings bestowed upon prophets and messengers, and that the accomplishment he will achieve surpasses the work of prophets. All of these and other matters lead to ambiguity and difficulty in accepting [the notion of the Imam in a state of *ghaybah*], especially in light of the fact that we are living in a time in which it is difficult to accept forms of knowledge dealing with the metaphysical and the Unseen[2].

However, we respond with the following: Indeed, every phenomenon we confront for the first time requires us to conceptualize and comprehend its components and modes. Because the human mind is skeptical, we require clear proof to be established. This is especially so because the *default principle* of *theoretical* and *practical reason* calls for investigation and not outrightly denying matters merely out of considering them odd or improbable. Reason's sense perception finds the existence of a world beyond the world of death to be improbable and rejects [the notions of] the

---

[1] T: Taraddud; hesitation in deciding between a number of possibilities. This is not to say that the mother's name was unknown by some but the fact that multiple names have been attributed to her gives the impression of uncertainty regarding her actual name. Of course, the uncertainty arises based on the assumption that only one name/title can apply to the mother. But that assumption is disputed -- perhaps the same mother was known by multiple names and titles, even if only for the purpose of maintaining the relative secrecy of her son's birth.

[2] T: *Ghaybīyah*; Hidden; beyond the physical senses or otherwise present but unrecognized.

resurrection[1] and the reckoning[2]. But there mere [fact of] ambiguity and obscurity pertaining to that which lies beyond this world does not call for [passing a judgment of] denial on reason's part. Rather, one must confront the epistemic channels appropriate to this piece of information until the fallaciousness or soundness of this proposition is revealed.[3] Similarly, reason's sense perception does not realize the necessity of having a *ḥujjah* on earth and that the impact of this *ḥujjah* is an impact on the [order of the] universe.

Has human reason's sense perception managed to comprehend the phenomenon of revelation or the existence of beings such as angels, jinn, and other worlds that are not subject to sense perception? Indeed, these examples and others are deemed improbable by the verdict of reason's sense perception, but not by abstract reason[4].

THE ESSENTIAL COMPONENTS OF THE MAHDĪ IDEA

In this light, we say the following. The Mahdī idea consists of a number of essential components:

1. The Mahdī, his features, attributes, and accomplishments.
2. The *ghaybah* (the *minor* [*ghaybah*] as well as the *major* [*ghaybah*]).

---

[1] T: *al-Nushūr.*

[2] T: *al-Ḥisāb.*

[3] T: This is not to say that one will never reach a point of uncertainty despite investigating thoroughly. If that occurs, one would be prudent to suspend judgment if precaution is, otherwise, not possible. However, the author's point is to fall back on the *default principle* of investigating and covering one's grounds properly before rushing to *any* conclusions. Apparently, this includes even the "conclusion" of inconclusiveness (i.e. the resolution to suspend judgment), at least in some cases with serious consequences.

[4] T: *al-ʿAql al-tajarrudī.*

3. The birth [of the Mahdī], the duration of the *ghaybah*, the unknown timing [of his public appearance], and the hidden personal identity [of the Mahdī].

The hesitant and the skeptical regarding the likes of these matters, and even the deniers [of these matters], do not claim that these phenomena are impossible, that they cannot be. Rather, they claim that there is no proof that they are a reality. Regarding these three matters, we say the following.

First: The Mahdī, his Features, Attributes, and Accomplishments

The reports are *mutawātir* about [the Mahdī, his features, attributes and accomplishments]. Surveying the vast quantity of [relevant] reports makes us concede that the Mahdī reality is an Islamic (if not also a [more generally] religious and innately intuitive) reality. These reports have discussed the distinct features of the Mahdī and his capabilities. Moreover, books that include discussions on the Mahdī have been written, such as *Ḥilyat al-Awliyāʾ* by Abū Naʿīm al-Iṣbahānī, *Sunan Abī Dāwūd*, the book *Āl Muḥammad* by Shaykh Ḥusām al-Dīn al-Murdī, *Sunan al-Tirmidhī*, the book *al-Fitan*, *Sunan Ibn Mājah*, and others.

Therefore, there is no room to apply expert skill in [a way that is in] opposition to the explicit text [revealed by God or spoken by the Divine representative]. [There is no room] to object by saying: Why would the community that did not heed [the prescriptions of] the prophets heed [the prescriptions of] the Mahdī? For there is an explicit text, in terms of its chain of transmission as well as its indication, that describes the one who carries out this grand and grave matter as the Mahdī. The [fact that the] prophets could not carry out this role does not entail that the Mahdī is prevented from doing so – the explicit text [revealed by God or spoken by the Divine representative] confirms it.

Sure, there is an [insignificant] slice[1] of scholars who denied the Mahdī [as an actual individual] due to *misconceptions in the face of intuitive notions*[2]. For example, they adopted some sociological theories that are not harmonious with the universal idea of a savior, or they interpreted the Mahdī phenomenon as a social phenomenon, not to be carried out by an individual. [Another reason why they denied the Mahdī is] because some ill-intentioned individuals exploited the Mahdī name for worldly aims; the governors of the ʿAbbāsid dynasty even sought to bestow some legitimacy and holiness upon themselves, so they gave their children names reserved for the Mahdī. However, even a quick review of the reports leads one to reject those theories, for the reports identify the Mahdī as the son of a given person, as having given personal features, and so on and so forth.

Moreover, if it comes to the point that one would be skeptical even of this vast quantity of reports, then no certainty would hold its ground regarding any *necessarily established* religious truth, doubt would seep into every phenomenon, and the end result would be skepticism and denial regarding all religious truths and notions taken for granted[3]. In addition, the underlying infrastructure denying these reports rests on *positivist theories*[4] that are of unknown validity. Even granting their validity, [for argument's sake], are they general and comprehensive enough to encompass all phenomena, including religious phenomena, or not? An *incomplete survey* alone does not establish a scientific *generality*.

---

[1] T: Shirdhimah.

[2] T: Shubuhāt fī muqābil al-badīhīyāt.

[3] T: al-Musallamāt (sing. al-musallam).

[4] T: Naẓarīyāt waḍʿīyah. The word "waḍʿī" can translate to "positive" (as in positive law, law established by human authority), or "positivist" (as in an empiricist approach to knowledge). The author is apparently using the phrase "naẓarīyāt waḍʿīyah" here to refer not only to secular, but to fallible, theories, whose validity is neither known to be conclusive/generalizable, empirically, nor endorsed by Divine revelation.

Second: The Ghaybah

The believers at the very beginning of the *ghaybah* were not surprised by the *ghaybah* phenomenon – let alone the believers of later generations. Rather, the *ghaybah* is [the natural expectation] based on the reports of [words by] Prophet Muḥammad and the Imams – the key to knowledge and proof.

For it has been reported that the most honorable Messenger said,

تكون له غيبة وحيرة حتّى تضلّ الخلق عن أديانهم

> *In relation to him, [the Mahdī, that is], there will be an absence (ghaybah) and a puzzlement (ḥayrah), in which [some] people will go astray from their religions [...]*[1]

Moreover, it has been reported that the Commander of the Faithful said,

تكون له غيبة وحيرة يضلّ فيها أقوام

> *In relation to him, [the Mahdī, that is], there will be an absence (ghaybah) and a puzzlement (ḥayrah), in which [some] groups of people will go astray [...]*[2]

It has also been reported that [Imam] Ḥasan said,

من ولد أخي الحسين بن سيدة الإماء، يطيل الله عمره في غيبته

> *[...] from among the descendants of my brother Ḥusayn; the son of the [noblewoman among those in service of God]*[3]*; God extends his life during his ghaybah [...]*[4]

Moreover, it has been reported that [Imam] Ḥusayn said,

---

[1] *Al-Imāmah wa al-Tabṣirah*: 120 / Bāb fī al-Ghaybah / Ḥ 114.

[2] *Al-Kāfī* 1:338 / Bāb fī al-Ghaybah / Ḥ 7.

[3] T: Sayyidat al-Imāʾ.

[4] *Kamāl al-Dīn*: 316 / Bāb 29 / Ḥ 2.

قائم هذه الأمّة هو التاسع من ولدي وهو صاحب الغيبة

The qāʾim of this community is the ninth [generation] of my descendents; and he is the one with the ghaybah [...][1]

Furthermore, it has been reported that [Imam ʿAlī] Zayn al-ʿĀbidīn said,

القائم منّا تخفى ولادته على الناس

[As for] the qāʾim from among us, his birth will be [relatively] hidden from the people [...][2]

As for [Imam Muḥammad] al-Bāqir, it has been reported that he said,

إمام يخنس في زمانه عند انقضاء من علمه سنة ستّين ومائتين، ثمّ يبدو كالشهاب الوقّاد

An Imam who [undergoes occultation][3] *during his time, when [much accessibility to]*[4] *knowledge of him ceases, in the year two hundred and sixty [AH]. Then he will appear like a radiant star*[5].[6]

Moreover, it has been reported that [Imam Jaʿfar] al-Ṣādiq said,

إنّ لصاحب هذا الأمر غيبة فليتّق الله عبد وليتمسّك بدينه

Indeed, the master of this amr will have a ghaybah; therefore, let each servant [of God] be God-conscious[7] *and hold on to his or her religion.*[8]

---

1 *Kamāl al-Dīn*: 317 / Bāb 31 / Ḥ 2.

2 *Kamāl al-Dīn*: 322-323 / Bāb 31 / Ḥ 6.

3 T: Yakhnis.

4 T: ʿInda inqiḍāʾin min ʿilmih.

5 T: al-Shihāb al-waqqād.

6 *Kamāl al-Dīn*: 325 / Bāb 32 / Ḥ 1.

7 T: Pious, vigilant regarding one's responsibility before God.

8 *Kamāl al-Dīn*: 343 / Bāb 33 / Ḥ 25.

Furthermore, it has been reported that [Imam Mūsá] al-Kāẓim said,

إنّه لا بدَّ لصاحب هذا الأمر من غيبة

> *Indeed, it is inevitable that the master of this amr will have a ghaybah […]*[1]

As for [Imam ʿAlī] al-Riḍā, it has been reported that he said,

كأنّي بالشيعة عند فقدهم الثالث من ولدي يطلبون المرعى ولا يجدونه

> *It is as if [I see] the Shīʿah – when they lose the third [generation of Imam] from my descendants – seeking out the pasture*[2]*, but they do not find him.*

The transmitter of the report then asked, "And why is that O son of God's Messenger?"

The Imam then replied,

لأنَّ إمامهم يغيب عنهم [...]

> *Because their Imam goes into ghaybah [relative] to them […]*[3]

As for [Imam Muḥammad] al-Jawād, it has been reported that he said,

هو الذي تخفى على الناس ولادته ويغيب عنهم شخصه

> *[…] He is the one whose birth is hidden [relative] to the people and his person goes into ghaybah [relative] to them […]*[4]

---

[1] *Al-Kāfī* 1:336 / Bāb fī al-Ghaybah / Ḥ 2.

[2] T: *al-Marʿá*; This might refer to how they seek out their Imam for spiritual nourishment like sheep seeking out the feeding ground.

[3] ʿUyūn Akhbār al-Riḍā 1:247 / Ḥ 6.

[4] *Kamāl al-Dīn*: 378 / Bāb 36 / Ḥ 2.

It has been reported that someone asked [Imam Muḥammad al-Jawād], "Who is the successor after you?" In response, he said,

ابني علي، وابنا علي،

My son ʿAlī, and the two descendants of ʿAlī

Then he [lowered his head in contemplation][1], after which he said,

إنّها ستكون حيرة

Indeed, there will be a [state of] puzzlement (ḥayrah) [...][2]

As for [Imam ʿAlī] al-Hādī, it has been reported that he said,

لولا من يبقى بعد غيبة قائمكم عليه السلام من العلماء الداعين إليه والدالّين عليه والذابّين عن دينه بحجج الله والمنقذين لضعفاء عباد الله من شباك إبليس ومردته ومن فخاخ النواصب لما بقي أحد إلاّ ارتدّ عن دين الله [...]

If it were not for those among the scholars who remain after the [commencement of the] ghaybah of your Qāʾim, who call [others] to him and instruct people about him, protect his religion with the ḥujaj of God, and save the weak among the servants of God [the Shīʿah] from the nets of Satan and his followers, and from the traps of the anti-Shīʿah[3]*, then nobody would remain who had not converted from*[4] *the religion of God [...]*[5]

As for [Imam Ḥasan] al-ʿAskarī, it has been reported that he said:

---

[1] T: Aṭraqa malīyan.

[2] *Al-Ghaybah* by al-Nuʿmānī: 191 / Ḥ 36.

[3] T: *al-Nawāṣib* (sing. *al-nāṣibī*); Those who are hostile toward Ahl al-Bayt.

[4] T: Irtadda ʿan.

[5] *Al-Iḥtijāj* 1:9.

ابني محمّد هو الإمام والحجّة بعدي، من مات ولم يعرفه مات ميتة جاهلية. أمَا إنَّ له غيبة يحار فيها الجاهلون، ويهلك فيها المبطلون، ويكذب فيها الوقّاتون، ثمّ يخرج فكأنّي أنظر إلى الأعلام البيض تخفق فوق رأسه بنجف الكوفة

My son Muḥammad is the Imam and the ḥujjah after me. One who dies without being acquainted with him has died a death of ignorance. Indeed, he will have a ghaybah in which the ignorant will be puzzled, the liars will perish, and those who [claim to specify a particular date of his public appearance][1] lie. Then he will mobilize. It is as if I can see the white flags fluttering above his head in the Najaf of Kūfah.[2]

This is all in addition to those who reported the *Ark ḥadīth*[3], *the safety for the people of earth* reports[4], the *one who dies without being acquainted*

[1] T: al-Waqqātūn (sing. al-waqqāt).

[2] *Kamāl al-Dīn*: 409 / Ḥ 9.

[3] The Messenger of God has said,

إنّما مثل أهل بيتي فيكم مثل سفينة نوح من ركب فيها نجى ومن تخلّف عنها غرق

The analogy of my Ahl al-Bayt among you is like the ark of Noah – those who got on board survived and those who fell behind drowned.

Baṣāʾir al-Darajāt: 317 / Bāb 13 / Ḥ 4.

[4] It has been reported that ʿAlī quoted the Messenger of God as having said the following,

النجوم أمان لأهل السماء،[...] وأهل بيتي أمان لأهل الأرض فإذا ذهب أهل بيتي ذهب أهل الأرض

The stars are a [source of] safety for the inhabitants of the heavens […] and my Ahl al-Bayt are a [source of safety] for the inhabitants of the earth; so, if my Ahl al-Bayt were to go away, then the inhabitants of the earth would go away.

Kamāl al-Dīn: 205 / Bāb 21 / Ḥ 19.

with his Imam reports[1], *the twelve caliphs and Imams* reports[2], the *thaqalayn* reports[3], the *whoever would be delighted* reports[1], the *return from the dead* reports[2], and the reports regarding the following quotation:

---

[1] Abū ʿAbd Allāh, [that is Imam Jaʿfar al-Ṣādiq], relayed that the Messenger of God said,

من مات وهو لا يعرف إمامه مات ميتة جاهلية

> *One who died without becoming acquainted with his Imam has died a death of ignorance [...]*

Al-Maḥāsin: 154 / Bāb 22 / Ḥ 78.

[2] It has been reported that Ibn Masʿūd relayed that the Prophet Muḥammad said,

الخلفاء بعدي اثنا عشر، كعدّة نقباء بني إسرائيل

> *There will be twelve caliphs after me, like the number of the chiefs (nuqabāʾ) of the Israelites.*

Amālī al-Ṣadūq: 387 / Ḥ (497/7).

It has also been reported that [Imam] al-Ṣādiq, [that is Imam] Jaʿfar, son of [Imam] Muḥammad [al-Bāqir], relayed from his father, [Imam Muḥammad al-Bāqir], who relayed from his grandfather, [Imam Ḥusayn], who relayed from [Imam] ʿAlī, that the Messenger of God said,

الأئمّة بعدي اثنا عشر أوّلهم علي بن أبي طالب وآخرهم القائم هم خلفائي وأوصيائي وأوليائي وحجج الله على أمّتي بعدي، المقرّ بهم مؤمن والمنكر لهم كافر

> *There are twelve Imams after me, the first of whom is ʿAlī son of Abū Ṭālib and the last of whom is the Qāʾim; they are my successors (khulafāʾ), my trustees (awṣiyāʾ), my guardians [over people, or my friends] (awliyāʾ), and the ḥujaj of God over my community after me. The one who confesses [faith] in them is a believer and the one who denies them is a disbeliever (kāfir).*

ʿUyūn Akhbār al-Riḍā 1:62 / Ḥ 28.

[3] It has been reported that Jābir said: Abū Jaʿfar, [that is Imam Muḥammad al-Bāqir], said,

دعا رسول الله أصحابه بمنى، قال: يا أيّها الناس إنّي تارك فيكم الثقلين أما إن تمسّكتم بهما لن تضلّوا، كتاب الله وعترتي أهل بيتي فإنّهما لن يفترقا حتّى يردا عليّ الحوض [...]

The Messenger of God called out to his companions in Miná, saying, "O people, I am indeed leaving with you two weighty things; so long as you hold on to the two of them, you will never go astray – the Book of God and my close kin, my Ahl al-Bayt; for, indeed, the two will never separate until they meet me at [a special stage beyond the life of this world] (al-ḥawḍ) […]

Baṣāʾir al-Darajāt: 433 / Bāb 17 / Ḥ 3.

[1] It has been reported that Abū al-Ḥasan, [Imam ʿAlī] al-Riḍā, said,

من سرّه أن ينظر إلى الله بغير حجاب وينظر الله إليه بغير حجاب فليتول آل محمّد، وليتبرّأ من عدوّهم، وليأتمّ بإمام المؤمنين منهم فإنّه إذا كان يوم القيامة نظر الله إليه بغير حجاب ونظر إلى الله بغير حجاب

Whoever would be delighted to look at [the excellent signs of] God without any veil [between him or her and God], and to have God look at him or her [so favorably] without any veil, then let him or her [pledge allegiance to the guardianship of] Muḥammad's progeny, disavow their enemies and take as leader (imam) the Imam of the faithful from among them. For, indeed, on the Day of Judgement, then, God will look at him or her without any veil [between them] and he or she will look at [the excellent signs of] God without any veil [between them].

Al-Maḥāsin 1:60 / Bāb 78 / Ḥ 101.

[2] It has been reported that Muḥammad ibn Muslim said: I heard Ḥumrān ibn Aʿyan and Abū al-Khaṭṭāb both relaying – before Abū al-Khaṭṭāb had brought about [misguidance] in the way he did – that they heard Abū ʿAbd Allāh, [that is Imam Jaʿfar al-Ṣādiq], saying:

أوّل من تنشق الأرض عنه ويرجع إلى الدنيا الحسين بن علي عليهما السلام وإنّ الرجعة ليست بعامّة وهي خاصّة لا يرجع إلاّ من محض الايمان محضاً أو محض الشرك محضاً

The first person who the earth will crack open revealing him, and [that is the first person to] return (yarjiʿ) to this world is [Imam] Ḥusayn, son of [Imam] ʿAlī. Indeed, the return from the dead (rajʿah) is not comprehensive and is, rather, specific [to certain individuals] – no one returns except those who had utterly pure faith or utterly pure [disbelief] (shirk).

Mukhtaṣar Baṣāʾir al-Darajāt: 24.

اللّهمّ بلى لا تخلو الأرض من قائم لله بحجّة، إمّا ظاهراً مشهوراً أو خائفاً مغموراً لئلاّ تبطل حجج الله وبيّناته

O God; indeed, the earth is never empty of one to uphold God's ḥujjah – either [publicly] apparent and famous or fearful [for others and/or the mission][1] and unrecognized, lest the ḥujaj and clear proofs of God be invalidated.[2]

Additionally, there are the *signs of the [public] appearance* reports.[3] Moreover, in this vein, books [related to the *ghaybah*] were written before and/or during the Imam's *ghaybah*. This confirms that the *ghaybah* phenomenon was familiar. For even though, as mentioned earlier, it would not have evoked an initial sense of familiarity, the Shīʿah gained a sense of familiarity with [the notion of the *ghaybah*] due to their inherited [heritage of relevant] reports and practice, [preserved by] ḥadīth scholars and legal scholars, and [kept] in the minds of the Shīʿah during that time period.

---

[1] T: *Khāʾif*, "Fearful," similar to how it is used Qurʾān 28:18 and 28:21, in a way that fits with the immaculate personality being described. Fear of God has many degrees and is not limited to fear of "sins" (in the legal classification sense). Fear can also be understood as a reference to observance of precautions related to the object of fear. Hence, when one is "fearful" for the fate of his or her mission to serve God by serving humanity and guiding the misguided, he or she becomes vigilant in action.

[2] *Nahj al-Balāghah* 4:37 / Ḥ 147.

[3] It has been reported that ʿUmar ibn Ḥanẓalah said: I heard Abū ʿAbd Allāh, [that is Imam Jaʿfar al-Ṣādiq], saying,

خمس علامات قبل قيام القائم: الصيحة والسفياني والخسف وقتل النفس الزكيّة واليماني

There are five signs before the rise of the Qāʾim: [1] the outcry (al-ṣayḥah); [2] the Sufyānī [personality]; [3] the swallow up [of the Sufyānī's army by the earth] (al-khasf); [4] the murder of the pure soul (qatl al-nafs al-zakīyah); and [5] the Yamānī [personality].

Al-Kāfī 8:310 / Ḥ 483; In addition to other reports.

Those books included, for example: *al-Ghaybah* by al-ʿAbbās ibn Hishām al-Nāshirī, who was one of the companions of [Imam ʿAlī] al-Riḍā; the book *al-Qāʾim* by al-Faḍl ibn Shādhān; a book by ʿAbd Allāh ibn Jaʿfar al-Ḥimyarī; a book by Muḥammad ibn al-Qāsim al-Baghdādī; a book by ʿAbd al-Wahhāb al-Mādarāʾī; the book by ʿAlī ibn Muḥammad ibn Riyāḥ al-Sawwāq; and the book *Akhbār al-Qāʾim* by Muḥammad ibn Ibrāhīm, known as ʿAllān al-Kulaynī.

Furthermore, the idea of the *ghaybah* and that the Shīʿah were headed toward the *ghaybah* phenomenon – the veil between [them and] their Imam – was deeply ingrained within the minds of [Imam Ḥasan] al-ʿAskarī's companions. These included [companions named]: Aḥmad ibn Isḥāq al-Ashʿarī; ʿUthmān ibn Saʿīd al-ʿAmrī; Aḥmad ibn Idrīs al-Ashʿarī, Abū ʿAlī; Muḥammad ibn ʿAlī ibn Bilāl, the trustworthy one; Muḥammad ibn al-Ḥusayn ibn Abī al-Khaṭṭāb al-Zayyāt; Muḥammad ibn al-Ḥasan al-Ṣaffār; Ḥamdān ibn Sulaymān al-Naysābūrī; ʿUrwah al-Wakīl al-Qummī; al-ʿAzīz ibn Zuhayr; Muḥammad ibn Bilāl; Muḥammad ibn Ṣāliḥ ibn Muḥammad al-Hamadānī al-Dahqān; ʿAlī ibn Ziyād al-Ṣaymarī; Abū Sulaymān al-Maḥmūdī; and Ibn Saʿdān al-Kātib al-Anbārī.

These individuals and others accepted the *ghaybah* with ease. Moreover, historically speaking, we see no indications that one of the companions of Imam al-Hādī or al-ʿAskarī experienced the phenomenon of puzzlement. The same goes for the *agents* of [Imam Mahdī during the minor *ghaybah*][1]: Muḥammad ibn Ibrāhīm, Dāwūd ibn al-Qāsim, and the two sons of ʿAlī ibn Ibrāhīm al-Hamadānī.

The same goes for the *agents* of the major *ghaybah*, such as al-Kulaynī and al-Ṭūsī – it being a phenomenon that the Shīʿah experienced and dealt

[1] T: *al-Nāḥiyah*; The place, direction toward, or side. The context makes it clear that this is a reference to the nāḥiyah of Imam Mahdī specifically.

with. Researchers and critics of the Shīʿah school of thought have not recorded a [single] case of coup d'état and rupture[1] due to the *ghaybah.*

Third: The Birth [of the Mahdī], The Duration of the Ghaybah, the Unknown Timing [of his Public Appearance], and the Hidden Personal Identity [of the Mahdī]

The reason for his *ghaybah* is an ongoing one, one that has caused the duration of the *ghaybah* to extend long enough to become a [pretense] for denying his birth. [So what is the reason?] Decisively sure proofs establish the necessity of a Divinely appointed Imam, on the one hand, and the fact that the Imams are limited to the twelve [historical] Imams [after Prophet Muḥammad], on the other hand. Moreover, we find that the [last] Imam is hidden from sight[2]. [In light of the established facts,] we know that there must be a reason why the Imam is in a state of *ghaybah.* But if one does not happen to be acquainted with the reason – even if the reports do [in fact] indicate it – that does not harm the Mahdī system of thought. For [such a scenario would be] analogous to lacking acquaintance with the intended meaning of *mutashābih* verses; [or] verses that give the impression of corporeal form; [or] verses giving the impression of fatalism; [or] others. [It would also be similar] to lacking acquaintance with the philosophy

---

[1] T: It appears that the author means there was no *lasting* schism due to the *ghaybah*, regardless of whatever claims existed here or there in the period directly following Imam Ḥasan al-ʿAskarī's passing, and regardless whether those claims were indicative of genuine division and/or part of the evasion to protect the twelfth Imam. For the only surviving community adhering to Imam Ḥasan al-ʿAskarī's *Imāmah* (in the specific sense) is the Twelver Shīʿah community, which believes in both the birth and *ghaybah* of the twelfth Imam.

[2] T: In the sense that his identity is hidden, not known as the person he actually is; in that sense, hidden in plain sight.

behind acts of worship, such as the number of prayer units[1], and the wisdom[2] behind the deeds and rituals of *pilgrimage*[3].

Some Pearls of Wisdom Behind the Ghaybah

The reports have pointed to some of the pearls of wisdom[4] behind the *ghaybah*. Some of these [wisdoms that function as potential] reasons are:

1. So that he would not have been [forced to be] under the pledge of allegiance[5] to any [tyrannical ruler]. For it has been reported that [Imam] ʿAlī said:

   إنَّ القائم منّا إذا قام لم يكن لأحد في عنقه بيعة فلذلك [تخفى] ولادته ويغيب شخصه

   Indeed, when the Qāʾim from among us rises, no one would have had a pledge of allegiance on his neck. That is why his birth will be [relatively] hidden and his person will be [in a state of ghaybah][6]

2. Fear [for others and/or the mission][7] over being killed before accomplishing the objective. For it has been reported that [Imam Muḥammad] al-Bāqir said,

   إنَّ للقائم غيبة قبل ظهوره

---

[1] T: *Rakaʿāt* (sing. *rakʿah*).

[2] T: al-Wajh; The aspect [explaining or giving a reason].

[3] T: al-Ḥajj.

[4] T: *Awjuh* (sing. *wajh*); The aspects [explaining or giving reasons].

[5] T: *Bayʿah*.

[6] *Kamāl al-Dīn*: 303 / Bāb 26 / Ḥ 14.

[7] T: "Fear," similar to how it is used Qurʾān 28:18 and 28:21, in a way that fits with the immaculate personality being described. Fear of God has many degrees and is not limited to fear of "sins" (in the legal classification sense). Fear can also be understood as a reference to observance of precautions related to the object of fear. Hence, when one is "fearful" for the fate of his or her mission to serve God by serving humanity and guiding the misguided, he or she becomes vigilant in action.

Indeed, the Qāʾim will have a ghaybah before his [public] appearance.

The transmitter of the report then asked, "Why is that?" [The Imam] replied,

يخاف

He is fearful [for others and/or the mission][1]

The transmitter of the report described the Imam as gesturing by pointing to his stomach, [indicating that Imam Mahdī fears he will be killed, thereby stopping him from achieving the objectives for which he exists].

3. Testing people and cleansing them. For it has been reported that [Imam Jaʿfar] al-Ṣādiq said:

كيف أنتم إذا بقيتم بلا إمام هدى ولا علم ؟ يتبرّأ بعضكم من بعض ؟ فعند ذلك تميّزون وتمحّصون وتغربلون، وعند ذلك اختلاف السيفين، وإمارة أوّل من النهار وقتل وخلع من آخر النهار

How will you be if you remain without an Imam of guidance and without a [public] authority[2]*? [How will you be when] you disavow one another? At that point, you will be distinguished, tested and sifted through. At that point, there will be conflict between the two swords, taking the reins of power at the beginning of the day, and killing and overthrowing by the end of the day.*[3]

4. So that he follows in the footsteps of the prophets [of old]. For it has been reported that [Imam Ḥasan] al-ʿAskarī said,

---

[1] *Kamāl al-Dīn*: 481 / Bāb 44 / Ḥ 9.

[2] T: ʿ*Alam.*

[3] *Al-Imāmah wa al-Tabṣirah*: 130 / Bāb fī Āyāt Ẓuhūrih / Ḥ 136.

إنَّ ابني هو القائم من بعدي وهو الذي يجري فيه سنن الأنبياء عليهم السلام بالتعمير والغيبة

Indeed, my son is the Qāʾim after me and he is the one who follows the footsteps of the prophets in [their] long lives and ghaybah.[1]

5. In order for believers to be born, [believers] who descend from [those who unreasonably reject what is right]. For it has been reported that [Imam Jaʿfar] al-Ṣādiq said,

لن يظهر أبداً حتَّى تظهر ودائع الله عز وجل فإذا ظهرت ظهر على من يظهر فقتله

He will not appear – not at all – until God Almighty's deposits[2] *appear. Once they appear, he will [appear and] prevail over those [tyrants] who prevail*[3] *and will inflict casualties.*[4]

---

[1] *Kamāl al-Dīn*: 524 / Bāb 46 / Ḥ 4.

[2] T: The author is conveying that, in this report, faithful individuals are described as "deposits" that God has deposited in their unfaithful ancestors. As the report indicates (see the author's coming footnote), one of the wisdoms behind the delay in the Mahdī's advent is to allow sufficient time for all the potential believers (i.e. God's "deposits" in their unbelieving ancestors) to be born ––for the faithful "deposits" to be "separated" from their unfaithful depositories.

[3] T: Ẓahara ʿalá man yaẓhar.

[4] It has been reported that Ibrāhīm al-Karkhī said:

قلت لأبي عبد الله عليه السلام - أو قال له رجل -: أصلحك الله ألم يكن علي عليه السلام قوياً في دين الله عز وجل؟ قال: (بلى)، قال: فكيف ظهر عليه القوم، وكيف لم يدفعهم وما يمنعه من ذلك؟ قال: (آية في كتاب الله عز وجل منعته)، قال: قلت: وأيّة آية هي؟ قال: (قوله عز وجل: (لَوْ تَزَيَّلُوا لَعَذَّبْنَا الَّذِينَ كَفَرُوا مِنْهُمْ عَذاباً أَلِيماً) إنَّه كان لله عز وجل ودائع مؤمنون في أصلاب قوم كافرين ومنافقين فلم يكن علي عليه السلام ليقتل الآباء حتَّى يخرج الودائع فلمَّا خرجت الودائع ظهر على من ظهر فقاتله. وكذلك قائمنا أهل البيت لن يظهر أبداً حتَّى تظهر ودائع الله عز وجل فإذا ظهرت ظهر على من يظهر فقتله)

6. In order to allow the opportunity for all types of people to take the reins of power. For it has been reported that [Imam Jaʿfar] al-Ṣādiq said,

ما يكون هذا الأمر حتَّى لا يبقى صنف من الناس إلاَّ وقد ولّوا على الناس حتَّى لا يقول قائل: إنّا لو ولّينا لعدلنا، ثمّ يقوم القائم بالحقّ والعدل

This amr will not occur until there remains no type of people who have not been given the reins of power over people. [This is] so that no one will say, "Indeed, if only we had been given the reins of power, then we would have

---

I or another man said the following to Abū ʿAbd Allāh, [that is, Imam Jaʿfar al-Ṣādiq], "God bless you; was not ʿAlī mighty when it came to the religion of God Almighty?" He replied, "Yes." [Then the transmitter] said, "Then how did [that group of people] prevail over him, how did he not fend them off, and what prevented him from doing so?" He replied, "A verse from the Book of God Almighty prevented him." Then I said, "Which verse is that?" Then he replied, "when God Almighty says,

[...] And had [the believers and the unreasonable rejectors of what is right] become separate, we would have surely punished the [unreasonable rejectors of what is right] among them with a painful punishment. [Qurʾān 48:25]

"Indeed, God Almighty had believers deposited in the loins of people who were [unreasonable rejectors of what is right] and hypocrites. So ʿAlī would not have killed the fathers until the deposits came out. Once the deposits came out, he prevailed over those [tyrants] who prevailed and fought them. Such is the case with our Qāʾim, [the Qāʾim] of Ahl al-Bayt. He will not appear – not at all – until God Almighty's deposits appear. Once they appear, he will [appear and] prevail over those [tyrants] who prevail[4] and will inflict casualties."

Kamāl al-Dīn: 642.

upheld justice." Then the Qā'im will bring about what is right and [will bring about] justice.[1]

7. A Divine matter of the Unseen. For it has been reported that ʿAbd Allāh ibn al-Faḍl al-Hāshimī said:

سمعت الصادق جعفر بن محمّد عليهما السلام يقول: (إنَّ لصاحب هذا الأمر غيبة لا بدَّ منها يرتاب فيها كلّ مبطل)، فقلت: ولِمَ جُعلت فداك؟ قال: (لأمر لم يؤذن لنا في كشفه)، قلت: فما وجه الحكمة في غيبته؟ قال: (وجه الحكمة في غيبته وجه الحكمة في غيبات من تقدَّمه من حجج الله تعالى ذكره، إنَّ وجه الحكمة في ذلك لا ينكشف إلاَّ بعد ظهوره كما لم ينكشف وجه الحكمة فيما أتاه الخضر عليه السلام من خرق السفينة، وقتل الغلام، وإقامة الجدار لموسى عليه السلام إلى وقت افتراقهما

I heard [Imam] al-Ṣādiq, Jaʿfar, son of Muḥammad, saying, "The master of this amr will have a ghaybah – one that is inevitable, in which every falsifier becomes skeptical." Then I said, "Why is that, may I be sacrificed for your sake?" He replied, "For a reason that we have not been granted permission to reveal." Then I said, "So, [if we cannot know the ultimate reason, then] what is the wisdom behind his ghaybah?" He said, "The wisdom behind his ghaybah is the wisdom behind the ghaybahs of God Almighty's ḥujaj who preceded him. Indeed, the [full] wisdom in that will not be revealed until after his [public] appearance, just as the wisdom of al-Khiḍr's actions – [when he] made a hole in the boat, slew the boy, and erected the wall for Moses – was not revealed until the time they were about to part ways.[2]

---

[1] *Al-Ghaybah* by al-Nuʿmānī: 282 / Bāb 14 / Ḥ 53.

[2] *Kamāl al-Dīn*: 482 / Bāb 45 / Ḥ 11.

We will later explain how to reconcile these reports, for they do not conflict – in terms of their wording – with the aforementioned pearls of wisdom.

The Report-Based Proof of the Birth

As for the reports that prove the [Mahdī's] birth, among these reports are the following:

1. Imam [Ḥasan] al-ʿAskarī was asked, "Do you have a son?" He replied,

   إي والله سيكون لي ولد يملأ الأرض قسطاً وعدلاً، فأمّا الآن فلا

   Indeed, by God, I will have a son who fills the earth with fairness and justice. But as for now, no.[1]

2. It has been reported that ʿAllān al-Rāzī said,

   أخبرني بعض أصحابنا أنّه لمّا حملت جارية أبي محمّد عليه السلام، قال: (ستحملين ذكراً واسمه محمّد وهو القائم من بعدي)

   Some of our [fellow Shīʿah] relayed to me that when the wife[2] *of Abū Muḥammad [i.e. Imam Ḥasan al-ʿAskarī] became pregnant, he said [to her], "You will carry a boy; his name is Muḥammad and he is the Qāʾim*[3] *after me."*[4]

3. It has been reported that Mūsá ibn Muḥammad ibn al-Qāsim ibn Ḥamzah ibn Mūsá ibn Jaʿfar said: Ḥakīmah bint Muḥammad ibn ʿAlī ibn Mūsá ibn Jaʿfar ibn Muḥammad ibn ʿAlī ibn al-Ḥusayn ibn ʿAlī ibn Abī Ṭālib relayed the following to me:

   بَعَثَ إِلَيَّ أَبُو مُحَمَّدٍ الْحَسَنُ بْنُ عَلِيٍّ عليهما السلام فَقَالَ: (يَا عَمَّةُ اجْعَلِي إِفْطَارَكِ اللَّيْلَةَ عِنْدَنَا فَإِنَّهَا لَيْلَةُ النِّصْفِ مِنْ شَعْبَانَ فَإِنَّ اللهَ تَبَارَكَ وَتَعَالَى سَيُظْهِرُ فِي

---

1 *Al-Kharāʾij wa al-Jarāʾiḥ* 1:478 / Bāb 13 / Ḥ 19.

2 T: Jāriyah.

3 T: In this context, the word "Qāʾim" can be read as more generally describing the role of taking on the station of Imāmah —without negating that it still applies in the more specific sense of the "rising one, the Mahdī."

4 *Kamāl al-Dīn*: 408 / Bāb 38 / Ḥ 4.

هَذِهِ اللَّيْلَةِ الْحُجَّةَ وَهُوَ حُجَّتُهُ فِي أَرْضِهِ)، قَالَتْ: فَقُلْتُ لَهُ: وَمَنْ أُمُّهُ؟ قَالَ لِي: (نَرْجِسُ)، قُلْتُ لَهُ: وَاللهِ جَعَلَنِيَ اللهُ فِدَاكَ مَا بِهَا أَثَرٌ، فَقَالَ: (هُوَ مَا أَقُولُ لَكِ)، قَالَتْ: فَجِئْتُ فَلَمَّا سَلَّمْتُ وَجَلَسْتُ جَاءَتْ تَنْزِعُ خُفِّي وَقَالَتْ لِي: يَا سَيِّدَتِي كَيْفَ أَمْسَيْتِ؟ فَقُلْتُ: بَلْ أَنْتِ سَيِّدَتِي وَسَيِّدَةُ أَهْلِي، قَالَتْ: فَأَنْكَرَتْ قَوْلِي وَقَالَتْ: مَا هَذَا يَا عَمَّةُ؟ قَالَتْ: فَقُلْتُ لَهَا: يَا بُنَيَّةُ إِنَّ اللهَ تَبَارَكَ وَتَعَالَى سَيَهَبُ لَكِ فِي لَيْلَتِكِ هَذِهِ غُلاَماً سَيِّداً فِي الدُّنْيَا وَالآخِرَةِ، قَالَتْ: فَجَلَسَتْ وَاسْتَحْيَتْ فَلَمَّا أَنْ فَرَغْتُ مِنْ صَلاَةِ الْعِشَاءِ الآخِرَةِ وَأَفْطَرْتُ وَأَخَذْتُ مَضْجَعِي فَرَقَدْتُ فَلَمَّا أَنْ كَانَ فِي جَوْفِ اللَّيْلِ قُمْتُ إِلَى الصَّلاَةِ فَفَرَغْتُ مِنْ صَلاَتِي وَهِيَ نَائِمَةٌ لَيْسَ بِهَا حَادِثٌ ثُمَّ جَلَسْتُ مُعَقِّبَةً ثُمَّ اضْطَجَعْتُ ثُمَّ انْتَبَهْتُ فَزِعَةً وَهِيَ رَاقِدَةٌ ثُمَّ قَامَتْ فَصَلَّتْ.

قَالَتْ حَكِيمَةُ: فَدَخَلَتْنِي الشُّكُوكُ فَصَاحَ بِي أَبُو مُحَمَّدٍ عليه السلام مِنَ الْمَجْلِسِ فَقَالَ: (لاَ تَعْجَلِي يَا عَمَّةُ فَإِنَّ الأَمْرَ قَدْ قَرُبَ)، قَالَتْ: فَقَرَأْتُ الم السَّجْدَةَ وَيس فَبَيْنَمَا أَنَا كَذَلِكِ إِذَا انْتَبَهَتْ فَزِعَةً فَوَثَبْتُ إِلَيْهَا فَقُلْتُ: اسْمُ اللهِ عَلَيْكِ، ثُمَّ قُلْتُ لَهَا: تُحِسِّينَ شَيْئاً؟ قَالَتْ: نَعَمْ يَا عَمَّةُ، فَقُلْتُ لَهَا: اجْمَعِي نَفْسَكِ وَاجْمَعِي قَلْبَكِ فَهُوَ مَا قُلْتُ لَكِ.

قَالَتْ حَكِيمَةُ: ثُمَّ أَخَذَتْنِي فَتْرَةٌ وَأَخَذَتْهَا فَتْرَةٌ فَانْتَبَهْتُ بِحِسِّ سَيِّدِي عليه السلام فَكَشَفْتُ الثَّوْبَ عَنْهُ فَإِذَا أَنَا بِهِ عليه السلام سَاجِداً يَتَلَقَّى الأَرْضَ بِمَسَاجِدِهِ فَضَمَمْتُهُ إِلَيَّ فَإِذَا أَنَا بِهِ نَظِيفٌ [مُنَظَّفٌ] فَصَاحَ بِي أَبُو مُحَمَّدٍ عليه السلام: (هَلُمِّي إِلَيَّ ابْنِي يَا عَمَّةُ)، فَجِئْتُ بِهِ إِلَيْهِ فَوَضَعَ يَدَيْهِ تَحْتَ أَلْيَتَيْهِ وَظَهْرِهِ وَوَضَعَ قَدَمَيْهِ عَلَى صَدْرِهِ ثُمَّ أَدْلَى لِسَانَهُ فِي فِيهِ وَأَمَرَّ يَدَهُ عَلَى عَيْنَيْهِ وَسَمْعِهِ وَمَفَاصِلِهِ ثُمَّ قَالَ: (تَكَلَّمْ يَا بُنَيَّ)، فَقَالَ: (أَشْهَدُ أَنْ لاَ إِلَهَ إِلاَّ اللهُ وَحْدَهُ لاَ شَرِيكَ لَهُ. وَأَشْهَدُ أَنَّ مُحَمَّداً رَسُولُ اللهِ صلى الله عليه وآله وسلم...) ثُمَّ صَلَّى عَلَى أَمِيرِ الْمُؤْمِنِينَ عليه السلام وَ عَلَى الأَئِمَّةِ إِلَى أَنْ وَقَفَ عَلَى أَبِيهِ ثُمَّ أَحْجَمَ.

قَالَ أَبُو مُحَمَّدٍ عليه السلام: (يَا عَمَّةُ اذْهَبِي بِهِ إِلَى أُمِّهِ لِيُسَلِّمَ عَلَيْهَا وَائْتِنِي بِهِ)، فَذَهَبْتُ بِهِ فَسَلَّمَ عَلَيْهَا وَرَدَدْتُهُ وَوَضَعْتُهُ فِي الْمَجْلِسِ، ثُمَّ قَالَ: (يَا عَمَّةُ إِذَا كَانَ يَوْمُ السَّابِعِ فَأْتِينَا).

قَالَتْ حَكِيمَةُ: فَلَمَّا أَصْبَحْتُ جِئْتُ لأُسَلِّمَ عَلَى أَبِي مُحَمَّدٍ عليه السلام فَكَشَفْتُ السِّتْرَ لأَفْتَقِدَ سَيِّدِي عليه السلام فَلَمْ أَرَهُ، فَقُلْتُ لَهُ: جُعِلْتُ فِدَاكَ مَا فَعَلَ سَيِّدِي؟ فَقَالَ: (يَا عَمَّةُ اسْتَوْدَعْنَاهُ الَّذِي اسْتَوْدَعَتْهُ أُمُّ مُوسَى عليه السلام).

قَالَتْ حَكِيمَةُ: فَلَمَّا كَانَ فِي الْيَوْمِ السَّابِعِ جِئْتُ وَسَلَّمْتُ وَجَلَسْتُ فَقَالَ: (هَلُمِّي إِلَيَّ ابْنِي)، فَجِئْتُ بِسَيِّدِي فِي الْخِرْقَةِ فَفَعَلَ بِهِ كَفَعْلَتِهِ الأُولَى ثُمَّ أَدْلَى لِسَانَهُ فِي فِيهِ كَأَنَّهُ يُغَذِّيهِ لَبَناً أَوْ عَسَلاً.

ثُمَّ قَالَ: (تَكَلَّمْ يَا بُنَيَّ)، فَقَالَ عليه السلام: (أَشْهَدُ أَنْ لاَ إِلَهَ إِلاَّ اللهُ...)، وَثَنَّى بِالصَّلاَةِ عَلَى مُحَمَّدٍ وَعَلَى أَمِيرِ الْمُؤْمِنِينَ وَالأَئِمَّةِ صَلَوَاتُ اللهِ عَلَيْهِمْ أَجْمَعِينَ حَتَّى وَقَفَ عَلَى أَبِيهِ عليه السلام ثُمَّ تَلاَ هَذِهِ الآيَةَ: ((بِسْمِ اللهِ الرَّحْمنِ الرَّحِيمِ * وَنُرِيدُ أَنْ نَمُنَّ عَلَى الَّذِينَ اسْتُضْعِفُوا فِي الأَرْضِ وَنَجْعَلَهُمْ أَئِمَّةً وَنَجْعَلَهُمُ الْوارِثِينَ * وَنُمَكِّنَ لَهُمْ فِي الأَرْضِ وَنُرِيَ فِرْعَوْنَ وَهامانَ وَجُنُودَهُما مِنْهُمْ ما كانُوا يَحْذَرُونَ) [القصص: ٥ و٦])

Abū Muḥammad, [that is, Imam al-ʿAskarī], Ḥasan, son of ʿAlī sent me [a message], saying, "O my [dear] aunt, have your fast-breaking meal[1] *at our place tonight, for, indeed, it is the eve of the fifteenth of Shaʿbān and, indeed, this night God Almighty will manifest the ḥujjah – and he is God's ḥujjah on earth." I then asked him, "Who is his mother?" Then he replied, "Narjis." I then said to him, "By God, may God make me a sacrifice for your sake, there are no signs [of pregnancy] on her." Then he said, "It is as I say to you." So I came [to the Imam's place]. When I said my greetings and sat down, [Narjis] came to remove my [leather socks]*[2] *and said to me, "My Lady*[3]*, how is your evening?" So I replied, "Rather, it is you who are my Lady and the Lady of my household." She refused what I said and then asked, "What it this [you are saying, O dear] aunt*

---

[1] T: *Ifṭār.*

[2] T: *Khuff.*

[3] T: *Sayyidatī*; My master, chief, leader (in the feminine form).

[of the Imam]?" Then I told her, "O daughter, indeed during this night of yours, God Almighty will grant you a boy who is a master in this world and the hereafter." So she sat and was bashful. I finished the evening prayer[1]*, broke my fast, lay down and fell asleep. In the midst of the night, I rose to pray. I finished my prayer while she was sleeping, nothing eventful happening to her. So I sat, reciting recommended supplications [after prayer]. Then I lay down. Next, I woke up alarmed while she was asleep. Then she rose and prayed.*

Skeptical thoughts crossed my mind, but then Abū Muḥammad, [that is, Imam Ḥasan al-ʿAskarī], called out to me from the sitting area[2]*, "O [dear] aunt, do not rush [it], for indeed the matter is near." So I recited Alif Lām Mīm al-Sajdah [Qurʾān 32] and Yā Sīn [Qurʾān 36]. While I was doing so, she woke up alarmed, so I leaped toward her saying, "May God's name bless you." Then I asked her, "Do you feel something?" She replied, "Yes, O [dear] aunt." So I said to her, "Gather yourself [together] and gather your heart [together], for it is what I told you."*

Then a [state of calm that occurs before sleep][3] *overtook me and a [state of birthing]*[4] *overtook her. I then emerged alert due to the movement of my [newborn] master*[5]*. So I revealed the cover off of him and, lo and behold, he was prostrating with his [points of prostration]*[6] *in contact*

---

[1] T: al-ʿIshāʾ al-Ākhirah.

[2] T: *al-Majlis*; Place where sitting occurs; assembly; gathering.

[3] T: *Fatrah.*

[4] T: If read *faṭrah* (as in the manuscript used by al-Majlisī in *Biḥār al-Anwār*, vol. 51, p. 3). Otherwise, if read *fatrah*, then it would mean a, "state of calm that occurs before sleep."

[5] T: Fa intabahtu bi ḥissi sayyidī.

[6] T: *Masājid*; Includes at least part of the forehead, palms, knees and toes.

with the ground. I then hugged him and, lo and behold, I noticed he was clean, [cleaned]. Then Abū Muḥammad, [that is Imam Ḥasan al-ʿAskarī], called out to me, "Bring me my son, O [dear] aunt." So I brought him to him. He placed his hands under his bottom and his back, and placed his feet on his chest. Then he [made contact between his tongue and his mouth][1] and passed his hand over his eyes, [ears][2], and joints, and said, "Speak, O my son." Then he said, "I bear witness that there is no god but God, alone without partner; and I bear witness that Muḥammad is the Messenger of God [...]" Then he prayed [to God, asking Him to shower blessings] upon the Commander of the Faithful [i.e. Imam ʿAlī], and upon the Imams, until he reached his father [i.e. Imam Ḥasan al-ʿAskarī]; then he stopped.

Abū Muḥammad, [that is Imam Ḥasan al-ʿAskarī], then said, "O [dear] aunt, take him to his mother so that he can greet her, then bring him [back] to me." So I took him, he greeted her, then I returned him and placed him in the sitting area [of Imam Ḥasan al-ʿAskarī]. Then he said, "O [dear] aunt, on the seventh day, do come [and see us]."

When morning came upon me, I came to greet Abū Muḥammad. So I uncovered the cover to check on my master but I did not see him. Then I said to him, "May I be sacrificed for your sake, what did my master do?" He replied, "O [dear] aunt, we have [entrusted him for safekeeping][3] with the One with whom the mother of Moses entrusted [her son Moses] for safekeeping."

---

1 T: Adlá lisānahu fī fīhi.

2 T: Samʿihi; his hearing.

3 T: Istawdaʿnāhu.

When it was the seventh day, I came, said my greetings and sat. Then he said, "Bring me my son." So I brought my master [wrapped] in the cloth, and he did to him what he had done the first time. Then he [made contact between his tongue and his mouth] as if he was feeding him yogurt or honey.

Then he said, "Speak, O my son." So he said, "I bear witness that there is no god but God [...]" Secondly, he made a prayer [that God shower blessings] upon Muḥammad, upon the Commander of the Faithful and the Imams, until he reached his father. Then he recited [these verses],

In the Name of God, the Compassionate, the Merciful,

And We wish to bestow favor upon those who were oppressed in the land; and to make them imams; and to make them the heirs;

and to establish them in the land; and to show Pharaoh and Hāmān and their soldiers from among them that which they dreaded from them. [Qurʾān 28:5-6][1]

4. Muḥammad ibn ʿAlī al-Shalmaghānī reported the following in the book *al-Awṣiyā*ʾ, saying:

حدَّثني حمزة بن نصر غلام أبي الحسن عليه السلام، عن أبيه، قال: لمَّا ولد السيّد عليه السلام تباشر أهل الدار بذلك فلمَّا نشأ خرج إليّ الأمر أن أبتاع في كلّ يوم مع اللحم قصب مخ، وقيل: إنَّ هذا لمولانا الصغير عليه السلام

Ḥamzah ibn Naṣr, the servant of Abū al-Ḥasan, [that is Imam ʿAlī al-Hādī], relayed that his father said, "When the master, [that is, the twelfth Imam], was born, the people of the household gave good tidings of [the birth to one

---

[1] *Kamāl al-Dīn*: 424-426 / Bāb 42 / Ḥ 1.

another]. When he grew up [a little], an order reached me [telling me] to purchase bone marrow along with meat every day, and it was said that this is for our little master."[1]

5. It has been reported that Abū Ghānim, the servant, said:

ولد لأبي محمّد عليه السلام ولد فسمّاه محمّداً، فعرضه على أصحابه يوم الثالث، وقال: (هذا صاحبكم من بعدي [...]

Abū Muḥammad, [that is, Imam Ḥasan al-'Askarī], had a son, so he named him Muḥammad. Then he showed him to his companions on the third day and said, "This is your master[2] *after me [...]"*[3]

6. It has been reported that al-Sayyārī relayed from Nasīm and Māriyah that when the master of the age was born, he fell to his knees, raising his two index fingers to the sky. Then he sneezed, and said:

الْحَمْدُ للهِ رَبِّ الْعالَمِينَ وَصَلَّى اللهُ عَلَى مُحَمَّدٍ وَآلِهِ، زَعَمَتِ الظَّلَمَةُ أَنَّ حُجَّةَ اللهِ دَاحِضَةٌ، وَلَوْ أُذِنَ لَنَا فِي الْكَلَامِ لَزَالَ الشَّكُّ

All praise is due to God, Lord of the Worlds; and may God shower blessings upon Muḥammad and his progeny. The oppressors claimed that God's ḥujjah has been refuted. But if we were given permission to speak, then the doubt would fade away."[4]

---

[1] *al-Ghaybah* by al-Ṭūsī: 245 / # 213.

[2] T: Ṣāḥib; Although this word can also mean companion, it is clear from the context that here it is used to mean master/Imam.

[3] *Kamāl al-Dīn*: 431 / Bāb 42 / Ḥ 8.

[4] *Kamāl al-Dīn*: 430 / Bāb 42 / Ḥ 5.

Gaining a sense of assurance[1] regarding any historical issue is done by [accumulating] testaments and clues, [by] the increased probability [of an occurrence] due to the [evidentiary] clues piling up.

In summary, the skepticism and hesitation regarding the likes of this phenomenon is due to the lack of [utilizing appropriate] epistemic approaches and due to sticking to objects of sense perception, or due to misconceptions and nonsense, or due to not referring to the reports because those [individuals] are not experts, and/or due to other issues. For, if not for such [issues], the matter is clear.

Therefore, those afflicted by puzzlement [in this regard] are the ones whose hearts are ill, whose minds are sick, whose faith is a place of temporary lodging[2], whose covenant is shaky, and whose beliefs are like a house of cobwebs – penetrated by the winds of affliction and blown away by the [icy] gales of misconception.

---

[1] T: al-Iṭmiʾnān.

[2] T: *Mustawdaʿ*; As opposed to an [enduring] abode (*mustaqarr*).

CHAPTER 7

THE MAHDĪ CULTURE

One of the major pitfalls when it comes to understanding the religion is for the followers of that religion to be caught between these two opposing phenomena: [1] being closed-minded; and [2] being so compromising as to be derailed from the path of equilibrium prescribed by God[1]. Choosing between these two is like choosing between a rock and a hard place. The dangers and negative repercussions of both can push others away from the faith, thinking that this impostor is the one who represents the religion's authentic thought, vision and deeds. The following are a number of instances manifesting this phenomenon.

THE RULE OF GOVERNMENTS BEFORE THE MAHDĪ

It has been reported that Abū Baṣīr said: Imam Jaʿfar al-Ṣādiq said,

كلّ راية ترفع قبل قيام القائم فصاحبها طاغوت يُعبد من دون الله عز وجل

Every banner that is raised before the rise of our Qāʾim is [the banner] of a tyrant[2] being worshipped aside from God Almighty.[3]

Some have understood this report to mean that the only just government is the government of Imam Mahdī. Hence, every government before the rise of the Mahdī is a government of misguidance. In reality, this idea is tantamount to secularism and isolating religion from the principle of

---

[1] T: al-Sharīʿah.

[2] T: *Ṭāghūt*; Evil one; idol taken as an object of worship; devil.

[3] *Al-Kāfī* 8:295 / Bāb al-Malāḥim wa al-Fitan / Ḥ 452.

government and managing people's affairs. This understanding of the report would deactivate a number of Qur᾽ānic verses and ḥadīth reports. Moreover, this understanding has become a reason for encouraging others not to recognize even a just government. It is as if this matter were not a matter of jurisprudence; [as if this matter] did not require the skill of an expert legal scholar to understand the religious text; [as if] it sufficed to take the *apparent meaning* of the report, if one were to grant such a reading [to begin with]; [as if it were acceptable to] neglect taking into consideration *conflicting* [*report(s)*]; [and as if it were acceptable to] run with it, intellectually-speaking, with an understanding of this text to mean that every banner [raised] claiming it is the banner of the Mahdī before [his public] appearance is a banner of deviation and misguidance. This ḥadīth is similar to another received ḥadīth relayed by al-Faḍl, in which he quotes Abū [ʿAbd Allāh] Jaʿfar, [that is, Imam al-Ṣādiq], as having said,

من ادّعى مقامنا ـ يعني الإمامة ـ فهو كافر ـ أو قال: مشرك ـ

> *One who claims our station, [i.e. the Imāmah], is an [unreasonable rejector of what is right]*[1]

[The transmitter of the report said: or the Imam said],

> *[…] is [one who ascribes partners to the Absolute]*[2]*."*[3]

Hence, what is meant by Abū Baṣīr's report is that every banner raised in the name of the Mahdī, claiming the Mahdī's legitimacy and considering its banner to be like that of the Mahdī, is [the banner] of a tyrant. As for raising the banner in the sense of pushing away a greater harm or upholding the *promotion of virtue and the prevention of vice* or the like, the report does not forbid that. This is on the one hand.

On the other hand, the other [extreme of] crooked understanding – despite not being extracted from the report according to the [earlier] crooked

---

[1] T: *Kāfir*.

[2] T: *Mushrik*; An idolater; one who practices *shirk*.

[3] *Al-Ghaybah* by al-Nuʿmānī: 115 / Bāb 5 / Ḥ 10.

understanding of it – gives legitimacy to every government and identifies no criteria for [classifying] governments. Consequently, [this crooked understanding] establishes an ideology of managing people to the exclusion of religious texts[1], out of a belief that this issue – administering people's affairs – does not require religious texts in order to define it, or that the religious text is silent in its regard, or that the religious text is foreign to such matters and so one must let such matters be sought after in other sources of knowledge. Rather, it might even be said [by those who think this way] that religious rhetoric regarding an intuitive matter is unbefitting – out of a belief that administering people's affairs is an intuitive matter.

THE FATE OF {PROTECTED COMMUNITIES}[2] DURING THE AGE OF THE IMAM

It has been reported that Abū Baṣīr relayed the following exchange between himself and Abū ʿAbd Allāh [i.e. Imam Jaʿfar al-Ṣādiq]:

> قلت: فما يكون من أهل الذمّة عنده _ أي عند الإمام المهدي عليه السلام _؟ قال: يسالمهم كما سالمهم رسول الله صلى الله عليه وآله وسلم ويؤدّون الجزية عن يد وهم صاغرون
>
> *I asked, "What will be [the fate of the protected communities when it comes to Imam Mahdī]?" He replied, "He will make peace with them just as the Messenger of God made peace with them; and they will pay the jizyah [tax] with a willing hand, humbly [accepting*

---

[1] T: *Bi maʿzil ʿan al-nuṣūṣ al-dīnīyah*; Regardless of religious texts; disregarding religious texts.

[2] T: *Ahl al-Dhimmah*; Such as Jews and Christians who pay the *jizyah* tax to an Islamic government, as opposed to Muslims who pay religious dues.

> *to live under Islamic rule as a protected community, without becoming Muslim]."*[1]

It has also been reported that Jābir quoted [Imam Muḥammad] al-Bāqir as having said,

> [...] ويحكم بين أهل التوراة بالتوراة، وبين أهل الإنجيل بالإنجيل، وبين أهل الزبور بالزبور، وبين أهل القرآن بالقرآن [...]
>
> *[...] And he will judge between the people of the Torah with the Torah; between the people of the Gospel*[2] *with the Gospel; between the people of the Psalms*[3] *with the Psalms; and between the people of the Qurʾān with the Qurʾān [...]*[4]

In light of these texts, some have understood that the people of various books are in line with *what is right.* [This interpretation] argues based on the following notion: the Mahdī will fill the earth with fairness and justice; one of the laws by which the Imam governs is to ratify other religions and judge according to their judgment; and although the rule of the Imam is entirely just, right and fair, he does not redirect them [to another religion], but instead ratifies their way. Hence, [some have argued for the interpretation] adopting the position that those religions are in line with *what is right.*[5] On the flipside, some argue that [the Imam] will exact the

---

[1] *Al-Mazār* by Ibn al-Mashhadī: 135 / Bāb 5 / Ḥ 7.

[2] T: *al-Injīl*; The Christian Bible; the Evangel.

[3] T: *al-Zabūr.*

[4] *Al-Ghaybah* by al-Nuʿmānī: 243 / Ḥ 26.

[5] T: This interpretation appears to assume that the Imam would ratify other approaches as equally valid to Islam's approach. However, this is a flawed assumption, because the ratification may be merely an administrative matter for upholding justice among the protected communities who do not accept Islam as the message of God. In other words, it is entirely just in those particular circumstances, but it is not the case that those individuals have reached the ultimate truth/right in their inherited paths.

severest punishment upon non-Shīʿah communities, referencing God Almighty's words,

وَقَاتِلُوهُمْ حَتَّىٰ لَا تَكُونَ فِتْنَةٌ وَيَكُونَ الدِّينُ لِلَّهِ ۖ [...]

And fight them so that there is no strife[1]*, and religion is for God. [...]*[2]

However, according to *common sense reconciliation*[3] of the different reports, the following *apparent meaning* surfaces: The ruling related to [taxes levied on protected communities, referred to as] the *jizyah*, applies in the first stage of his rule and before his government becomes well-established [enough to serve its purpose of decisively establishing *what is right*]; or it is an established ruling up until the complete argument[4] is established [to convince others]; or [it is an established ruling] up until the *return from the dead*[5] occurs.

THE DILEMMA OF THE MAHDĪ IDEA

Religious phenomena, including the Mahdī idea, experience two dilemmas: the dilemma of myth, of marketing absolute, unchecked [notions] of the Unseen, on the one hand, and the dilemma of [completely] rejecting the world beyond the natural world, on the other hand. For example, the issue of jinn, angels, and Satan has been explained in the religious circles of ignorant zealots based on myth and human foolishness; it has led people to play with minds, take advantage of the naïve, demolish systematic areas of knowledge, and go after monetary and political gains. For example, this

---

[1] T: *Fitnah.*

[2] T: Qurʾān 2:193.

[3] T: al-Jamʿ al-ʿurfī.

[4] T: *al-Ḥujjah.*

[5] T: *al-Rajʿah.*

includes stories about "the one killed by the jinn,"[1] making use of the jinn[2], information from the jinn, and [notions of] widescale interventions by the jinn in our world, on the one hand. On the other hand, there are explanations of religious phenomena based on purely physical laws, rejecting the very notion of jinn and draping it with a new scientific garb under the notion of physical phenomena unpredicted by the mind. For instance, we might have explained why an apple falls from a tree by [proposing] that the jinn made it fall – until the theory of gravity appeared. We might have also explained tooth cavities as being caused by jinn staying in them – until germs and the like were discovered. This has been mentioned in *Tafsīr al-Manār*.

As such, the Mahdī proposition has been afflicted with the phenomenon of myth – in terms of thought and action, intentionally and out of ignorance – and has been exploited for political or personal, subjective objectives. It is influenced by the sentiments of the masses, which create stories for it, such that it is has become an asset for the bankrupt to acquire holiness and prestige. [In its state of affliction,] it has gone after the deactivation of sciences and fields of specialization, or has taken the position of a counterpart and alternative, such that the captivating idea has been exploited in order to traffic human beings to the grinder of ignorance. It has subverted realistic and correct concepts, exaggerating when it comes to the Unseen, casting the Unseen into the lap of myth. It has shut down the gauge [of right and wrong], has shut down knowledge, and has pushed people to travel toward the Unseen, in an all-encompassing sense, far from the natural and existential causes that we ourselves believe God has made the universal order in this world of testing and examination. Indeed, we do say that the Unseen should have its [fair] share, but it is not everything. Rather, the fields of knowledge and the arts have their province. This is on the one hand.

---

[1] T: Saʿd ibn ʿUbādah, who did not pledge allegiance to Abū Bakr, was found dead and was said to have been killed by the jinn.

[2] T: Taskhīr al-jinn.

On the other hand, the Mahdī proposition has been rejected wholesale, if only because of unconscious reactions to the position taken by those confining themselves to Unseen factors in the all-encompassing sense[1], as described on the aforementioned hand. Thus, the Mahdī idea was rejected, and the rejection was framed in intellectual terms, such as [framing the Mahdī as] a phenomenon of general social reform and a domination of Quraysh over all nations, instead of reform done by a particular individual. Alternatively, [the framing in intellectual terms has attempted] a blurring of the phenomenon to the extent of making it out to be a claim just like the many other claims out there; or emptying it of the benefit of believing in it, delaying discussion about it to the time that it occurs, and deferring it to the future; or [casting it as] a figment of imagination, a matter of legend, and a notion inherited from other societies. The pioneers of this theory can be found in [the likes of] Aḥmad Amīn al-Miṣrī, or Saʿd Muḥammad Ḥasan, or Muḥammad ʿAbd Allāh [ʿInān], or [ʿAbd al-Karīm Maḥmūd] al-Khaṭīb, or Ibn Khaldūn.

[In response,] I say the following: The invitation toward reasonability and being realistic does not mean a rejection of the Unseen. Similarly, belief in the Unseen does not mean that matters should go unchecked and that various fields of knowledge should be deactivated. Rather, reconciling between the two notions – reasonability and the Unseen – is possible and is, indeed, a matter of fact.

For the standard is reality, [the criterion is] *what is right*. However, the domain of reality, as a criterion, is not limited to objects of sense perception. Rather, the criterion is *matter-of-fact reality*[2], which embraces the world of the Unseen, accepts religious fields of knowledge, and

---

[1] T: Arbāb al-ghayb al-muṭlaq.

[2] T: *al-Wāqiʿ al-nafs amrī*; Related to *nafs al-amr*, which is arguably the intelligible plane on which existing beings and true statements are described to be as such, even if they their referents do not have an actual existence in the mind or externally. For further details and other opinions, see Ṭabāṭabāʾī's *Nihāyat al-Ḥikmah* (al-Marḥalah al-ūlá, al-faṣl al-thānī).

identifies a path for such knowledge that does not conflict with scientific principles and output. Indeed, the [true] Mahdī proposition lives in the spirit of the systematic Unseen. For the Mahdī's *ghaybah*, in principle, the philosophy behind it, and some of the details related to the Unseen, such as his sudden mobilization, are [all] aspects of the Unseen. However, because the scientific approach [to the available evidence] establishes the existence of the Imam and his influence, there is no room to reject such matters [outright]. God Almighty says,

تِلْكَ مِنْ أَنباءِ الغَيبِ نوحيها إِلَيكَ [...]

> *These are accounts of the Unseen which We reveal to you. [...]*[1]

It is of the systematic Unseen, not the imaginary Unseen. It is of the Unseen that does not conflict with knowledge and thought. It is not of the Unseen that impounds and blocks knowledge and thought. For we do not approve of deferring scientific, social, political reform to the hands of the Unseen, or the hands of the future, until the Imam and savior appears. Rather, it is necessary to strive diligently in order to activate the economic, scientific and social junctions that bring about his [public] appearance – or, rather, make it take place sooner.

THE RELIGIOUS VIEW – *SALAFISM* VS. *MUʿTAZILISM*

From some, religious understanding is represented by the *Salafism*, *Ashʿarīsm* view, which has limited itself to the [face value of scripture's] words. [Moreover, even] if those words have conflicted with reason, this vision has prohibited reinterpretation[2]. This vision's repercussions have extended to [various] manifestations of attributing corporeal form [to

---

[1] Qurʾān 11:49.

[2] T: *al-Taʾwīl*; In this context, it refers to a more holistic interpretation, beyond the face value of specific statements; a form of figurative interpretation.

God][1], excessively using the term "*[heretical/misguided] innovation*[2]" [in the context of accusing others of it], refusing reform, and insisting on *[all] behavior as devotionally reserved [for detailed, Divinely endowed prescriptions]*[3].

For others, religious understanding is represented by the *Muʿtazilism* vision, which has exaggerated abilities and jurisdiction of reason as extending to all propositions. This, in turn, has led to the phenomenon of [utilizing] *reason's [capacity for] suppositional perception*[4], *al-qiyās* and *al-istiḥsān.* The matter even went as far as to deny [the authoritativeness of] any case in which reason has no say, and to deactivate – practically speaking – the domain of the religious text. [This was the case] to such an extent that the views of [those who deny prophethood][5] were reborn with a new wardrobe, in order to underestimate the standing of a religious text that conflicts with *istiḥsān*-based reason. Thus, this vision unwittingly distanced itself from the Unseen, from occultation, sailed toward [solely] empirical reality, and described the holy Qurʾān as a human production.

[In response,] we say that *what is right,* in our view, is the following: The religious subject matter is actualized through human *theoretical* and *practical reason,* [on the one hand], and *revelation*'s *reason*[6] – meaning, what has reached us by Divine means, by revelation – [on the other hand]. Indeed, religious wording and rhetoric are the means of *revelation's reason,* but: They are governed by linguistic methods [customarily used]; *apparent meanings* are taken into account and deemed reliable so long as there are

---

[1] T: al-Tajsīm.

[2] T: *al-Bidʿah.*

[3] T: *al-Tawqīfīyah al-sulūkīyah*; Behavior/practice that is [specifically] prescribed/coined/defined by Divine legislation, in detail (as opposed to allowing behavior/practice to fall within a range of Divinely authorized options having several degrees of freedom).

[4] T: al-ʿAql al-ẓunnī.

[5] T: al-Barāhimah.

[6] T: al-ʿAql al-waḥyānī.

no *clues* – [from the *immediately connected context* or] even from *beyond the immediately connected context* – dictating that the intended meaning is contrary to the *apparent meaning*; and *linguistic metaphor*[1] and the like, such as *al-kināyah*, *al-isti'ārah*[2] and *al-tamthīl*[3], are befitting in religious texts once there exists a *clue* [indicating the intended meaning] and the text is crafted with attentive care to the dictates of the situation for an age in which the people of that age were being catered to. Hence there is to be no *salafism* in [interpreting] the text, no *mu'tazilism* in the authority of reason, no rejection of human reason, and no deactivation of *practical reason*'s activity that culminates in submission, conviction and faith. Referring back to *revelation's reason*, according to its standards and within its outlined domain, is a must. This is a must both for those who accept the religion and those who do not accept it[4] – because [the yields of *revelation's reason*] are constitutions that have been legislated not only from the core of *revelation's reason* but from the core of scientific objectivity, and the latter encompasses both individuals within the sphere of the religion – those who approve of it – and those who are outside the folds of the religion – those who do not approve of it.

The Mahdī phenomenon is something to be realized and practiced according to the approach of *theoretical* and *practical reason*, as well as *revelation's reason* based on the methodology described earlier. However,

---

[1] T: *al-Majāz al-lughawī*; Using a word in a different sense than its literal meaning that it was designated for, due to a suitable relationship; as opposed to *al*-majāz *al-'aqlī*, in which the literal meaning is maintained but the application of the meaning extends to metaphorical instances.

[2] T: A metaphor in which the relationship between the literal meaning and the metaphorical meaning is the similarity between the two.

[3] T: A type of *isti'ārah* in which the aspect of similarity is extracted from a composite of meanings.

[4] T: Those who do not accept the religion would still need to refer to the teachings of the religion to understand it properly, to see its internal logic, how it defines its boundaries, etc. There may also be dimensions to the religion's teachings that are of interest to society more broadly, regardless whether or not the religion is of Divine origin.

some harms and deviations might plague certain concepts pertaining to the Mahdī phenomenon due to [what one might call,] "salafist Shīʿah" reasons. These are reasons brought about by ignorant, narrow-minded [individuals who make certain fallible individuals/notions out to be untouchable holy figures/principles][1]. Thus, they hang on to the superficial and become distant from the secrets[2] of the Mahdī movement. [The plaguing] may alternatively be due to [what one might call,] "*muʿtazilist* Shīʿah" reasons. These are reasons brought about by those whose judgments withdraw from all but the path of human *theoretical reason*. Alternatively, [still, the plaguing] may be due to [what one might call,] "dry Shīʿah" reasons. These are reasons brought about by those who are distant from the spiritual[3] dimensions that we come to realize through [the path of] *practical reason*. Thus, they judge the Mahdī phenomenon and make conclusions regarding it using a form of reason that is far from being spiritually in-tune[4].

THE DILEMMA OF MAHDĪ RHETORIC

Although the Mahdī proposition is sound in terms of its content and thought, sometimes the authors and creators of Mahdī rhetoric cause it to be become obscure and lose its solid quality. This leads to ambiguity in thought and the absence of an interactive relationship with it. The weakness of rhetoric has many examples, [some of which we will now consider].

Rhetoric, with its complicated terms, old approaches, worn-out sequences of speech, sticking to [addressing] old misconceptions, especially when

---

1 T: *al-Muqaddisūn* (sing. *al-muqaddis*); The ones who consider [something/someone] holy. In this context, the problem is that the object of holiness here is not worthy of such sanctification. Hence, the individuals dealing with such notions or individuals as holy are doing so out of ignorance, not a well-reasoned expression of veneration.

2 T: The hidden pearls of wisdom; reasons.

3 T: al-Maʿnawīyah; Depending on the context, this can refer to sentimental, meaningful, token, moral, symbolic, and other meanings…

4 T: al-Ṭarāwah al-maʿnawīyah; spiritual/meaningful tenderness/sensitivity.

coupled with behavior of this sort, entails old rhetoric. This ancientness makes the idea come off as ancient as well, making it out to be part of an inherited [tradition] that is incapable of keeping up with the present and the future, and thus must be rebelled against and isolated away from scientific arenas. Some even go as far as to become ashamed of having a sense of belonging to the idea, thinking that there is a conflict between the badge of being educated, [on the one hand], and Mahdī rhetoric, [on the other hand]. This is because such individuals do not have confidence in the idea and because others accuse them of being [at odds with being educated for affiliating with the idea]. Hence, such individuals unconsciously disavow Mahdī thought due to the dilemma of old Mahdī rhetoric.

[The weakness of Mahdī rhetoric] also manifests in new rhetoric that is harmonious with people's views and fills the void for the youth, but only satisfies the needs of a specific layer and generation of people. Thus, it provides Mahdī thought with contemporary badges of honor and titles, such as: "The Democracy of the Mahdī," when describing how the Mahdī consults with his companions and puts forth the majority opinion ahead of his own, even if the majority opinion conflicts with his own opinion, or "The Socialism of the Mahdī," or "The Communism of the Mahdī," or "The Modernism of the Mahdī," or "The Post-modernism [of the Mahdī]," or "The Technocracy of the Mahdī's Government," and the like.

The problem with such rhetoric is that, in our view, these ideas are not entirely approvable. To reduce a Divine idea to a *secular*[1] framework is problematic. Sure, these terms might be used to designate new meanings, different than the ones intended by those who [use the terms in their original senses] which are rejected by the principle of *submission* [to God] (*Islam*). However, even if these new meanings were to be accepted Islamically, it remains a phenomenon of picking up [and uncommendably

[1] T: *Waḍʿīyah/waḍʿī*; The word "waḍʿī" can translate to "positive" (as in positive law, law established by human authority), or "positivist" (as in an empiricist approach to knowledge). The author appears to be using the word in a broad sense here to describe fallible, particularly secular, human theories/studies.

repeating] non-Islamic phrases.[1] Indeed, sometimes [practicing] the theory [which advocates] for [so-called] modernizing [of Islamic concepts] and Islamizing Western phrases leads to a disruption of the meanings, let alone it being a weak approach that is not [indicative of] confidence in Islamic civilization's [more traditional] phrases. In any case, there is no crisis of phrase [shortage] such that one would [make it a point to] seek the assistance of terms from other cultures. If it must be done by some individuals, then a very clear *clue* must be indicated, [specifying the intended meaning], in order to avoid a confusion of meaning and an ailing interpretation. For example, if "democracy" were to be defined as consulting with others and seeking the help of some of their expertise, then – although this is an acceptable Islamic principle – the usage of the term "democracy" may nonetheless cause the illusion that the other meaning is intended, that the majority's opinion overrules the opinion of the Divine.

[The weakness of Mahdī rhetoric] also manifests when presenting Mahdī rhetoric in an excessively mystical tone or an extremely imaginative manner that goes over one's head except after exertion, interpretation and dealing with it contrary to the *apparent [meaning]* – that is by [ostensibly] ascertaining the *hidden meanings* and subtleties of truths. For it has been reported that, one day, [Imam] ʿAlī said the following to Ḥudhayfah ibn al-Yamān,

يا حذيفة لا تحدّث الناس بما لا يعرفون فيطغوا ويكفروا [...]

> *O Ḥudhayfah, do not speak to people of that which they are not acquainted, lest they transgress and [unreasonably reject what is right] [...]*[2]

The Mahdī system of thought has several levels of knowledge, some of which only the few and far between are prepared to digest. Thus, the general public would reject [such matters of knowledge that are difficult to

---

[1] T: Ẓāhirah iltiqāṭīyah.

[2] *Al-Ghaybah* by al-Nuʿmānī: 144 / Bāb 10 / Ḥ 3.

digest]. Hence, it would be senseless to discuss the likes of such matters, for it has been reported that the Prophet Muḥammad said,

إنّا معاشر الأنبياء أمرنا أن نكلّم الناس على قدر عقولهم

> *Indeed, we – the likes of the prophets – have been commanded to speak to people according to the extent of their intellects.*[1]

Among the additional pitfalls of Mahdī rhetoric are: the utilization of exaggerations and metaphors; deferring the idea to the fatalistic Unseen, taking away the believer's will to change and have an impact [on the world] and deactivating the Divine commands *to promote virtue and prevent vice* – from the aspect of the Divine command; describing Mahdī thought using rhetoric which gives the impression that its proposition is an ordinary one, reproducible by many, and does not require Divinely ordained aptitudes and support; revamping rhetoric that attempts to glorify personalities of particular periods of time; keeping Mahdī rhetoric away from real life experiences; systematizing rhetoric that breeds extremism, violence, militarization, conscription, bigotry, close-mindedness, marginalization; and creating a spirit of despair and irresponsibility.

However, Mahdī rhetoric must be: [capable of defending itself]; up-to-date; authentic; scientific; meaningful; reasonable; related to the world beyond; Qurʾānic; [capable of delivering people] to the peaks of civilization; and neither rightist Salafist, nor leftist modernist which would blur correct Islamic concepts. For it has been reported that [Imam] ʿAlī said the following in the context of describing battles [to come, referring to a Divinely guided leader][2]:

يعطف الهوى على الهدى إذا عطفوا الهدى على الهوى، ويعطف الرأي على القرآن إذا عطفوا القرآن على الرأي [...]

---

[1] *Al-Kāfī* 1:23 / Kitāb al-ʿAql wa al-Jahl / Ḥ 15.

[2] T: al-Malāḥim (sing. al-malḥamah).

> *He steers [whimsical] desire toward guidance when they steer guidance toward [whimsical] desire; he steers personal-opinion toward the Qur'ān when they steer the Qur'ān toward personal-opinion [...]*[1]

Indeed, [Imam] ʿAlī rejects the notion of crushing desire. Rather, he guides desire on the path toward the goal and prohibits the opposite from occurring. This is contrary to others who politicize goals in order to achieve [the objects of] their desires. [Imam] ʿAlī prohibits *personal-opinion* from overruling the Qur'ān and, rather, sees that the matter must be reversed – the Qur'ān must overrule the subjective mind.

EXAMPLES OF MAHDĪ RHETORIC

The following are some brief examples of Mahdī rhetoric that explains [relevant] beliefs, jurisprudence, individual and congregational practice, rituals and traditions:

1. God Almighty says,

   وَنُرِيدُ أَن نَمُنَّ عَلَى الَّذِينَ اسْتُضْعِفُوا فِي الأَرْضِ وَنَجْعَلَهُمْ أَئِمَّةً وَنَجْعَلَهُمُ الوارِثِينَ

   And We wish to bestow favor upon those who were oppressed in the land, and to make them imams, and to make them the heirs.[2]

2. God Almighty says,

   وَلَقَد كَتَبنا فِي الزَّبورِ مِن بَعدِ الذِّكرِ أَنَّ الأَرضَ يَرِثُها عِبادِيَ الصّالِحونَ

   And We have indeed written in the Psalms, after the Remembrance, that My righteous servants shall inherit the earth.[3]

---

[1] *Nahj al-Balāghah* 2:21 / Ḥ 138.

[2] Qur'ān 28:5-6.

[3] Qur'ān 21:105.

3. God Almighty says,

وَعَدَ اللَّهُ الَّذِينَ آمَنوا مِنكُم وَعَمِلُوا الصَّالِحاتِ لَيَستَخلِفَنَّهُم فِي الأَرضِ [...]

God has promised those of you who have faith and do righteous deeds that He will surely make them successors in the land [...][1]

4. God Almighty says,

هُوَ الَّذي أَرسَلَ رَسولَهُ بِالهُدىٰ وَدينِ الحَقِّ لِيُظهِرَهُ عَلَى الدّينِ كُلِّهِ وَلَو كَرِهَ المُشرِكونَ

It is He who has sent His Messenger with the guidance and the religion of what is right to make it prevail over all religion, though [those who ascribe partners to the Absolute][2] *be averse.*[3]

5. God Almighty says,

وَما خَلَقتُ الجِنَّ وَالإِنسَ إِلّا لِيَعبُدونِ

I did not create the jinn and the humans except that they may worship Me.[4]

In order to be brief, we have limited the examples to those of Qurʾānic rhetoric. However, Mahdī rhetoric extends beyond Qurʾānic examples to include the [Mahdī] rhetoric of: the Prophet Muḥammad; the Imams; the companions of the Prophet such as Abū Bakr, ʿUmar, ʿUthmān, ʿAbd Allāh ibn ʿUmar, Abū Hurayrah, Samurah ibn Jundub, Salmān, Abū Dharr and ʿAmmār; the wives the Prophet ʿĀʾishah, Ḥafṣah and Umm Salamah; the followers[5] [of the companions] ʿAwn ibn Abī Juḥayfah, ʿAbāyah ibn Ribʿī and Qatādah; the *deputies* [of Imam Mahdī during the *minor ghaybah*], the *agents* [of Imam Mahdī during the *minor ghaybah*], the

---

[1] Qurʾān 24:55.

[2] T: al-Mushrikūn.

[3] Qurʾān 9:33.

[4] Qurʾān 51:56.

[5] T: *al-Tābiʿūn* (sing. *al-tābiʿī*).

scholars, the educated, and the politicians; academic [discourse]; even the Torah, the Gospel and the Psalms; Sunnī exegetes such as al-Ṭabarī, al-Rāzī, al-Khāzin, al-Ālūsī, Ibn Kathīr, al-Suyūṭī and the like; the [Sunnī] *six authentic collections* (al-Bukhārī, Muslim, Ibn Mājah, Abū Dāwūd, al-Nisāʾī, and [al-Tirmidhī]); and [Sunnī] ḥadīth books such as *al-Mustadrak ʿalá al-Ṣaḥīḥayn, Majmaʿ al-Zawāʾid, Musnad al-Shāfiʿī, Sunan al-Dāraquṭnī, Sunan al-Bayhaqī, Musnad Abī Ḥanīfah,* and *Kanz al-ʿUmmāl.*

Moreover, it is necessary to conduct a study surveying the time periods and stages [when it comes to Mahdī rhetoric. It is also necessary] to conduct a comprehensive comparative study; to investigate the commonalities in [extended as well as abridged works][1]; to search for the causes behind rhetoric [choices] in each stage, the rhetoric examples, as well as the rhetoric objectives such as fortification, unification and invitation [to the faith and/or a campaign of some sort]; to present an internal analysis of the rhetoric, [on the one hand], and an external analysis of the rhetoric that compares it to religious rhetoric at large, [on the other hand]; and to seriously get to the bottom of the influence of theology, jurisprudence and exegesis on [Mahdī rhetoric].

---

[1] T: al-Muṭawwalāt wa al-munfaridāt. Al-munfaridāt may refer to works that are not necessarily summarized but focused and in relative isolation when contrasted with al-muṭawwalāt.

CHAPTER 8

SIGNS OF THE PUBLIC APPEARANCE (*AL-ẒUHŪR*)

THE TERM "*SIGN*"

The term "*sign*,"[1] in the context of religion, appears in several cases. Not to be exhaustive, some of these include:

1. A sign that is recorded in one of the books of Divine origins[2], such as the Torah and the Gospel, indicating an attribute of the noblest Messenger [Prophet Muḥammad]. Such signs are called glad tidings. God Almighty says,

   [...] وَمُبَشِّرًا بِرَسولٍ يَأتي مِن بَعدِي اسمُهُ أَحمَدُ [...]

   And [remember] when Jesus son of Mary said, "[...] and bearing glad tidings of a Messenger to come after me, whose name is Aḥmad[3]."[4]

   God Almighty also says,

   الَّذينَ آتَيناهُمُ الكِتابَ يَعرِفونَهُ كَما يَعرِفونَ أَبناءَهُم [...]

   Those whom We have given the Book recognize him just as they recognize their sons [...][5]

---

[1] T: ʿAlāmah.

[2] T: al-Kutub al-samāwīyah (sing. al-Kitāb al-samāwī).

[3] T: Another name of Prophet Muḥammad.

[4] Qurʾān 61:6.

[5] Qurʾān 2:146.

For it has been reported in *Tafsīr al-Qummī* that [Imam Jaʿfar] al-Ṣādiq said the following regarding the latter verse:

لأنَّ الله عز وجل قد أنزل عليهم في التوراة والزبور والإنجيل صفة محمّد صلى الله عليه وآله وسلم وصفة أصحابه [...]

[They recognize him] because God Almighty revealed to them, in the Torah, the Psalms and the Gospel, the description of Muḥammad and the description of his companions [...][1]

Moreover, *al-Kāfī*[2] mentions a report attributed to [Imam Jaʿfar] al-Ṣādiq in which he says:

[...] فلمّا أن بعث الله عز وجل المسيح عليه السلام قال المسيح لهم: إنّه سوف يأتي من بعدي نبيّ اسمه أحمد من ولد إسماعيل عليه السلام يجيء بتصديقي وتصديقكم، وعذري وعذركم [...]

[...] Then when God Almighty sent the Messiah, [Jesus, son of Mary], the Messiah said to them, "Indeed, there will come after me a prophet whose name is Aḥmad, from the descendants of Ishmael. He will come with a confirmation of what I profess and what you believe[3]*, and [mercy for me as well as you]*[4]*.*

---

[1] *Tafsīr al-Qummī* 1:33.

[2] *Al-Kāfī* 1:293 / Bāb al-Ishārah wa al-Naṣṣ ʿalá Amīr al-Muʾminīn / Ḥ 3.

[3] T: Bi taṣdīqī wa taṣdīqikum. The confirmation is of the truth that Jesus professed and that truth which people believed in (e.g., Jesus is the Messiah and a Messenger sent by God). Of course, if people believed things that Jesus did not profess, and/or they misinterpreted Jesus, that would not be confirmed.

[4] T: ʿUdhrī wa ʿudhrikum. This reading indicates that Prophet Muḥammad has a role in helping even the prophets to come closer to God. It does not at all conflict with the Shīʿah Muslim view of Jesus's infallibility (in the sense of immaculacy/ *ʿiṣmah*). It merely highlights the endless journey of coming closer to God Almighty and the distinct status of Prophet Muḥammad – even relative to other prophets – as a means for channeling Divine mercy.

Furthermore, it has been reported that [Imam Muḥammad] al-Bāqir said,

[...] فلم تزل الأنبياء تبشّر بمحمّد صلى الله عليه وآله وسلم حتّى بعث الله تبارك وتعالى المسيح عيسى بن مريم فبشَّر بمحمّد صلى الله عليه وآله وسلم وذلك قوله تعالى: (يَجِدُونَهُ) يعني اليهود والنصارى (مَكْتُوباً) يعني صفة محمّد صلى الله عليه وآله وسلم (عِنْدَهُمْ) يعني (في التوراة والإنجيل يأمرهم بالمعروف وينهاهم عن المنكر) [...]

[...] The prophets kept giving glad tidings about the coming of Muḥammad up until God Almighty sent the Messiah, Jesus, son of Mary, who then [also] gave glad tidings of Muḥammad's coming. That is [what is meant when, in the holy Qu'ān,] God Almighty says, "[the unschooled Prophet,] whom they find," meaning the Jews and the Christians [find him], "written," meaning they find the description of Muḥammad, "with them," meaning, "in the Torah and the Gospel, [he] who enjoins them to do what is right and forbids them from what is wrong[1]"[2] [...][3]

The report [from which this is an excerpt] is a lengthy one and is relayed in many sources. It is a beneficial report and we have cited this excerpt from it as needed. In addition, the Qur'ān has addressed the People of the Book, which include the Jews and the Christians who disobeyed the Messenger [Prophet Muḥammad] with regard to his prescription for them and invitation to them. God Almighty addressed them, saying,

يا أَهلَ الكِتابِ قَد جاءَكُم رَسولُنا يُبَيِّنُ لَكُم كَثيرًا مِمّا كُنتُم تُخفونَ [...]

---

[1] T: He promotes virtue among them and prevents vice among them.

[2] Qur'ān 7:157.

[3] *Al-Kāfī* 8:117 / Bāb Amrihi Subḥānahu Rasūlihi bil-Waṣīyah [...] / Ḥ 92.

O People of the Book! Our Messenger has come to you, clarifying for you much of what you used to hide [...][1]

It has also been reported that [Imam ʿAlī] al-Riḍā said the following to a Christian religious leader:

فخذ عليّ السِفْر الثالث فيه ذكر محمّد وبشارة عيسى بمحمّد،

Then [consider] the third book [of the Gospel], which includes the mention of Muḥammad and the glad tidings of Jesus regarding Muḥammad.

The Christian religious leader replied, "[Go ahead.]" So [Imam ʿAlī] al-Riḍā began to recite from that book in the Gospel, until he reached the mention of Muḥammad. At that point, he asked the Christian leader,

يا جاثليق، من هذا النبيّ الموصوف؟

O [Christian religious head][2]*, who is this prophet who is being described?*

The Christian leader replied, "[You] describe him." Then [Imam al-Riḍā] said:

لا أصفه إلاّ بما وصفه الله تعالى، هو صاحب الناقة والعصا والكساء، (النَّبِيَّ الْأُمِّيَّ الَّذِي يَجِدُونَهُ مَكْتُوباً عِنْدَهُمْ فِي التَّوْرَاةِ وَالْإِنْجِيلِ يَأْمُرُهُمْ بِالْمَعْرُوفِ وَيَنْهَاهُمْ عَنِ الْمُنْكَرِ وَيُحِلُّ لَهُمُ الطَّيِّبَاتِ وَيُحَرِّمُ عَلَيْهِمُ الْخَبَائِثَ وَيَضَعُ عَنْهُمْ إِصْرَهُمْ وَالْأَغْلَالَ الَّتِي كَانَتْ عَلَيْهِمْ) (الأعراف: ١٥٧)، يهدي إلى الطريق الأفضل، والمنهاج الأعدل، والصراط الأقوم [...]

I do not describe him except as God Almighty has described him. He is the one with the she-camel, the staff, and the cloak, "the unschooled[3] *Prophet whom they find*

[1] Qurʾān 5:15.

[2] T: Jāthalīq.

[3] T: Ummī.

written with them in the Torah and the Gospel, who enjoins them to do what is right and forbids them from what is wrong, makes lawful to them all the good things and forbids them from all vicious things, and relieves them of their burden and the shackles that were upon them […]"[1] *He guides to the best way, the most just approach, and the most upright path […]*[2]

2. *Signs* of the worldwide reformer, mentioned in books of Divine origins. God Almighty says,

   وَلَقَد كَتَبنا فِي الزَّبورِ مِن بَعدِ الذِّكرِ أَنَّ الأَرضَ يَرِثُها عِبادِيَ الصّالِحونَ

   And We have indeed written in the Psalms, after the Remembrance, that My righteous servants shall inherit the earth.[3]

   Prophet Muḥammad used to recite this verse before his staunchest opponents among the Jews, [who would have been familiar with the scripture being referred to], while they watched him in silence. Silence [in such a context] is a sign of approval. [Given that the noblest Prophet Muḥammad's staunchest opponents were just waiting for a time when he would seem to slip so that they could undermine him], had this content not been in the Torah, then they would have objected and denied it. Had such a reaction occurred at the time, it would have shown up in the records.

3. The Day of Judgment *signs*. These are of two types:

   First type: *Signs* that occur before the Day of Judgment. These are called *signs of the Day of Judgment*[4]. The reports mention the following among such *signs*: the commencement of Prophet

---

[1] Qur᾽ān 7:157.

[2] *Al-Thāqib fī al-Manāqib*: 190 / Bāb 2 / Ḥ (1/171).

[3] Qur᾽ān 21:105.

[4] T: *Ashrāṭ al-sā῾ah.*

Muḥammad's mission; the destruction of the barrier and the mobilization of Gog and Magog[1]; the sky bringing forth manifest smoke; the descent of the master, the Messiah [Jesus, son of Mary]; a creature[2] coming out of the earth; [the emergence of] the *Fāṭimī*[3] figure; and killing the *Dajjāl*[4]. In his *al-Yawāqīt wa al-Jawāhir fī Bayān ʿAqāʾid al-Akābir*[5], ʿAbd al-Wahhāb al-Shaʿrānī states the following:

إنَّ جميع أشراط الساعة التي أخبرنا بها الشارع حقّ لا بدَّ أن تقع كلّها قبل قيام الساعة، وذلك كخروج المهدي عليه السلام، ثمّ الدجّال، ثمّ نزول عيسى، وخروج الدابة، وطلوع الشمس من مغربها، ورفع القرآن، وفتح سدّ يأجوج ومأجوج، حتَّى لو لم يبق من الدنيا إلاَّ مقدار يوم واحد لوقع ذلك كلّه

Indeed, all the signs of the Day of Judgment that the Divine Legislator told us about are true – all of them must occur before the [Day of Judgment]. That includes, for instance, the coming of the Mahdī, then the Dajjāl, then the descent of Jesus, the creature coming out [of the earth], the rise of the Sun from its sunset, raising the Qurʾān up, and opening up the barrier of Gog and Magog. Even if nothing remained from the [lifetime of] the world except for a single day, all of that would occur.

God Almighty says,

فَهَل يَنظُرونَ إِلَّا السّاعَةَ أَن تَأتِيَهُم بَغتَةً ۖ فَقَد جاءَ أَشراطُها [...]

---

[1] T: Yaʾjūj wa Maʾjūj.

[2] T: *Dābbah.*

[3] T: Descendant of Fāṭimah; understood to be the Mahdī.

[4] T: A figure who practices deception.

[5] See: *al-Imām al-Thānī ʿAshar* / by Sayyid Muḥammad Saʿīd al-Mūsawī: 42, relaying [from al-Shaʿrānī's text].

Do they await anything except that the Hour should come upon them suddenly? Certainly its signs[1] *have come. [...]*[2]

The Arabic "*ashrāṭ*" is the plural form of "*sharaṭ,*" meaning "*sign.*" Hence, "*ashrāṭ al-sāʿah*" refers to *signs* that the Day of Judgment is near. Most exegetes believe that what is meant by *ashrāṭ al-sāʿah* [in this verse] is the appearance of the noblest Prophet in the person [of Muḥammad]. That is because Prophet Muḥammad, bringing his [two fingers][3] together, said,

بعثت أنا والساعة كهاتين _ ويجمع بين سبابتيه _

I have been sent forth while I and the [Day of Judgment] are like these two.[4]

Moreover, there are many reports explaining the *signs of the Day of Judgment,* noting, for instance, the spread of many sins among people. It has been reported that the Prophet Muḥammad said,

إنَّ من أشراط الساعة أن يرفع العلم ويظهر الجهل ويشرب الخمر ويفشو الزنا [...]

Indeed, among the signs of the Day of Judgment are that knowledge will be raised up[5]*, ignorance will manifest, wine will be drunk, fornication will be widespread [...]*[6]

---

[1] T: *Ashrāṭ* (sing. *sharaṭ*).

[2] Qurʾān 47:18.

[3] T: *wa yajmaʿu bayna sabbābatayh*; Although "*sabbābatayh*" or "*sabbāḥatayh*" can refer to the dual plural of his "index finger" (*sabbābah* or *sabbāḥah*), other sources indicate that the Prophet Muḥammad referred to his index and middle finger (*al-sabbābah wa al-wusṭá*), not his two index fingers. The point that has been understood from this gesture is that Prophet Muḥammad's message is directly followed by the Day of Judgment – that there is no more updated message to come before the Day of Judgment.

[4] *Amālī al-Mufīd*: 211-212 / Ḥ 1.

[5] T: *yurfaʿ al-ʿilm*; [The blessing of] knowledge lifted up [off of the people].

[6] *Rawḍat al-Wāʿiẓīn*: 485.

It has also been reported that Ibn ʿAbbās said the following:

حججنا مع رسول الله صلى الله عليه وآله وسلم حجة الوداع فأخذ بحلقة باب الكعبة ثمّ أقبل علينا بوجهه، فقال: (ألا أخبركم بأشراط الساعة؟)، وكان أدنى الناس منه يومئذٍ سلمان رحمة الله عليه، فقال: بلى يا رسول الله! فقال صلى الله عليه وآله وسلم: (إنّ من أشراط القيامة إضاعة الصلوات واتّباع الشهوات، والميل إلى الأهواء، وتعظيم أصحاب المال، وبيع الدين بالدنيا، فعندها يذوب قلب المؤمن في جوفه كما يذاب الملح في الماء ممّا يرى من المنكر فلا يستطيع أن يغيّره [...]

We performed the pilgrimage with the Messenger of God on his farewell pilgrimage. [At one point], he took the ring of the Kaʿbah's door, then turned to us face forward and said, "Should I not tell you the signs of the Day of Judgment?" The nearest person to him that day was Salmān, God bless him with mercy, who said, "Yes, O Messenger of God!" So [Prophet Muḥammad] said, "Indeed, among the signs of the Day of Judgment are wasting [opportunities regarding] prayers, following base desires, inclining toward [whimsical] desires, venerating people of wealth and selling religion in exchange for the worldly life. At that point, the heart of a believer dissolves inside of him or her – just like salt dissolves in water – due to the wrongdoing he or she sees but is not capable of changing." [...][1]

The report [from which this is only an excerpt] is a lengthy one.

Second type: *Signs* and events such as the disruption of the universal order, the fall of the current world order, and the rise of a new world order, as are mentioned in the following chapters [of the Qurʾān]: *al-Takwīr*, *al-Zalzalah*, *al-Inshiqāq*, and *al-Infiṭār*.

---

[1] See: *Tafsīr al-Qummī* 2:303-307.

4. *Signs* of the [public] appearance of the *Ḥujjah*, [that is, Imam Mahdī]. For, indeed, Muslims of all schools of thought have relayed ḥadīths attributed to the Messenger of God about the Mahdī, the signs of his [public] appearance, and what occurs during his days. *Ahl al-Bayt* have similarly reported in that regard.

   For it has been reported that Imam [Jaʿfar] al-Ṣādiq was asked about the [public] appearance of the *Qāʾim*. In response, he took a deep breath and said,

   يا لها من طامة _ وبكى _ إذا حكمت في الدولة الخصيان والنسوان والسودان، وأخذت الإمارة الشبان والصبيان، وخرب جامع الكوفة من العمران، وانعقد الجسران، فذلك الوقت زوال ملك بني عمّي العبّاس، وظهور قائمنا أهل البيت عليهم السلام)

   O what a calamity!

   [And he wept. He continued to say,]

   When castrates, women and blacks rule in the government, [when] the youth and young boys take command, [when] the Kūfah mosque is [left in ruins][1], and [when] the two bridges are assembled[2] --at that time will be the end to the rule of my uncle ʿAbbās's descendants, and [at that time will be the public] appearance of our Qāʾim, [the Qāʾim] from among us, Ahl al-Bayt.[3]

   It has also been mentioned in some reports that the *signs* of his [public] appearance include the following:

   خسف يكون ببغداد، [وخسف...] وخسف قرية (جابية) بالشام، وخسف بالبصرة، ونار تظهر بالمشرق طولاً وتبقى في الجوّ ثلاثة أيّام أو سبعة أيّام،

[1] T: *khariba* [...] *min al-ʿumrān*; In ruins and/or uninhabited.

[2] T: inʿaqada.

[3] *Al-Malāḥim wa al-Fitan*: 369 / Ḥ 532.

ونار تظهر من أذربيجان لا يقوم لها شيء، وخراب الشام، وعقد الجسر ممّا يلي الكرخ ببغداد، وارتفاع ريح سوداء بها في أوّل النهار، وزلزلة حتَّى ينخسف كثير منها، واختلاف صنفين من العجم، وسفك دماء كثيرة بينهم، وغلبة العبيد على بلاد الشام، ونداء من السماء يسمعه أهل الأرض كلّ أهل لغة بلغتهم [...]

A khasf[1] *that will be in Baghdad [and a khasf...]*[2]*; a khasf of the village of "Jābiyah" in Shām; a khasf in Baṣrah; a flame that appears in the east, [at its length]*[3]*, and remains in the atmosphere for three or seven days; a flame that appears from Azerbaijan – nothing can stand up to it; desolation in Shām; the assembling of a bridge near al-Karkh in Baghdad; the rise of black wind in it at the beginning of the day; a quake until much of it is swallowed up; a disagreement between two types of [non-Arabs],*[4] *and much bloodshed between them; the domination of slaves over the Shām region; a call from the sky that is*

---

[1] T: A description taken to refer to the earth swallowing up something; collapsing and caving in. The root kh-s-f can also be associated with a lunar eclipse and would be identified as such typically if the word for "moon (qamar)" follows it.

[2] T: This phrase is from the printed edition of Ibn Ṭāwūs's *al-Tashrīf bil-Minan fī al-Taʿrīf bil-Fitan* [*al-Malāḥim wa al-Fitan*].

[3] T: *Ṭūlan*; this could be referring to the length of the eastern horizon, for instance. It might also be referring to a vertical length describing a column-shaped phenomenon witnessed in the direction of the east. In other references, "similar to an immense thing dyed with [turmeric or red clay] (shibh al-hurdī al-ʿaẓīm)" appears instead of "ṭūlan."
Ibn Abī Zaynab al-Nuʿmānī (d. ca 360 AH / 970 CE), *al-Ghaybah*, ed. Fāris Ḥassūn Karīm, 1st ed. (Qom: Muhr, 1422 AH), 262.
Another reference reads, "like the form of an immense lasso (ka-hayʾat al-miradd al-ʿaẓīm)."
Al-Faḍl ibn al-Ḥasan al-Ṭabrisī (fl. 6th century AH), *Iʿlām al-Wará bi-Aʿlām al-Hudá*, vol. 2, 2 vols. (Qom: Muʾassasat Āl al-Bayt (ʿ) li-Iḥyāʾ al-Turāth, 1417 AH), 283.

[4] T: *al-ʿAjam*; non-Arabs generally, or people from the land of Persia, specifically.

heard by the people of earth – all peoples with a language hear it in their own language […][1]

Among the reports that have mentioned *signs* of the [Mahdī's public] appearance, the following have been mentioned:

خروج راية من المشرق، وراية من المغرب، وفتنة تُضِلُّ أهل الزوراء، وخروج رجل من ولد عمّي زيد باليمن، وانتهاب ستارة البيت [...]

The coming of a banner from the east; a banner from the west; strife that misleads the people of al-Zawrāʾ; the coming of a man from the descendants of my uncle Zayd in Yemen; and the theft of the curtain of the House [of God, the Kaʿbah][…].[2]

Moreover, [Imam Muḥammad] al-Bāqir has said:

لا بدَّ أن يملك بنو العبّاس، فإذا ملكوا واختلفوا وتشتَّت أمرهم خرج عليهم الخراساني والسفياني، هذا من المشرق، وهذا من المغرب [...]

It is inevitable that the descendants of al-ʿAbbās will rule. Once they have ruled, disagreed and their affair has become dispersed, then the Khurāsānī as well as the Sufyānī will mobilize against them – the former from the east and the latter from the west […][3]

The *signs* of the [public] appearance can be divided into [so-called] *inevitable signs* ([albeit still ultimately] subject to *badāʾ*[4]) and *non-inevitable signs*. They may also be divided into *near signs* and *distant signs*. They may additionally be divided into *pre-public-*

---

[1] *Al-Malāḥim wa al-Fitan*: 370.

[2] *Biḥār al-Anwār* 83:63 / Ḥ 1.

[3] *Al-Ghaybah* by al-Nuʿmānī: 267 / Bāb 14 / Ḥ 18.

[4] T: The change in outcomes, within some layers of destiny, based on a human's exercise of freedom in making choices. Of course, from God's perspective, transcending all variables and layers of reality, all final outcomes are inevitable, albeit some inevitable with a free-will trajectory to get there.

appearance signs and *post-public-appearance signs*. They may, moreover, be divided into *vertical*[1] *signs* and *horizontal*[2] *signs*; *signs that have already occurred* and *signs that have not yet occurred*; *signs coinciding with signs of the Day of Judgment* and *signs specific to the public appearance of the Qāʾim*; *signs having an aspect of generality* and *signs not having an aspect of generality*; *signs mentioned repeatedly in the reports* and *signs mentioned only in some reports*; *signs that the reports indicate are exclusive* and *signs that the reports do not indicate in terms of exclusivity*.

Furthermore, Sunnī books have also mentioned the *signs* of the Mahdī's [public] appearance. This includes books such as *Sunan Ibn Mājah*, *Sunan Abī Dāwūd*, and books by al-Suyūṭī, al-Ṭabarānī, al-Shāfiʿī and others.

Our objective behind this study is to point out that in examining the *signs* of the [Mahdī's public] appearance, the research should be based on [considering] similar and analogical [notions], such as the *signs* of the gospels and the *signs* of the Day of Judgment.

THE PHILOSOPHY BEHIND MENTIONING THE *SIGNS*

In order to delve into the philosophy behind mentioning these *signs*, one must pay attention to the following matters:

1. Indeed, the objective behind mentioning examples of these *signs* is to point out that the term *signs* of the [public] appearance of the Imam is not entirely exclusive to this phenomenon. Rather, there are analogical and similar [notions. There must be] emphasis on reading the *signs* of the [public] appearance similar to how and to the extent that other *signs* are read, while noting the differences.

---

[1] T: *Ṭūlīyah*; apparently, a reference to *signs* occurring in a causal series, one after the other.

[2] T: *ʿArḍīyah*; apparently, a reference to *signs* occurring contemporaneously.

2. A number of the [public] appearance *signs* are among the *signs* of the Day of Judgment.

3. The *signs* of the [public] appearance are not [all] on the same level. For some of those *signs* (*the general signs*) have occurred and some of them may have occurred to some extent but are of a gradated nature, one with potential to increase or decrease. As for the latter, it has been reported, for instance, [that the Mahdī appears], "after [the world] has been filled with inequity and tyranny," or [after people's] inclinations go with whimsical desires, or [after people] sell their religion in exchange for the worldly life. As for the former, [that is, *signs* which have already occurred], one of those *signs* of the [public] appearance is the commencement of the Noblest Messenger's prophetic mission. [Another example of the former type of *sign*] is the fall of ʿAbbāsid[1] rule – if one assumes that the ʿAbbāsids will not return to power. Hence, [in light of these two categories of *signs*] the mere occurrence of a *sign* does not entail that the [public] appearance occurs [immediately thereafter].

4. Indeed, some of the *signs* have a miraculous dimension to them, [leading to] conviction regarding the [public] appearance of the Mahdī, while other *signs* do not. Moreover, this is all with regard to the *signs* that are coupled with the [public] appearance, not the *signs* that precede the [public] appearance.

   Moreover, when it comes to such a *sign* that has a miraculous dimension to it, apparently the greater portion of [this type of *sign*] is meant for specialists, not the general public. For, indeed, a *sign* has two aspects: [one whose occurrence is within] realistic means; and another [whose occurrence] is beyond realistic means.[2] A

---

[1] T: *Banū al-ʿAbbās*; the descendants of ʿAbbās, the Prophet Muḥammad's uncle.

[2] T: When each aspect is discerned from the other, the relevant occurrences fall into place as *sign(s)*, which could not simply be explained by coincidence. For example, there would be a dimension to the occurrence which could not have followed the foretold sequence/pattern if not for it indeed being a *sign*. This

skilled specialist can discern each aspect from the other. [This applies] even to an *inevitable sign*, such as [the one referred to in] the following report transmitted by al-Mufaḍḍal, in which it is reported that a group, "known as 'Zaydīyah'," will then say, "This is nothing but mighty sorcery." This is, moreover, like the [response some had to the] *signs* of the Prophet Muḥammad. As affirmed in al-Mufaḍḍal's report, relaying the words of Abū ʿAbd Allāh [i.e. Imam Jaʿfar al-Ṣādiq] regarding the [Mahdī's public] appearance,

ويتَّصل به وبأصحابه خبر المهدي عليه السلام

News of the Mahdī reaches [the Ḥasanī[1]] and his companions.

This means the news reaches the Ḥasanī figure and his companions, who are treasures of God – treasures neither of gold nor of silver, but of men like blocks of iron.[2] The report continues:

فيقولون: يا بن رسول الله من هذا الذي نزل بساحتنا؟ فيقول: أخرجوا بنا إليه حتَّى ننظره من هو وما يريد وهو يعلم أنَّه المهدي [...]

They will then ask [the Ḥasanī], "O descendant of God's Messenger, who is this individual who has descended into our courtyard?" Then he replies, "Take us out to him so that we may see who he is and what he wants." And he knows that he is the Mahdī [...][3]

For, apparently, [in the future time described by the report], when news of the Mahdī reached the companions of the Ḥasanī – who

---

dimension of the *sign* is not something that experts of humanity would have been able to predict realistically beforehand. A relevant specialist can discern the two dimensions of a supposed *sign*, thereby confirming it as a true *sign* or not.

[1] T: Descendant of Imam Ḥasan.

[2] T: This description is from an earlier line in the source of the excerpt here.

[3] *Al-Hidāyah al-Kubrá*: 403.

are treasures of God with prior knowledge of those *signs* – they went out to [the Mahdī] in order to become acquainted with what he wanted and who he was. Hence, news of him is one thing, and what he wants is another thing. Merely receiving news [about the Mahdī] does not entail that one has necessarily become acquainted with him personally and become acquainted with his platform.

5. It has been reported, [as ascribed to Jesus, the Messiah, in an earlier reference], that the secret behind mentioning glad tidings [of *signs* to come] is,

   [...]تصديقي وتصديقكم، وعذري وعذركم [...]

   [...] a confirmation of what I profess and what you believe, and [mercy for me as well as you].[1]

   [When applying it to the glad tidings regarding the Mahdī,] this means the following: First, by means of miracles associated with the Imams, there is a confirmation of what the Imams told about the distinct features of the Mahdī and establishing that the truth is with them; second, there is a confirmation for the Mahdī [himself]. In other words, we will have confirmation of what the Imams have told about the *ghaybah* by witnessing [the actualization of those *signs*]. Then we will [see that those *signs*] apply to Imam Mahdī. Hence, conviction will arise regarding the universals, the *signs*, and then one will apply those [universals, those signs] to the [particular] instance, to the application, to the matter which becomes an argument making a case for others [to have conviction]. That is how [the *signs*] become the substance for systematic argumentation [in this regard].

6. Reconciling two distinct features, "arriving suddenly," and, "arriving after the *signs*." For the holy verse indicates this:

   فَهَل يَنظُرونَ إِلَّا السّاعَةَ أَن تَأتِيَهُم بَغتَةً ۖ فَقَد جاءَ أَشراطُها [...]

---

[1] *Al-Kāfī* 1:293 / Bāb al-Ishārah wa al-Naṣṣ ʿalá Amīr al-Muʾminīn / Ḥ 3.

> *Do they await (yanẓurūna) anything except that the Hour should come upon them suddenly? Certainly its signs*[1] *have come. […]*[2]

To clarify: The Arabic [verb] *yanẓurūna* [refers to the meaning understood] from [the noun] *al-intiẓār* [i.e. *awaiting*]. As for the Arabic *ashrāṭ*, it is the plural form of *sharaṭ*, meaning *sign*. What are meant by the *signs* of *the Hour* (*ashrāṭ al-sāʿah*) are the *signs* of the Day of Judgment approaching. When God Almighty says, "Certainly, its signs have come," that does not mean all of the *signs* have occurred. Rather, what is meant is that some of them have appeared. This refers to how the matter to which the *signs* point [i.e. *the Hour*] is approaching and the verse wants to explicate a matter of fact – that the arrival of the Day of Judgment will be sudden [i.e. Despite the fact that they already know it is approaching, due to the *signs*, it will still occur suddenly when the time comes]. This does not mean that they are -- suddenly -- awaiting it to come, such that the qualifier "suddenly" would be qualifying the awaiting. For it is the matter to which the signs point [i.e. *the Hour*] that occurs suddenly, and not the coming upon them that is sudden. Rather, [awaiting] the coming upon them should be from the get-go [i.e. upon witnessing some of the *signs* that have already come], not [suddenly] at the occurrence of the matter to which the signs point --that is *the Hour*. [*The Hour*] has been explained [elsewhere] as the awaited Mahdī [himself], as reported in *Mukhtaṣar Baṣāʾir al-Darajāt*[3]. Moreover, it has been reported that the Prophet Muḥammad said,

---

[1] T: *Ashrāṭ* (sing. *sharaṭ*).

[2] Qurʾān 47:18

[3] It has been reported that al-Mufaḍḍal ibn ʿUmar said:

> سألت سيّدي الصادق عليه السلام: هل للمأمول المنتظر المهدي عليه السلام من وقت موقَّت يعلمه الناس؟ فقال: (حاش لله أن يوقّت ظهوره بوقت يعلمه شيعتنا)، قلت: يا سيّدي ولِمَ ذاك؟ قال:

[...] إنّما مثله (أي المهدي) كمثل الساعة [...] لا تأتيكم إلاّ بغتة [...]

[...] Indeed, [the Mahdī's] parable is that of the Hour [...] It shall not come upon you but suddenly [...][1]

(لأنّه هو الساعة التي قال الله تعالى: (يَسْئَلُونَكَ عَنِ السَّاعَةِ أَيَّانَ مُرْساها قُلْ إِنَّما عِلْمُها عِنْدَ رَبِّي لا يُجَلِّيها لِوَقْتِها إِلاَّ هُوَ ثَقُلَتْ فِي السَّماواتِ وَالأَرْضِ...)

I asked my master, [Imam Jaʿfar] al-Ṣādiq, "Is there a scheduled time that people can know regarding the object of hopes, the awaited Mahdī?" He replied, "Glory be to God; [God would not] schedule his [public] appearance for a time that our Shīʿah would know." I said, "My master, why is that?" He replied, "Because he himself is the Hour that God Almighty described when He said,

They question you concerning the Hour, when will it set in? Say, 'Its knowledge is only with my Lord: none except Him shall manifest it at its time. It will weigh heavy on the heavens and the earth. [...] [Qurʾān 7:187]

Mukhtaṣar Baṣāʾir al-Darajāt: 179.

[1] It has been reported that Aḥmad ibn Muḥammad ibn al-Mundhir ibn [Jayfar or Ḥayfar] relayed that [Imam] Ḥasan, son of ʿAlī, said,

سألت جدّي رسول الله صلى الله عليه وآله وسلم عن الأئمّة بعده، فقال: الأئمّة بعدي عدد نقباء بني إسرائيل اثنا عشر، أعطاهم الله علمي وفهمي، وأنت منهم يا حسن، قلت: يا رسول الله فمتى يخرج قائمنا أهل البيت؟ قال: يا حسن إنّما مثله كمثل الساعة (ثَقُلَتْ فِي السَّماواتِ وَالأَرْضِ لا تَأْتِيكُمْ إِلاَّ بَغْتَةً) (كفاية الأثر: ١٦٨).

I asked my grandfather, the Messenger of God, about the Imams after him. So he replied, "The Imams after me are [of] the number of the chiefs (nuqabāʾ) of the Israelites – twelve. God has given them my knowledge and understanding, and you are one of them O Ḥasan." I then asked, "O Messenger of God, when will our Qāʾim – from among us, Ahl al-Bayt – mobilize?" He then replied, "O Ḥasan, his parable is that of the Hour, 'It will weigh heavy on the heavens and the earth. It shall not come upon you but suddenly. [...]' [Qurʾān 7:187]."

Hence, the verse comes with a hint of sarcasm, questioning how they will benefit from the reminder once that which the *signs* point to has come to pass suddenly. For at that point, there would be no more room for [preparatory] deeds. Rather, one should benefit from the reminder now – after the [conditions and *signs*] of the Day of Judgment and the Mahdī have come. Thus, after one's conviction regarding the [truth about] and the approaching of Judgment Day and the Mahdī, [conviction] which has come about due to the preceding [conditions and *signs*], one must act now. For one should suppose that at any moment the Day of Judgment will come suddenly. Once it has come, there is no more [chance to] benefit from acting. Therefore, the verse comes to require the principle of action and taking initiative immediately. It also includes an indication [that] there is no need to delay [preparation] for the [fulfilment] of its *signs*. For the *signs* are prerequisites for the *obligation*[1] that are beyond the scope of religious accountability[2]. They are not prerequisites for the *existence*[3] [of the obligatory act externally] such that they would be within the scope of religious accountability and for which preparation would be due. Thus, the case of these *signs* is like the case of the proposition, "If the Sun goes past its zenith, then pray." For although the Sun going past its zenith is a *sign* for the obligation of prayer, what is it that is entirely important? It is not the Sun going past its zenith that matters, [for that is beyond the person's control]. Rather, what matter are the prayer and preparing the prerequisite steps for the *existence* of the prayer act, such as the *ritual ablution*[4] and purity, and preparing all the prerequisite steps that the action of prayer hinges on. Similarly, one who wishes to

---

Kifāyat al-Athar: 168.

[1] T: [*Muqaddimāt lil-wujūb*; *muqaddimāt wujūbīyah*].

[2] T: *al-Taklīf*.

[3] T: [*Muqaddimāt lil-wujūd*; *muqaddimāt wujūdīyah*].

[4] T: *al-Wuḍū'*.

perform the *pilgrimage* must provide all matters that the [existence of the] *pilgrimage* [act] depends on before the ninth of Dhū al-Ḥijjah. He or she must buy the ticket, and prepare the passport and other matters, immediately, in order for him or her to have the chance to perform the pilgrimage at its time.

EXPLAINING THE SITUATION WITHIN THE MAHDĪ SYSTEM OF THOUGHT

In light of the aforementioned, the situation within the Mahdī system of thought becomes clear:

1. When the Mahdī appears [publicly, the appearance] will not be hidden to anyone. That is because [his public appearance] is preceded by [reports regarding] *signs* of his [public] appearance and, rather, the actual occurrence of some such *signs* before and upon his [public] appearance. Moreover, the philosophy of the *signs* is to safeguard the phenomenon of *awaiting*, as the aforementioned verse states.

2. [In one report, Prophet Muḥammad described the Mahdī as follows,]

   المهدي منّا أهل البيت يصلح الله أمره في ليلة

   As for the Mahdī from among us, Ahl al-Bayt, God will make ready his affair in a [single] night.

   Another report reads,

   يصلحه الله في ليلة

   God will make him ready in a [single] night.[1]

   In other words, the [public] appearance will be sudden. As we mentioned earlier, there is no conflict between the [fact that there are] *signs* and the [fact of the public] appearance being sudden.

---

[1] *Kamāl al-Dīn*: 152 / Bāb 6 / Ḥ 15.

3. The approach to dealing with the Mahdī issue has been reported in *Mukhtaṣar Baṣāʾir al-Darajāt* upon commenting on the following Qurʾānic verse:

[...] أَلَا إِنَّ الَّذِينَ يُمَارُونَ فِي السَّاعَةِ لَفِي ضَلَالٍ بَعِيدٍ

[...] Indeed those who [unreasonably] dispute about the Hour are surely far astray![1]

[The transmitter of the report asked], "What does '[unreasonably] dispute (*yumārūna*)' mean?" [Imam Jaʿfar al-Ṣādiq] then replied:

يقولون: متى ولد، ومن رآه، وأين يكون، ومتى يظهر، وكلّ ذلك استعجالاً لأمر الله وشكّاً في قضائه ودخولاً في قدرته

They would say, "When was he born? And who saw him? And where is he? And when will he appear?" – all of that out of rushing the command of God, doubting His decree, and having skepticisms[2] *about His Ability.*[3]

Furthermore, that people do not know the time in which the [public] appearance will occur, on the one hand, and the implication that the [public] appearance will come suddenly, on the other hand, mean that the [public] appearance might occur at any time and that one must await it and prepare for it. Indeed, not being acquainted with the [time in which it will occur] leaves a profound and clear mark on the soul.

4. The wording of some [other] reports is as such. For example, [it has been reported that Prophet Muḥammad said],

لو لم يبق من الدنيا إلاّ ليلة لملك فيها رجل من أهل بيتي

---

[1] Qurʾān 42:18.

[2] T: Dukhūl; If taken as the plural form of "dakhl/dakhal," meaning doubt.

[3] *Mukhtaṣar Baṣāʾir al-Darajāt*: 179.

Even if nothing remained from the [lifetime of] the world except for a single night, a man from my Ahl al-Bayt would rule in it.[1]

This wording comes up frequently in the reports, [not only] pertaining to the Mahdī's story, [but] also for instance in the following report:

إنَّ رسول الله صلى الله عليه وآله وسلم كان يوماً بارزاً للناس إذ أتاه رجل يمشي فقال: [...] يا رسول الله متى الساعة ؟ قال: (ما المسؤول عنها بأعلم من السائل ولكن سأحدّثك عن أشراطها)

One day, the Messenger of God was out in the open before people when a man walked up to him and asked, "[...] O Messenger of God, when is the Hour?" He replied, "The one being asked is not more knowledgeable of [when it is] than the one asking, but I will tell you about its signs."[2]

This is similar to prohibiting that one specify a time [for the public appearance of the Mahdī] and how the time of the Imam's mobilization is unknown – even to someone like the Imam. For the following has been mentioned in al-Mufaḍḍal's report as recounted in *Mukhtaṣar Baṣāʾir al-Darajāt*:

قلت: أفلا يوقّت له وقت، فقال: (يا مفضَّل لا أوقّت له وقتاً ولا يوقّت له وقت، إنَّ من وقَّت لمهدينا وقتاً فقد شارك الله تعالى في علمه وادّعى أنّه ظهر على سرّه)

[al-Mufaḍḍal asked], "Is there no scheduled time for [his public appearance that can be specified]?" [Imam Jaʿfar al-Ṣādiq] replied, "O Mufaḍḍal, neither do I specify a time for him nor can a time be specified for him. Indeed, the one who specifies a time for our Mahdī has [in doing so

---

[1] *Kashf al-Ghummah* 3:273; *Biḥār al-Anwār* 51:83.

[2] *Ṣaḥīḥ al-Bukhārī* 6:20-21.

allegedly] become a partner to God Almighty in His knowledge and has claimed that he or she has uncovered God's hidden [essence]."[1]

The reasoning [provided by the Imam] apparently denies such knowledge even to the Imams – and God knows [the reality of the matter]. Of course, this [must be understood in such a way that does not conflict with givens regarding the nature of a Divinely appointed] Imam's knowledge[2].

Moreover, God Almighty says:

يَسأَلونَكَ عَنِ السّاعَةِ أَيّانَ مُرساها ۖ قُل إِنَّما عِلمُها عِندَ رَبّي [...]

They question you concerning the Hour, when will it set in? Say, 'Its knowledge is only with my Lord [...]'[3]

God Almighty continues,

[...] يَسأَلونَكَ كَأَنَّكَ حَفِيٌّ عَنها [...]

[...] They ask you as if you were in the know of it [...][4]

It has been said – for example, by al-Zamakhsharī in his *al-Kashshāf* – that this [verse means],

تختصّهم بتعليم وقتها لأجل القرابة

[as if you, O Muḥammad] would specifically let them [alone] in on the knowledge of its timing because of the close [kin] relationship [with them][5]

In any case, the *apparent meaning* of the holy verse means that the Prophet was not acquainted with the time of the Hour and it denies

[1] *Mukhtaṣar Bāṣā'ir al-Darajāt*: 179.

[2] See: the book *Ḥaqīqat 'Ilm 'Āl Muḥammad wa Jihātuh* by Sayyid 'Alī 'Āshūr.

[3] Qur'ān 7:187.

[4] Qur'ān 7:187.

[5] *Al-Kashshāf* 2:135.

[that he had made an exception by] informing some of his relatives and no one else.

5. One report mentions [that Prophet Muḥammad said],

من سرَّه أن ينظر إلى يوم القيامة كأنّه رأي عين فليقرأ: (إِذَا الشَّمْسُ كُوِّرَتْ) [...]

Whoever would be delighted to look at the Day of Judgment as if it were before his or her eyes, then he or she should recite [the Qur'ānic chapter starting with], "When the Sun is enfolded, [...][1]"[2]

[That has been encouraged] because this chapter presents the *signs* of Judgment Day. Moreover, it goes without saying that having conviction regarding Judgment Day entails that the religiously accountable individual would have prepared him or herself for this voyage, especially since [its ship] will be arriving suddenly.

We can say something similar regarding the *signs* of the [Mahdī's public] appearance. For there is no inherent objective that is accomplished by being on the watch for the *signs*. Rather, being on the watch for the *signs* is sought after as a means to be on the watch for the master of the age, [that is, Imam Mahdī]. Hence, let one who reads the *signs* of the [Mahdī's public] appearance read them from the angle of conviction, and in the sphere of *practical reason*, not *theoretical reason*. For it has been reported that [the immaculate ones] have recommended frequent remembrance [of God] by reciting, "God is greater,"[3] or, "Glory be to God,"[4] or, "Praise be to God."[5] According to the *apparent [meaning]*, the goal

---

[1] Qur'ān 81:1–

[2] *Al-Durr al-Manthūr* 6:318.

[3] T: Allāhu Akbar.

[4] T: Subḥān Allāh.

[5] T: al-Ḥamdu lil-Lāh.

is to get *practical reason* in motion and arrive at the shores of faith, conviction and engaging heart in order to enlighten thought.

6. History has not recorded the existence of a school of thought that strives to bring about the features of Judgment Day for the purpose of expediting its arrival. Hence, it is befitting that we take the same approach when it comes to the *signs* of the [Mahdī's public] appearance. It would be flowery [but empty] discourse [to suggest] that we rush to commit sins in order [for the earth to be filled with injustice and thus] to have the Imam appear [publicly sooner]. For [the spread of sinning and the like], as we have discussed earlier, are *prerequisites for the obligation*[1] [to set in] and not *prerequisites for the existence*[2] [of the obligatory act]. Indeed, when it comes to [the spread of sinning and the like], it is an obligation *to stop* bringing about those things. One should strive to expedite the [Mahdī's public] appearance and *not* expedite the occurrence of the *sign* – the difference between the two is obvious.[3]

7. The following exchange with the Messenger of God has been reported:

[رجلاً أتى رسول الله صلى الله عليه وآله وسلم] فقال: متى قيام الساعة؟ [...] فقال له رسول الله صلى الله عليه وآله وسلم: (فما أعددت لها؟)، قال الأعرابي: ما أعددت لها من كثير عمل لا صلاة ولا صوم إلاّ أنّني أحبّ الله ورسوله، فقال له النبيّ صلى الله عليه وآله وسلم: (المرء مع من أحبّ)

---

[1] T: *Muqaddimāt wujūbīyah.*

[2] T: *Muqaddimāt wujūdīyah.*

[3] T: The author is particularly highlighting the problem of wishing for evil to occur. Just because the evil of the Sufyānī figure, for instance, is a *sign* for the impending appearance of the Mahdī does not mean that one should wish for the Sufyānī's evil to occur, let alone contribute to the Sufyānī's rise. Sure, when it comes to *signs* or other forms of preparation that are in line with moral and religious prescriptions, one would be encouraged to wish for and contribute to those. But the standard to be referred to, when in doubt, would remain a religiously legal one, defined by the leading Twelver Shīʿah religious authorities (i.e. *marājiʿ*).

[A man came to the Messenger of God and asked,] "When will the occurrence of the Hour be?" [...] The Messenger of God then said to him, "What have you prepared for it?" [The man then replied], "I have not prepared much good deeds – neither prayer nor fasting – but, indeed, I love God and His Messenger." The Prophet then said, "A person is with whom he or she loves."[1]

[This report makes the following points:] Firstly, shifting the question from "when?" to "what?" is a way to address the question appropriately by means of taking the position of [asking a redirecting] question. [For the response to the person asking] is to forbid [asking] about this time. [The right thing] is not to ask about the date and time [of the Hour].[2]

Secondly, the Prophet confirmed that what is important is for a person to identify *what is right*[3], love [*what is right*] and love the people of [*what is right*], such that doing so would be followed by action according to [*what is right*], leading to being resurrected with [*what is right*] and the people of [*what is right*].

Thirdly, the timing is unknown. It is a timing that God has in store because He knows that the [ultimate] well-being of creation resides in having their religious accountability last until that time.

Fourthly, reaffirming the inevitability of this matter.

Fifthly, paying attention to the educational dimension of being on the watch for those *signs*. For based on the *absolute indication in*

---

[1] *ʿIlal al-Sharāʾiʿ* 1:139-140 / Bāb 117 / Ḥ 2.

[2] T: That is, the Prophet Muḥammad redirected the person asking the question by asking him a question to shift the focus. Thus, the Prophet implicitly made it clear that it is not the right question to ask about the time of the Hour.

[3] T: al-Ḥaqq.

context[1] and the [fact that the] speaker is *in the context of explaining* that the matter to be asked about should be the preparation of good deeds, it is obvious that not mentioning the *signs* and [instead] limiting importance to, "What have you prepared for it?" indicate that [preparing good deeds] is exclusively important [in this regard] – nothing else.

In this light, one can understand the ḥadīth transmitted by ʿUmar ibn Abān, in which he relays that Abū ʿAbd Allāh [that is, Imam Jaʿfar al-Ṣādiq] said:

اعرف العلامة فإذا عرفتها لم يضرّك تقدّم هذا الأمر أو تأخّر [...]

Become acquainted with the sign. For once you have become acquainted with it, it will not harm you, whether this amr comes sooner or later [...][2]

What supports this is that the occurrence of some of those *signs* coincides with the concept of *awaiting*, and that after the occurrence of a *sign,* its benefit fades – as it becomes negated with the negation of its subject matter. For that which continues to accompany a person is the *awaiting* – as it is the object of one's religious accountability. Hence, what matters in the religious view is activating the *awaiting* phenomenon and preparing for [the Mahdī]. It is not important to figure out a *sign* except to the extent that it reveals [the truth, leading to] conviction.

8. It is possible that foretelling about events to come, such as the *signs* of the [Mahdī's public] appearance, may be [itself intended to fall]

---

[1] T: *al-Iṭlāq al-maqāmī*; The type of *unqualified/absolute indication* (*iṭlāq*) that allows one to understand that the speaker only intended to include the listed subject matter(s) of the ruling in question, unless proven otherwise. This depends on the speaker being in the context of listing the subject matter(s) of the ruling in question.

[2] *Al-Kāfī* 1:372 / Bāb Annahu Man ʿArafa Imāmahu [...] / Ḥ 7.

in the sequence of miraculous and otherworldly information, and so we reap the benefits that [such things have].

9. It is necessary to pay attention to [the fact] that, when in the face of dangerous events, some naïve people express their interest in the topic of Imam Mahdī and the *signs* of the [Mahdī's public] appearance, searching for more of that which may give them a glimmer of hope. Rather, some writers have even attempted to satisfy this desire, dedicating great efforts in order to sketch the future according to the easily accessible [religious] texts available to him or her – [the problems with this being that] most of those cited are ambiguous and vague; reliable reports among them are mixed up with unreliable reports; and many of them have been exposed to distortion, having been added to, removed from and segmented. Instead [of such attempts], a believer should savor the sweetness of *awaiting* – indeed, this is the meaning of his words,

   اعرف العلامة فإذا عرفتها لم يضرّك تقدّم هذا الأمر أو تأخّر [...]

   Become acquainted with the sign. For once you have become acquainted with it, it will not harm you, whether this amr comes sooner or later [...][1]

   Some have attempted to argue that being acquainted with the *signs* of the [Mahdī's public] appearance is an obligation, claiming that this follows from the obligation to become acquainted with the person of [the Imam], since such acquaintance would not be possible except by becoming acquainted with the *signs*. [The following points refute this claim]:

   Firstly, this argument does not apply to the *non-inevitable signs* and the *signs* that occur before his [public] appearance.

   Secondly, becoming acquainted with the person of the Imam is not limited to going through those *signs*, even if they are *inevitable*

---

[1] *Al-Ghaybah* by al-Nuʿmānī: 352 / Bāb 25 / Ḥ 6.

signs and coincide with his [public] appearance. This is analogous to how the Muslims became acquainted with the Messenger of God at the commencement of his prophetic mission despite lacking knowledge regarding the glad tidings [of previously anticipated *signs* pertaining to his prophethood]. Furthermore, the Imam will come with miracles through which others will be able to become acquainted with him. Similarly, he will have the inherited artifacts of the prophets[1].

[Some might argue that] the imperative form in the verb, "become" [acquainted] indicates a [religious] obligation or [at least a] recommendation to become acquainted [with the *signs*]. However, the *apparent meaning* of this command is that it is meant in the sense of *mentorship*[2], [guiding toward becoming acquainted with the Imam], not a *stand-alone*[3] [command, requiring acquaintance with the *signs* for their own sake].

10. Within the Mahdī system of thought, there are [several] terms that one should place importance on. Among these terms is the *pledge of allegiance*[4]. It has been reported in *Ṣaḥīḥ Muslim* that the Messenger of God said,

    [...]من مات وليس في عنقه بيعة مات ميتة جاهلية

    [...] Whoever dies without a pledge of allegiance on his neck has died a death of ignorance.[5]

---

[1] T: *Mawārīth al-anbiyā'*; Historical artifacts and/or miraculous items inherited from the prophets of old.

[2] T: *al-Irshādīyah.*

[3] T: *al-Nafsīyah.*

[4] T: al-Bay'ah.

[5] It has been reported that 'Abd Allāh ibn 'Umar said: I heard the Messenger of God saying,

من خلع يداً من طاعة لقي الله يوم القيامة لا حجّة له، ومن مات وليس في عنقه بيعة مات ميتة جاهلية

The following has also been reported [as part of a supplication recommended by Imam Jaʿfar al-Ṣādiq]:

[...] اللَّهُمَّ إِنِّي أُجَدِّدُ لَهُ فِي صَبِيحَةِ يَوْمِي هَذَا وَمَا عِشْتُ مِنْ أَيَّامِي عَهْداً وَعَقْداً وَبَيْعَةً لَهُ فِي عُنُقِي [...]

[...] O God, in the morning of this day of mine and for all the days that I live, I renew a covenant [with him], a contract [with him], and a pledge of allegiance to him on my neck [...][1]

Another important term is *love*[2] for him. This draws on the words of God Almighty when He says,

[...] قُل لا أَسأَلُكُم عَلَيهِ أَجرًا إِلَّا المَوَدَّةَ فِي القُربىٰ [...]

[...] Say, "I do not ask you any reward for it except love of [my] relatives." [...][3]

In a ḥadīth attributed to [Imam Jaʿfar] al-Ṣādiq, when [a group of his companions] entered into his presence, they saw him weeping and saying,

سيّدي غيبتك نفت رقادي [...]

My master, your ghaybah has left me sleepless [...]

Whoever revokes a covenant of obedience will meet God on the Day of Judgment without an argument [establishing a case in his or her favor]; and whoever dies without a pledge of allegiance on his neck has died a death of ignorance.

Ṣaḥīḥ Muslim 6:22 / Bāb Ḥukm Man Farraqa Amr al-Muslimīn [...].

[1] *Biḥār al-Anwār* 53:96 / Ḥ 110 Duʿāʾ al-ʿAhd.

[2] T: al-Mawaddah.

[3] Qurʾān 42:23.

Notice that Imam al-Ṣādiq uses the expression, “your *ghaybah.*” This points to something he mentions in the latter part of the report:

[...] نظرت في كتاب الجفر صبيحة هذا اليوم ـــ وهو الكتاب المشتمل على علم المنايا والبلايا والرزايا وعلم ما كان وما يكون إلى يوم القيامة الذي خصَّ الله به محمّداً والأئمّة من بعده عليهم السلام ـــ وتأمّلت منه مولد [غائبنا] وغيبته وإبطاءه وطول عمره وبلوى المؤمنين في ذلك الزمان [...] فأخذتني الرقّة، واستولت عليَّ الأحزان

[…] I looked into the Jafr book this morning. [The Jafr is the book which includes knowledge of deaths, calamities and tragedies, and knowledge of what was and what will be until the Day of Judgment – that God gave specifically to Muḥammad and the Imams after him]. I contemplated on the part of it regarding the birth of our [Qāʾim][1], his ghaybah, his delay [before appearing publicly], his long life, the affliction of the faithful during that age […] so I was moved and sorrows overcame me.[2]

Yet another important term is: *praying* for him. As one prayer goes,

[...] اللّهمّ أيّده بنصرك وانصر عبدك وقوّ أصحابك وصبّرهم وافتح لهم من لدنك سلطاناً نصيراً وعجّل فرجه وأمكنه من أعدائك وأعداء رسولك يا أرحم الراحمين

[…] O God, support him with your victory; grant your servant victory; strengthen [your][3] companions, grant them patience and initiate for them – from Your presence – an authority to help them; expedite his relief; and enable

---

[1] T: Some versions read, “our *Qāʾim* (rising one),” while others read, “our *Ghāʾib* (one who is in a state of *ghaybah*).”

[2] *Kamāl al-Dīn*: 353-354 / Bāb 33 / Ḥ 50.

[3] T: Another version reads, “his companions.”

him [to overcome] your enemies and the enemies of Your Messenger, O most Merciful of the merficul.[1]

An additional important term is *saluting* him. For example, [this is done by reciting] the *visit of Āl Yāsīn*[2].

---

[1] Miṣbāḥ al-Mutahajjid: 61 / Ḥ (96/69).

[2] T: Ziyārat Āl Yāsīn.

CHAPTER 9

THE SAVIOR ACROSS FAITH TRADITIONS

There is a consensus among the three religions with Divine origins (Judaism, Christianity, and Islam) and even other religions, on the recognition of and belief in a Godsent savior who will inaugurate Divine values and deliver the world – the material dimension included – to the shores of peace.

This savior has been mentioned within the following general descriptions:

1. The savior [who aids the] spirit from God and the soul, the upright, and the servant of God. ([See references within the] Gospel of John [such as John 14:10-30]).
2. The world in its entirety will follow him, [for he is the leader/chief ruler/prince of the world]. ([John 14:30])
3. The just savior, and the just ruler. (John 14 and Psalm 94).
4. Removing oppression and wicked [oppressors]. (Isaiah 11).
5. He does not speak out of [his own] desire, but rather speaks what comes from God and what he had heard from the Prophet and the friends of God, [the appointed *guardians*]. (John 14).

   Moreover, it has been mentioned in the appropriate place elsewhere that the Imam knows things like the Prophet knows them, even if the way in which he comes to know them differs. For instance, [the Imam] might come to know things through revelation [albeit non-prophetic revelation]. This is, [of course], assuming – as is the correct position – that revelation that is not exclusive to prophets. [That is, there are non-prophetic forms of revelation]. Moreover, [the Imam] might come to know things through mystical experience[1] or other means.

6. General guidance for people. (Psalm 37 and Daniel 12).
7. Extracting the treasures of the earth for him. (Psalm 37 and Daniel 12).
8. He dwells amongst people; he sees them but they do not recognize him due to their absentmindedness. (John 14).
9. Before him, the earth will be ruled by inequity and tyranny. (Daniel 12).

That is in addition to other relevant references from religious texts of Divine origins. For example, [the savior figure is] described in terms of [his] excellence in [the various] sciences; being a scholar of [the various] sciences; having access to the Unseen; passing judgments according to [the facts] in reality, [not merely the *apparent* evidence]; not [needing to act] out of *precautionary secrecy*[2]; clearing [up] the station of Jesus in the eyes of his supporters, testifying to his prophethood; Jesus being present with him; the Christians believing in him before those of other misguided groups; no one knowing his [public] appearance [timing], not even the angels; and that he will have a *return* [*from the dead*][3].

For additional references in this regard, see the following sources:

1. *Al-Barāhīn al-Sābāṭīyah [fī al-Radd ʿalá al-Naṣārá]* by Jawād al-Sābāṭī, a scholar from the 12th century AH;
2. The study *al-Kitāb al-Muqaddas Taḥt al-Mijhar* by Odeh Muhawesh, a Jordanian author also known as Abū Muḥammad al-Urdunī;

---

[1] T: *al-Kashf*; Revealing/unveiling.

[2] T: *al-Taqīyah.*

[3] T: *Rajʿah.*

3. *Anīs al-Aʿlām fī al-Radd ʿalá al-Yahūd wa al-Naṣārá* by Muḥammad Ṣādiq Fakhr al-Islām and [The book][1] by Muḥammad Riḍā [Riḍāʾī], [the two] who embraced Islam;
4. Also refer to *al-Masīḥ al-Dajjāl* by Mr. Saʿīd Ayyūb al-Miṣrī.

As for references from Books of Divine Origins, see the following:

1. John 15:[26]-27; 14:16; 16:7.
2. Matthew 24:27.
3. Mark 13:26.
4. Luke 21.
5. Psalm 37 and others.
6. Daniel 7.

However, despite their agreement on the inevitability of a savior, [the concept of a savior], they disagree over [who that savior is,] the application of [that concept]. Is it Ezra[2] or the Messiah? Is it someone from the lineage of the Messenger [of God, Prophet Muḥammad], or someone from the lineage of Abraham, God's friend?

The basis of this disagreement is the disagreement over interpreting the religious text – for the religious text outlines *general* descriptions, [much like] those referred to earlier. The application of [a given] textual description to specific persons is not a far-fetched occurrence when brought about by factors such as political [motivations], bigotry, love, emotional influences, and seeking to score points of pride for one's religion

---

[1] T: It appears that the author is referring to a version of the book described as *Manqūl Riḍāʾī*, written in Hebrew by Muḥammad Riḍā al-Yazdī, a convert to Islam in 1238 AH. The original Hebrew version, which is apparently not available, was translated into Persian as *Iqāmat al-Shuhūd* [*fī Radd al-Yahūd*] by ʿAlī ibn al-Ḥusayn al-Ḥusaynī al-Ṭihrānī.
See: Āghā Buzurg al-Ṭihrānī, *al-Dharīʿah Ilá Taṣānīf al-Shīʿah*, 2nd ed. Vol. 23, (Beirut: Dār al-Aḍwāʾ), 152.

[2] T: al-ʿUzayr.

after [realizing that] glad tidings of Divine origins spelled out that the [savior][1] would have exalted attributes and intensely high forms of excellence.

Furthermore, it is advisable to make note of the following matters:

1. One must distinguish between and not mix up the glad tidings [of *signs*] regarding the savior, on the one hand, and the glad tidings [of *signs*] regarding the Prophet [Muḥammad], on the other hand. For, indeed, even though the Prophet was a savior, his salvation is not [yet] world-wide, effectively-speaking.
2. One should pause, be careful, and study all the descriptions of the world-wide savior before making an identification of him as a particular individual. Then one should take into account the historical facts and the clues from the [religious] texts in order to make note of the [individual who the descriptions apply to], while including in the assessment all those who might [reasonably] be the world-wide savior.

For example, [if] in some [religious] texts it is mentioned that the Messiah, [Jesus, son of Mary], mentions the attributes of the savior, then it would be senseless to consider that the savior figure [being described by him] is the person of the Messiah, [Jesus], himself. Moreover, for the purpose of identifying the person of the world-wide savior as Imam Mahdī, it suffices [as an additional clue corroborating other proof] to cite the [meaning conveyed by a] holy text within the book of Revelation,

[... إنَّ السلطة كانت تريد قتل هذا الغلام ولكن بعد ولادة الطفل غيب]

[... Indeed, the authorities wanted to kill this boy, but after the child was born, he was made to disappear][2]

---

[1] T: *al-Muṣliḥ*; The reformer.

[2] T: The author appears to be paraphrasing a reading of Revelation 12:1-5. Noteworthy for the author is that this is from the New Testament and that the description plausibly applies to the Twelver Shīʿah Mahdī.

The researcher Saʿīd Ayyūb mentions the following in his book *al-Masīḥ al-Dajjāl*, third edition, p. 379-380,

ويقول كعب: مكتوب في أسفار الأنبياء: (المهدي ما في عمله عيب)

Kaʿb says, "It is written in the books of the prophets that there is no flaw in the actions of the Mahdī."

Then Ayyūb comments on this saying:

وأشهد أنّني وجدته كذلك في كتب أهل الكتاب. لقد تتبّع أهل الكتاب أخبار المهدي كما تتبّعوا أخبار جدّه صلى الله عليه وآله وسلم. فدلّت أخبار سفر الرؤيا إلى امرأة يخرج من صلبها اثنا عشر رجلاً، ثمّ أشار إلى امرأة أخرى، أي: التي تلد الرجل الأخير الذي هو من صلب جدّته. وقال السفر: إنَّ هذه المرأة الأخيرة ستحيط بها المخاطر، ورمز للمخاطر باسم التنّين وقال: (والتنّين وقف أمام المرأة العتيدة حتّى تلد ليبتلع ولدها متى ولدت) سفر الرؤيا ١٢: ٤، أي: أنَّ السلطة كانت تريد قتل هذا الغلام. ولكن بعد ولادة الطفل، يقول باركلي في تفسيره، عندما هجمت عليها المخاطر اختطف الله ولدها وحفظه [...]

And I bear witness that I have, indeed, found [the Mahdī mentioned] in that way in the books of the People of the Book. The People of the Book have tracked the reports regarding the Mahdī like they have tracked the reports regarding his ancestor, [Prophet Muḥammad]. Indeed, the news relayed in the Book of Revelation points to [the existence of] a woman who is the maternal ancestor of twelve men. Then it points to another [vision of a] woman – the one who gives birth to the last man [of the twelve, the man] who descends from the line of his maternal ancestor. As the Book [of Revelation] describes, indeed this latter woman [giving birth] would be surrounded by dangers,

> *and [the book] used the name "dragon" to symbolize these dangers. The Book of Revelation states, "[...] and the dragon stood before the woman who was about to give birth, so that when she bore her child he might devour it." (Revelation 12:4). Meaning, the authorities wanted to kill this boy. But after the birth of the child, as Barkley says in his commentary, when the dangers attacked her, God snatched her child and protected him.[1] [...]*[2]

Two Questions:

First question: How can one make an argument using religious texts from books that have been deemed distorted without a doubt?

Answer:

Firstly: The proof is the noble Sunnah. [That is the real authoritative source to establish the facts]. As for what has been cited [of the religious texts from books of Divine origins], it is fitting to consider that [supplementary] support [for the main proof which comes from the Sunnah]. Moreover, [citing such references from other books of Divine origins] is a way to convince the people of those books regarding the truth of Islam and the [Twelver Shīʿah] school of thought.

Secondly: Not everything in those books has been distorted. Indeed, rather, the Qurʾān has cited some of the books of Divine origins when it came to the glad tidings [of signs] regarding Prophet Muḥammad.

Thirdly: The books have mentioned distinct features associated with the savior. In particular, they have mentioned them before their occurrence.

---

[11] T: Barclay's commentary on Revelation 12:5 states, "When the child was born, he was rescued from the dragon by being snatched up to heaven, even to the throne of God."

[2] *Al-Mahdī al-Muntaẓar fī al-Fikr al-Islāmī* / Markaz al-Risālah: 13.

Hence, it is valid to rely on them from the aspect that they have foretold of [otherwise] Unseen matters which were proven to be true when measured up against the historical facts.

Second question: How can the Mahdī idea be an Islamic one when all of these religious texts indicate that it is an idea of Israelite origins, has been imported from outside the sphere of Islamic legislation and thought, and, furthermore, is not from the core of the Islamic religious reality?

Answer:

Firstly: The mere existence of glad tidings [of *signs*] for the Prophet and Islamic concepts does not entail their invalidation. Moreover, [if the objection were to be granted,] then it would follow from the mention of distinct features specific to the noblest Messenger in the books of Divine origins that Islam [itself] and, likewise, the Prophet [Muḥammad] are ideas of Israelite origins.

Secondly: It has been mentioned earlier that there is no corollary relationship between [the fact of] an idea being mentioned in the books of Divine origins, on the one hand, and it being an invalid Israelite notion, on the other hand. God Almighty says:

وَلَقَدْ نَعْلَمُ أَنَّهُمْ يَقُولُونَ إِنَّمَا يُعَلِّمُهُ بَشَرٌ ۗ لِسَانُ الَّذِي يُلْحِدُونَ إِلَيْهِ أَعْجَمِيٌّ وَهَٰذَا لِسَانٌ عَرَبِيٌّ مُبِينٌ

> *We certainly know that they say, 'It is only a human that instructs him.' The language of the one to whom they refer is non-Arabic, while this is a clear Arabic language.*[1]

For the *apparent [meaning]* here is that [those who unreasonably rejected what was right] realized that some of the Qur᾿ānic concepts matched up with those in the books of Divine origins, so they accused the Messenger of [learning] what he had from the People of the Book. Thus, the verse comes in the sequence of an *absolute indication in context* [to address their

---

[1] Qur᾿ān 16:103.

accusation, coupled with] not denying that what he has was *not* in the [earlier] books of Divine origins. Rather, the verse points out that a human being is not fit to be the source of the Qur᾽ān and, furthermore, that humanity is incapable of bringing it about – especially if those [supposed sources] do not know Arabic well. In light of the *absolute indication in context* here, there is no problem with [the notion of] a common idea among reports [of various sources].

Moreover, there are many testaments in favor of this case of ours regarding common ideas. For, indeed, the Mahdī system of thought, as an idea, precedes the message of the noblest Prophet, but Islam – in its authentic, Shīʿah thought – has transformed this idea from the proposition and talk of the innately anticipated future into a platform on the path of implementation after having conviction regarding [the Mahdī system of thought. This means conviction regarding the Mahdī's] existence as well as his influence [on multiple levels]: existential; legislative; spiritual; and guidance-related. [It also means] taking the [Mahdī idea] out of the Unseen and into reality; out of the future and into the present; and out of a dream and into an actuality. [This is such that] we savor it [by the moment]. It, thus, influences us and we are influenced by it. In this light, the Mahdī reports in our sources – contrary to those in Sunnī sources – are not merely the talk of a future [to come], but are rather talk of the present.

Thus, we savor life experiencing the Mahdī and the Mahdī lives with us, bearing our concerns and vigilantly awaiting the Divine promise as we too vigilantly await him with a passion. Moreover, the [relationship of] *guardianship* in our [school of thought] is vibrant and continuous. God Almighty says,

إِنَّهُمْ يَرَوْنَهُ بَعِيدًا

وَنَرَاهُ قَرِيبًا

Indeed they see [that][1] to be far off,

and We see [that] to be near.[2]

[1] T: I replaced "it" with "that" for the third person masculine pronoun in "*yarawnahu*" and in "*narāhu*" because the Qur᾿ānic verse is referring to forms of a Divine promise (i.e. punishment or the Day of Judgement), on the one hand, but the author is using this verse to evoke contemplation on the Mahdī, on the other hand.

[2] Qur᾿ān 70:6-7.

CHAPTER 10

SECRETS OF WAITING

Indeed, one of the concepts that coincides with the Mahdī idea is the concept of awaiting [the Mahdī's public appearance] – so much so that the two are like inseparable twins. Hence, one cannot be understood without understanding the other. Furthermore, a flimsy understanding of one of them seeps into the other. In light of this, it is necessary to explain the correct meaning of awaiting both for its own sake and for the soundness of the Mahdī system of thought. Hence, we will now discuss the secrets of awaiting. Among these are the following:

1. The hope, steadfastness and vitality that the *ghaybah* evokes in the hearts of oppressed who have faith in the [true] creed.

2. Instilling [deterrent] fear in the hearts of enemies, disturbing their sleep – for, indeed, he will come after them whence they are not aware. God Almighty says,

   [...] يَحْسَبُونَ كُلَّ صَيْحَةٍ عَلَيْهِمْ [...]

   [...] They suppose every cry [is directed] against them. [...][1]

3. The utmost warning and the full preparation of the public's rank and file for their Imam by means of embodying Islamic character traits according to the methodology of Ahl al-Bayt.

4. Promises [of reward] and warning [of punishment], glad tidings and cautioning. For, indeed, awaiting leaves the public's rank and file with [sentiments of] fear as well as hope resulting from the

---

[1] Qur'ān 63:4.

cautioning and [glad tidings] dimension of this idea and the Mahdī culture.

5. Indeed, in awaiting, there is an indication regarding the way of life [that we describe as] fighting for survival. God Almighty says,

[...] وَلَولا دَفعُ اللَّهِ النّاسَ بَعضَهُم بِبَعضٍ لَهُدِّمَت صَوامِعُ وَبِيَعٌ وَصَلَواتٌ وَمَساجِدُ يُذكَرُ فيهَا اسمُ اللَّهِ [...]

[...] Had not God repelled the people, some by means of others, ruin would have befallen monasteries, churches, synagogues and mosques in which God's name is mentioned [...][1]

For one of the attributes and characteristics of this world is the [phenomenon of] competing and conflicting forces. This is why the world of matter has been called the world of competing forces[2]. Through [competing forces], motion is put in order and the course from starting point to destination is set. Through its motion, the world is headed toward this destination and end point – that is, the government of the righteous, according to Mahdī thought. So long as we are in this [state of] motion, we are in a state of awaiting. For it is the hope of exchanging one culture for another, one life for another, and one goal for another. Moreover, there is an opposition between the notion of awaiting and [the notion of] despair. For the one who loses touch with [living the experience of] awaiting experiences despair, and the one who lives the experience of awaiting defeats despair. Furthermore, awaiting, [in this sense], is a notion that requires an object [which is awaited], and the best object to be awaited is the promised Mahdī – in light of who he is and what his platform is. Moreover, there is no conflict between the notion of awaiting the Mahdī and the words of God that state,

[...]إِنّا لِلَّهِ وَإِنّا إِلَيهِ راجِعونَ

---

[1] Qur'ān 22:40.

[2] T: al-Tazāḥum.

[...] Indeed we belong to Allah, and to Him do we indeed return.[1]

In a word, human society must advance, and the epitome of that advancement manifests with the [public] appearance of Imam Mahdī. For his age is the age of humankind's human excellence, and the community vigilantly awaits that advancement of human society. Indeed, [the community] is taking its course in order to achieve that advancement. For its role has not been deactivated. Rather, [it has an active role –] its role is to pave the way for that advancement.

In light of this explanation, it becomes clear that the Mahdī idea – with its treasures in terms of creed, education and human [values] for humanity's advancement and ascension toward rectitude, happiness and justice – motivates all of humanity. Its language is inclusive, inviting all religions of Divine origins. For it is not an idea that is exclusive to the right school of thought, the Shīʿah school. Indeed, a faithful human being and a faithful community must have a goal, believe in it and sacrifice for it – so long as the goal is possible and can be achieved. This is the meaning of the saying [attributed to one of the Imams],

انتظار الفرج من الفرج

Awaiting the relief[2] *is [part] of the relief.*[3]

---

[1] Qurʾān 2:156.

[2] T: The prime instance of relief (*faraj*) is the public appearance of Imam Mahdī. Hence, when the Mahdī's name is mentioned in Shīʿah circles, it is followed by the prayer, "May God Almighty expedite his relief (*ʿajjala Allāhu taʿālá farajahu*)," meaning, "may God make his public appearance sooner."

[3] *Al-Ghaybah* by al-Ṭūsī: 459 / Ḥ 471.

CHAPTER 11

ADDRESSING NON-SHĪʿAH DILEMMAS

THE DILEMMA OF ORIENTALIST THOUGHT REGARDING THE MAHDĪ SYSTEM OF THOUGHT

By this, we mean [the dilemma of] those who have denied the idea of Imam Mahdī altogether through various tactics, such as:

1. The tactic of casting doubt.
2. The tactic of reform and scientific critique.
3. The tactic of excavating[1] [a tradition's] heritage.
4. The tactic of modernity and post-modernity.
5. The tactic of globalization.

For, indeed, they have accused the idea of [being] myth and legend, used the language of mockery and have confined themselves to [accounts of] some bizarre conduct that was performed without legitimate religious basis.

Among the deniers are:

Donaldson, who in his book *The Shi'ite Religion* writes, "It is very probable that the dismal failure of the Muhammadan Empire to attain to equity and justice during the period of the Umayyad caliphate (41-132 AH) may have had something to do with the rise of the tradition that one absolutely

---

[1] T: Tanqīb.

guided by God would come in the End of Time."[1] He is also of the view that the Mahdī reports were fabricated before the compilation of any of the standard books of the Prophetic Sunnah, and [relays Ibn Khaldūn's view] that the major Sunnī collections of ḥadīth [i.e. those of Bukhārī and Muslim] do not include these reports [about the Mahdī]. Moreover, he writes, "But with the Shi'ites also the Ḳoran has not been regarded as sufficiently explicit [when it comes to mentioning Imam Mahdī], and what is lacking has been supplied in the traditions."[2]

[Another is] Goldziher, who in his book *Mohammed and Islam* writes, ["That which God tolerates, man may not oppose. He may cling to the hope that God will in the future fill with righteousness the world which now is filled with unrighteousness. Out of these silent hopes arose the Mahdī idea, the firm belief in the future resurrection of a theocratic ruler divinely guided (*as a reconciliation between the actual and the ideal*)."[3]] Yet another claims that the Mahdī idea is [a product of the] imagination present among the tribes of North Africa --[an imagination] based on ignorance, bigotry and inclinations toward the worship of idols. Moreover, Aḥmad Amīn al-Miṣrī, in his *al-Mahdī wa al-Mahdawīyah*[4], and Saʿd Muḥammad Ḥasan, in his *al-Mahdī fī al-Islām mundhu [Aqdam al-ʿUṣūr ḥattá al-Yawm]*[5],

---

[1] T: Dwight M. Donaldson, *The Shi'ite Religion* (London: Luzac & Company, 1933), 227.

[2] T: Donaldson, *The Shi'ite Religion*, 228.

Referring to the Mahdī idea on p. 227, he writes, "At the same time the very fact that the Ḳoran did not warrant any such hopes made it all the more necessary that they should be confirmed by appropriate and reassuring traditions."

[3] T: Ignaz Goldziher, *Mohammed and Islam*, trans. Kate Chambers Seelye (Yale University Press, 1917), 90.

[4] T: See:

Aḥmad Amīn, *al-Mahdī wa al-Mahdawīyah* (Cairo: Muʾassasat Hindāwī lil-Taʿlīm wa al-Thaqāfah, 2012), 12.

[5] T: Consider:

Saʿd Muḥammad Ḥasan, *al-Mahdī fī al-Islām mundhu Aqdam al-ʿUṣūr ḥattá al-Yawm* (Dār al-Kitāb al-ʿArabī bi-Miṣr, 1953), 48; 138.

claim that the Mahdī idea [as a developed term, not the mere phrase] was formulated by the Fāṭimids.[1]

THE DILEMMA OF SUNNĪ THOUGHT REGARDING THE MAHDĪ SYSTEM OF THOUGHT

Sunnī scholars of ḥadīth and exegesis have recorded the occurrence of the *ghaybah* in such a manner that leaves no room for doubt regarding it.[2] Moreover, they have accused those who deny it of lacking insight, expertise and acquaintance with even the most basic measures used in the field. Still, they have disagreed with the Shī'ah over the matter when it comes to a number of inquiries – despite conceding the *possibility* of committing to what has been reported by the Shī'ah [regarding the Mahdī]. We will now point out some of those inquiries:

1. The fact that his birth was not known to people leads to skepticism regarding [Shī'ah] Imāmī thought and the Mahdī proposition.

   The answer to this is two-fold:

   Firstly, even the birth of [some] prophets was unknown [to people]. Take, for instance, the unknown birth of Moses, son of Amram, and the unknown birth of Abraham.

   Secondly, even if it is out of the ordinary to keep birth a secret from both those who are close and those who are distant, history is filled with issues that require keeping birth a secret due to

---

[1] T: Assuming there is no printing error here, these latter two references are apparently included in this segment due to their views resonating with those described earlier (as opposed to their geographic or national backgrounds, for instance).

[2] T: The author appears to be referring to Sunnī scholars who believe in the Mahdī's birth and *ghaybah* and/or Sunnī scholars who believe in the principle of the *ghaybah* occurring when it comes to other personalities in religious history, such as prophets and friends of God.

numerous reasons. For example, consider the case of a man who had married a second wife in secret – she had borne children from him and the matter was kept under wraps for a lifetime.

2. Jaʿfar, the brother of Imam Ḥasan al-ʿAskarī, denied [the existence of a son of Imam Ḥasan al-ʿAskarī]. For Jaʿfar took the wealth of his brother as [his own] inheritance, implying that [Imam Ḥasan] al-ʿAskarī had no heir of the first tier.

   Answer: Citing the action of Jaʿfar – who is not immaculate – is not authoritative in order to make an argument. It is possible that he committed a sin – let alone made a mistake. Merely being the son of an Imam does not entail his immaculacy or that he is to be believed [in his claims]. The brothers of [Prophet] Joseph are the best testament to this. Furthermore, Jaʿfar had motives for denying the birth and claiming that there was no other heir – [the inheritance] and the eminent station of [Imam Ḥasan] al-ʿAskarī, a station which [people] go to great lengths for, souls are tempted by and men strive for. Thus, denying [the birth] would have been a matter of significant consequence for him – it would have been [self-serving][1].

   Moreover, had the likes of this argumentation been valid, then the claim of Abū Lahab – the Prophet's uncle – in denying the message [of Islam] would have been valid.[2] Granted, there is a [significant] difference between the birth [of the Mahdī as a fact] and the message [of Islam as a whole].

---

[1] T: Yajurru al-nāra ilá qurṣihi; he draws the flame toward his [own] round-shaped piece [of dough for bread].

[2] T: Meaning, if Jaʿfar's word should be taken because he is a close blood relative of an Imam, then Abū Lahab's word should be taken as well – for he too was a close blood relative of the Prophet Muḥammad himself.

3. The will[1] of Imam Ḥasan al-ʿAskarī to his mother, making her the executor[2] of his [will, trustee over his] wealth, without mentioning the Qāʾim in his will regarding all his wealth. This indicates that the child did not exist, as he did not mention his child in the will.

   Answer: Indeed, after Imam [Ḥasan] al-ʿAskarī wanted to give legal value to his will, he had some supporters of the government witness his will. These included, for example: al-Wāthiq's *mawlá*; Muḥammad ibn al-Maʾmūn's *mawlá*; and al-Fatḥ ibn ʿAbd Rabbih.[3] This would have required that he not mention his son in the will – in order to protect his life.

4. If the reason was fear for his son's life, then why did not the other Imams also resort to the same measures that Imam Ḥasan al-ʿAskarī resorted to in hiding [his son's birth]? For there is no difference between them when it comes to the necessity of protecting life.

   Answer: It is known to all, based on the reports about the savior, that the twelfth Imam will exercise a very active political role. Moreover, the timing of his blessed movement[4] has not been specified. Hence, every ruler entertains the possibility that his number one adversary will be Imam Mahdī. For his *primary* mission is to oppose tyrants – contrary to the case of other Imams. Indeed, the general character of [the remaining Imams'] legacies was to emphasize the [principle of] *precautionary secrecy*. Furthermore, reports have [been attributed to them which] prohibited getting involved in political conflict – for reasons that are mentioned in the appropriate places elsewhere. In addition, the reasons for keeping [the birth] secret did not

---

[1] T: Waṣīyah.

[2] T: Waṣīyah; Waṣīy in the feminine form.

[3] T: See al-Mufīd's *al-Fuṣūl al-ʿAsharah fī al-Ghaybah*, 69.

[4] T: Nahḍah.

apply in a necessary fashion to the cases of earlier Imams. For in their cases, there existed subsequent links in the chain of Imāmah – the series would not have died out. With the awaited Mahdī, on the other hand, the matter is different. That is, had the Mahdī not gone into *ghaybah*, and had he subsequently been killed similar to how his forebears were killed, then the series of Imāmah would have died out and the Divine plan would have [fallen through][1] – since he is the final Imam in the chain. Moreover, [Divinely] ordaining Imams only to the [specific number of] twelve Imams [after Prophet Muḥammad] is similar to how the prophets are [Divinely] ordained only to a specific number [ending with Prophet Muḥammad].

5. With this lengthy duration [of waiting], how can it be possible that the Imam does not contact anyone and that no one knows of his whereabouts?

   Answer: The same response given about al-Khiḍr who was mentioned in the Qur'ān[2] [and dwells amongst people without them recognizing his Divinely ordained role. The same response given about] Moses. For after Moses left for Midian, he was a prophet before being commanded to confront the Pharoah. No one was acquainted with him [as a prophet] until God commanded him to call people [toward God]. Similar was the case [of his *ghaybah*] during his travel for the term appointed by his Lord[3] and the deviation of his people in the Sāmirī incident. [The *ghaybah* was such a *ghaybah* that] even his successor Aaron[4] did not know the details of what Moses was doing [during his travel. The same response given about] the story of Joseph – even his father [Jacob] was not acquainted with his

---

[1] T: If the Arabic reads, "*inkharama*."

[2] T: He is referred to in Qur'ān 18:65, albeit not mentioned by name.

[3] T: Mīqāt Rabbihi.

[4] T: Hārūn.

whereabouts. [The same response given about] Dhū al-Nūn, Jonah the Prophet, [who remained in the belly of a fish for some time].

6. With the [extended] passage of time, the Imam's genealogy is forgotten. So the only[1] way he will be accepted [as the twelfth Imam and Mahdī] when he rises is if a miracle accompanies him. But miracles are for prophets, [not Imams]. Therefore, the notion of the Imāmah conflicts with the notion of a [final Imam][2].[3]

   Answer: The occurrence of a miracle is not exclusive to a prophet. Sure, as for the occurrence of a miracle coupled with the claim of being a prophet, that *is* something exclusive to a prophet. Moreover, the occurrence of a miracle, [coupled with a feasible claim], entails the truthfulness of the one making the claim.[4] Indeed, miracles and [Divinely-bestowed] honors have

---

[1] T: Because those who once knew him personally have not survived to identify him and, hence, people are not able to identify him as the son of Imam Ḥasan al-ʿAskarī. Unless, of course, there is some other technological means and evidence to identify his genealogy.

[2] T: *al-Khātimīyah/al-Khātamīyah*; Conclusion/sealing [of the Imāmah, in this context].

[3] T: For if there were a final Imam who must live for so long in *ghaybah*, then he would not be identified as an Imam at any point in the future for people to follow him and have his public mission accomplished. If the only way to identify him is through a miracle, and only prophets have such miracles, then there can be no such thing as a *final* Imam with these variables. Of course, the flaw in this line of reasoning is in not realizing that identifying the Imam can occur in more than one way and that the miracle potentially required is not specific to a prophet.

[4] T: Because God would not leave people to be fooled by such a wonderous feat if they had no reasonable way to figure it out on their own. Alternatively, looking at the bigger picture, the accumulation of evidence and context clues would increase the likelihood of the occurrence being a miracle until a certain threshold is reached – at which point one becomes decisively sure that it is indeed a miracle.

occurred in association with individuals who are not prophets. As God Almighty mentions:

[...] كُلَّمَا دَخَلَ عَلَيْهَا زَكَرِيَّا الْمِحْرَابَ وَجَدَ عِنْدَهَا رِزْقًا ۖ قَالَ يَا مَرْيَمُ أَنَّىٰ لَكِ هَٰذَا ۖ قَالَتْ هُوَ مِنْ عِنْدِ اللَّهِ [...]

[...] Whenever Zechariah visited her in the sanctuary, he would find provisions with her. He said, 'O Mary, from where does this come to you?' She said, 'It comes from God. [...]'[1]

[Thus, Imam] Muḥammad the son of [Imam] Ḥasan [al-ʿAskarī] who was born in 255 AH and inaugurated to the position of Imāmah in 260 AH, is alive. He lives through the various conflicts [of humanity] and the bankruptcy of [various] civilizations when it comes to achieving [humanity's noble] goals. All nations must advance with their hearts and minds in order to become [a single] community of the Mahdī and the Seal of Guardians[2]. Moreover, he has a *major ghaybah* that began in the year 329 AH and continues till this very day. With this [Imāmah], the disparity between Shīʿah thought and other thought is revealed.

For, indeed, the Sunnī belief in the Mahdī does not have the slightest influence on their conduct and the positions they take. That is because the Mahdī figure is ambiguous [in their thought] and lacks the notion of Imāmah in its correct, legitimate form. Thus, the Mahdī proposition [in their thought] is a superficial proposition that ends up left out in the cold – even if some of them acknowledge his birth.

This is contrary to what one finds within the school of Ahl al-Bayt, [the Shīʿah school of thought], where he is the [missing] link. He is the one who establishes the legitimacy of *ijtihād* and connects the Shīʿah to the Mahdī with a connection of spirit, jurisprudence

---

[1] Qurʾān 3:37.

[2] T: *Khātam/Khātim al-Awliyāʾ*; The Seal of God's Friends; The Last Guardian.

and conduct. Furthermore, to the Shīʿah, the period of awaiting [the Mahdī] is a period of change, development and the survival of the Mahdī spirit within them. This means that his objectives become manifest: refusing injustice, [refusing] the ascription of partners [to the Absolute, refusing] corruption and [refusing] falsehood; and undertaking the Mahdī idea as an undertaking of hope, victory and achievement.

In conclusion, to the Sunnīs, the Mahdī is a future occurrence that has no impact on their present. To the Shīʿah, on the other hand, the Mahdī is the past, present and future. For he is a principle among the principles of the religion or [at least] the school of thought. Moreover, he is the key to the legal scholar's legitimacy. Therefore, he is alive in the Shīʿah conscience, intuition and thought.

CHAPTER 12

CRITERIA FOR ADOPTION OF THE MAHDĪ VISION

The following has been reported as [part of] holy supplication [literature],

[...] اللّهمّ عرّفني حجّتك فإنّك إن لم تعرّفني حجّتك ضللت عن ديني [...]

[...] O God, make me acquainted with your Ḥujjah; for, indeed, if you do not make me acquainted with your Ḥujjah, I will stray away from my religion. [...][1]

Indeed, the richness of the Mahdī proposition, its indisputable historicity, and its acceptability to the religious mind, of its various sorts, have been linked to a dangerous phenomenon – [the phenomenon of false] claimants. This link has not been broken since the moment of the [Mahdī's] birth and [will not break] until the accomplishment [of his mission]. This is no surprise, for the phenomenon of prophethood and messengership has also been accompanied by impostors all along.

The following are some amusing [stories of relevance]. Someone once claimed to be a prophet and his [supposed] miracle was that when he would cast pebbles into water, they would break up [into pieces]. When he was asked to use different pebbles, he said, "You are harsher than Pharaoh, for he did not ask Moses to use a different staff." Another person made the claim [of being a prophet] and when he was asked to show his miracle, he said, "Whose miracle do you want?" They replied, "The miracle of Moses." He then asked them, "And what was it?" They replied, "The staff." Then he said, "Give me something easier." They replied, "The miracle of Abraham

---

[1] *Miṣbāḥ al-Mutahajjid*: 411 / Ḥ (536/146).

– for the fire to become coolness and peace." He then said, "I want something easier." Then the ruler said, "The miracle of Jesus – to raise the dead." Then he said, "That is what I will give you. For, indeed, I will kill the ruler and then bring him back to life." The ruler then said, "Indeed, I believe in your miracle, so there is no need for you to do that." The situation is similar when it comes to impostors of the Mahdī proposition. For some claim to be the Mahdī, or his specifically appointed *deputy*, or the Yamānī, or the Khurāsānī, or *the Pure Soul*, or the one with the black banner, or the son of the Imam, or one of the *Abdāl*, or some other title mentioned in the religious texts.

What is important is to note the following.

TYPES OF [FALSE] CLAIMANTS

Firstly: [It is important] to realize the types of [false] claimants or those for whom a claim was made in that regard. For they are of several types:

First Type: The likes of Muḥammad ibn al-Ḥanafīyah; Zayd the Martyr; and Muḥammad ibn ʿAbd Allāh, referred to as *al-Nafs al-Zakīyah.* Furthermore, it has even been claimed for some of the [other] Imams that they are the Mahdī – the *Wāqifīyah* and the *Bāqirīyah* making such claims, for instance.

Second Type: The likes of the ʿAbbāsid [caliph] al-Mahdī, or those of the *Bābīyah* movement, or Muḥammad Aḥmad ibn ʿAbd Allāh, the Sudanese Mahdī, and from among the Umayyad and ʿAbbāsid rulers, and others.

ROOT CAUSES OF [FALSE] CLAIMS

Secondly: [It is important] to realize the root causes for the deviation of those with this [false] claim. Among these causes are:

1. Adopting some aspects of [Mahdī] thought while abandoning other aspects. As God Almighty says,

[...] أَفَتُؤْمِنونَ بِبَعضِ الكِتابِ وَتَكفُرونَ بِبَعضٍ [...]

[...] Do you believe in part of the Book and defy another part? [...]

2. Adopting the *mutashābih* [verses] of the Qur'ān while abandoning its *muḥkam* [verses]. As God Almighty says:

[...] مِنهُ آياتٌ مُحكَماتٌ هُنَّ أُمُّ الكِتابِ وَأُخَرُ مُتَشابِهاتٌ فَأَمَّا الَّذينَ في قُلوبِهِم زَيغٌ فَيَتَّبِعونَ ما تَشابَهَ مِنهُ ابتِغاءَ الفِتنَةِ وَابتِغاءَ تَأويلِهِ [...]

[...] Parts of it are muḥkam verses, which are the mother of the Book, while others are mutashābih. As for those in whose hearts is deviance, they follow what tashābaha[1] in it, in pursuit of mischief and in pursuit of its ta'wīl [...][2]

3. Clinging to the adoption of particular [applications] without referring them back to the relevant universal [propositions].

4. Adopting bizarre, unusual or disregarded [religious] texts, or those that conflict with the [*famously adopted view*][3].

5. Seeking to engage in thorny, specialist studies while being a superficial and, [albeit] educated, [still a] non-specialist. This is like a person who, [as the saying goes], memorizes one thing but misses many.[4]

6. Not keeping track of, referring back to, and relying on the constants, [the steadfast principles]. Hence, they move around on the variable's horizon, regardless of the constant.

7. Not establishing a theory of knowledge for the subject matter under study, or mixing up between epistemic methodologies. [This occurs,] for example, in relying on dreams, *occult sciences*[5]

---

[1] T: *Tashābaha*; The past tense verb related to *mutashābih*.

[2] Qur'ān 3:7.

[3] T: *al-Mashhūr*.

[4] T: Ḥafiẓa shay'an wa ghābat 'anhu ashā'u.

[5] T: *al-'Ulūm al-gharībah*.

or *mystical experiences*[1]. Even if one were to grant, [for argument's sake], the validity of such matters – as major premises[2] [in principle] and as minor premises[3] [in particular instances] – and grant that they are authoritative to the person who experiences them, [the one who realizes their truth, the experiences of one person] still do not count as authoritative to other individuals [who have not experienced the truth of such matters. Thus], this is especially the case when it comes to someone who wants to prove his or her claim [about things beyond his or her own person] by such means – let alone prove him or herself to be true [in his or her claim about his or her own person] by means of [the former claim].

Moreover, it has been mentioned in the appropriate place elsewhere that even those who rely on the likes of these means know that some of them are among the schemes of Satan or are confused dreams or satanic delusions. Furthermore, had it been valid to rely on these means, then it would entail the adoption of conflicting notions and [notions] that belie one another.

8. Relying on invalid foundations, such as the [invalid] approaches of the Ṣūfīs[4] and sciences that are intruders[5] to Islam. It has been reported that Imam [ʿAlī] al-Hādī said:

---

[1] T: *al-Mukāshafāt* (sing. *al-mukāshafah*); Associated with extrasensory perception.

[2] T: *Kubrawīyan.*

[3] T: *Ṣughrawīyan.*

[4] T: It must be noted that by "Ṣūfī," the author is not referring to Islamic spirituality and disciplined practice – for that is the core of Shīʿah Islam. Rather, the author is referring to misguided beliefs and illegitimate practices associated with the label "Ṣūfī/Ṣūfism/Taṣawwuf."

[5] T: This is not referring to advancements in technology and fields of knowledge. It is specifically referring to claims of knowledge that contradict established Islamic principles and teachings. For, in principle, Islam encourages learning and even traveling to the far reaches of the earth in order to advance knowledge.

لا تلتفتوا إلى هؤلاء الخدّاعين فإنّهم خلفاء الشيطان ومخرّبو قواعد الدين، يتزهّدون لراحة الأجسام، ويتهجّدون لصيد الأنعام [يتجوّعون] عمراً حتّى يديخوا للايكاف حمراً لا يهلّلون إلاّ لغرور الناس ولا يقلّلون الغذاء إلاّ لملأ العساس واختلاس قلوب الدفناس، يكلّمون الناس بإملائهم في الحبّ ويطرحون باذليلائهم في الجبّ أورادهم الرقص والتصدية، وأذكارهم الترنّم والتغنية فلا يتبعهم إلاّ السفهاء ولا يعتقدهم إلاّ الحمقاء، فمن ذهب إلى زيارة أحد منهم حيّاً وميّتاً فكأنّما ذهب إلى زيارة الشيطان وعبادة الأوثان، ومن أعان أحداً منهم فكأنّما أعان يزيد ومعاوية وأبا سفيان

Do not pay attention to those deceivers – for, indeed, they are the successors of Satan and the destroyers of the foundations of religion. They take up asceticism for the relief of [their] physical bodies and keep vigil in order to hunt cattle. They starve themselves for a lifetime in order to bring donkeys under [their] control to saddle them up. They do not chant, "there is no god but God," except to deceive people, and do not decrease food [consumption] except to fill [their] huge bowls and steal the hearts of the [foolish, stingy, or lazy][1]. They speak to people by means of them dictating [to people] about love and, [the people], with their hearts broken, are cast into the well[2]. Their litanies are dance and clapping, and their invocations are but vocal tunes and singing [associated with distraction][3]. Thus, no one would follow them except for the feeble-

---

[1] T: al-Difnās.

[2] T: Or, "submitting themselves are cast into the well." These two translations assuming *bi idhlīlāʾihim* is the correct reading of the original manuscript and that *idhlīlāʾ* is a derivative of *idhlawlá*, as expressed by al-Ḥurr al-ʿĀmilī in his words following this report.

[3] T: I have added this clarification in brackets because, according to Twelver Shīʿah Islamic jurisprudence, the definition of *ghināʾ* is understood by leading scholars to include the idea of it being done in tunes that are commensurate for gatherings of distraction [away from God] and play (*al-lahw wa al-laʿib*).

minded and no one would believe [in] them except for the foolish. Whoever had gone to visit any of them alive and[/or] dead, it is as if he or she had gone to visit Satan and worship idols, and whoever had assisted any of them, it is as if he or she had assisted Yazīd, Muʿāwiyah and Abū Sufyān.

Then one of his companions asked him,

وإن كان معترفاً بحقوقكم ؟

Is that so even if he or she[1] *[faithfully] acknowledges your rights?*

[The Imam] then looked at him while seeming to be upset[2] and said:

دع ذا عنك، من اعترف بحقوقنا لم يذهب في عقوقنا أمَا تدري أنّهم أخس طوائف الصوفية والصوفية كلّهم مخالفونا وطريقتهم مغايرة لطريقتنا وإن هم إلاّ نصارى أو مجوس هذه الأمّة أولئك الذين يجهدون في إطفاء نور الله بأفواههم والله متمّ نوره ولو كره الكافرون

Relieve yourself of [the burden of considering] that [scenario. For] the one who [faithfully] acknowledges our rights would not go on the path of [abandoning dutifulness][3] *toward us. Do you not know that they are the most contemptible group among the Ṣūfīs, and [that] all*[4]

---

[1] T: Meaning, the Ṣūfī who is being visited.

[2] T: Shibh al-mughḍab.

[3] T: *ʿUqūq.*

[4] T: There are indications from other reports and the commentaries by scholars that, in certain cases, a Shīʿah would be excused for calling him or herself a "Ṣūfī" (e.g., in cases of *taqīyah*). But it goes without saying that such a Shīʿah individual should not adopt non-Shīʿah beliefs. Core issues to address in this regard are both the adoption of unreasonable beliefs and practices associated with Ṣūfism, and

of the Ṣūfis are in opposition to us and their way is contrary to our way? They are but the Christians or the Magi of this community. They are the ones who exhaust [themselves] in trying to extinguish the light of God with their mouths, and God refuses but to complete His light, though [those who unreasonably reject what is right][1] *be averse.*[2]

ROOT CAUSES FOR THE INFLUENCE OF [FALSE] CLAIMS ON THE PUBLIC'S RANK AND FILE

Thirdly: [It is important] to realize the causes for the influence of these forces of darkness on the public's rank and file. Among these causes are:

1. Ignorance, exaggerating [notions] of the Unseen, divorcing the world of competing forces from the natural causes [that actually govern it], and explaining natural phenomena based on guesswork.

2. Poverty. But poverty itself is not the cause. Rather, the cause is to feel poor, oppressed and deprived, to record it and blame it on the religious establishment, or to consider that the political establishment is the religious establishment, or [the cause is] an illusionary psychological feeling.

   For, indeed, to feel poor – with a negative outlook – can be a cause for the infiltration of this thinking. This is done either by: pumping in masses of wealth and buying people's souls; or by having poverty be an assisting factor in developing phony spiritual connections —even if only [by having such phony

---

being associated with what has come to represent those invalid beliefs and practices.

[1] T: al-Kāfirūn.

[2] *Al-Ithnā ʿAsharīyah* by al-Ḥurr al-ʿĀmilī: 28-29.

spiritual connections evoke] a numbing effect, or [in that such phony spiritual connections reinforce a sense of] inability to fight poverty through natural means, which in turn causes the person to seek out [either solely] supernatural means or [solely] natural means in order to overcome poverty, or [in that such phony spiritual connections lead the person on] a quest for a patron to fight poverty, like a knight in shining armor.

3. Activating the rhethoric of treason accusations and *takfīr*[1]; adding movement spirit to one's rhetoric; using a halo of holiness; and distributing symbolic badges [of honor] to members.

4. Utilizing attractive tactics in one's rhetoric and education. This includes notions such as: "annihilation in God"[2]; or "the return to God"[3]; or "the eye of certainty"[4] and "the truth of certainty."[5] For, indeed, even though some of the usages of such rhetoric are [referring to] true [realities], these terms are being passed out for the cheapest of prices and are being dealt with based on a fallacious mystical [approach]. Alternatively, [this includes] the invitation to exaggerate in one's love for Ahl al-Bayt to such an extent that reaches the degree of the Bāṭinīyah[6].

---

[1] T: Typically understood to mean the excessive, extremist, unconventional, and malicious judgment that a given person who professes Islam is not to be considered a Muslim. This is invoked in order to rid the person of his or her *Muslim* rights within the Muslim community.

[2] T: al-Fanāʾ fī Allāh.

[3] T: al-ʿAwdah ilá Allāh.

[4] T: ʿAyn al-yaqīn.

[5] T: Ḥaqq al-yaqīn.

[6] T: In this context, the point is that the love should not be independent of love for God. The love for Ahl al-Bayt flows from one's love for God, because they are the excellent examples of devotion to God and of putting Divine teachings into action – the epitome of excellence as human beings. Going beyond that would not merely be an exaggeration and a failure to properly honor Ahl al-Bayt – it would be falling

5. Systematic destruction of one's personality – thoughts, beliefs, values and conduct. This is done by repetition, [blind] following, employing the tactic of herd mentality[1], blind compliance, indoctrination[2], and creating a spirit of rebellion against [true] intellectual sources.
6. Isolation [of a person, keeping him or her] away from scholars and bringing about a spirit of hatred and enmity toward them. Furthermore, [bringing about a spirit] authorizing their bloodshed by distorting their image, portraying them as a reason for why the Imam has not yet appeared [publicly] or claiming that killing the scholars will expedite his [public] appearance.
7. Double standards in action. On the one hand, they are invited toward special rituals that are intruders [to Islam]. On the other hand, the [tradition's] religious commandments are [deemed] deactivated under the pretext that they are commandments based [merely] on the *apparent [meanings* of the religious texts] and that one must arrive at the *hidden* [*meanings]* of the Sharīʿah. When it comes to committing forbidden acts, some of them even went as far as to forbid that which is known -- as a *necessarily established truth* -- to be lawful, or to deem lawful that which is known -- likewise -- to be forbidden.

NEGATIVE CORRELATIONS OF [FALSE] CLAIMS

Fourthly: [It is important] to realize the correlations of this [false] claim. Among these are:

---

short of the absolute love and devotion due to God Almighty as the One and Only. The author mentions Bāṭinīyah here in the sense that they conceal blasphemous views despite outwardly professing love for Ahl al-Bayt.

[1] T: *al-ʿAql al-jamʿī*; In a different context, this term might be used in the sense of collective intelligence.

[2] T: al-Talqīn.

1. Lying.
2. Temptation toward ignorance.[1]
3. Depreciating[2] *what is right.*
4. Secrecy and stealth in approach, conduct and thought.
5. Deception, misguidance and foolishness.
6. Exaggeration.

CAUSES OF GOING ASTRAY

Fifthly: [It is important] to realize the causes of going astray. Among these are:

1. The psychological and emotional factor.
2. The philosophical factor and going astray in terms of thought.
3. The political factors, such as infiltration by foreign agencies for various motives; bringing about discord and conflict; embarrassing the Shīʿah school of thought; bringing about groups that pressure the Shīʿah [into a certain] position; and activation by internal governing bodies for many purposes such as keeping people distracted, eliminating the opposition through them, and justifying their failure.
4. The materialistic factor, the perks of fame, and acquiring [what will eventually become] the wreckage[3] of the worldly life.
5. Rushing, lacking patience, and running after the attainment of euphoria – even if it be illusory – of the Mahdī cause.

---

[1] T: al-Ighrāʾ bil-Jahl.

[2] T: Bakhs.

[3] T: Ḥuṭām.

TREATMENT MECHANISMS FOR GOING ASTRAY

Sixthly: [It is important] to realize the forms of immunity-building that can treat these forms of going astray. Among these are:

1. Adopting knowledge:

   Firstly: Knowing that deviant movements have existed throughout history.

   Secondly: Knowledge and awareness to comprehend the Mahdī proposition, to comprehend the roles, and to comprehend how *awaiting* [should be].

2. Adopting the principle of not trusting hidden, strange, bizarre and illusory thought; also [not trusting] movements and leadership [figures] that are [not known but merely] suppositional[1] and unknown; and [not trusting] secret meetings.

3. Adopting the [principle] that the default is to [defer to] action covered by [religious] legitimacy, and the endorsement of the law that, "God is not obeyed from whence He is disobeyed." Steadfast religious principles include, for example: *prayer*; *fasting*; *promoting virtue and preventing vice*; avoiding sins such as harming oneself without a legal justification; and detesting terrorist thought that [attempts to justify] *takfir*, authorizing the bloodshed and violation of people's honor[2]. Such steadfast principles are to be deferred to by default and are to be relied upon in actions, legislations and approvals.

4. Adopting the approach of warning [others] against Ṣūfī conduct, rhetoric and methodology.

---

[1] T: *al-Maẓnūnah*; Related to *ẓann*; probable, likely, but not known in a way that would make one sure and content.

[2] T: *A'rāḍ* (sing. *'irḍ*).

5. Conviction that Shīʿah thought is authentic and that it has had [deep] roots and a methodology since the time of the Prophet until this very day. This is the path that the Prophet and his close, pure kin outlined. Hence, the [approaches of those] without authoritative status and with thought that is incomplete and sterile are rejected. For, indeed, we are [in] a time period between past that is known, and a future that is outlined and known. Any trend of thought must be measured based on this criterion. As for an unknown [figure] who does not have deeply-rooted jurisprudence, well-defined thought, or a comprehensive and steadfast platform[1], it is not possible to accept [his or her claims] and lean on him or her [in that regard].
6. Adopting the culture of not accepting [the claims of] those who claim [to have special] *knowledge by God's presence*[2], those of bizarre scientific claims, and those of rationally, reasonably, and religiously unheard-of approaches.
7. Spreading a culture of *not* identifying the Mahdī proposition [descriptions of characters/elements] with specific persons [except for the Mahdī himself; a culture of *not*] restricting it to and embodying it in individual and personal forms.[3]

---

[1] T: Mashrūʿ; Project, campaign, mission.

[2] T: *al-ʿIlm al-Ladunnī*; Knowledge *from* God in a way that is not commonly accessible.

[3] T: It is also possible that the author means to encourage seeing even the Mahdī concept itself as beyond the person of the twelfth Imam. In other words, even though the Mahdī is the twelfth Imam, the son of Imam Ḥasan al-ʿAskarī, the ideals that the Mahdī represents are goals that everyone should play a part in achieving. In that sense, then, the Mahdī proposition goes beyond the individual person of the twelfth Imam.

REFERENCES

The Holy Qur'ān

Al-Ithnā 'Asharīyah by al-Ḥurr al-'Āmilī / edited by[1] Sayyid Mahdī al-Lāzawardī / Dār al-Kutub al-'Ilmīyah / Qom.

Al-Iḥtijāj by al-Ṭabarsī / edited by Muḥammad Bāqir al-Kharsān / printing press: al-Nu'mān / Dār al-Nu'mān.

Al-Ikhtiṣāṣ by Shaykh al-Mufīd / edited by 'Alī Akbar Ghaffārī / Jamā'at al-Mudarrisīn / Qom.

Ikhtiyār Ma'rifat al-Rijāl by Shaykh al-Ṭūsī / 1404 AH edition / Mu'assasat Ahl al-Bayt / Qom.

Al-Irshād by al-Mufīd / edited by Mu'assasat Āl al-Bayt / 2nd edition / 1414 AH.

Al-Asfār al-Arba'ah by Mullā Ṣadr al-Dīn Muḥammad al-Shīrāzī / Beirut.

Al-Uṣūl al-'Āmmah lil-Fiqh al-Muqāran by Muḥammad Taqī al-Ḥakīm / 2nd edition / 1979 CE / Āl al-Bayt.

Aḍwā' 'alá al-Ṣaḥīḥayn by Muḥammad Ṣādiq al-Najmī / 1st edition / 1419 AH / Mu'assasat al-Ma'ārif al-Islāmīyah / Qom.

Al-Amālī by Shaykh al-Mufīd / edited by 'Alī Akbar al-Ghaffārī / published by Jamā'at al-Mudarrisīn Qom.

---

1 T: "Edited by" in the references here is a rendering of the Arabic *taḥqīq* (investigation), so it often involves some commentary and much research related to the text and references.

Al-Imām al-Thānī ʿAshar by Sayyid Muḥammad Saʿīd al-Mūsawī / Manshūrāt Maktabat Nīnawá / Karbalāʾ / Maṭbaʿat al-Qaḍāʾ / Najaf 1393 AH / 1973 CE.

Al-Imāmah wa al-Tabṣirah by Ibn Bābawayh / 1st edition / 1409 CE / Muʾassasat Āl al-Bayt li-Iḥyāʾ al-Turāth.

Al-Anwār al-Qudsīyah by Muḥammad Ḥusayn al-Iṣfahānī / 1st edition / 1415 AH / Muʾassasat al-Maʿārif al-Islāmīyah / Qom.

Biḥār al-Anwār by al-Majlisī / Muʾassasat al-Wafāʾ / Beirut / 1403 AH.

Baṣāʾir al-Darajāt by Muḥammad ibn al-Ḥasan al-Ṣaffār / 1404 AH edition / printing press: Aḥmadī / Tehran.

Al-Bayān fī Tafsīr al-Qurʾān by Sayyid al-Khūʾī / 4th edition / 1395 AH / Dār al-Zahrāʾ / Beirut.

Tārīkh Ibn Khaldūn by Ibn Khaldūn / 4th edition / Dār Iḥyāʾ al-Turāth al-ʿArabī / Beirut.

Al-Tārīkh al-Kabīr by al-Bukhārī / al-Maktabah al-Islāmīyah / Turkey.

Tadhkirat al-Ḥuffāẓ by al-Dhahabī / Dār Iḥyāʾ al-Turāth al-ʿArabī / Beirut.

Tafsīr al-ʿAyyāshī by al-ʿAyyāshī / al-Maktabah al-ʿIlmīyah al-Islāmīyah / Tehran / 1380 AH.

Tafsīr al-Qummī by ʿAlī ibn Ibrāhīm al-Qummī / Muʾassasat Dār al-Kitāb Qom / 3rd edition.

Al-Thāqib fī al-Manāqib by Ibn Ḥamzah al-Ṭūsī / edited by Nabīl Riḍā ʿAlawān / 2nd edition.

Al-Kharāʾij wa al-Jarāʾiḥ by Quṭb al-Dīn al-Rāwandī / Muʾassasat al-Imām al-Mahdī / Qom.

Al-Khiṣāl by Shaykh al-Ṣadūq / edited by ʿAlī Akbar Ghaffārī / published by Jamāʿat al-Mudarrisīn Qom.

Al-Durr al-Manthūr by Jalāl al-Dīn al-Suyūṭī / 1st edition / 1365 AH / Dār al-Maʿrifah.

Rijāl al-Najāshī by Abū al-ʿAbbās Aḥmad al-Najāshī / edited by al-Zanjānī / 5th edition / 1416 AH / printed and published by Jamāʿat al-Mudarrisīn / Qom.

Rawḍat al-Wāʿiẓīn by Muḥammad ibn al-Fattāl al-Naysābūrī / Manshūrāt al-Raḍī / Qom.

Sunan Abī Dāwūd by Abū Dāwūd al-Sijistānī / printing press: Dār al-Fikr Beirut / 1st edition / 1410 AH.

Sharḥ al-Asmāʾ al-Ḥusná by Mullā Hādī al-Sabzawārī / Manshūrāt Maktabat Baṣīratī / Qom.

Sharḥ Muslim by al-Nawawī / 1407 AH edition / Dār al-Kitāb al-ʿArabī / Beirut.

Ṣaḥīḥ al-Bukhārī by al-Bukhārī / Dār al-Fikr / 1st edition / 1411 AH.

Ṣaḥīḥ Muslim by Muslim ibn al-Ḥajjāj al-Naysābūrī / Dār al-Fikr / Beirut.

Al-Ṣirāṭ al-Mustaqīm by ʿAlī al-ʿĀmilī / edited by Muḥammad Bāqir al-Bihbūdī / 1st edition.

Al-Ṭabaqāt al-Kubrá by Muḥammad ibn Saʿd / Dār Ṣādir / Beirut.

ʿIlal al-Sharāʾiʿ by Shaykh al-Ṣadūq / printing press: al-Ḥaydarīyah / Najaf / 1386 AH.

ʿAwālī al-Laʾālīʾ by Ibn Abī Jumhūr al-Aḥsāʾī / 1st edition / 1403 AH / Qom.

ʿUyūn Akhbār al-Riḍā by Shaykh al-Ṣadūq / printing press: al-Aʿlamī / 1404 AH / Beirut.

Al-Ghaybah by al-Ṭūsī / Muʾassasat al-Maʿārif al-Islāmīyah / 1st edition / 1411 AH.

Al-Ghaybah by Muḥammad ibn Ibrāhīm al-Nuʿmānī / Manshūrāt Anwār al-Hudá / Qom / 1st edition.

Fatḥ al-Bārī by Ibn Ḥajar / Dār al-Maʿrifah / Beirut / 2nd edition.

Farāʾid al-Uṣūl by Shaykh al-Anṣārī / 1st edition / 1419 AH / Majmaʿ al-Fikr al-Islāmī / Qom.

Al-Fuṣūl al-Muhimmah by Ibn al-Ṣabbāgh al-Mālikī / printing press: al-ʿAdl / 1st edition / 1950 CE.

Al-Kāfī by Shaykh al-Kulaynī / 3rd edition / 1388 AH / [edited by] ʿAlī Akbar Ghaffārī / Dār al-Kutub al-Islāmīyah.

Al-Kashshāf by al-Zamakhsharī / Dār al-Kitāb al-ʿArabī / Beirut.

Kashf al-Ghummah by al-Irbilī / 2nd edition / 1405 AH / Dār al-Aḍwāʾ / Beirut.

Kifāyat al-Athar by al-Khazzāz al-Qummī / Manshūrāt Bīdār / Qom / 1401 AH.

Kamāl al-Dīn by Shaykh al-Ṣadūq / edited by ʿAlī Akbar Ghaffārī / 1405 AH edition.

Kanz al-ʿUmmāl by al-Muttaqī al-Hindī / edited by a group / printed and published by / Muʾassasat al-Risālah / Beirut.

Majmaʿ al-Bayān by al-Ṭabarsī / Muʾassasat al-Aʿlamī / Beirut / 1st edition / 1415 AH.

Al-Maḥāsin by al-Barqī / edited by Jalāl al-Dīn al-Ḥusaynī / Dār al-Kutub al-Islāmīyah.

Mukhtaṣar Baṣāʾir al-Darajāt by al-Ḥasan ibn Sulaymān al-Ḥillī / 1st edition / 1380 AH / printing press: al-Ḥaydarīyah / Najaf.

Al-Mazār by Muḥammad ibn al-Mashhadī / 1st edition / 1419 AH / Muʾassasat al-Nashr al-Islāmī / Qom.

Miṣbāḥ al-Mutahajjid by Shaykh al-Ṭūsī / 1st edition / 1411 AH / Muʾassasat Fiqh al-Shīʿah / Beirut.

Al-Miṣbāḥ by al-Kafʿamī / 3rd edition / 1403 AH / Muʾassasat al-Aʿlamī / Beirut.

Maṭālib al-Saʾūl by Ibn Ṭalḥah al-Shāfiʿī / edited by Mājid Aḥmad al-ʿAṭīyah / Tehran edition.

Maʿānī al-Akhbār by Shaykh al-Ṣadūq / edited by ʿAlī Akbar Ghaffārī / 1361 AH edition.

Muʿjam Aḥādīth al-Imām al-Mahdī by ʿAlī al-Kūrānī / 1st edition / 1411 AH / Muʾassasat al-Maʿārif.

Muʿjam Rijāl al-Ḥadīth by Sayyid al-Khūʾī / 5th edition / 1413 AH / Lajnah edition.

Al-Malāḥim wa al-Fitan by Ibn Ṭāwūs / 1st edition / 1416 AH / Muʾassasat Ṣāḥib al-Amr / Iṣfahān.

Al-Mahdī al-Muntaẓar fī al-Fikr al-Islāmī by Markaz al-Risālah / 1st edition / 1417 AH / printing press: Muhr / Qom.

Al-Mahdī al-Muntaẓar fī Ḍawʾ al-Aḥādīth wa al-Āthār al-Ṣaḥīḥah by al-Bastawī / 1st edition / 1420 AH / Dār Ibn Ḥazm / Beirut.

Al-Mīzān fī Tafsīr al-Qurʾān by Sayyid al-Ṭabāṭabāʾī / Muʾassasat al-Nashr al-Islāmī / Jamāʿat al-Mudarrisīn / Qom.

Nahj al-Balāghah: Khuṭab al-Imām ʿAlī / edited by Muḥammad ʿAbduh / Dār al-Maʿrifah / Beirut.

Al-Hidāyah al-Kubrá by al-Khaṣībī / 4th edition / 1411 AH / Muʾassasat al-Balāgh / Beirut.

Wasāʾil al-Shīʿah by al-Ḥurr al-ʿĀmilī / printing press: Muhr / Qom / 2nd edition / 1414 AH / edited by Muʾassasat Āl al-Bayt.

Wafiyāt al-Aʿyān by Ibn Khallikān / edited by Muḥammad Muḥyī al-Dīn ʿAbd al-Ḥamīd / printing press: al-Saʿādah / 1st edition / 1367 AH / Egypt.

Manufactured by Amazon.ca
Bolton, ON

38419397R00219